Learning LibGDX Game Development

Second Edition

Wield the power of the LibGDX framework to create a cross-platform game

Suryakumar Balakrishnan Nair

Andreas Oehlke

BIRMINGHAM - MUMBAI

Learning LibGDX Game Development
Second Edition

Copyright © 2015 Packt Publishing

All rights reserved. No part of this book may be reproduced, stored in a retrieval system, or transmitted in any form or by any means, without the prior written permission of the publisher, except in the case of brief quotations embedded in critical articles or reviews.

Every effort has been made in the preparation of this book to ensure the accuracy of the information presented. However, the information contained in this book is sold without warranty, either express or implied. Neither the authors, nor Packt Publishing, and its dealers and distributors will be held liable for any damages caused or alleged to be caused directly or indirectly by this book.

Packt Publishing has endeavored to provide trademark information about all of the companies and products mentioned in this book by the appropriate use of capitals. However, Packt Publishing cannot guarantee the accuracy of this information.

First published: September 2013

Second edition: January 2015

Production reference: 1220115

Published by Packt Publishing Ltd.
Livery Place
35 Livery Street
Birmingham B3 2PB, UK.

ISBN 978-1-78355-477-5

www.packtpub.com

Credits

Authors
Suryakumar Balakrishnan Nair
Andreas Oehlke

Reviewers
Juwal Bose
Yunkun Huang
Stéphane Meylemans
Chris Moeller

Commissioning Editor
Kartikey Pandey

Acquisition Editors
Subho Gupta
Kartikey Pandey

Content Development Editor
Arun Nadar

Technical Editor
Shashank Desai

Copy Editors
Relin Hedly
Neha Karnani
Nithya P

Project Coordinator
Neha Bhatnagar

Proofreaders
Ting Baker
Simran Bhogal
Maria Gould
Ameesha Green
Paul Hindle

Indexer
Mariammal Chettiyar

Graphics
Abhinash Sahu

Production Coordinator
Alwin Roy

Cover Work
Alwin Roy

About the Authors

Suryakumar Balakrishnan Nair is an engineering graduate from Cochin University of Science and Technology, Cochin, India with a specialization in computer science. He just loves programming and likes to keep on experimenting. He has designed a dozen games on the Android platform using LibGDX.

He loves traveling and visiting various places. He reads articles and books on a range of issues from politics to environment. He is currently working as a full-time Android game developer for an Indian game company, Csharks (`http://csharks.com/site/`).

> I would like to thank my colleagues in Csharks for providing me with moral support, especially Vipin TP and Dheeraj S. I would also like to thank my dear friend Rahul Satish who helped me with the Blender models. Most importantly, I want to thank my mentor, Juwal Bose, who guided me and motivated me for this project.

Andreas Oehlke is a professional software engineer and computer scientist who feels very much at home on any Linux/UNIX machine. He holds a bachelor's degree in Computer Science and loves to assemble and disassemble software and hardware alike. The exorbitant affinity for electronics and computers has always been his trademark. His hobbies include game and web development, programming in general (software design and new languages), programming embedded systems with microcontrollers, playing sports, and making music.

He currently works full time as a software engineer for a German financial institution. Furthermore, he has worked as a consultant and game developer in San Francisco, CA. In his spare time, he provides his expertise to a German start-up called Gamerald (`http://www.gamerald.com/`).

> I want to thank my parents, Michael and Sigrid, and my brother Dennis for their constant and invaluable support, which definitely kept me on the go while writing this book. I also want to thank my close friends for giving me lots of helpful feedback, notably Sascha Björn Bolz for providing the artwork for Canyon Bunny. Last but not least, I want to thank Klaus "keith303" Spang for providing the music track, the whole team of Packt Publishing, and all the numerous reviewers for their great work who helped me produce a high-quality book.

About the Reviewers

Juwal Bose is a game developer, game designer, and technology consultant from the incredibly beautiful state of Kerala in India. He is an active figure in social media and game development SIGs and never misses a chance to speak at technical conferences and BarCamps. He conducts technical workshops for engineering students at professional colleges as part of open source initiatives. Juwal is the Director at Csharks Games and Solutions Pvt. Ltd., where he manages research and development as well as training and pipeline integration in his area of expertise.

He has been developing games since 2004 using multiple technologies, including ActionScript, Objective-C, Java, Unity, LibGDX, Cocos2D, OpenFL, Unity, and Starling. His team has created more than 400 games to date, and many of the job management games are listed at the top of leading portals worldwide. He has been part of the development of more than 20 LibGDX games primarily for the Android platform.

Juwal writes game development tutorials for GameDevTuts+ and manages the blog of Csharks' games. His isometric tutorial for GameDevTuts+ was well received and is considered a thorough guide to developing tile-based isometric games. Juwal has written *LibGDX Game Development Essentials, Packt Publishing*, and reviewed a couple of books as well. The first book he had written, *Starling Game Development Essentials, Packt Publishing*, is based on another exceptional cross-platform game development framework called Starling.

Juwal is a voracious reader and likes to travel. His future plans also include writing fiction.

Yunkun Huang is a senior software engineer with more than 7 years of experience in Java development. His research interests include game development, swarm intelligence, automated trading, and enterprise application development.

He works for ThoughtWorks as a Java developer now. For more information about his background and research, you can visit his home page http://www.huangyunkun.com/.

Stéphane Meylemans has a bachelor's degree in information technology. He worked in web development for 8 years and then decided to move on to game development (mobile and desktop). He has learned Unreal Engine and Unity Game development and is currently working on a LibGDX-based point n click adventure game for which he is writing the story.

> I would like to thank the author for this great book. It's very useful and well written. It helped me a lot to develop in LibGDX and I recommend it to anyone with Java knowledge who wants to start developing in LibGDX.

Chris Moeller is a founder of the game studio Ackmi Design and Engineering. He has been building computers since the age of 9 and has been programming for more than 10 years. He has had the opportunity to work for software companies as a PHP developer, Java QA engineer, and a Flash developer, and he currently works primarily in Java on LibGDX-based applications.

He has been an enthusiastic gamer for most of his life and loves many of John Carmack's and early Blizzard games. From these inspirations, he has created many games and game prototypes in several different programming languages. He writes game programming tutorials on his blog at http://chris-moeller.blogspot.in/, and most of his new games can be found on his company website at http://ackmi.com/, which he runs with his wife, Megan.

www.PacktPub.com

Support files, eBooks, discount offers, and more

For support files and downloads related to your book, please visit www.PacktPub.com.

Did you know that Packt offers eBook versions of every book published, with PDF and ePub files available? You can upgrade to the eBook version at www.PacktPub.com and as a print book customer, you are entitled to a discount on the eBook copy. Get in touch with us at service@packtpub.com for more details.

At www.PacktPub.com, you can also read a collection of free technical articles, sign up for a range of free newsletters and receive exclusive discounts and offers on Packt books and eBooks.

https://www2.packtpub.com/books/subscription/packtlib

Do you need instant solutions to your IT questions? PacktLib is Packt's online digital book library. Here, you can search, access, and read Packt's entire library of books.

Why subscribe?

- Fully searchable across every book published by Packt
- Copy and paste, print, and bookmark content
- On demand and accessible via a web browser

Free access for Packt account holders

If you have an account with Packt at www.PacktPub.com, you can use this to access PacktLib today and view 9 entirely free books. Simply use your login credentials for immediate access.

Table of Contents

Preface	**1**
Chapter 1: Introduction to LibGDX and Project Setup	**9**
Diving into LibGDX	**10**
Features of LibGDX 1.2.0	**11**
Graphics	11
Audio	12
Input handling	12
File I/O and storage	12
Math and physics	13
Utilities	13
Tools	13
Getting in touch with the community	**14**
Prerequisites to install and configure LibGDX	**14**
Java Development Kit	15
Eclipse – Integrated Development Environment	19
Downloading LibGDX	20
Installing Android SDK	21
Running Eclipse and installing plugins	30
Creating a new application	**37**
Using the old setup tool	37
Using the Gradle-based setup	46
gdx-setup versus gdx-setup-ui	**52**
Kicking your game to life	**54**
Key to success lies in planning	**56**
Game project – Canyon Bunny	**57**
Description of the game	58
Summary	**59**

Table of Contents

Chapter 2: Cross-platform Development – Build Once, Deploy Anywhere   61
The demo application – how the projects work together   62
LibGDX backends   65
    Lightweight Java Game Library   66
    Android   66
    WebGL   66
    RoboVM (iOS backend)   67
LibGDX core modules   67
    The application module   68
       Logging   68
       Shutting down gracefully   68
       Persisting data   69
       Querying the Android API level   69
       Querying the platform type   70
       Querying the memory usage   70
       Multithreading   70
    The graphics module   71
       Querying delta time   71
       Querying display size   71
       Querying the frames per second (FPS) counter   71
    The audio module   71
       Sound playback   71
       Music streaming   72
    The input module   72
       Reading the keyboard/touch/mouse input   72
       Reading the accelerometer   72
       Starting and canceling vibrator   72
       Catching Android's soft keys   73
    The files module   73
       Getting an internal file handle   73
       Getting an external file handle   73
    The network module   73
       HTTP requests   73
       Client/server sockets   74
       Opening a URI in a web browser   74
LibGDX's application life cycle and interface   74
Starter classes   76
    Running the demo application on a desktop   76
    Running the demo application on Android   79
    Running the demo application in a WebGL-capable web browser   83
    Running the demo application on an iOS device   88

The demo application – time for code	**94**
Inspecting an example code of the demo application	94
The create() method	95
The render() method	97
The dispose() method	98
Having fun with the debugger and Code Hot Swapping	100
Summary	**106**
Chapter 3: Configuring the Game	**107**
Setting up the Canyon Bunny project	**108**
Using a class diagram for Canyon Bunny	**110**
Laying foundations	**113**
Implementing the Constants class	113
Implementing the CanyonBunnyMain class	114
Implementing the WorldController class	115
Implementing the WorldRenderer class	116
Putting it all together	**117**
Building the game loop	117
Adding the test sprites	121
Adding the game world's debug controls	126
Adding the CameraHelper class	130
Adding the camera debug controls using CameraHelper	132
Summary	**136**
Chapter 4: Gathering Resources	**137**
Setting up a custom Android application icon	**138**
Setting up a custom iOS application icon	**140**
Creating the texture atlases	**141**
Loading and tracking assets	**148**
Organizing the assets	**149**
Testing the assets	**157**
Handling level data	**161**
Summary	**163**
Chapter 5: Making a Scene	**165**
Creating game objects	**166**
The rock object	167
The mountains object	171
The water overlay object	173
The clouds object	174

Implementing the level loader	177
Assembling the game world	182
Implementing the game GUI	186
The GUI score	190
The GUI extra lives	191
The GUI FPS counter	192
Rendering the GUI	193
Summary	194
Chapter 6: Adding the Actors	**195**
Implementing the actor game objects	195
Creating the gold coin object	198
Creating the feather object	200
Creating the bunny head object	201
Updating the rock object	210
Completing the level loader	210
Adding the game logic	213
Adding collision detection	213
Losing lives, game over, and fixing the camera	220
Adding the game over text and the feather icon to the GUI	222
Summary	226
Chapter 7: Menus and Options	**227**
Managing multiple screens	227
Exploring Scene2D UI, TableLayout, and skins	235
Using LibGDX's scene graph for the menu UI	236
Building the scene for the menu screen	240
Adding the background layer	246
Adding the objects layer	246
Adding the logos layer	247
Adding the controls layer	247
Adding the Options window layer	249
Building the Options window	253
Using the game settings	260
Summary	262
Chapter 8: Special Effects	**263**
Creating complex effects with particle systems	264
Adding a dust particle effect to the player character	270
Moving the clouds	274
Smoothing with linear interpolation (Lerp)	275
Letting the rocks float on the water	276

Adding parallax scrolling to the mountains in the background	**278**
Enhancing the game screen's GUI	**280**
Event – player lost a life	280
Event – score increased	283
Summary	**285**
Chapter 9: Screen Transitions	**287**
Adding the screen transition capability	**287**
Implementing the transition effects	296
Knowing about interpolation algorithms	296
Creating a fade transition effect	298
Creating a slide transition effect	301
Creating a slice transition effect	304
Summary	**307**
Chapter 10: Managing the Music and Sound Effects	**309**
Playing back the music and sound effects	**309**
Exploring the Sound interface	310
Exploring the Music interface	312
Accessing the audio device directly	**312**
Exploring the AudioDevice interface	313
Exploring the AudioRecorder interface	314
Using sound generators	**314**
The sfxr generator	315
The cfxr generator	316
The bfxr generator	317
Adding music and sounds to Canyon Bunny	**318**
Summary	**327**
Chapter 11: Advanced Programming Techniques	**329**
Simulating physics with Box2D	**330**
Exploring the concepts of Box2D	331
Understanding the rigid bodies	331
Choosing the body types	331
Using shapes	332
Using fixtures	332
Simulating physics in the world	332
Physics body editor	333
Adding Box2D	333
Adding Box2D dependency in Gradle	334
For non-Gradle users	337
Preparing Canyon Bunny for raining carrots	338
Adding the new assets	338
Adding the carrot game object	339

Adding the goal game object	340
Extending the level	342
Letting it rain carrots	345
Working with shaders in LibGDX	**357**
Creating a monochrome filter shader program	358
Using the monochrome filter shader program in Canyon Bunny	360
Adding alternative input controls	**364**
Summary	**368**

Chapter 12: Animations — 369

Manipulating actors through actions	**369**
Actions for manipulating actors	371
Controlling the order and time of execution	372
Animating the menu screen	**372**
Animating the gold coins and bunny head actors	374
Animating the menu buttons and Options window	375
Using sequences of images for animations	**378**
Packing animations using TexturePacker	379
Choosing between animation play modes	380
Animating the game screen	**381**
Defining and preparing new animations	381
Animating the gold coin game object	384
Animating the bunny head game object	387
Summary	**392**

Chapter 13: Basic 3D Programming — 393

Light sources	**393**
Environment and materials	**394**
Basic 3D using LibGDX	**394**
The project setup	394
The camera	398
Model and ModelInstances	399
The ModelBatch class	399
The environment	400
Loading a model	**400**
Model formats and the FBX converter	403
3D frustum culling	**404**
Ray picking	**411**
Summary	**413**

Chapter 14: Bullet Physics — 415

About Bullet Physics	**415**
A few basic concepts	**416**

Understanding rigid bodies	417
Static, dynamic, and kinematic rigid bodies	417
Collision shapes	417
MotionStates	418
Simulating physics	418
Learning Bullet with LibGDX	**419**
Setting up a project	419
Creating a basic 3D scene	421
Initializing Bullet	426
Creating a dynamics world	426
A custom MotionState class	427
A simple ContactListener class	427
Adding some rigid bodies	**428**
Stepping the world	**429**
Ray casting in Bullet	430
A simple test game	430
Having fun with shadows	**445**
Summary	**447**
Index	**449**

Preface

As personal computers have conquered our private homes, video games have become more and more popular and eventually a multimillion dollar business for big video game companies. With the introduction of mobile devices such as smartphones and tablets, the market for video games has experienced another significant increase; in particular, it has now become open to independent game developers with small budgets.

For game developers, it is essential to have tools at hand that provide fundamentals that allow rapid prototyping and cost-effective implementation of their creative ideas. This is where LibGDX comes into play. LibGDX, as a Java-based game development framework, provides a unified access layer to handle all the supported platforms. LibGDX also makes use of C/C++ to achieve cross-platform support as well as to boost the application performance for mission critical tasks.

This book will show you how easy it is to develop cross-platform games by walking you through a complete game development cycle using the free and open source library—LibGDX. Besides this, you will also learn about common game structure and the involved requirements.

You will be introduced to the key features of LibGDX. You will also learn how to develop a game with ease and speed up your development cycles. In ten easy-to-follow chapters, you will develop your first LibGDX cross-platform game and add more and more game functionalities as you progress further through this book.

The special features will also make you acquainted with advanced programming techniques such as animations, physics simulations, and shader programs that enhance your games in both their gameplay and visual presentation.

By the end of this book, you will have a fully working 2D game that will run on Windows, Linux, Mac OS X, WebGL-capable browsers, Android, and iOS. You will also have all the skills required to extend the game further or to start developing your own cross-platform games.

Preface

What this book covers

Chapter 1, Introduction to LibGDX and Project Setup, covers how to install and configure the development environment and introduces you to the project setup tool that comes with LibGDX. Then, we will take a first look at the basics of what a game needs to come alive.

Chapter 2, Cross-platform Development – Build Once, Deploy Anywhere, explains the supported target platforms and how to deploy and run our application on each platform using a demo application. For the first overview of LibGDX's API, we will take a glance at each module. Then, the application cycle will be introduced, and we will take a look at how to debug and manipulate our code at runtime.

Chapter 3, Configuring the Game, takes us from our demo application to a real game by setting up a new project called Canyon Bunny. We will work on this project throughout the rest of the book and extend it from chapter to chapter with new features. As LibGDX is a framework, we will first have to build our program architecture using UML class diagrams to structure our game engine.

Chapter 4, Gathering Resources, describes how to gather all the resources (assets) needed for Canyon Bunny, including graphics, audio files, level data, and so on. We will also find out how to load, track, and organize assets efficiently. Finally, it is time to think about how level data is going to be handled so that we are able to populate our game world with objects.

Chapter 5, Making a Scene, will implement the game objects such as rocks, mountains, and clouds. We will put the new code into action using a level loader. We will also add a Graphical User Interface (GUI) to the game scene to show the player's score, extra lives and frames per second to measure the games performance.

Chapter 6, Adding the Actors, explains how to add the remaining game objects for Canyon Bunny, including the player character and collectible items to complete our game. We will also add simple physics for player movement and basic collision detection. Additionally, the game logic will be extended so that it is able to detect the "life lost" and "game over" conditions.

Chapter 7, Menus and Options, describes how to create a menu system with widgets such as buttons, labels, and checkboxes to enrich the overall game experience. Furthermore, we will add an Options window where the player can adjust the game settings.

Chapter 8, Special Effects, covers how to make use of particle systems and how to apply interpolation algorithms to create impressive effects such as dust clouds, a smooth, following camera, floating rocks, and parallax scrolling for mountains in the background. Using special effects will spice up the appearance of your game.

Chapter 9, Screen Transitions, introduces screen transitions. We will dive into enhanced visual effects using OpenGL's Framebuffer Objects for off-screen rendering into video memory. This will allow us to create seamless transitions for an improved user experience while switching from one screen to another. For Canyon Bunny, we will create a variety of transition effects.

Chapter 10, Managing the Music and Sound Effects, will walk you through a list of recommended sound generators and discuss their differences. Then, we will take a look at the LibGDX's Audio API and demonstrate how to use it by creating an audio manager. We do this so that handling our entire audio playback needs become a breeze.

Chapter 11, Advanced Programming Techniques, introduces you to some advanced programming techniques that will guide you to the next level of game programming. We will build basic knowledge about the Box2D API that enables us to create believable physics simulations in games. Additionally, we will discuss the topic of shader programs with the example of a monochrome image filter effect. Lastly, we will show you how to make use of the accelerometer hardware that is commonly available in modern smartphones and tablets, which allows controlling the game by tilting the device.

Chapter 12, Animations, explains how to polish the game by adding animations. In this chapter, we will cover two different approaches to animate the game menu and the game world. Finally, we will implement a state machine to allow event-based animations for the player character.

Chapter 13, Basic 3D Programming, introduces the new LibGDX's 3D API. You will learn how to use the 3D API to create basic models such as sphere, cube, cylinder, and so on, and load models exported from modeling software such as Blender. You will also learn about ray picking, an important concept used to develop first person shooter games.

Chapter 14, Bullet Physics, will walk you through the basics of 3D physics using Bullet. Finally, we will create a simple application to simulate physics using Bullet.

What you need for this book

LibGDX is a cross-platform game development framework. For development, you will need a computer running either Windows (Vista/7/8), Linux (for example, Ubuntu), or Mac OS X (10.9+).

Additionally, you will need to download the LibGDX framework for game development. You can download LibGDX from `http://libgdx.badlogicgames.com/releases/`. Download the version 0.1.2 of LibGDX as this is the version that is used in this book.

The Integrated Development Environment (IDE) used in this book is Eclipse. You can download the Eclipse IDE from `http://www.eclipse.org/`.

To develop games for the Android platform, you will need an Android device running Android 2.2 (Froyo) or higher, supporting OpenGL ES 2.0, and the official Android Software Development Kit (SDK) that can be downloaded from `http://developer.android.com/sdk/index.html`.

To develop games for an iOS platform, you will need Mac OS X (10.9+) and an iOS device.

Who this book is for

This book is written for software developers who are new to game development and to LibGDX in particular. It is assumed that you have some experience in Java to be able to follow the discussed code in this book.

Conventions

In this book, you will find a number of styles of text that distinguish between different kinds of information. Here are some examples of these styles, and an explanation of their meaning.

Code words in text, database table names, folder names, filenames, file extensions, pathnames, dummy URLs, user input, and Twitter handles are shown as follows: "The starter class for iOS application is `RobovmLauncher.java`."

A block of code is set as follows:

```
prefs.putInteger("sound_volume", 100); // volume @ 100%
prefs.flush();
```

When we wish to draw your attention to a particular part of a code block, the relevant lines or items are set in bold:

```
package com.packtpub.libgdx.demo;
import com.badlogic.gdx.backends.lwjgl.LwjglApplication;
import com.badlogic.gdx.backends.lwjgl.LwjglApplicationConfiguration;
public class Main {
public static void main(String[] args) {

LwjglApplicationConfiguration cfg = new
LwjglApplicationConfiguration();
cfg.title = "demo";
cfg.width = 480;
cfg.height = 320;
new LwjglApplication(new MyDemo(), cfg);
    }
}
```

New terms and **important words** are shown in bold. Words that you see on the screen, in menus or dialog boxes for example, appear in the text like this: "You can quickly check this by going to the **Project** menu."

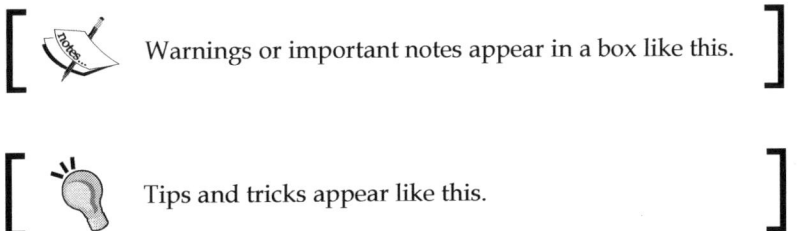

> Warnings or important notes appear in a box like this.

> Tips and tricks appear like this.

Reader feedback

Feedback from our readers is always welcome. Let us know what you think about this book—what you liked or may have disliked. Reader feedback is important for us to develop titles that you really get the most out of.

To send us general feedback, simply send an e-mail to `feedback@packtpub.com`, and mention the book title via the subject of your message.

If there is a topic that you have expertise in and you are interested in either writing or contributing to a book, see our author guide on `www.packtpub.com/authors`.

Customer support

Now that you are the proud owner of a Packt book, we have a number of things to help you to get the most from your purchase.

Downloading the example code

You can download the example code files for all Packt books you have purchased from your account at http://www.packtpub.com. If you purchased this book elsewhere, you can visit http://www.packtpub.com/support and register to have the files e-mailed directly to you.

Downloading the color images of this book

We also provide you a PDF file that has color images of the screenshots/diagrams used in this book. The color images will help you better understand the changes in the output. You can download this file from: https://www.packtpub.com/sites/default/files/downloads/4775OS_ColoredImages.pdf

Errata

Although we have taken every care to ensure the accuracy of our content, mistakes do happen. If you find a mistake in one of our books—maybe a mistake in the text or the code—we would be grateful if you would report this to us. By doing so, you can save other readers from frustration and help us improve subsequent versions of this book. If you find any errata, please report them by visiting http://www.packtpub.com/submit-errata, selecting your book, clicking on the **Errata Submission Form** link, and entering the details of your errata. Once your errata are verified, your submission will be accepted and the errata will be uploaded on our website, or added to any list of existing errata, under the Errata section of that title.

To view the previously submitted errata, go to https://www.packtpub.com/books/content/support and enter the name of the book in the search field. The required information will appear under the **Errata** section.

Piracy

Piracy of copyright material on the Internet is an ongoing problem across all media. At Packt, we take the protection of our copyright and licenses very seriously. If you come across any illegal copies of our works, in any form, on the Internet, please provide us with the location address or website name immediately so that we can pursue a remedy.

Please contact us at `copyright@packtpub.com` with a link to the suspected pirated material.

We appreciate your help in protecting our authors, and our ability to bring you valuable content.

Questions

You can contact us at `questions@packtpub.com` if you are having a problem with any aspect of the book, and we will do our best to address it.

1
Introduction to LibGDX and Project Setup

This book will take you on an exciting tour to show and teach you about game development using the open source LibGDX framework. Actually, you have chosen just the right time to read about game development as the game industry is in a remarkable state of change. With the advent of increasingly powerful smartphones and tablets as well as the ever-growing application stores for desktop computers and mobile platforms serving millions of users a day, it has never been easier for **Independent Game Developers** (also known as **Indies**) to enter the market with virtually no risks and very low budgets.

In this chapter, you will learn about what LibGDX is and the advantages that it provides when developing your own games. You will also get a brief overview of the feature set that LibGDX provides.

Before you can start developing games with LibGDX, you have to install and set up your development environment accordingly. You will be using the freely available and open source software **Eclipse** as your **Integrated Development Environment** (**IDE**) to set up a basic project that uses LibGDX. It will feature a runnable example application for every currently supported target platform. These platforms are as follows:

- Windows
- Linux
- Mac OS X
- Android (2.2+)
- iOS
- HTML5 (using JavaScript and WebGL)

>  The target platforms, namely, Windows, Linux, and Mac OS X will from now on be referred to as desktop and also share a project in our development environment.

You are going to explore what a game needs by looking at it from a technical standpoint, and why it is so important to plan a game project before the development starts.

At the end of this chapter, you will be introduced to the game project that is going to be developed and enhanced throughout this book.

Diving into LibGDX

LibGDX is an open source, cross-platform development framework, which is designed mainly, but not exclusively, to create games using the Java programming language. Besides Java, LibGDX also makes heavy use of the C programming language for performance-critical tasks to incorporate other C-based libraries and to enable cross-platform capabilities. Moreover, the framework abstracts the complex nature of all its supported target platforms by combining them into one common **Application Programming Interface (API)**. One of the highlights of LibGDX is the ability to run and debug your code on the desktop as a native application. This enables you to use very comfortable functions of the **Java Virtual Machine (JVM)**, such as Code Hot Swapping, which in turn lets you immediately see the effect of your changed code at runtime. Therefore, it will significantly reduce your time to iterate through different ideas or even to find and fix nasty bugs more quickly.

Another critical point is to understand that LibGDX is a framework and not a game engine that usually comes with lots of tools, such as a full-blown level editor and a completely predefined workflow. This might sound like a disadvantage at first, but actually it turns out to be an advantage that enables you to freely define your own workflow for each project. For example, LibGDX allows you to go low-level so you could add your own OpenGL calls if that really became necessary at some point. However, most of the time it should be sufficient enough to stay high-level and use the already built-in functionalities of LibGDX to realize your ideas.

Features of LibGDX 1.2.0

Since the release of LibGDX Version 0.1 back in March 2010, a lot of work has been contributed in order to improve this library. The latest stable release of LibGDX is Version 1.2.0 from June 2014, which we are going to use throughout this book.

Here is a list of features taken from the official website (`http://libgdx.badlogicgames.com/features.html`).

Graphics

The graphic features are as follows:

- Render through OpenGL ES 2.0 on all platforms
- Custom OpenGL ES 2.0 bindings for Android 2.0 and higher versions
- Low-level OpenGL helpers:
    - Vertex arrays and vertex buffer objects
    - Meshes
    - Textures
    - Framebuffer objects (GLES 2.0 only)
    - Shaders, integrating easily with meshes
    - Immediate mode rendering emulation
    - Simple shape rendering
    - Automatic software or hardware mipmap generation
    - ETC1 support (not available in JavaScript backend)
    - Automatic handling of OpenGL ES context loss that restores all textures, shaders, and other OpenGL resources
- High-level 2D APIs:
    - Custom CPU side bitmap manipulation library
    - Orthographic camera
    - High-performance sprite batching and caching
    - Texture atlases with whitespace stripping support, which are either generated offline or online

- Bitmap fonts (does not support complex scripts such as Arabic or Chinese), which are either generated offline or loaded from TTF files (unsupported in JavaScript backend)
- 2D particle system
- TMX tile map support
- 2D scene-graph API
- 2D UI library, based on the scene-graph API, fully skinable
- High-level 3D APIs:
  - Perspective camera
  - Decal batching for 3D billboards or particle systems
  - Basic loaders for Wavefront OBJ and MD5
  - 3D rendering API with materials and lighting system and support to load FBX models via fbx-conv

Audio

The following are the audio features:

- Streaming music and sound effect playback for WAV, MP3, and OGG
- Direct access to audio device for PCM sample playback and recording (unsupported in JavaScript backend)

Input handling

The various input features are as follows:

- Using abstractions for mouse and touchscreen, keyboard, accelerometer, and compass
- The gesture detector that detects taps, panning, flinging, and pinch zooming

File I/O and storage

The following are the features for the file I/O and storage:

- Filesystem abstraction for all platforms
- Read-only filesystem emulation for JavaScript backend
- Binary file support for JavaScript backend
- Preferences for lightweight setting storage

Math and physics

The math and physics features for LibGDX are as follows:

- Matrix, vector, and quaternion classes. Matrix and vector operations are accelerated via native C code where possible.
- Bounding shapes and volumes.
- Frustum class to pick and cull.
- Catmull-Rom splines.
- Common interpolators.
- Concave polygon triangulator.
- Intersection and overlap testing.
- JNI wrapper for Box2D physics. It is so awesome that other engines use it as well.
- JNI wrapper for bullet physics.

Utilities

The different utilities in LibGDX are as follows:

- Custom collections with primitive support
- JSON writer and reader with POJO (de-)serialization support
- XML writer and reader

Tools

The following are the different tools in LibGDX:

- Particle editor
- Texture packer
- Bitmap font generator

Getting in touch with the community

The LibGDX project enjoys a steadily growing and active community. If you ever find yourself stuck with a problem and you just cannot figure out how to solve it, check out the official forum at `http://badlogicgames.com/forum/`. There is a great chance someone else has already asked your question and has even found a solution with the help of the community. Otherwise, do not hesitate to ask your question on the forums.

There is also an official IRC channel (`#libgdx`) on Freenode (`https://freenode.net/`) where you can find some of the users and developers to talk about LibGDX.

If you want to read about the latest news on development of LibGDX, visit the blog of Mario Zechner who is the founder of the LibGDX project, or follow him on Twitter using the following links:

- LibGDX website (`http://libgdx.badlogicgames.com/`)
- Mario Zechner's blog (`http://www.badlogicgames.com/`) and the Twitter link (`http://www.twitter.com/badlogicgames/`)

Also, check out the following links for more in-depth information:

- Wiki (`https://github.com/libgdx/libgdx/wiki`)
- API overview (`http://libgdx.badlogicgames.com/nightlies/docs/api/`)

Prerequisites to install and configure LibGDX

Before you can start writing any application or game with LibGDX, you need to download and install the library and some additional software.

To target Windows, Linux, Mac OS X, Android, and HTML5, you will need to install the following software:

- Java Development Kit 7+ (JDK) (v6 will not work!).
- Eclipse (the Eclipse IDE for Java developers is usually sufficient).
- Android SDK; you only need the SDK, not the ADT bundle, which includes Eclipse. Install all platforms via the SDK Manager.

- Android Development Tools for Eclipse, also known as ADT Plugin. Use this updated site (https://dl-ssl.google.com/android/eclipse/).
- Eclipse Integration Gradle, use this updated site (http://dist.springsource.com/release/TOOLS/gradle).

To additionally target iOS, you will also need:

- Mac, as iOS Development does not work on Windows/Linux, thanks to Apple
- The latest Xcode, which you can get from the Mac OS X App Store for free
- The RoboVM plugin

Java Development Kit

Due to the fact that LibGDX is a framework based on Java, it is necessary to download **Java Development Kit (JDK)**. To install it, follow these steps:

1. The software is freely available on Oracle's website: http://www.oracle.com/technetwork/java/javase/downloads/index.html.
   Enter this address and you will see the following page:

Introduction to LibGDX and Project Setup

2. Click on the **DOWNLOAD** button to start downloading the latest JDK.

 It is important to choose the JDK instead of the JRE package. The reason is that the JDK package contains the **Java Runtime Environment (JRE)** to run Java applications and everything else that is required to develop them.

You will have to accept the license agreement and choose the version that is appropriate for your platform. For example, if you are using a 64-bit version of Windows, choose the download labeled as **Windows x64**. Here, we are using the 32-bit version that is labeled **window-i586**:

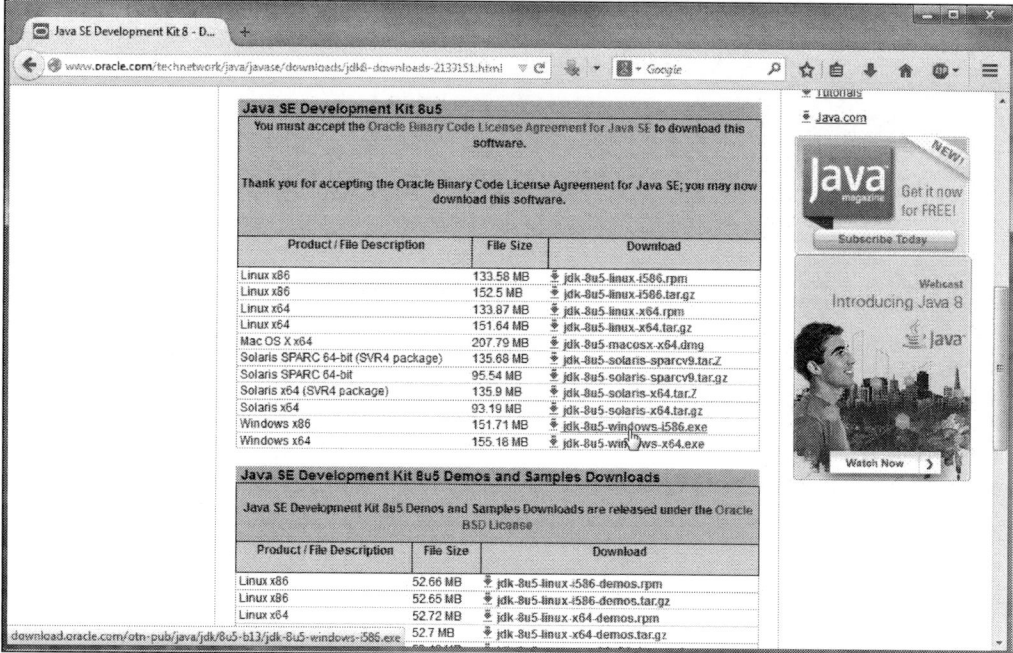

[16]

3. To install the JDK, simply run the downloaded installer file (for example, `jdk-8u5-windows-i586.exe`) and follow the instructions on the screen:

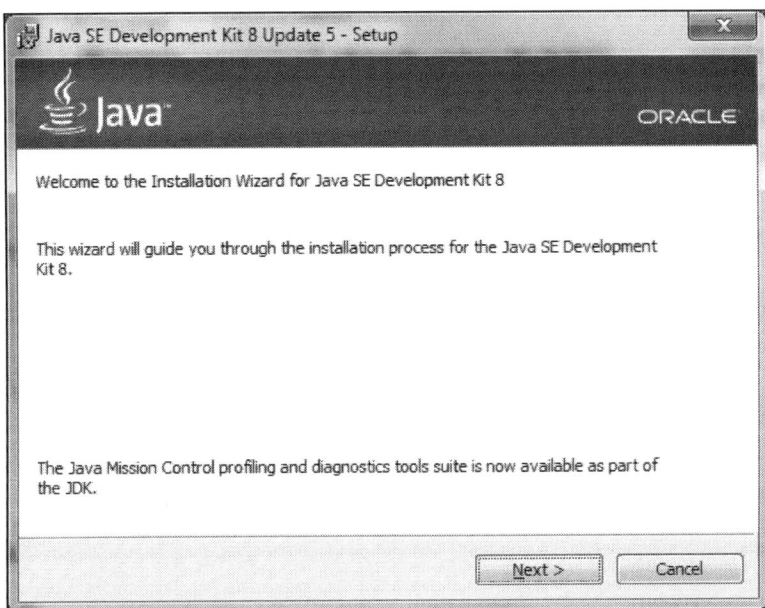

4. On the welcome screen of the installer, click on **Next** to continue:

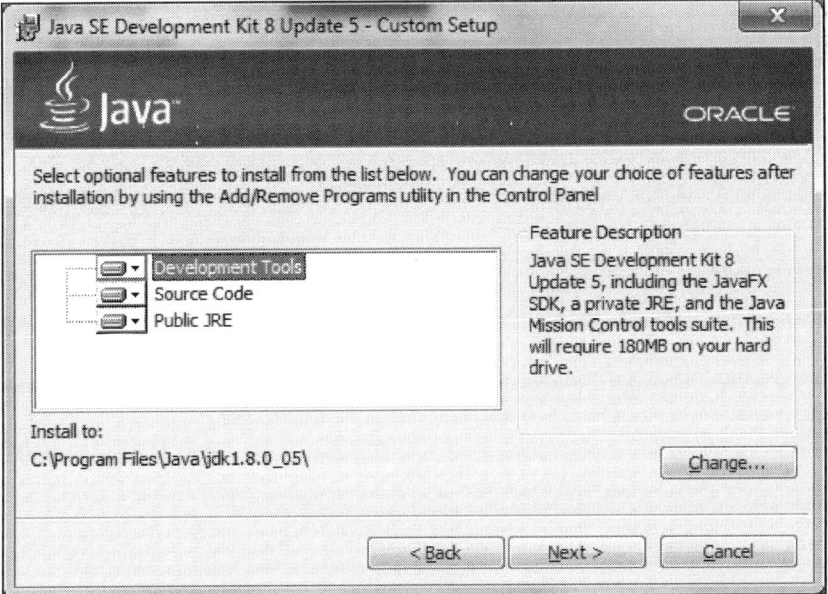

5. Then, keep all the features selected to be installed, and click on **Next** again to continue, as shown in the following screenshot:

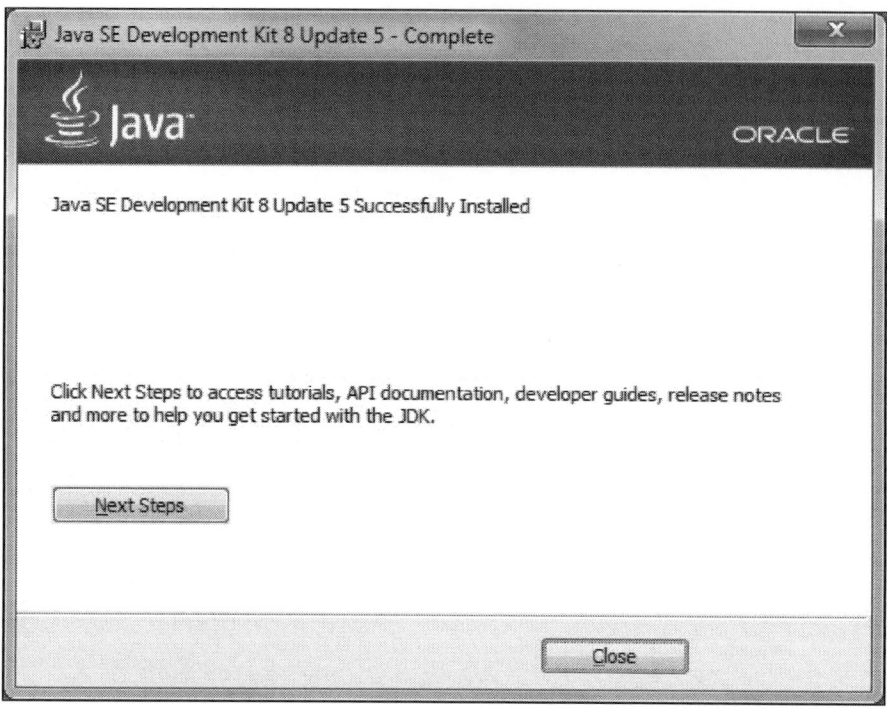

6. Once the installation is complete, click on the **Close** button to exit the installer.

Eclipse – Integrated Development Environment

The next step is to download and install Eclipse, a freely available and open source **Integrated Development Environment (IDE)** in order to develop applications in Java. Go to `http://www.eclipse.org/downloads/` and choose **Eclipse IDE for Java Developers**, as shown in the following screenshot, to download for the platform you are using:

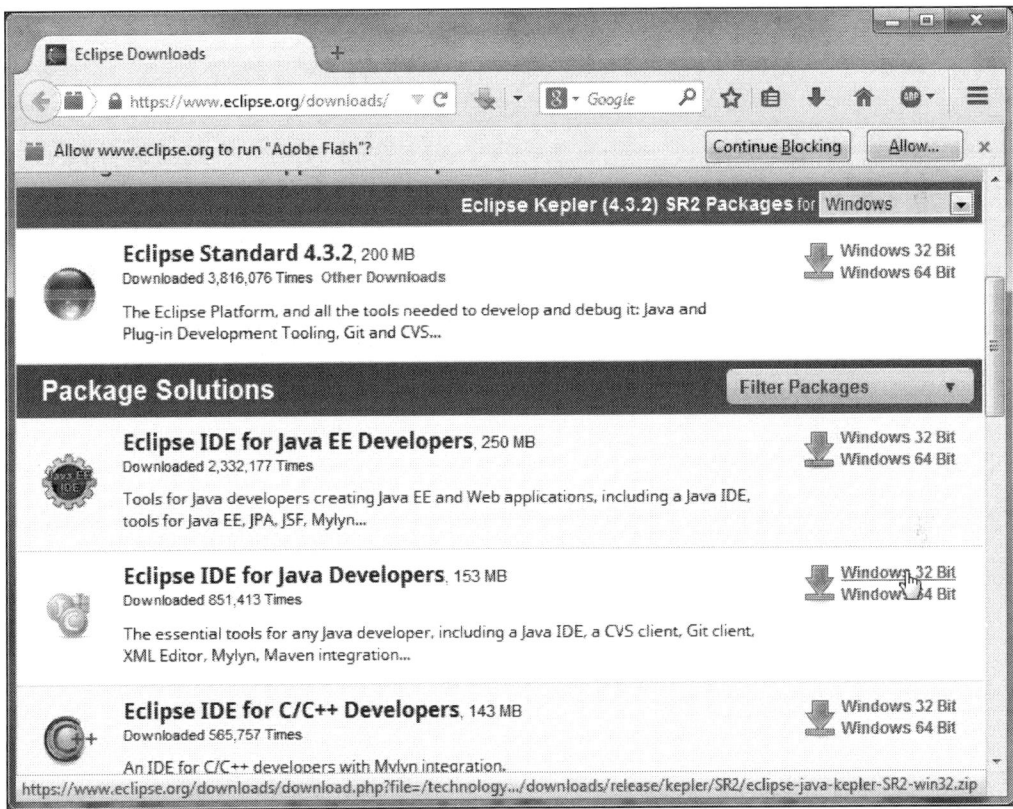

Once the download is finished, extract the archive to `C:\eclipse\`.

Downloading LibGDX

Go to `http://libgdx.badlogicgames.com/releases/` and choose the `libgdx-1.2.0.zip` file to download LibGDX.

At the time of writing this book, the latest stable version of LibGDX is 1.2.0. It is recommended to use the same version while working with this book.

The following screenshot shows a list of all the available files:

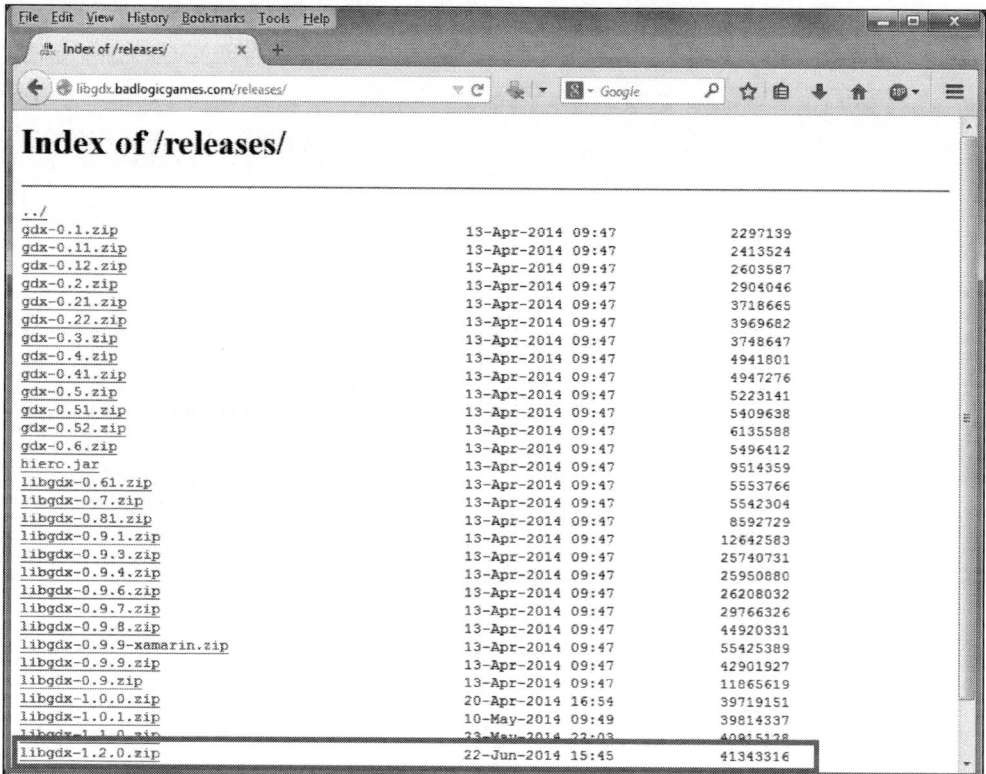

In the meantime, create a new folder inside the root folder of your C drive with the name `libgdx`. Once the download is finished, move the archive to `C:\libgdx\`.

Installing Android SDK

The Android mobile OS is one of LibGDX's supported target platforms. Before you can create Android applications, you have to download and install the Android SDK.

1. Go to `http://developer.android.com/sdk/index.html` and click on the **Download the stand-alone Android SDK Tools for Windows** button, as shown in the following screenshot. In case you are using an OS other than Windows, you will have to scroll down a bit further, click on **Download for other platforms** and choose the appropriate platform.

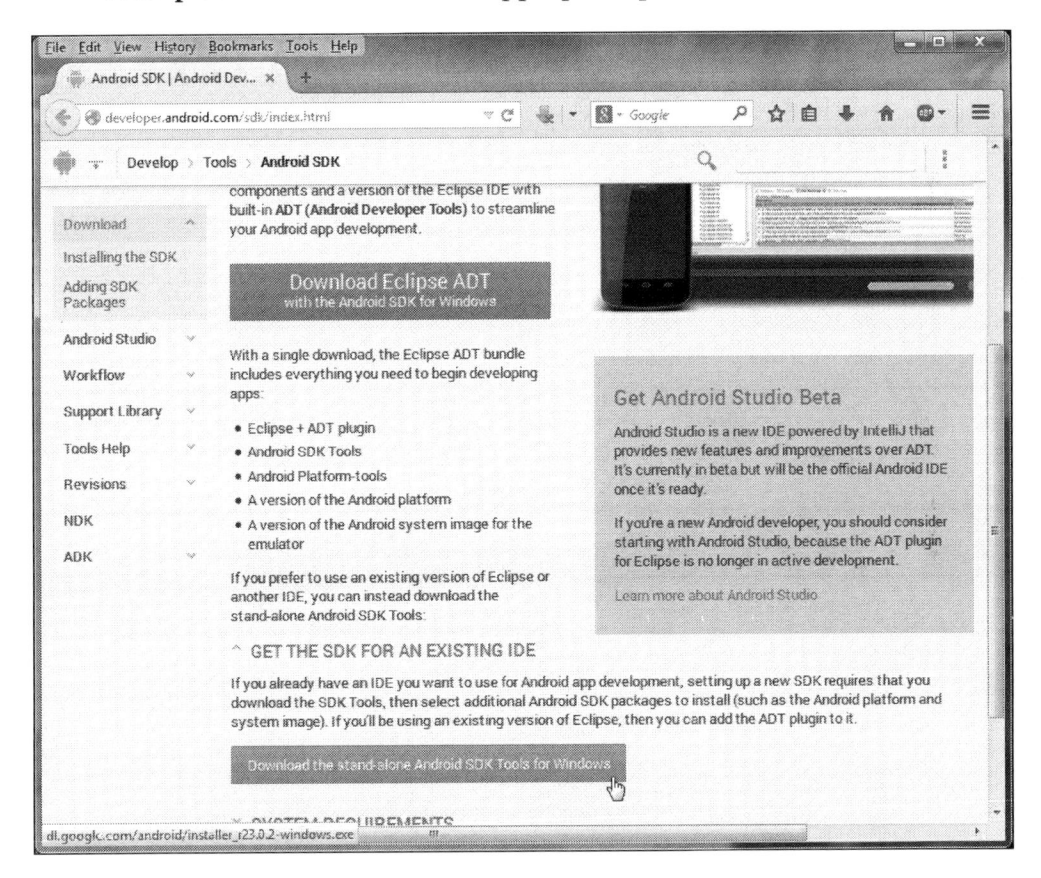

Introduction to LibGDX and Project Setup

2. Once the download is finished, run the installer (for example, `installer_r22.0.4-windows.exe`) and follow the instructions on the screen.

3. You will see the following screen when you try to install the Android SDK. This is because the installer cannot find the JDK although you have already installed it.

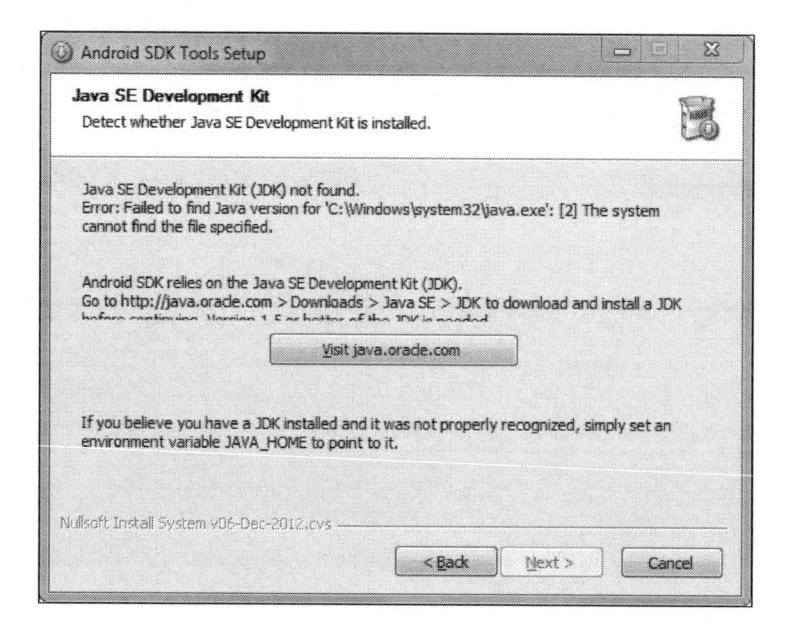

[22]

4. You need to set the value of the environment variable JAVA_HOME to the installation path of the JDK. To find the correct path, go to `C:\Program Files\Java\`. You will see a folder starting with `jdk`. Take the full name of this folder (here, it is `jdk1.8.0_05`) and append it to its path, as shown in the following screenshot:

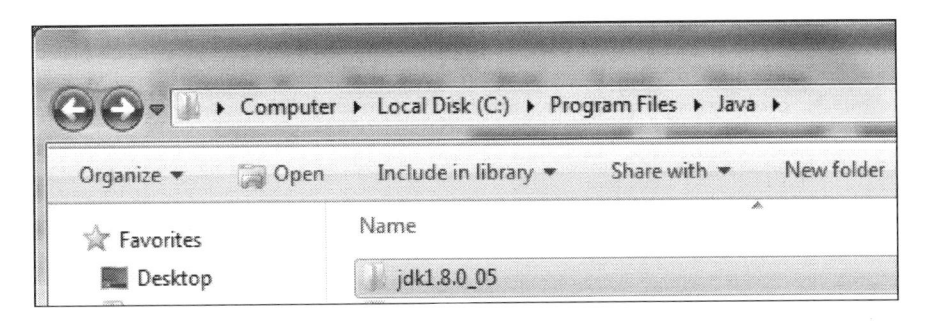

5. The complete path will now look like `C:\Program Files\Java\jdk1.8.0_05`. Now you have to set the environment variable. Click on the Windows **Start** button and right-click on **Computer**. Then click on **Properties** to open the control panel system window, as shown in the following screenshot:

Introduction to LibGDX and Project Setup

6. Click on **Advanced system settings** on the left-hand side of the window, as shown here:

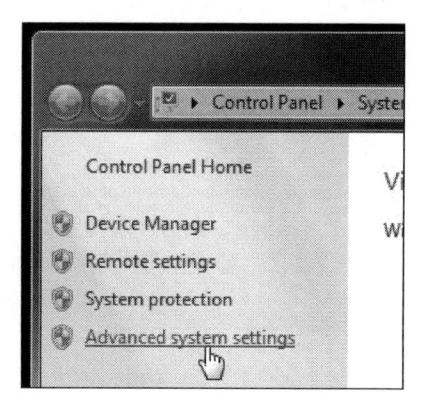

7. The **System Properties** window will appear. Click on the **Environment Variables** button:

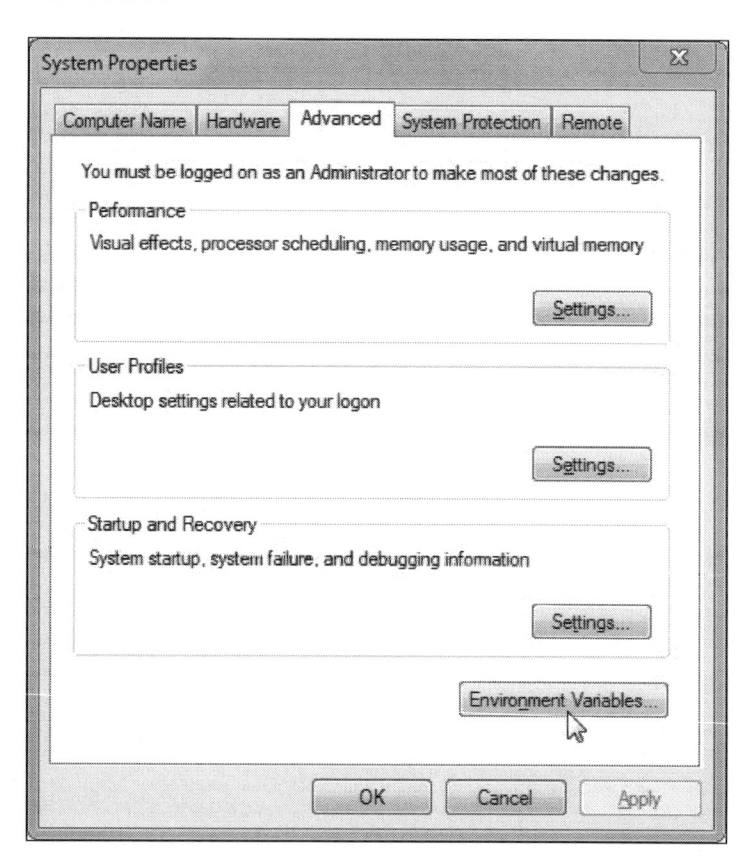

8. The **Environment Variables** window will appear. Click on the **New** button (at the top) that corresponds to **User variables for <USERNAME>** (the username in this case is **andreas**), as shown here:

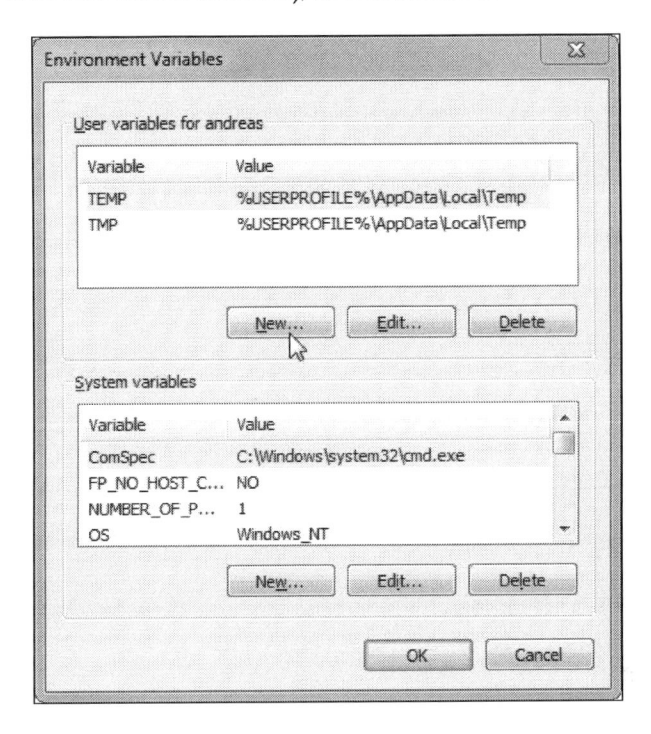

9. A window with the title **New User Variable** will appear. Now, fill in the two text fields. Enter `JAVA_HOME` in the **Variable name** field and the JDK's path you found earlier in the **Variable value** field, as shown in the following screenshot:

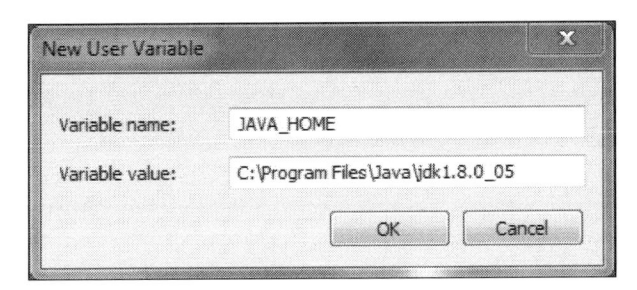

Great! Now your system is prepared for the Android SDK installer. Make sure to exit the Android SDK installer if it is still running to let the change take effect. You will be presented with the next screen after the installer has restarted.

Introduction to LibGDX and Project Setup

10. Now, back in the Android SDK setup, click on **Next** to continue the installation, as shown here:

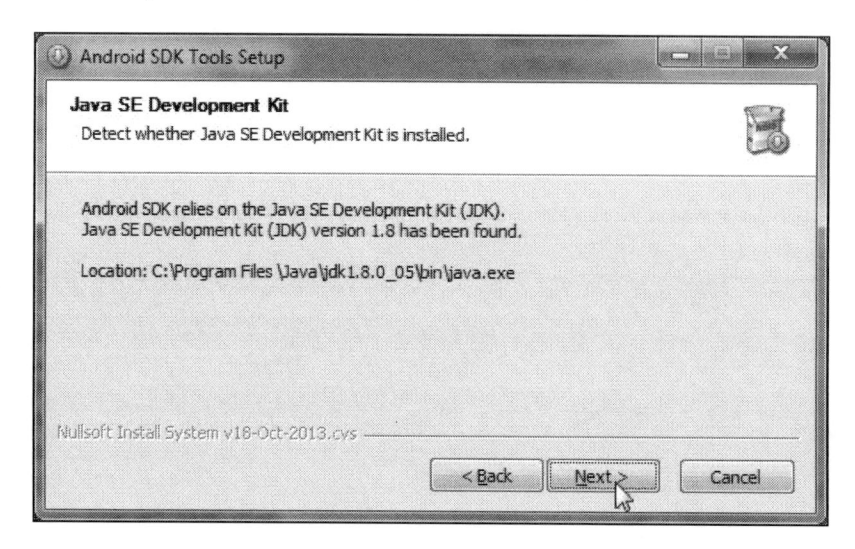

11. The following screenshot will ask you to choose the users for which the Android SDK should be installed. Usually, the suggested **Install for anyone using this computer** selection is perfectly fine, so just click on **Next** to continue.

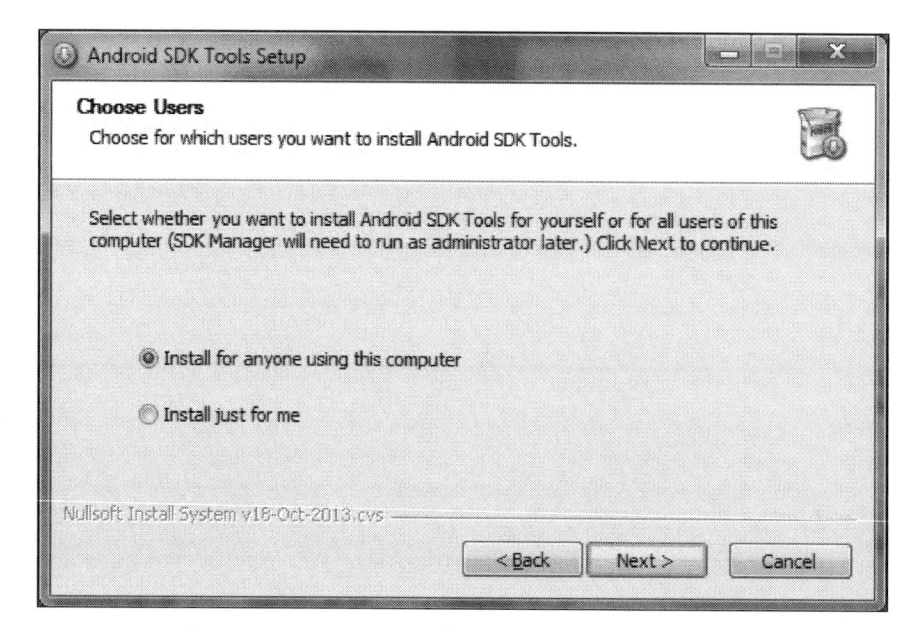

12. Now, choose the installation location on your computer. You can safely keep the suggested location and click on **Next** to continue:

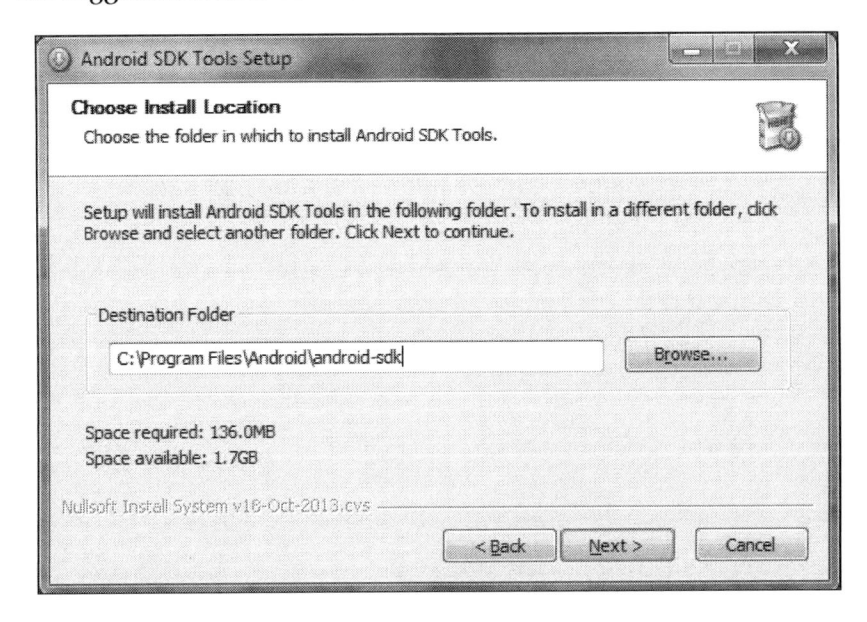

13. After this, you will be asked to choose a start menu folder. Again, you can safely keep the suggestion and click on **Install** to start the installation process:

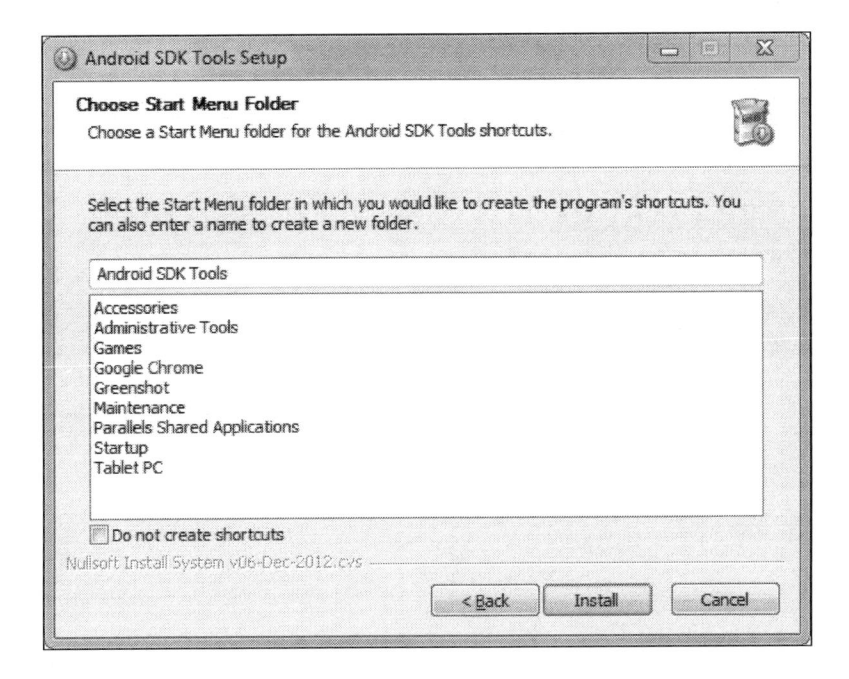

14. After the installation is complete, click on **Next** to continue:

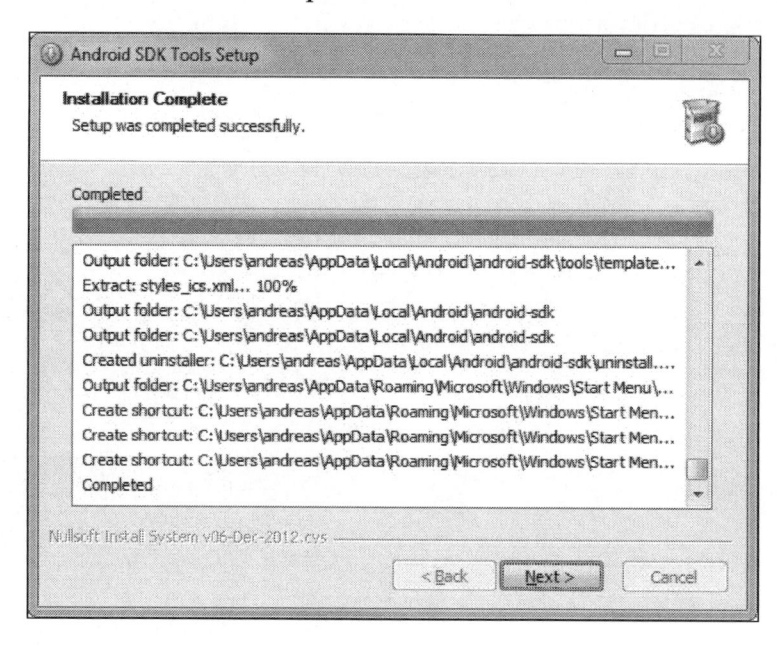

15. Once the installation is finished, you can choose to start the Android SDK Manager. Leave the **Start SDK Manager (to download system images, etc.)** checkbox enabled and click on **Finish** to start the manager:

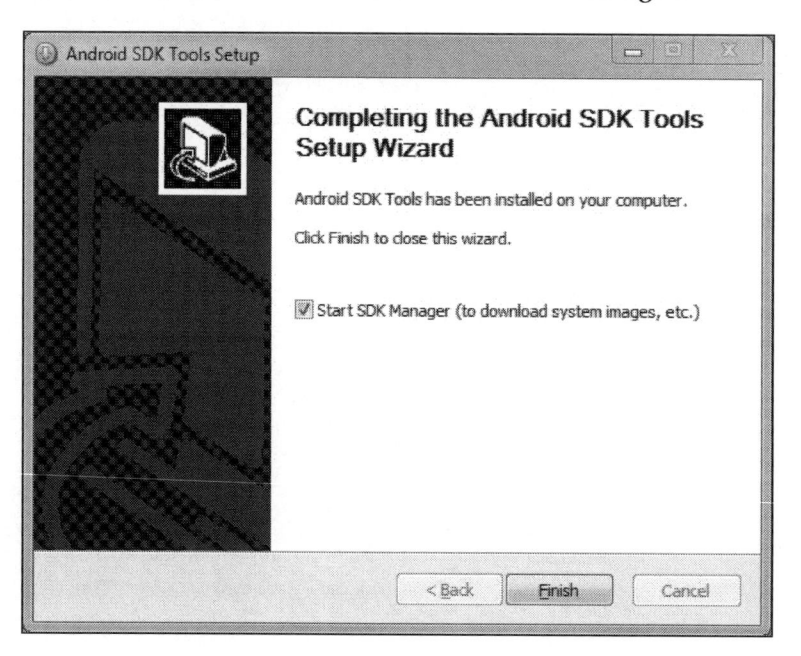

The Android SDK Manager enables you to download system images for the specific API levels you want to develop applications for. For up-to-date and detailed information about Android API levels, check out the link `http://developer.android.com/guide/topics/manifest/uses-sdk-element.html#ApiLevels`.

16. Now, choose at least **Android 2.2 (API 8)** and/or any other higher API levels that you might need and click on the **Install 7 packages** button to automatically download and install all the relevant files, as shown in the following screenshot. The reason why we want to use at least API level 8 is that the earlier versions before Android 2.2 do not support OpenGL ES 2.0, which we will need in later chapters. Using a certain API level also allows you to control the range of devices that you will be able to see and install on your application via the Google Play Store.

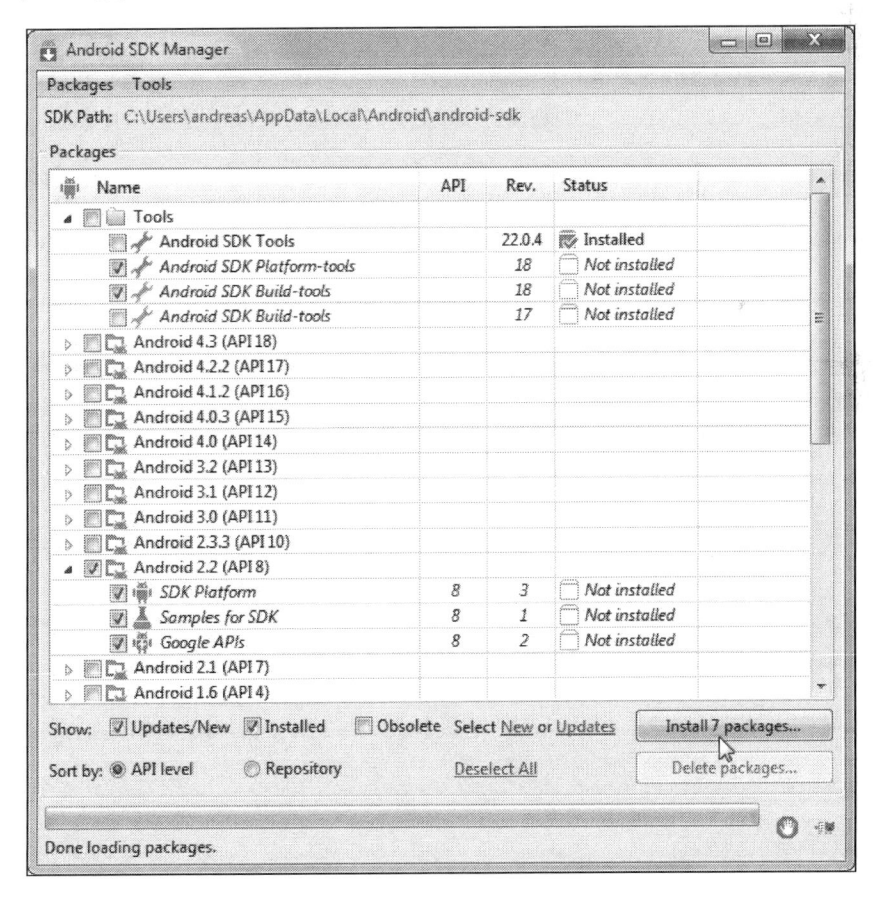

17. Once the download and installation process is finished, close the **Android SDK Manager** window.

Introduction to LibGDX and Project Setup

Running Eclipse and installing plugins

Great! You are almost done setting everything up. The remaining steps involve running Eclipse for the first time and installing important plugins, which are required to develop applications for Android, iOS, and HTML5/GWT with Eclipse.

Open Windows Explorer, and go to the location where you extracted Eclipse (here, `C:\eclipse\`), and simply run the program by double-clicking on the executable called `eclipse`.

Eclipse will ask you to select a so-called workspace. This is the folder where all your projects will be saved. We want to use the `C:\libgdx\` folder we created a bit earlier:

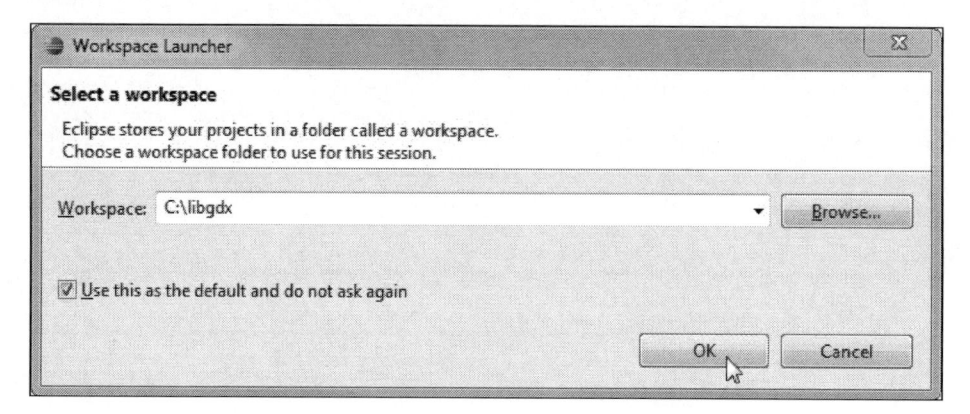

Select the **Use this as the default and do not ask again** checkbox if you don't want to see this dialog box every time you start Eclipse. To proceed, confirm the dialog box by clicking on the **OK** button.

The first time Eclipse is started with a new workspace, it will greet you with a welcome screen. Simply click on the small cross (**x**) of the **Welcome** tab to close it:

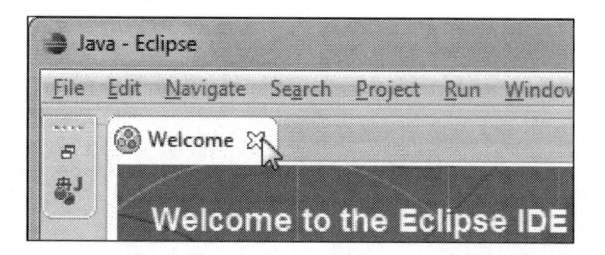

You should now see the standard view of Eclipse, which is also called the **Java Perspective**. On the left-hand side, you can see the **Package Explorer** section, as shown in the following screenshot. This is where you will see and manage your different projects. This is all you need to know about Eclipse for the moment.

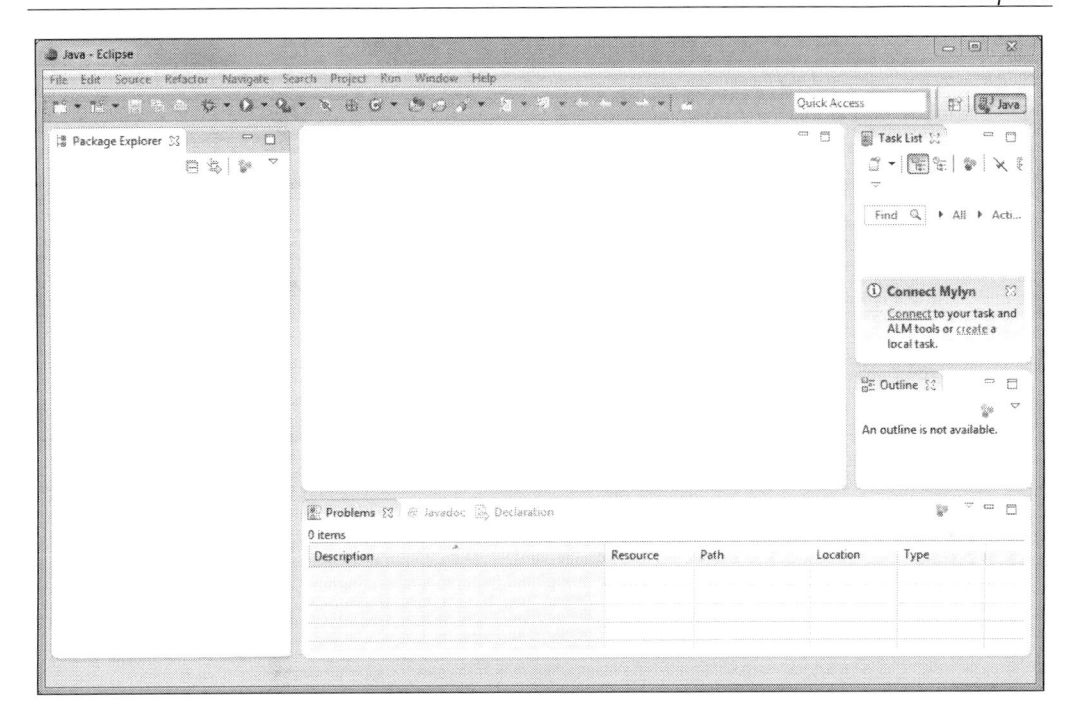

If you have never worked with Eclipse before, it might seem quite overwhelming with all these windows, toolbars, huge context menus, and so on. However, be rest assured that all the steps will be discussed in detail as required to make it easy for you to follow.

To install new plugins, go to the menu bar, and click on **Help**, and then click on **Install New Software**. This will open the **Install** window, where you can type the special repository URLs to browse for new plugins. Google provides a list of such URLs at `https://developers.google.com/eclipse/docs/getting_started`. You have to choose the correct URL that corresponds with your Eclipse installation.

At the time of writing this book, Eclipse 4.3.2 (Kepler) was the most current version available. According to Google's website, the suggested URL for our version is `http://dl.google.com/eclipse/plugin/4.3`.

Type the URL in the text field that is labeled **Work with** and press return to let Eclipse request a list of available downloads. Select everything in the list that is shown in **Developer Tools** to add support for Android applications. Then, select everything in **Google Plugin for Eclipse (required)** to install the required Eclipse plugin. Lastly, select **Google Web Toolkit SDK 2.5.1 in SDKs** to add support for HTML5/GWT applications and click on **Next** to continue:

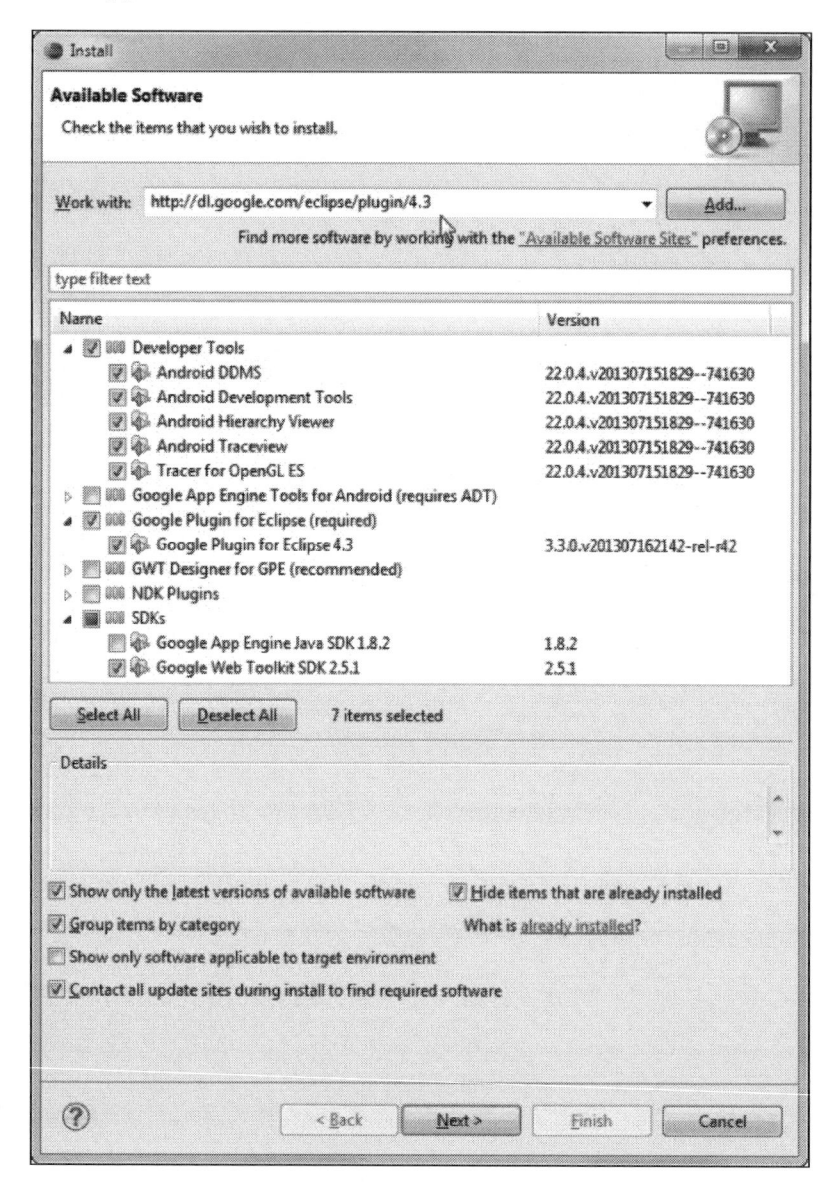

Now, click on **Next** to start the installation:

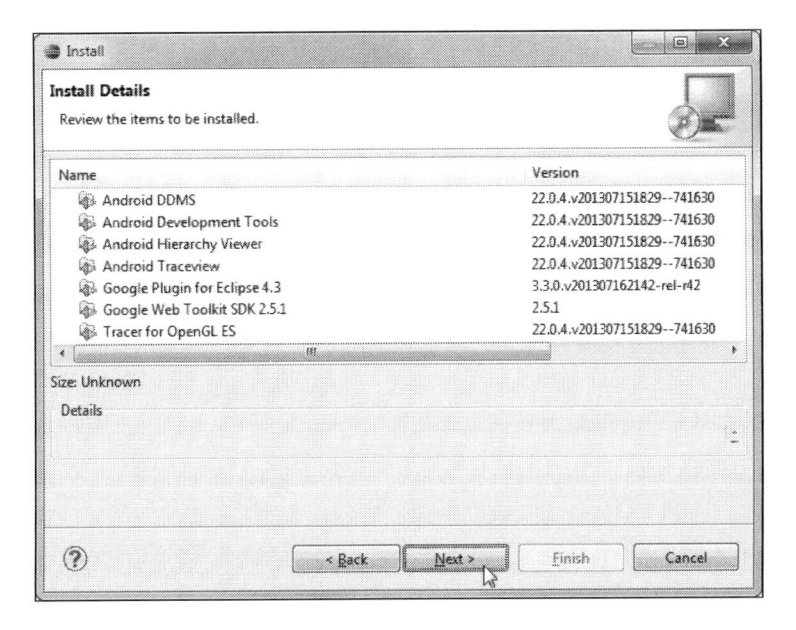

You will now be prompted to accept the terms of the license agreements by selecting the **I accept the terms of the license agreements** option. You have to do this before you can click on **Finish** to continue, as shown in the following screenshot:

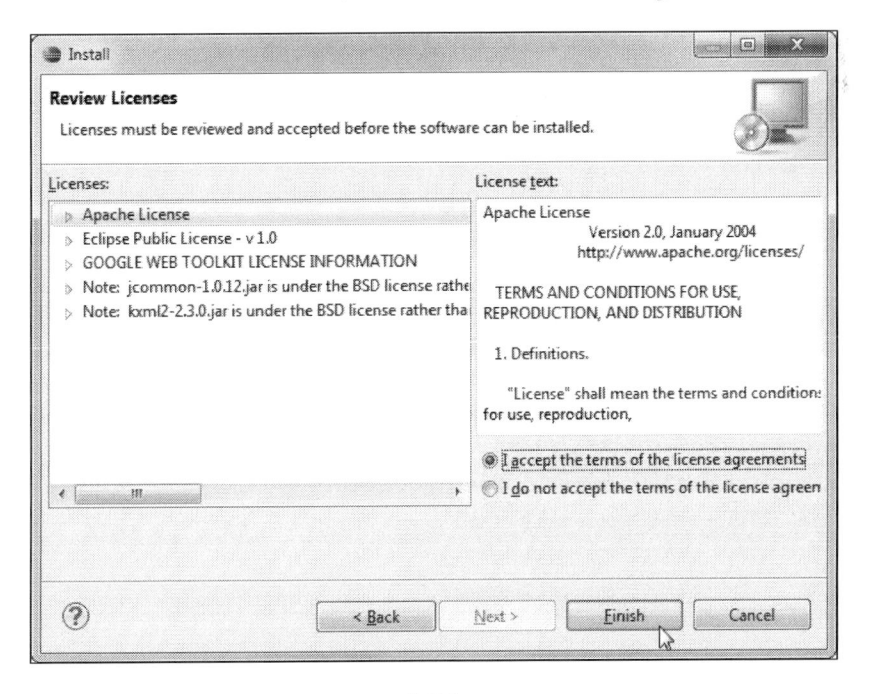

Introduction to LibGDX and Project Setup

The download process should only take a couple of minutes, depending on the speed of your network connection. When downloading is finished, Eclipse will show a security warning that you are about to install unsigned content and wants to know whether it should continue or abort. There is always a potential risk of installing malicious software. However, in this case, the download is provided by Google, a well-known company, which is trustworthy enough. Click on the **OK** button to accept the warning and continue the installation, as shown in the following screenshot:

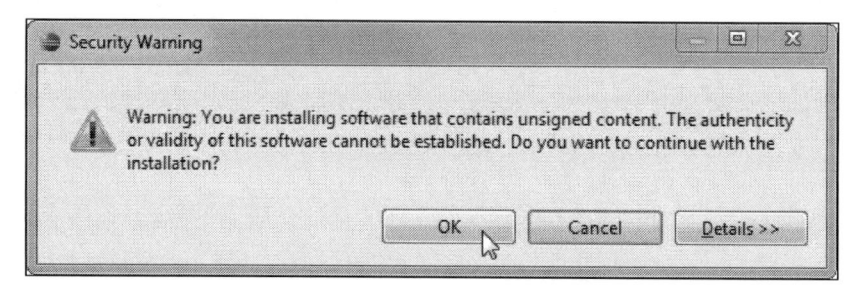

After the installation is finished, a final restart of Eclipse is required. Click on the **Yes** button to confirm the restart:

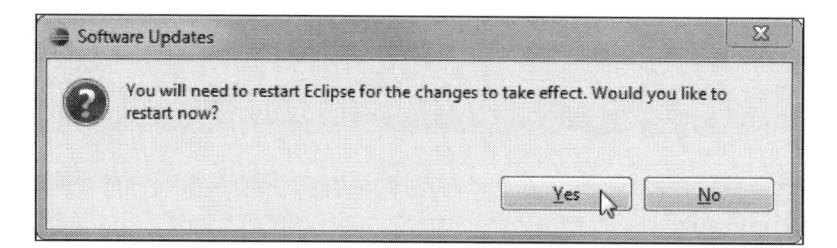

Now, let's install the Gradle plugin for Eclipse so that we can import the project into Eclipse via Gradle. For this, let's perform the previous steps again. Go to the **Install New Software** option in the **Help** menu.

Enter the URL `http://dist.springsource.com/release/TOOLS/gradle` in the **Work with** field:

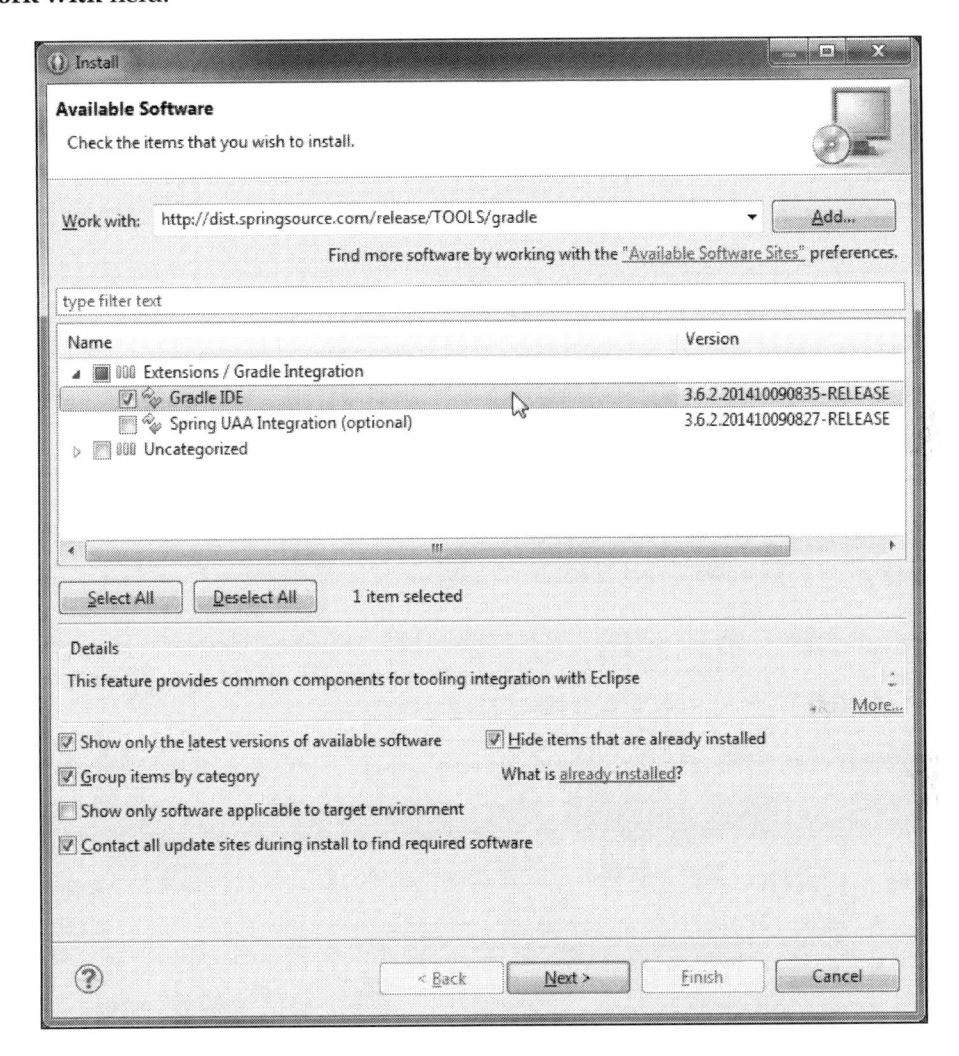

Select **Gradle IDE** under **Extensions / Gradle Integration** and click on **Next**. Continue as you did while installing Eclipse plugins to finish the process.

Additionally, in order to enable the iOS development, you need to install the RoboVM plugin in Eclipse. RoboVM for Eclipse integrates the RoboVM AOT (ahead-of-time) compiler with the Eclipse Java IDE. With this plugin, you will be able to develop native iOS apps in Java and launch them on the iOS simulator and iOS devices from within Eclipse.

> To execute an application using RoboVM as backend, you need a Mac with Mac OS X 10.9 or higher version with Xcode 5.0 or higher version installed. However, you can construct the project in Windows and later copy it to Mac for execution.

To download and install the latest RoboVM plugin, we will perform the same steps that we did to install Eclipse plugins earlier. Go to the **Install New Software** option in the **Help** menu.

Enter the URL `http://download.robovm.org/eclipse/` and continue, as shown in the following screenshot:

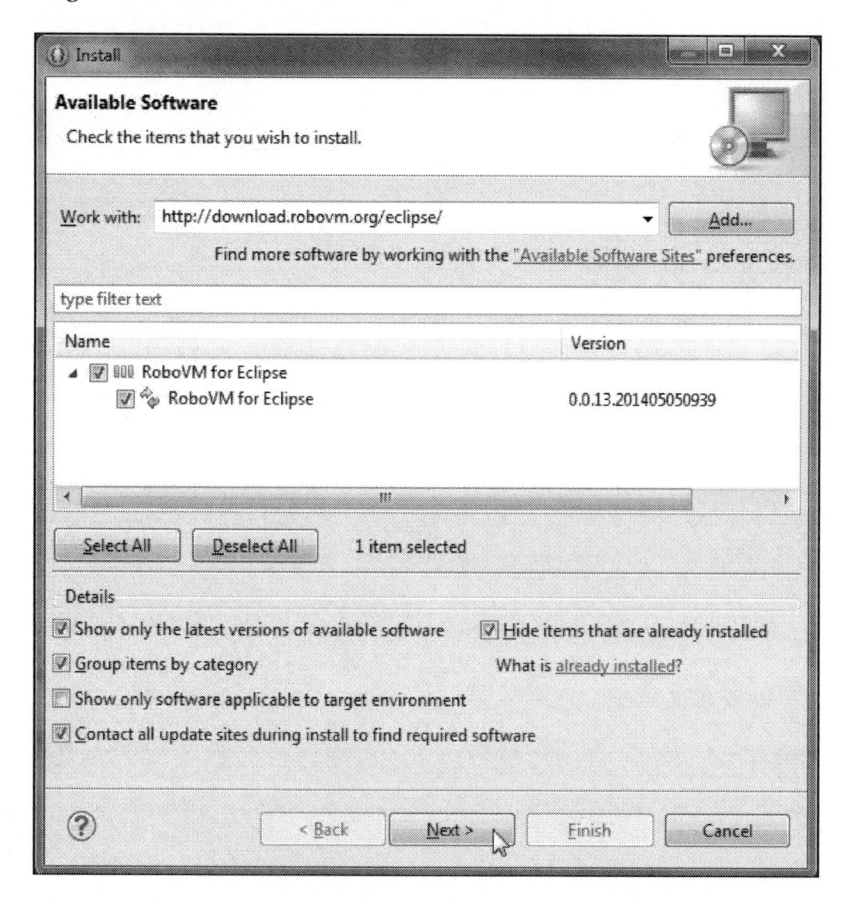

The latest RoboVM release while writing the book was v0.0.13.

Congratulations! You have just finished the installation of everything that you will need to develop and build your own games with LibGDX.

Creating a new application

The next step is to create a new application. Usually, you would have to create several projects in Eclipse: one project for the shared game code, another one for the desktop launcher, and more for the Android, iOS, and HTML5/GWT launchers. Furthermore, the projects would also have to be configured and linked together in a certain way. This is quite a time-consuming task and more or less an error-prone process for inexperienced users.

Luckily, LibGDX provides tools to generate preconfigured projects for a new application that can be directly imported into Eclipse. There are two tools to create a LibGDX project, the latest one is using Gradle, and the old project setup tool written by Aurelien Ribon. First, we will learn about the old setup tool and then about the Gradle setup tool.

Using the old setup tool

The old project setup tool is an executable JAR file called `gdx-setup-ui.jar`.

Step 1

You can download the old setup tool from `https://github.com/libgdx/libgdx-old-setup-ui`, as shown here:

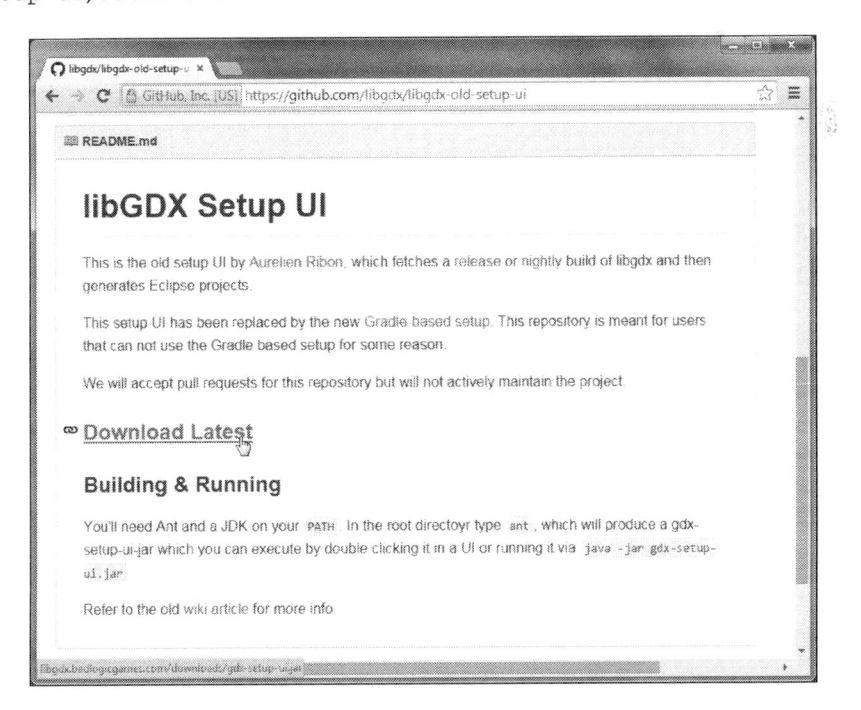

Step 2

To run the tool, double-click on the `gdx-setup-ui` file. When the program starts, click on the big **Create** button:

Step 3

In the next window, you will see a box labeled **CONFIGURATION** on the left-hand side. Here, you can configure what the tool will generate.

Enter `demo` in the **Name** field, which defines a common project name for your application. Each launcher project will add its own suffix to it, such as `-desktop`, `-android`, or `-html`. A preview of the outcome is shown in the **OVERVIEW** box on the right-hand side of the window.

The **Package** field defines the name of your Java package. This needs to be a unique identifier written in lowercase, which is usually derived from a reversed domain name. You do not have to own a domain name nor does it have to really exist, but it helps in choosing nonconflicting namespaces for Java applications. This is especially important on Android, as identical package names for two separate applications would mean that the already installed application is going to be overwritten by the second one while trying to install it. For this demo application, use `com.packtpub.libgdx.demo` as the package name for now.

The **Game class** field defines the name of the main class in the shared game code project. Enter `MyDemo` as the game class name.

Chapter 1

The **Destination** field defines the destination folder where all the projects will be generated. Click on the blue folder button (just next to the field) and set the destination folder to `C:\libgdx\`.

In another box called **LIBRARY SELECTION**, the status of required libraries is shown. If there is any item listed in red, it needs to be fixed before any project can be generated. You will see **LibGDX** being listed in red in the **Required** section. Click on the blue folder icon next to it:

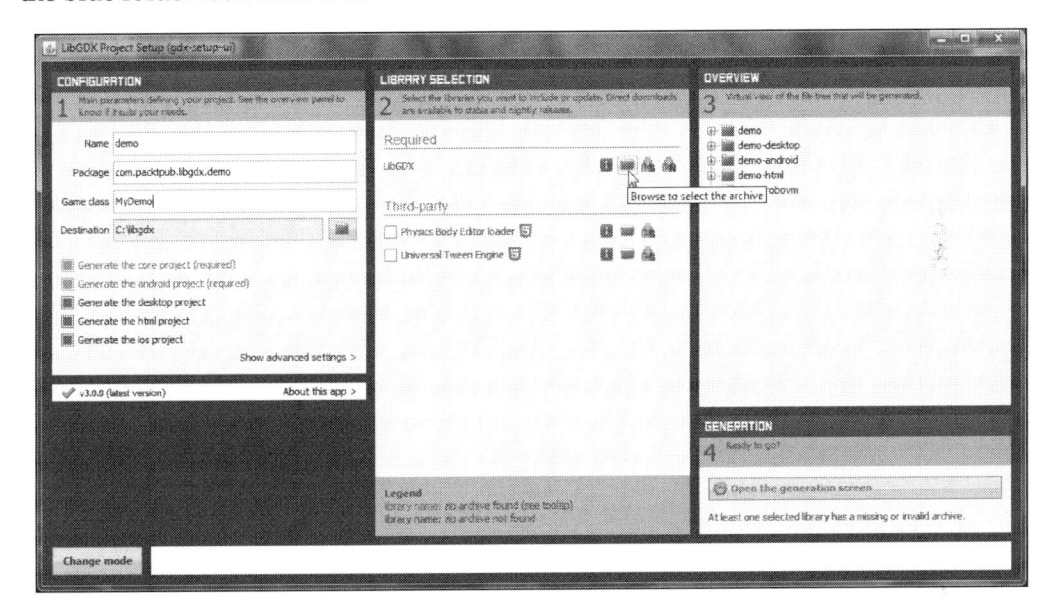

Step 4

Then, choose the downloaded archive file `libgdx-1.2.0.zip` from `C:\libgdx\` and click on **Open**, as shown in the following screenshot:

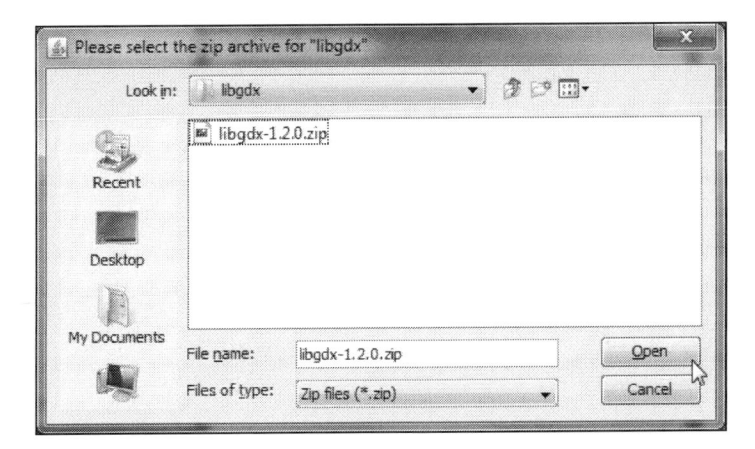

Introduction to LibGDX and Project Setup

Step 5

The text color of the **LibGDX** label should have changed from red to green by now. Click on the **Open the generation screen** button to continue:

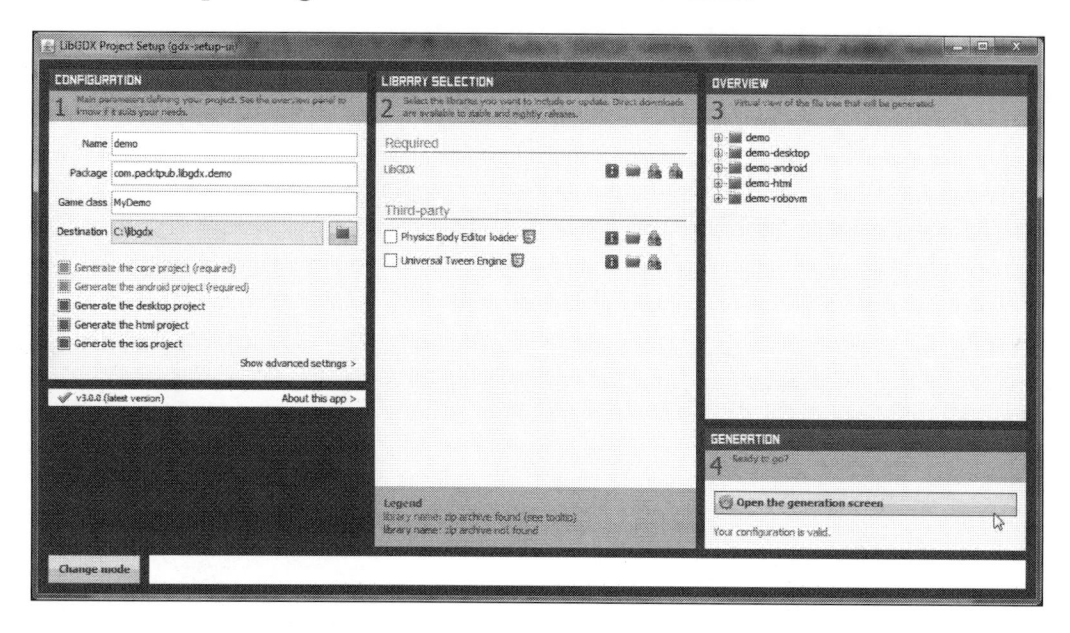

Step 6

Next, click on the **Launch!** button to generate all the projects, as shown here:

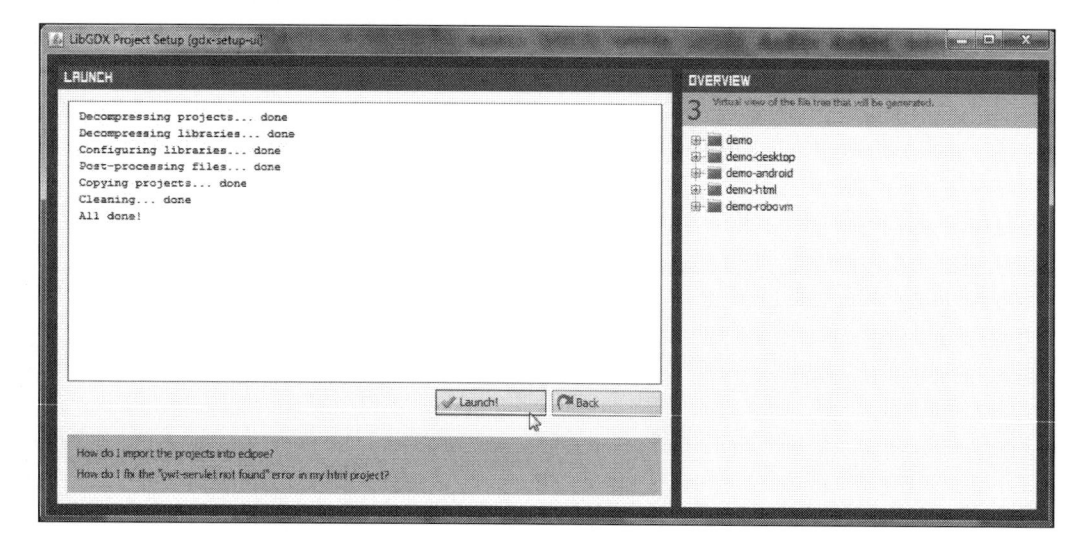

Step 7

All done! You can now go to Eclipse and start importing the generated projects into your workspace. To do this, simply navigate to the **Import** option in the **File** menu.

Step 8

In the **Import** dialog box, open the **General** category, select **Existing Projects into Workspace**, and click on the **Next** button, as shown here:

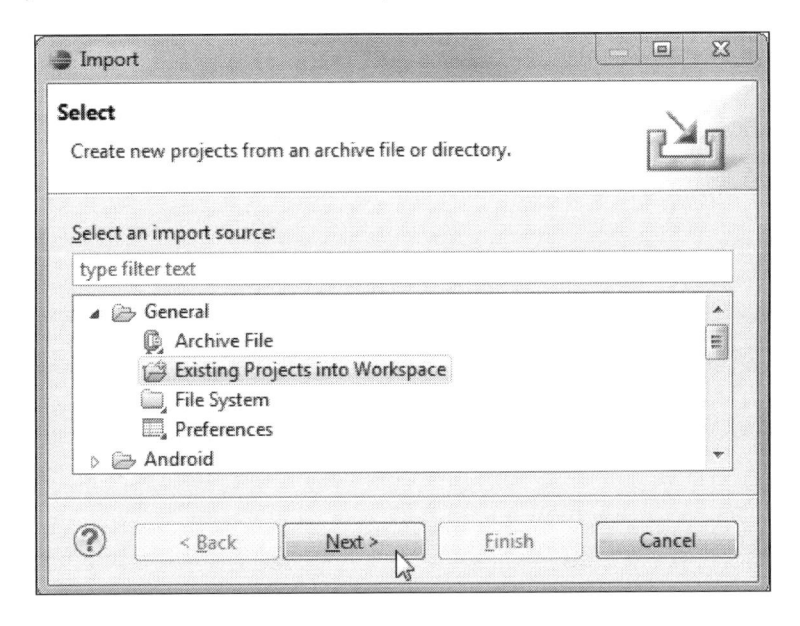

Step 9

Click on the radio button **Select root directory** and enter `C:\libgdx` in the text field. This is the directory where all your generated projects were created. You need to confirm your text input by pressing the return key once. Eclipse will start to scan the directory for your projects and list them. Leave all checkboxes selected and click on the **Finish** button, as shown in the following screenshot:

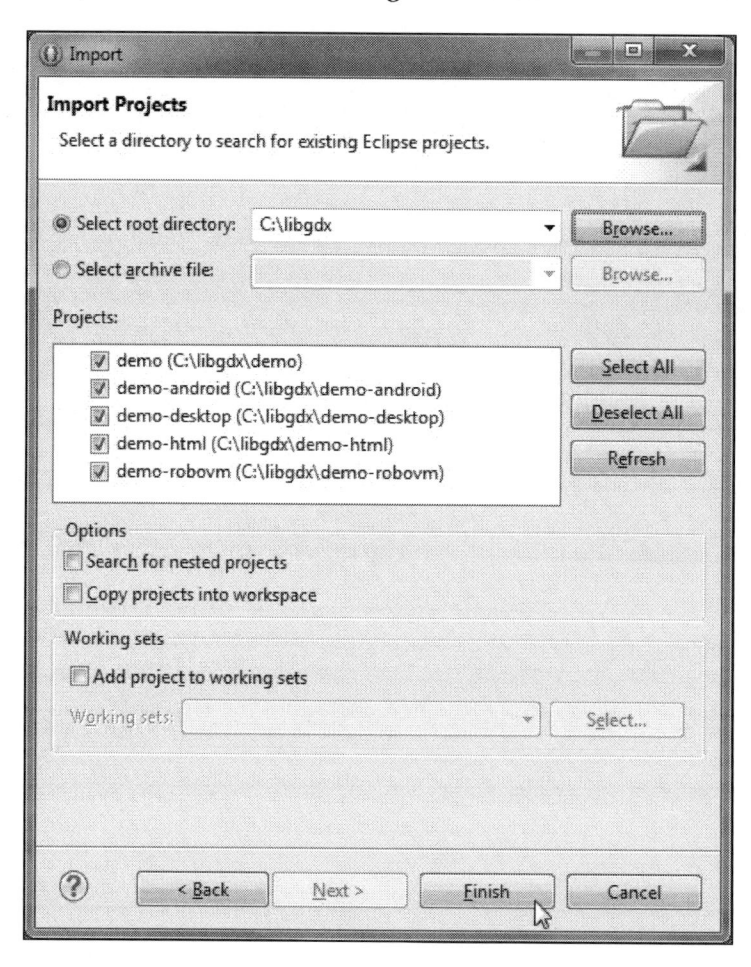

Step 10

Eclipse will automatically try to build (compile) all the four newly imported projects in your workspace and probably fail. There are two issues that need to be resolved manually after the import. The first one is reported directly to the **Console** window in Eclipse. It complains about being unable to resolve the target android-15, as shown in the following screenshot:

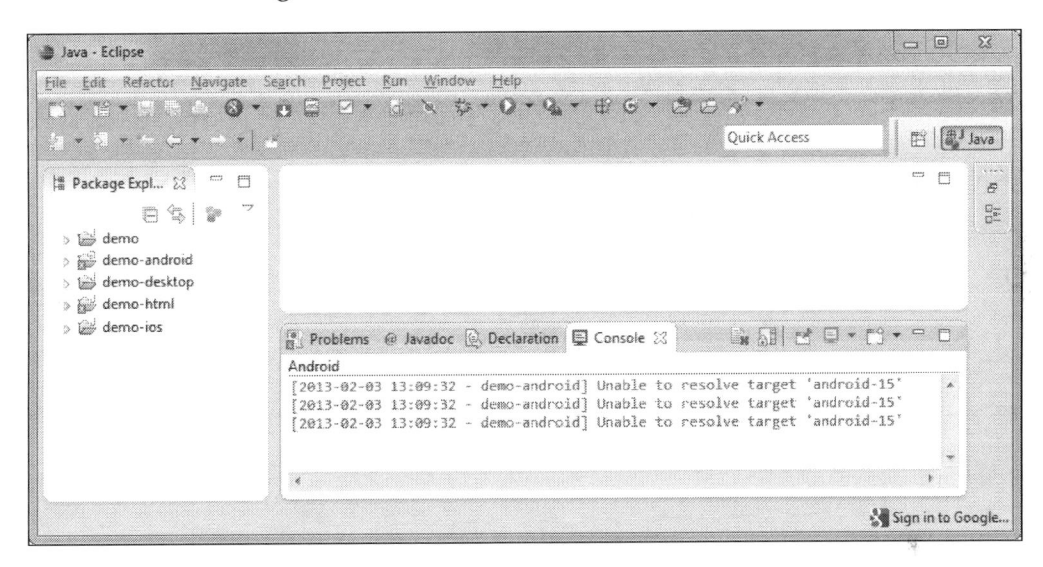

You have to open the project properties of the `demo-android` project. First, select it in the **Package Explorer** box on the left-hand side. Then, go to the menu bar and navigate to **Properties** option in the **Project** menu:

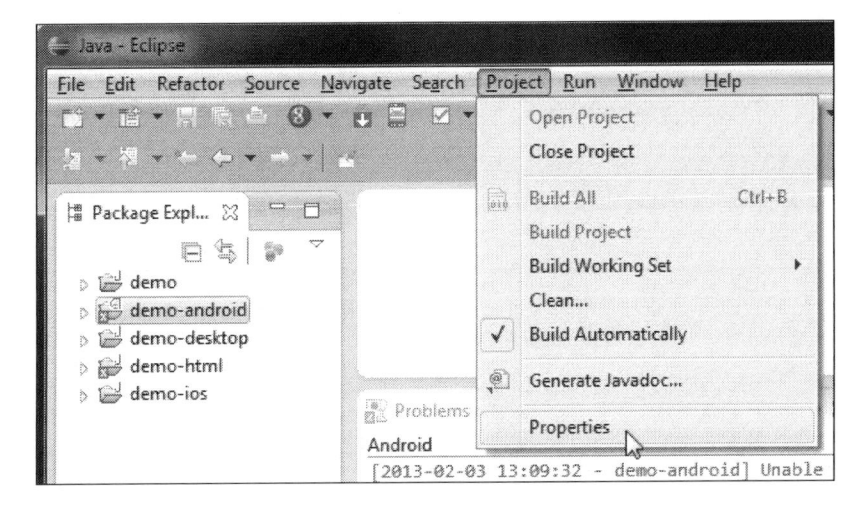

Step 11

The title of the window will say **Properties for demo-android**. If this is not the case, close the window and make sure you have selected the correct project and try again. Next, select **Android** from the list on the left-hand side. You will see a list of targets that are available on your system. Select **Android 2.2**, which uses API level 8, and click on the **OK** button, as shown here:

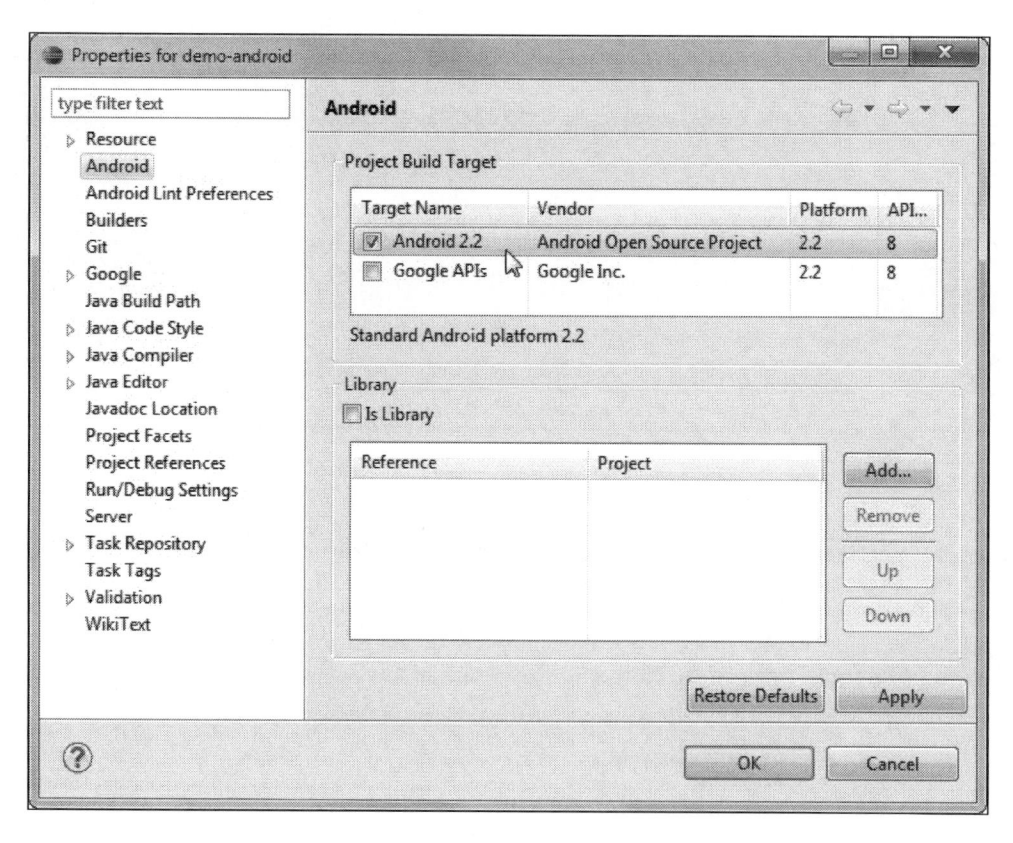

Step 12

Eclipse will recognize the change and successfully build the Android project this time.

The second issue requires you to click on the **Problems** tab in Eclipse. Open the **Errors** list and right-click on the reported problem, which will say **The GWT SDK JAR gwt-servlet.jar is missing in the WEB-INF/lib directory**. Choose **Quick Fix** from the context menu, as shown in the following screenshot:

Chapter 1

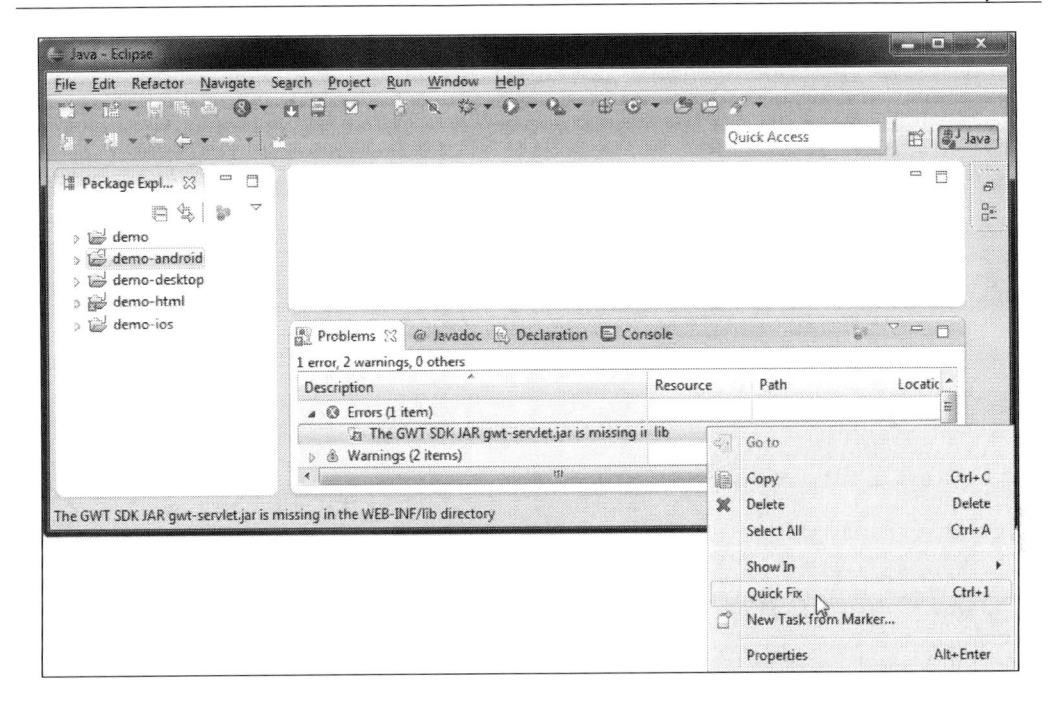

Step 13

In the **Quick Fix** dialog box, select **Synchronize <WAR>/WEB-INF/lib with SDK libraries** as the desired fix and click on the **Finish** button, as shown here:

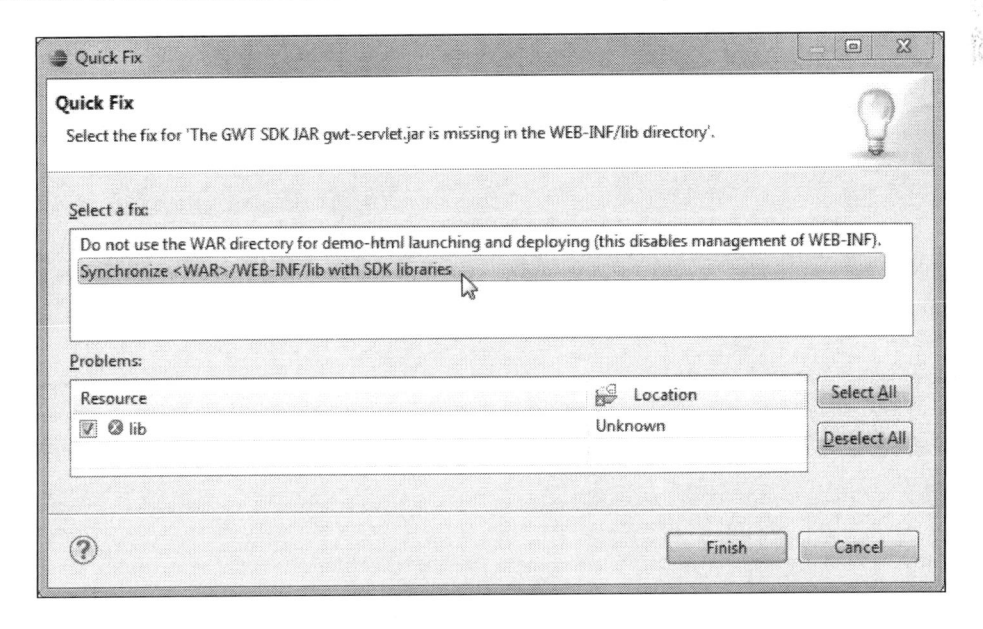

Introduction to LibGDX and Project Setup

The two issues will be solved by now, which means that all the projects are now automatically built without failure and can be compiled.

> Though the steps to create a project using `gdx-setup-ui` might seem difficult, actually it's very easy. In our book, we will generate the project setup for our first game using this setup tool, and later in *Chapter 14, Bullet Physics*, we will use the Gradle-based tool to generate the project, thereby mastering the two technologies.

Using the Gradle-based setup

For the first game, we will use the projects generated using the old setup tool; however, read this section and understand how it works, so that we can use it later in *Chapter 14, Bullet Physics*.

You can download the `gdx-setup.jar` file from `http://libgdx.badlogicgames.com/download.html` and then click on **Download Setup App**, as shown in the following screenshot:

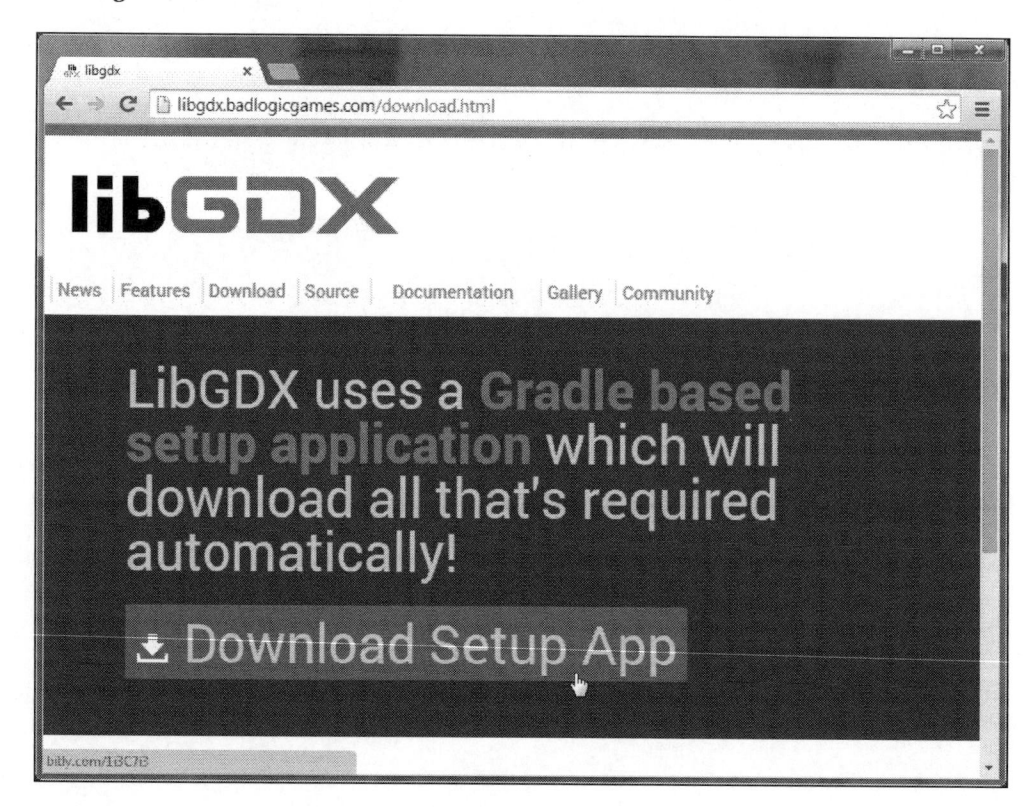

However, we have already downloaded the `libgdx-1.2.0.zip` file, which contains `gdx-setup.jar`; hence, we will extract `gdx-setup` from the archive. To run the tool, double-click on `gdx-setup` to get the following screenshot:

The **Name**, **Package**, **Game Class**, and **Destination** fields are the same that we learned for the old project setup tool.

The **Android SDK** field defines the path to where you have installed your `android sdk`. Click on the **Browse** button and set it to the `android sdk` folder. Here, it's `C:\Program Files\Android\android-sdk`.

We will now select **Release 1.2.0** from the drop-down list in the **Libgdx Version** field. Next under the **Sub Projects** tab, you can select the hardware platforms that you want to support. Here, we select all four, namely, **Desktop**, **Android**, **Ios**, and **Html**.

Introduction to LibGDX and Project Setup

Finally, you can select the extensions (for example, `box2d`, `physics bullet`, and so on) to be included in your app. Some might not work on all the platforms for which you'll get a warning. For the demo, we don't need any extensions, hence ignore this part.

> Once chosen and created, you will have to add new hardware platforms or extensions manually. For manually adding dependencies, visit https://github.com/libgdx/libgdx/wiki/Dependency-management-with-Gradle.

Now, click on the **Advanced** button, enable **Eclipse**, and then click on **Save**, as shown in the following screenshot:

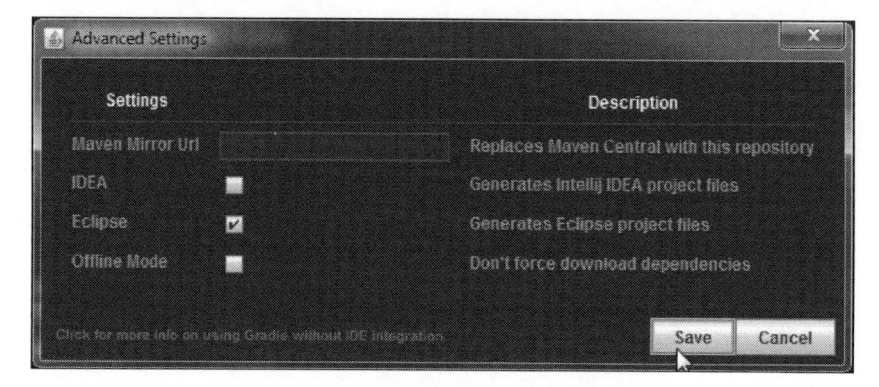

Now that we have set everything, click on **Generate**.

> The `gdx-setup` option will prompt you to download and install the latest SDK platform and build tools. Just ignore this. While writing the book, the SDK platform was 19 and build tools were 19.0.3.

It will take a while to download and generate the projects. Make sure that you are connected to the Internet. Finally, it will display **BUILD SUCCESSFUL** like this:

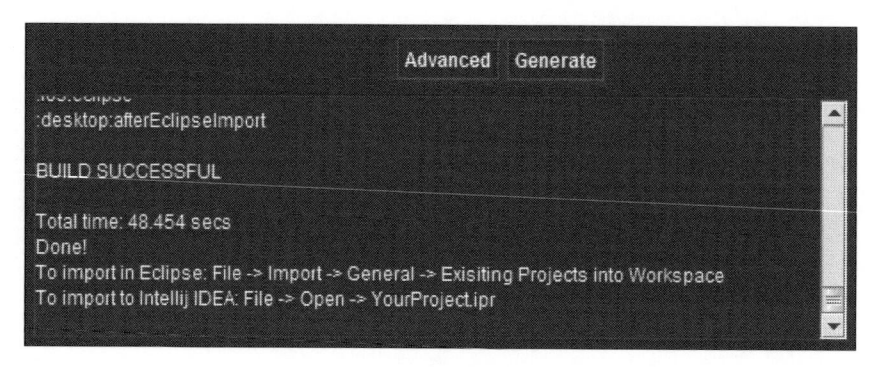

This means you are now ready to import the project into your IDE, run, debug, and package it! All done! You can now go to Eclipse and start importing the generated projects into your workspace.

You can import projects to Eclipse as in the old project setup by following *Step 7* to *Step 9*. However, in order to access the features of the Gradle plugin, you need to import it quite differently. Navigate to the **Import** option in the **File** menu. In the **Import** dialog box, select the `Gradle Project` subfolder from the `Gradle` folder, as shown in the following screenshot:

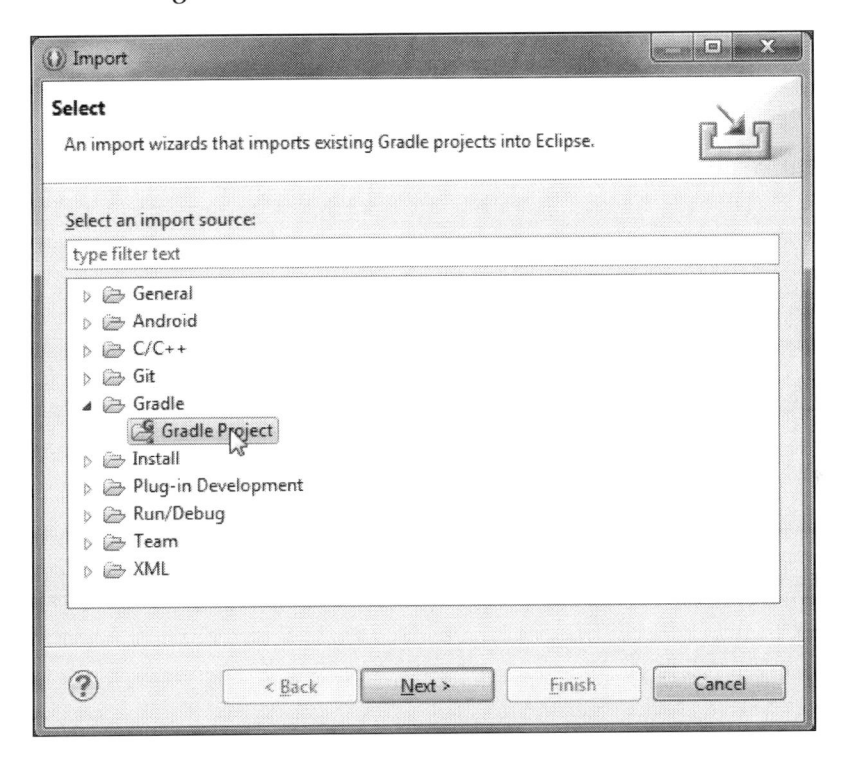

Introduction to LibGDX and Project Setup

Now in the **Import Gradle Project** window, click on **Browse** and select the folder where you created the demo project. Here, it's `C:\libgdx`. Then, click on the **Build Model** button:

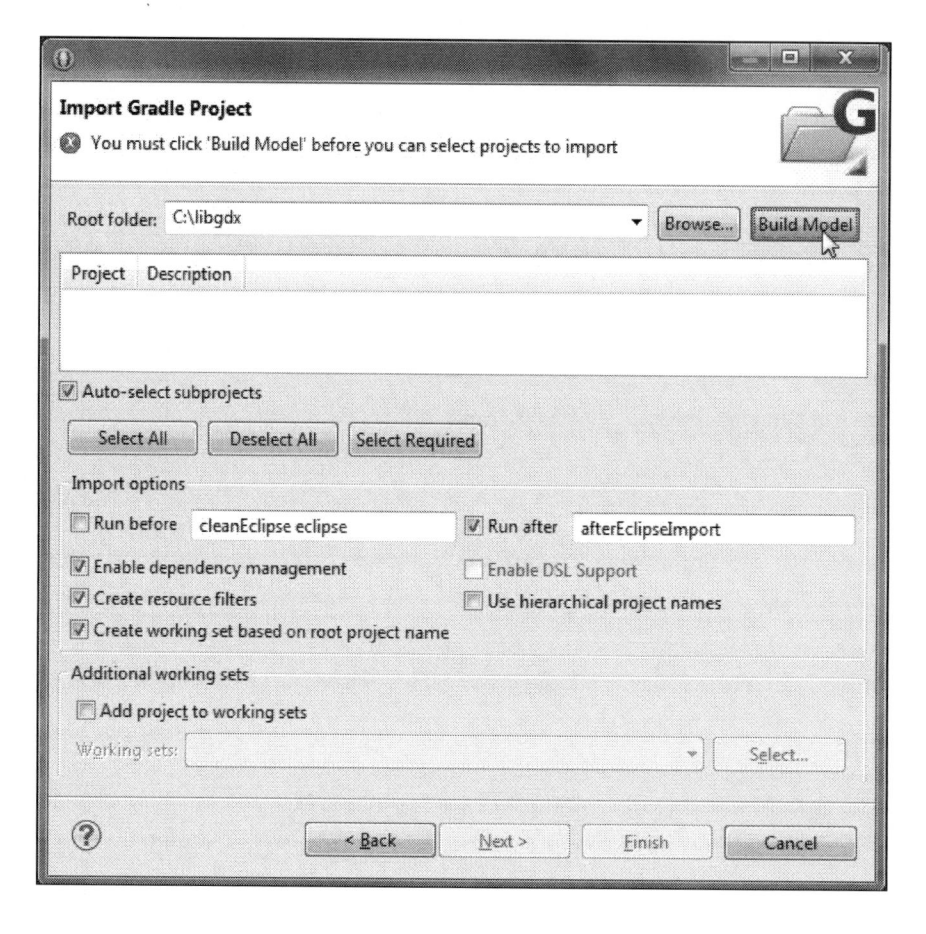

It will take a while to build the project. After this, select the different projects and click on **Finish**, as shown in the following screenshot:

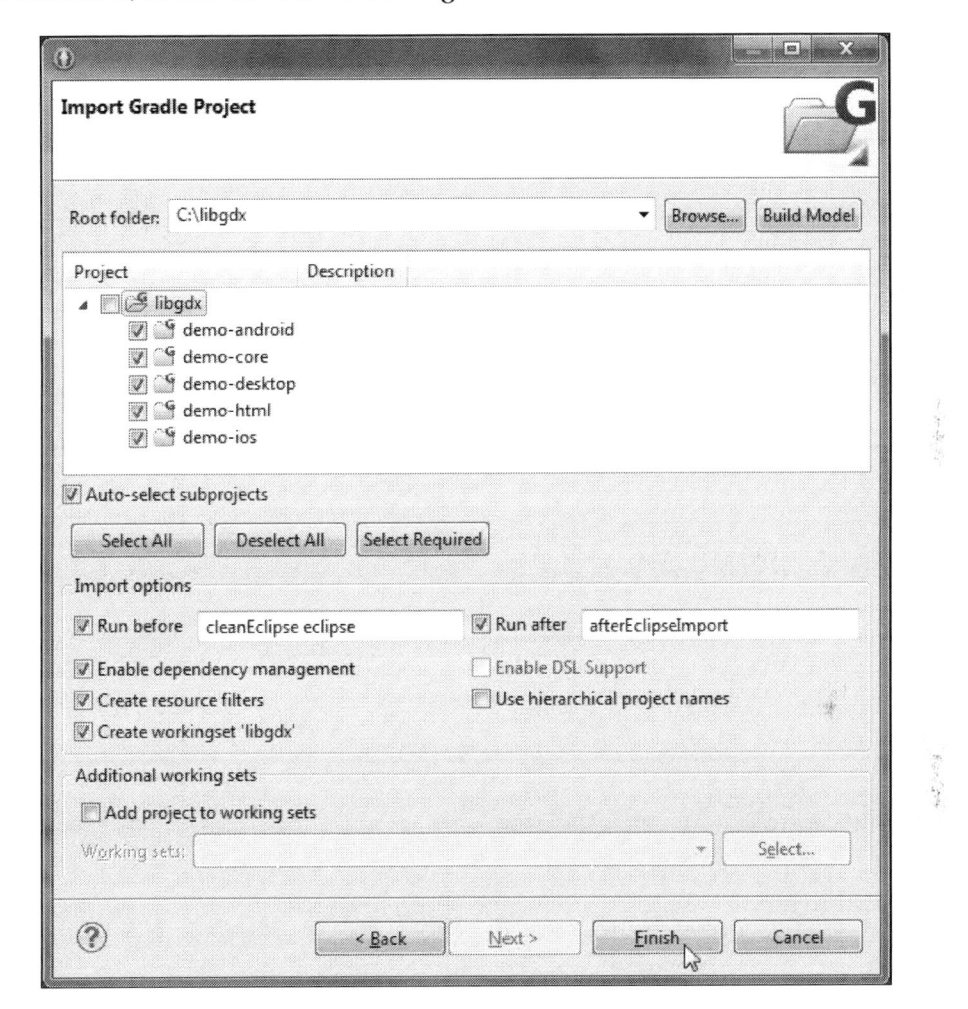

All done! After importing, change the API level of **Android** to **8** by following *Step 10* and *Step 11* from the old project setup.

gdx-setup versus gdx-setup-ui

Before entering into the game, let's make a quite distinction between the two project setup tools. Why choose one over the other?

There is no doubt that the Gradle-based setup tool is the best. One of the biggest advantages of using Gradle is the dependency management system. The dependency management system is quick, simple, efficient, and easy. If you are developing a simple project without any extensions such as Box2d, you might use the old setup tool; however, if you are developing a multi-platform project, which might be updated soon, then you can use the Gradle-based setup tool.

The projects generated using Gradle and the old setup tool have some minor naming differences that are illustrated in the following figure:

Gradle Based Setup Tool (gdx-setup)	Old Project Setup Tool (gdx-setup-ui)

demo-core
  src
    com.packtpub.libgdx.demo
      MyDemo.java
      MyDemo.gwt.xml
demo-android
  src
    com.packtpub.libgdx.demo.android
      AndroidLauncher.java
demo-desktop
  src
    com.packtpub.libgdx.demo.desktop
      DesktopLauncher.java
demo-html
  src
    com.packtpub.libgdx.demo
      GdxDefinition.gwt.xml
      GdxDefinitionSuperdev.gwt.xml
    com.packtpub.libgdx.demo.client
      HtmlLauncher.java
demo-ios
  src
    com.packtpub.libgdx.demo
      IOSLauncher.java
	demo
	  src
	    com.packtpub.libgdx.demo
	      MyDemo.java
	      MyDemo.gwt.xml
	demo-android
	  src
	    com.packtpub.libgdx.demo
	      MainActivity.java
	demo-desktop
	  src
	    com.packtpub.libgdx.demo
	      Main.java
	demo-html
	  src
	    com.packtpub.libgdx.demo
	      GwtDefinition.gwt.xml
	    com.packtpub.libgdx.demo.client
	      GwtLauncher.java
	demo-robovm
	  src
	    com.packtpub.libgdx.demo
	      RobovmLauncher.java

Chapter 1

The Java classes shown in the preceding figure are starter classes; we will learn about them in the next chapter. Although the names for projects, packages, and classes generated by the two tools are slightly different, other aspects of the projects such as the assets folder, manifest files, and project wiring are the same.

> All the chapters in this book will be explained based on the projects generated from the old setup tool. However, understanding projects generated from Gradle is very easy because the names are easily comparable.
>
> The old setup tool (gdx-setup-ui) is now not encouraged by LibGDX and it might be phased out later; however, it is included in this book because it will be useful for smaller projects.

You can also see that the projects generated and organized under the C:\libgdx path are different for both tools. The old setup tool (gdx-setup-ui) creates all the five projects in the respective folders, as shown in the following screenshot:

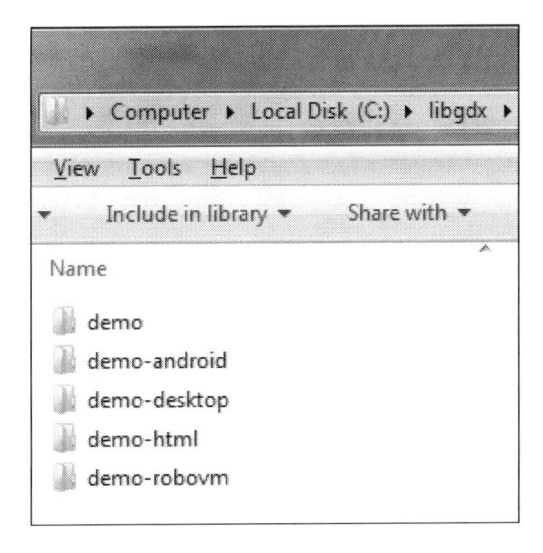

[53]

However, the Gradle-based tool (`gdx-setup`) creates a lot file, as shown here:

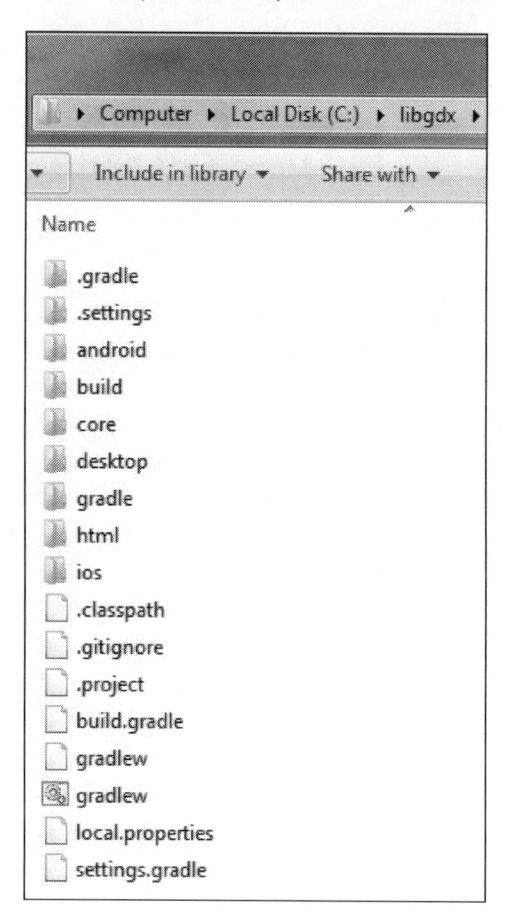

```
Computer ▶ Local Disk (C:) ▶ libgdx
Name
    .gradle
    .settings
    android
    build
    core
    desktop
    gradle
    html
    ios
    .classpath
    .gitignore
    .project
    build.gradle
    gradlew
    gradlew
    local.properties
    settings.gradle
```

Observe that our projects are named `core`, `android`, `desktop`, `html`, and `ios`. Additionally, take a note of the `build.gradle` file. This file is important because this is the file you need to edit in order to add more dependencies (such as hardware platform) or new extensions (such as Box2D or Bullet).

Kicking your game to life

Let's take a moment to discuss what a game basically consists of. From a very high-level point of view, a game can be split up into two parts: game assets and game logic.

Game assets include everything that is going to be used as a kind of working material in your game, such as images, sound effects, background music, and level data.

Game logic is responsible for keeping track of the current game state and to only allow a defined set of state transitions. These states will change a lot over time due to the events triggered either by the player or by the game logic itself. For example, when a player presses a button, picks up an item, or an enemy hits the player, the game logic will decide the appropriate action to be taken. All this is better known as gameplay. It constrains the ways of action in which a player can interact with the game world, and also how the game world would react to the player's actions.

To give you a better idea of this, take a look at the following diagram:

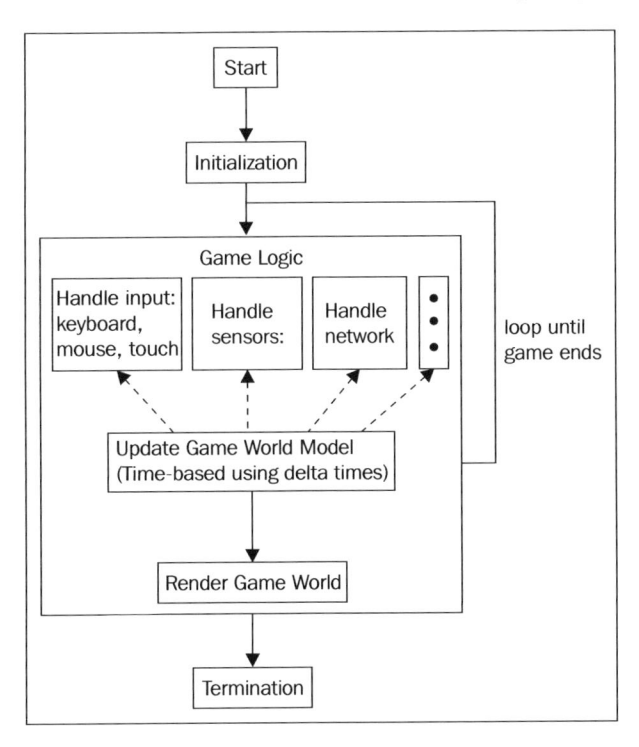

```
                    ┌───────┐
                    │ Start │
                    └───┬───┘
                        ▼
                ┌──────────────┐
                │ Initialization│
                └──────┬───────┘
                       ▼
        ┌─────────── Game Logic ───────────┐
        │ ┌──────────┐ ┌──────┐ ┌──────┐ • │
        │ │Handle    │ │Handle│ │Handle│ • │  loop until
        │ │input:    │ │sensors│ │network│ •│  game ends
        │ │keyboard, │ │      │ │      │   │
        │ │mouse,    │ │      │ │      │   │
        │ │touch     │ │      │ │      │   │
        │ └─────▲────┘ └──▲───┘ └──▲───┘   │
        │       └────┬────┴────┬───┘       │
        │       ┌────┴─────────────┐       │
        │       │Update Game World │       │
        │       │Model (Time-based │       │
        │       │using delta times)│       │
        │       └────────┬─────────┘       │
        │                ▼                 │
        │       ┌─────────────────┐        │
        │       │Render Game World│        │
        │       └─────────────────┘        │
        └────────────────┬─────────────────┘
                         ▼
                 ┌─────────────┐
                 │ Termination │
                 └─────────────┘
```

The very first step is to initialize the game, that is, loading assets into memory, creating the initial state of the game world, and registering with a couple of subsystems, such as input handlers for keyboard, mouse and touch input, audio for playback and recording, sensors, and network communication.

When everything is up and running, the game logic is ready to take over and will loop for the rest of the time until the game ends and will then be terminated. This kind of looping is also referred to as the game loop. Inside the game loop, the game logic accumulates all (new) data it is interested in and updates the game-world model accordingly.

It is very important to consider the speed at which updates will occur in the game world. Currently, the game will just run at the maximum speed of the available hardware. In most cases, this is not a desirable effect because it makes your game dependent on the processing power and the complexity of the scene to be rendered, which will vary from computer to computer. This implies that your game world will also progress at different speeds on different computers with an almost always negative impact on the gameplay.

The key to tackle this issue is to use delta times in order to calculate the fractional progress of the game world. The delta time is the real time between the last rendered frame and current frame. Now, every update to the game world will occur in relation to real time that is passed since the last frame was rendered. You will see how this actually works with LibGDX in the later examples.

What you have just read was an overview of the basic concept to create games. Yes, it is that simple! Frankly speaking, there is a lot more to learn before your application becomes a real game. There are lots of topics and concepts waiting to be discovered in this book. For instance, you will need to understand how to use and manage different images in an efficient manner. Efficiency becomes even more important if you plan to target mobile devices such as Android or iOS smartphones, where the available resources are constantly scarce.

Key to success lies in planning

Great! Now you have your development environment set up and a basic understanding of what a game is and what it might need. It appears to be a good idea to dedicate some additional time to think about your first game project and create a plan for it. In general, planning your game projects is what you should always do in the first place before any actual work is done. For novice game developers, it might be very tempting to skip this planning phase, which admittedly is a lot more fun in the beginning, but this approach is very likely to fall short in the long run. You will need some sort of outline of what you want to achieve. It does not have to be a very long and detailed description.

A simple and brief feature list of your design goals will do just fine for this purpose. The reason behind this is that you will make yourself aware of each single feature that is a part of your game. In addition, this list will also serve you as a great tool to measure and compare your progress in the game during the development phase. Bear in mind that game development is a very dynamic and iterative process. Although, you should try to adhere to your list of design goals for most of the time, there should always be room to adapt to shifting requirements. Just keep in mind that adhering to the list will make sure that you are going to push development in the right direction. Conversely, it will let you focus on the important parts first, while also protecting you from running out of time and taking too many detours, which prevents you from reaching the finish line due to unclear goals.

Game project – Canyon Bunny

To make this guide both easy and fun to read, it makes perfect sense to show you how to plan and develop a whole game project throughout this book. As we now know, planning should be the first step to take on the journey of any new game project.

So, let's begin with the outline:

- The name or working title for the game will be Canyon Bunny
- The genre will be 2D side-scrolling jump and run
- The list of actors are as follows:
    - The player character (can jump and move forward and will be controlled by the player)
    - Rocks will be serving as platforms for the player character and items
    - Canyons in the background (for level decoration)
    - Clouds in the sky (for level decoration)
    - Water at the bottom of the level (which will be deadly for the player character)
    - Collectible items (such as gold coins and feather power-up) for the player

Next, it is always helpful to write down some supporting text to further describe the overall behavior of the game, and how the features should be implemented.

Introduction to LibGDX and Project Setup

Description of the game

The game world is presented in a 2D-side view to the player. The view will scroll horizontally to the right-hand side when the player character moves forward. The background shows distant canyons and clouds in the sky. The bottom of the level is filled with water and will instantly kill the player character if both get in touch with each other.

The player character will move on and jump over to random rocks, sticking out of the water. The width and height will be different to make the game more challenging. The player is only in control of a jump button, which will keep the automatically forward-moving player character from falling down into the deadly water.

The level will be randomly populated with collectible items consisting of gold coins and feather power-ups. Collecting the gold coins will increase the player's high score. The feather power-up grants the player character the ability to fly for a limited time and can be used by repeatedly pressing the jump button. The player's goal is to beat the last high score.

As a picture is worth a thousand words, creating a sketch based on our outline can help us even more to get a better idea of the resulting game. Moreover, changing a sketch is usually a lot easier than having to change (complex) game code. So, you really want to keep it very simple; just grab your pen and paper and start to draw. If you feel lucky or have some time to spend, you can do something more elaborate, of course.

Here is a mock-up for Canyon Bunny:

The previous mock-up has been created entirely by using vector graphics. Using vector graphics in favor of raster graphics for your sketches can be an advantage as they are infinitely scalable to any size without losing the image quality. However, the final graphics used in games are almost, always, rasterized graphics, simply because vector graphics are costly to render in real time. So, the common approach is to create vector graphics and later on export them choosing an appropriate rasterized graphics file format, such as **Portable Network Graphics** (**PNG**) for lossless compression with alpha channel support, or **Joint Photographic Experts Group** (**JPEG**) for lossy but high compression without alpha channel support.

For more details, check out the following Wikipedia articles:

- For information on raster graphics, visit `http://en.wikipedia.org/wiki/Raster_graphics`
- For information on vector graphics, visit `http://en.wikipedia.org/wiki/Vector_graphics`
- For information on PNG file format, visit `http://en.wikipedia.org/wiki/.png`
- For information on JPEG file format, visit `http://en.wikipedia.org/wiki/.jpg`

There is a free and open source tool called Inkscape similar to Adobe Illustrator. It allows you to easily create your own drawings as vector graphics and is available for Windows, Linux, and Mac OS X. Check out the project's website `http://inkscape.org/`.

Summary

We learned a lot about LibGDX in this chapter and all the other bits and bobs to prepare your system for multi-platform game development, specifically on the following points:

- We discussed every step in great detail to successfully download, install, and configure all the required software components: JDK, Eclipse, LibGDX, Android SDK, and additional Eclipse plugins for Android, HTML5/GWT, and RoboVM.
- We learned how to use the project setup tool that comes with LibGDX to easily generate all the required Eclipse projects for a new application and how to import them. We also learned what a game needs to come alive.

- We found out why planning game projects is so important.
- We also saw how to plan a game project by writing an outline.

In *Chapter 2, Cross-platform Development – Build Once, Deploy Anywhere*, we will learn more about how to deploy and run a LibGDX application on all supported target platforms. Building on this knowledge, we will finally jump to the first code examples where the magic happens and take a closer look at it to find out how it works.

2
Cross-platform Development – Build Once, Deploy Anywhere

In this chapter, you will learn more about the generated Eclipse projects and how they work together. Also, you will learn the following components of the LibGDX framework:

- Backends
- Modules
- Application life cycle and interface
- Starter classes

At the end of this chapter, you will take a closer look at the demo application and inspect the generated code of the Main class in great detail. You will learn how to set breakpoints, run the application in the debug mode, and speed up your overall productivity with the awesome **JVM Code Hot Swapping** feature. The discussion on the demo application ends with some simple and fun modifications to the code accompanied by a demonstration of the JVM Code Hot Swapping feature.

After completing this chapter, you will be able to deploy, run, and debug the demo application from *Chapter 1, Introduction to LibGDX and Project Setup*, on a desktop (including Windows, Linux, and Mac OS X), on Android, iOS, and in a WebGL-capable web browser such as Google Chrome.

The demo application – how the projects work together

In *Chapter 1, Introduction to LibGDX and Project Setup*, we successfully created our `demo` application, but we did not look at how all the Eclipse projects work together. Take a look at the following figure to understand and familiarize yourself with the configuration pattern that all your LibGDX applications will have in common:

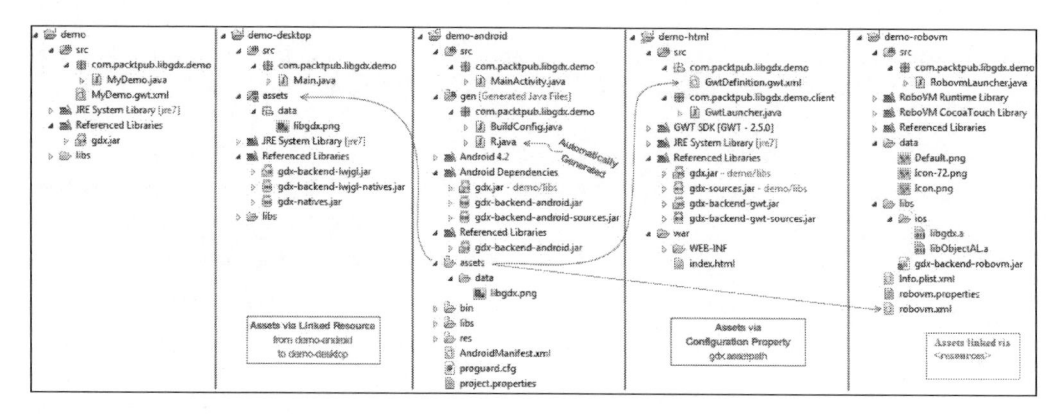

What you see here is a compact view of four projects. The `demo` project to the very left contains the shared code that is referenced (added to the build path) by all other platform-specific projects. The main class of the `demo` application is `MyDemo.java`. However, there is a different main class where an application gets started by the operating system, which will be referred to as starter classes from now on. Notice that LibGDX uses the term starter class to distinguish between these two types of main classes in order to avoid confusion. We will cover everything related to the topic of starter classes later.

While taking a closer look at all these directories in the preceding figure, you might have spotted that there are two `assets` folders: one in the `demo-desktop` project and another in the `demo-android` project. This brings us to the question, where should we put all the application's assets? The `demo-android` project plays a special role in this case. In the preceding screenshot, you can see a subfolder called `data`, which contains an image named `libgdx.png`. This image also appears in the `demo-desktop` project in the same place.

> Just remember to always put all your assets into the `assets` folder under the `demo-android` project. The reason behind this is that the Android build process requires direct access to the application's `assets` folder. During its build process, a Java source file, `R.java`, will be automatically generated under the `gen` folder. It contains special information for Android about the available assets. It will be the usual way to access assets through the Java code if you were explicitly writing an Android application. However, in LibGDX, you will want to stay independent of the platform as much as possible and access any resource such as assets only through the methods provided by LibGDX. You will learn more about accessing resources in the last section of this chapter.

You might wonder how other platform-specific projects will be able to access the very same assets without having to maintain several copies per project. Needless to say this would require you to keep all copies manually synchronized each time the assets change.

Luckily, this problem has already been taken care of by the generator. The `demo-desktop` project uses a linked resource—a feature by Eclipse—to add existing files or folders to other places in a workspace. You can check this out by right-clicking on the `demo-desktop` project, navigating to **Properties** | **Resource** | **Linked Resources**, and then clicking on the **Linked Resources** tab.

The `demo-html` project requires another approach as **Google Web Toolkit (GWT)** has a different build process compared to other projects. There is a special file called `GwtDefinition.gwt.xml` that allows you to set the asset path by setting the `gdx.assetpath` configuration property to the `assets` folder of the Android project. Notice that it is good practice to use relative paths such as `../android/assets` so that the reference does not get broken if the workspace is moved from its original location. Take this advice as a precaution to protect you and your fellow developers from wasting precious time on something that can be easily avoided by using the right setup, right from the beginning.

The following is the code listing for `GwtDefinition.gwt.xml` from `demo-html`:

```
<?xml version="1.0" encoding="UTF-8"?>
<!DOCTYPE module PUBLIC "-//Google Inc.//DTD Google Web Toolkit
trunk//EN" "http://google-web-toolkit.googlecode.com/svn/trunk/
distro-source/core/src/gwt-module.dtd">
<module>
```

```
        <inherits name='com.badlogic.gdx.backends.gdx_backends_gwt' />
        <inherits name='MyDemo' />
        <entry-point
        class='com.packtpub.libgdx.demo.client.GwtLauncher'
        />
        <set-configuration-property name="gdx.assetpath"
        value="../ android/assets" />
</module>
```

Similar to the `demo-html` project, the `demo-robovm` project has a special file called `robovm.xml` that saves the path to the `assets` folder in `demo-android`. Notice the `<directory>` key under `<resources>`, where the relative path to the `assets` folder is set. However, this is not the end of resource setting for `demo-robovm`. In iOS projects, there will be some resources specific to iOS, such as icons and default splash images. You don't want to put this in your Android `assets` folder. So, put this in the folder named `data` in your `demo-robovm` project. The path of the folder is also linked in the `robovm.xml` file under `<resources>`.

> Unlike Android, iOS version needs specific names for icons to show in respective devices. For example, `Icon-72.png` is the name for the app icon on iPad. You can find specifics of the icon name and size at https://developer.apple.com/library/iOs/qa/qa1686/_index.html.

The following code snippet is taken from `robovm.xml` in our `demo-robovm` project:

```
<config>
  <executableName>${app.executable}</executableName>
  <mainClass>${app.mainclass}</mainClass>
  <os>ios</os>
  <arch>thumbv7</arch>
  <target>ios</target>
  <iosInfoPList>Info.plist.xml</iosInfoPList>
  <resources>
    <resource>
      <directory>../android/assets</directory>
      <includes>
        <include>**</include>
      </includes>
      <skipPngCrush>true</skipPngCrush>
    </resource>
```

```xml
  <resource>
    <directory>data</directory>
  </resource>
</resources>
<forceLinkClasses>
  <pattern>com.badlogic.gdx.scenes.scene2d.ui.*</pattern>
</forceLinkClasses>
<libs>
  <lib>libs/ios/libgdx.a</lib>
  <lib>libs/ios/libObjectAL.a</lib>
</libs>
<frameworks>
  <framework>UIKit</framework>
  <framework>OpenGLES</framework>
  <framework>QuartzCore</framework>
  <framework>CoreGraphics</framework>
  <framework>OpenAL</framework>
  <framework>AudioToolbox</framework>
  <framework>AVFoundation</framework>
</frameworks>
</config>
```

LibGDX backends

LibGDX makes use of several other libraries to interface the specifics of each platform in order to provide cross-platform support for your applications. Generally, a backend is what enables LibgGDX to access the corresponding platform functionalities when one of the abstracted (platform-independent) LibGDX methods is called; for example, drawing an image in the upper-left corner of the screen, playing a sound file at a volume of 80 percent, or reading and writing from/to a file.

LibGDX currently provides the following four backends:

- Lightweight Java Game Library (LWJGL)
- Android
- JavaScript/WebGL
- iOS/RoboVM

Lightweight Java Game Library

Lightweight Java Game Library (**LWJGL**) is an open source Java library originally started by Caspian Rychlik-Prince to ease game development in terms of accessing the hardware resources on desktop systems. In LibGDX, LWJGL is used for the desktop backend to support all the major desktop operating systems, such as Windows, Linux, and Mac OS X.

For more details, check out the official LWJGL website `http://www.lwjgl.org/`.

Android

Google frequently releases and updates its official Android SDK. This represents the foundation for LibGDX to support Android in the form of a backend.

There is an API guide available, which explains everything the Android SDK has to offer to Android developers. You can find this at `http://developer.android.com/guide/components/index.html`.

WebGL

The WebGL support is one of the latest additions to the LibGDX framework. This backend uses the GWT to translate the Java code into JavaScript and **SoundManager2** (**SM2**) among others in order to add a combined support for HTML5, WebGL, and audio playback. Note that this backend requires a WebGL-capable web browser to run the application.

The following are some useful links that will help you get a detailed description:

- Check out the official website of GWT at `https://developers.google.com/web-toolkit/`

- Check out the official website of SM2 at `http://www.schillmania.com/projects/soundmanager2/`
- Check out the official website of WebGL at `http://www.khronos.org/webgl/`
- There is also a list of unresolved issues at `https://github.com/libgdx/libgdx/blob/master/backends/gdx-backends-gwt/issues.txt` that you might want to check out

RoboVM (iOS backend)

The goal of the RoboVM open source project is to bring Java and other JVM languages to iOS. RoboVM's ahead-of-time compiler translates the Java bytecode into a native ARM or x86 machine code that runs directly on the target CPU without being interpreted. The runtime is based on Android's runtime classes and includes a Java to Objective-C bridge, which makes it easy to use the native Cocoa Touch APIs from Java.

You can find more about RoboVM at `http://www.robovm.com`, and you can check the currently working code at `https://github.com/robovm/robovm`.

LibGDX core modules

LibGDX provides six core modules that allow you to access various parts of the system your application will run on. What makes these modules so great for you as a developer is that they provide you with a single **Application Programming Interface** (**API**) to achieve the same effect on more than just one platform. This is extremely powerful because you can now focus on your own application and do not have to bother with the specialties that each platform inevitably brings, including the nasty little bugs that might require tricky workarounds. This is all going to be transparently handled in a straightforward API, which is categorized into logic modules and is globally available anywhere in your code as every module is accessible as a `static` field in the `Gdx` class.

> LibGDX allows you to create multiple code paths for per-platform decisions. For example, you can increase the complexity of a desktop game as desktops have a lot more computing power than mobile devices.

The application module

The application module can be accessed through `Gdx.app`. It gives you access to the logging facility, a method to shutdown gracefully, persist data, query the Android API version, query the platform type, and query the memory usage.

Logging

LibGDX employs its own logging facility. You can choose a log level to filter what should be printed to the platform's console. The default log level is `LOG_INFO`. You can use a settings file and/or change the log level dynamically at runtime using the following code:

```
Gdx.app.setLogLevel(Application.LOG_DEBUG);
```

The available log levels are as follows:

- `LOG_NONE`: This prints no logs and the logging is completely disabled
- `LOG_ERROR`: This prints error logs only
- `LOG_INFO`: This prints error and info logs
- `LOG_DEBUG`: This prints error, info, and debug logs

To write an info, debug, or error log to the console, use the following listings:

```
Gdx.app.log("MyDemoTag", "This is an info log.");
Gdx.app.debug("MyDemoTag", "This is a debug log.");
Gdx.app.error("MyDemoTag", "This is an error log.");
```

Shutting down gracefully

You can tell LibGDX to shut down the running application. The framework will then stop the execution in the correct order as soon as possible and completely deallocate any memory that is still in use, freeing both Java and the native heap. Use the following listing to initiate a graceful shutdown of your application:

```
Gdx.app.exit();
```

> You should always do a graceful shutdown when you want to terminate your application. Otherwise, you will risk creating memory leaks, which is a really bad thing. On mobile devices, memory leaks will probably have the biggest negative impact due to their limited resources. Note that in an Android device, it will call the `pause()` and `dispose()` functions sometime later and won't immediately finish the application.

Persisting data

If you want your data to persist after exit, you should use the `Preferences` class. It is merely a dictionary or a hash map data type that stores multiple key-value pairs in a file. LibGDX will create a new preferences file on the fly if it does not exist. You can have several preference files using unique names in order to split up data into categories. To get access to a preference file, you need to request a `Preferences` instance by its filename as follows:

```
Preferences prefs = Gdx.app.getPreferences("settings.prefs");
```

To write a (new) value, you have to choose a key under which the value should be stored. If this key already exists in a preferences file, it will be overwritten. Do not forget to call `flush()` afterwards, as shown in the following code, to persist the data, or else all the changes will be lost:

```
prefs.putInteger("sound_volume", 100); // volume @ 100%
prefs.flush();
```

> Persisting data needs a lot more time than just modifying values in memory (without flushing). Therefore, it is always better to modify as many values as possible before a final `flush()` method is executed.

To read back a certain value from the preferences file, you need to know the corresponding key. If this key does not exist, it will be set to the default value. You can optionally pass your own default value as the second argument (for example, in the following listing, 50 is the default sound volume):

```
int soundVolume = prefs.getInteger("sound_volume", 50);
```

Querying the Android API level

On Android, you can query the Android API level that allows you to handle things differently for certain versions of the Android OS. Use the following listing to find out the version:

```
Gdx.app.getVersion();
```

> On platforms other than Android, the version returned is always 0.

Querying the platform type

You might want to write a platform-specific code where it is necessary to know the current platform type. The following example shows how it can be done:

```
switch (Gdx.app.getType()) {
case Desktop:
  // Code for Desktop application
break;
case Android:
  // Code for Android application
break;
case WebGL:
  // Code for WebGL application
break;
case iOS:
  // Code for IOS application
break;
default:
  // Unhandled (new?) platform application
break;
}
```

Querying the memory usage

You can query the system to find out its current memory footprint of your application. This might help you find excessive memory allocations that could lead to application crashes. The following functions return the amount of memory (in bytes) that is in use by the corresponding heap:

```
long memUsageJavaHeap = Gdx.app.getJavaHeap();
long memUsageNativeHeap = Gdx.app.getNativeHeap();
```

Multithreading

When our game is created, LibGDX creates a separate thread called the **Main loop thread** and OpenGL context is attached to it. The entire event processing or rendering happens within this thread and not in the UI thread. Hence to pass data to the rendering thread from another thread, we use `Application.postRunnable()`. This will run the code in the `Runnable` function in the rendering thread in the next frame, as shown in the following code:

```
Gdx.app.postRunnable(new Runnable() {
    @Override
    public void run() {
```

```
                    //do something
            }
    });
```

The graphics module

The graphics module can be accessed either through `Gdx.getGraphics()` or using the shortcut variable `Gdx.graphics`.

Querying delta time

Query LibGDX for the time span between the current and the last frame in seconds by calling `Gdx.graphics.getDeltaTime()`.

Querying display size

Query the device's display size returned in pixels by calling `Gdx.graphics.getWidth()` and `Gdx.graphics.getHeight()`.

Querying the frames per second (FPS) counter

Query a built-in frame counter provided by LibGDX to find the average number of frames per second by calling `Gdx.graphics.getFramesPerSecond()`.

The audio module

The audio module can be accessed either through `Gdx.getAudio()` or using the shortcut variable `Gdx.audio`.

Sound playback

To load sounds for playback, call `Gdx.audio.newSound()`.

The supported file formats are WAV, MP3, and OGC. However, for the iOS version, OGG is not supported. There is an upper limit of 1 MB for the decoded audio data. Consider the sounds to be short effects such as bullets or explosions so that the size limitation is not really an issue.

Music streaming

To stream music for playback, call `Gdx.audio.newMusic()`. The supported file formats are WAV, MP3, and OGG. However, the iOS version currently supports the WAV and MP3 formats only.

The input module

The input module can be accessed either through `Gdx.getInput()` or using the shortcut variable `Gdx.input`.

In order to receive and handle the input properly, you should always implement the `InputProcessor` interface and set it as the global handler for the input in LibGDX by calling `Gdx.input.setInputProcessor()`.

Reading the keyboard/touch/mouse input

Query the system for the last *x* or *y* coordinate in the screen coordinates, where the screen origin is at the top-left corner by calling either `Gdx.input.getX()` or `Gdx.input.getY()`. The different conditions are as follows:

- To find out whether the screen is touched either by a finger or by mouse, call `Gdx.input.isTouched()`
- To find out whether the mouse button is pressed, call `Gdx.input.isButtonPressed()`
- To find out whether the keyboard key is pressed, call `Gdx.input.isKeyPressed()`

Reading the accelerometer

Query the accelerometer for its value on the *x* axis by calling `Gdx.input.getAccelerometerX()`. Replace X in the method's name with Y or Z to query the other two axes. Be aware that there will be no accelerometer present on a desktop, so LibGDX always returns 0.

Starting and canceling vibrator

On Android, you can let the device vibrate by calling `Gdx.input.vibrate()`. A running vibration can be canceled by calling `Gdx.input.cancelVibrate()`.

Catching Android's soft keys

You might want to catch Android's soft keys to add an extra handling code for them. If you want to catch the back button, call `Gdx.input.setCatchBackKey(true)`, and if you want to catch the menu button, call `Gdx.input.setCatchMenuKey(true)`.

On a desktop where you have a mouse pointer, you can tell LibGDX to catch it so that you get a permanent mouse input without having the mouse ever leave the application window. To catch the mouse cursor, call `Gdx.input.setCursorCatched(true)`.

The files module

The files module can be accessed either through `Gdx.getFiles()` or using the shortcut variable: `Gdx.files`.

Getting an internal file handle

You can get a file handle for an internal file by calling `Gdx.files.internal()`. An internal file is relative to the `assets` folder on the Android and WebGL platforms. On a desktop, it is relative to the `root` folder of the application.

Getting an external file handle

You can get a file handle for an external file by calling `Gdx.files.external()`. An external file is relative to the SD card on the Android platform. On a desktop, it is relative to the user's home folder. Note that this is not available for WebGL applications.

The network module

The network module can be accessed either through `Gdx.getNet()` or using the shortcut variable: `Gdx.net`.

HTTP requests

You can make HTTP requests by calling `Gdx.net.sendHttpRequest()` or cancel them by calling `Gdx.net.cancelHttpRequest()`.

Client/server sockets

You can create client/server sockets by calling either `Gdx.net.newClientSocket()` or `Gdx.net.newServerSocket()`.

Opening a URI in a web browser

To open a **Uniform Resource Identifier (URI)** in the default web browser, call `Gdx.net.openURI(URI)`.

LibGDX's application life cycle and interface

The application life cycle in LibGDX is a well-defined set of distinct system states. The list of these states is pretty short: create, resize, render, pause, resume, and dispose.

LibGDX defines an `ApplicationListener` interface that contains six methods, one for each system state. The following code listing is a copy that is directly taken from LibGDX's sources. For the sake of readability, all comments have been stripped:

```
public interface ApplicationListener {
public void create ();
public void resize (int width, int height);
public void render ();
public void pause ();
public void resume ();
public void dispose ();
}
```

All you need to do is implement these methods in your main class of the shared game code project. LibGDX will then call each of these methods at the right time.

> **Downloading the example code**
> You can download the example code files for all Packt books you have purchased from your account at http://www.packtpub.com. If you purchased this book elsewhere, you can visit http://www.packtpub.com/support and register to have the files e-mailed directly to you.

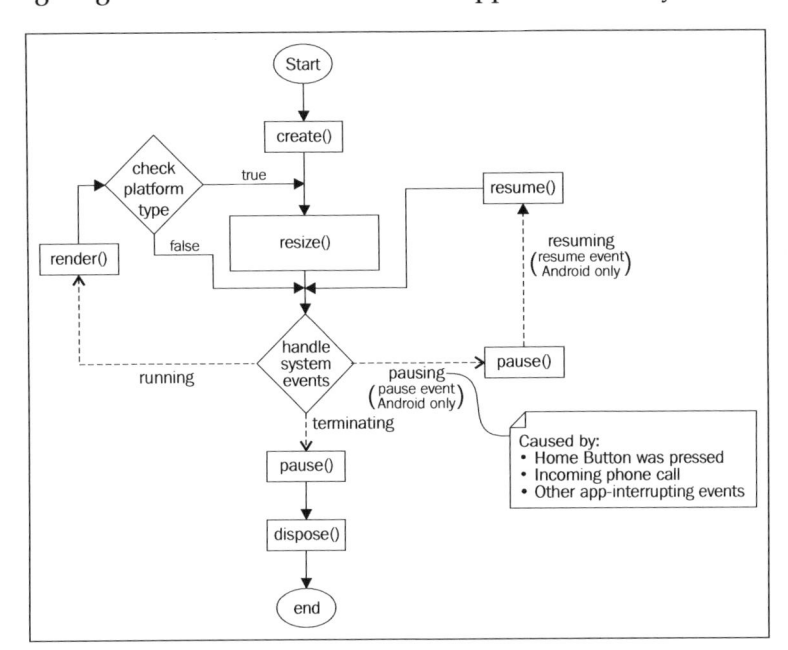

The following diagram visualizes the LibGDX's application life cycle:

Note that a full and dotted line basically has the same meaning in the preceding diagram. They both connect two consecutive states and have a direction of flow indicated by a little arrowhead on one end of the line. A dotted line additionally denotes a system event.

When an application starts, it will always begin with create(). This is where the initialization of the application should happen, such as loading assets into memory and creating an initial state of the game world. Subsequently, the next state that follows is resize(). This is the first opportunity for an application to adjust itself to the available display size (width and height) given in pixels.

Next, LibGDX will handle system events. If no event has occurred in the meanwhile, it is assumed that the application is (still) running. The next state would be render(). This is where a game application will mainly do the following two things:

- Update the game world model
- Draw the scene on the screen using the updated game world model

Afterwards, a decision is made on which the platform type is detected by LibGDX. On a desktop or in a web browser, the displaying application window can be virtually resized at any time. LibGDX compares the last and current sizes on every cycle so that resize() is only called if the display size is changed. This makes sure that the running application is able to accommodate a changed display size.

Now, the cycle starts over by handling (new) system events once again. Another system event that can occur during runtime is the `exit` event. When it occurs, LibGDX will first change to the `pause()` state, which is a very good place to save any data that would be lost otherwise, after the application is terminated. Subsequently, LibGDX changes to the `dispose()` state where an application should do its final cleanup to free all the resources that it is still using.

This is also almost true for Android, except that `pause()` is an intermediate state that is not directly followed by the `dispose()` state at first. Be aware that this event might occur anytime during an application runtime when the user has pressed the *Home* button or if there is an incoming phone call in the meanwhile. In fact, as long as the Android operating system does not need the occupied memory of the paused application, its state will not be changed to `dispose()`. Moreover, it is possible that a paused application might receive a `resume` system event, which in this case would change its state to `resume()`, and it would eventually arrive at the system event handler again.

Starter classes

A starter class defines the entry point (starting point) of a LibGDX application. It is specifically written for a certain platform. Usually, these kinds of classes are very simple and mostly consist of not more than a few lines of code to set certain parameters that apply to the corresponding platform. Think of them as a kind of bootup sequence for each platform. Once booting is finished, the LibGDX framework hands over control from the starter class (for example, the `demo-desktop` project) to your shared application code (for example, the `demo/demo-core` project) by calling different methods from the `ApplicationListener` interface that the `MyDemo` class implements. Remember that the `MyDemo` class is where the shared application code begins.

We will now take a look at each of the starter classes that were generated during the project setup.

Running the demo application on a desktop

The starter class for the desktop application is called `Main.java`. The following listing is `Main.java` from the `demo-desktop` project:

```
package com.packtpub.libgdx.demo;
import com.badlogic.gdx.backends.lwjgl.LwjglApplication;
import com.badlogic.gdx.backends.lwjgl.LwjglApplicationConfiguration;
public class Main {
```

```
public static void main(String[] args) {

LwjglApplicationConfiguration cfg = new
LwjglApplicationConfiguration();
cfg.title = "demo";
cfg.width = 480;
cfg.height = 320;
new LwjglApplication(new MyDemo(), cfg);
    }
}
```

In the preceding code listing, you can see the `Main` class: a plain Java class without the need to implement an interface or inherit from another class. Instead, a new instance of the `LwjglApplication` class is created. This class provides a couple of overloaded constructors to choose from. Here, we pass a new instance of the `MyDemo` class as the first argument to the constructor. Optionally, an instance of the `LwjglApplicationConfiguration` class can be passed as the second argument. The configuration class allows you to set every parameter that is configurable for a LibGDX desktop application. In this case, the window title is set to `demo`, and the window's width and height is set to `480` by `320` pixels.

This is all you need to write and configure a starter class for a desktop project. Let's try to run the application now. To do this, right-click on the `demo-desktop` project in **Project Explorer** in Eclipse and then select the **Java Application** option from the **Run As** menu. Eclipse might ask you to select the `Main` class when you do this for the first time. Simply select the `Main` class, and also check whether the correct package name (`com.packtpub.libgdx.demo`) is displayed next to it, as shown in the following screenshot:

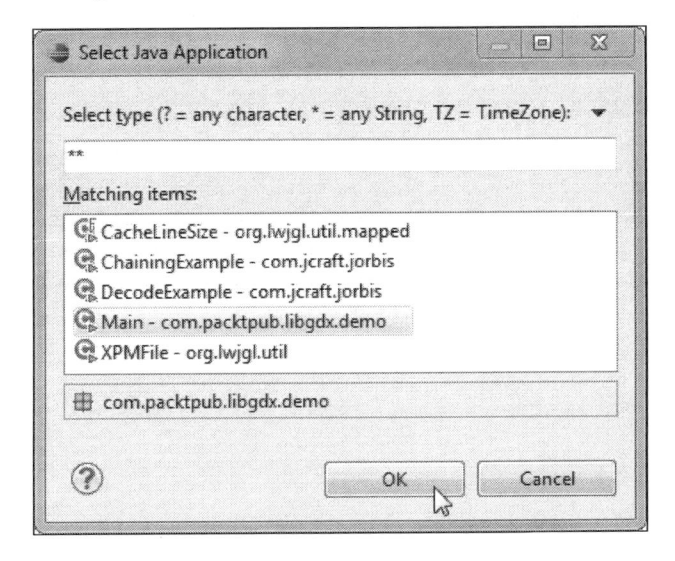

For those who use Gradle to set up the project, remember that the starter class of the desktop project will be `DesktopLauncher.java` and the correct package name will be `com.packtpub.libgdx.demo.desktop`.

The desktop application should now be up and running on your computer. If you are working on Windows, you should see the following window:

For Gradle users, this image will be displayed:

Running the demo application on Android

The starter class for the Android application is called `MainActivity.java`. For a Gradle-based project, the starter class will be `AndroidLauncher.java`.

The following listing is `MainActivity.java` from `demo-android`:

```
package com.packtpub.libgdx.demo;
import android.os.Bundle;
import com.badlogic.gdx.backends.android.AndroidApplication;
import com.badlogic.gdx.backends.android.
AndroidApplicationConfiguration;
public class MainActivity extends AndroidApplication {
@Override
public void onCreate(Bundle savedInstanceState) {
super.onCreate(savedInstanceState);
AndroidApplicationConfiguration cfg = new
AndroidApplicationConfiguration();
initialize(new MyDemo(), cfg);
    }
}
```

In the preceding code listing, you can see the `MainActivity` class that is inherited from the `AndroidApplication` class. This is how LibGDX encapsulates tasks such as creating a so-called activity that registers handlers to process touch input, read sensor data, and much more. What is left to do for you is to create an instance of a class that implements the `ApplicationListener` interface. In this case, it is an instance of the `MyDemo` class. The instances of `MyDemo` and `AndroidApplicationConfiguration` are passed as arguments to the `initialize()` method. If you are interested in the latest development of Android hardware statistics, be sure to check out the **Dashboards** section on the official Android developer website (http://developer.android.com/about/dashboards/index.html#OpenGL).

The following screenshot of the OpenGL statistics was taken in May 2014 from the preceding mentioned website:

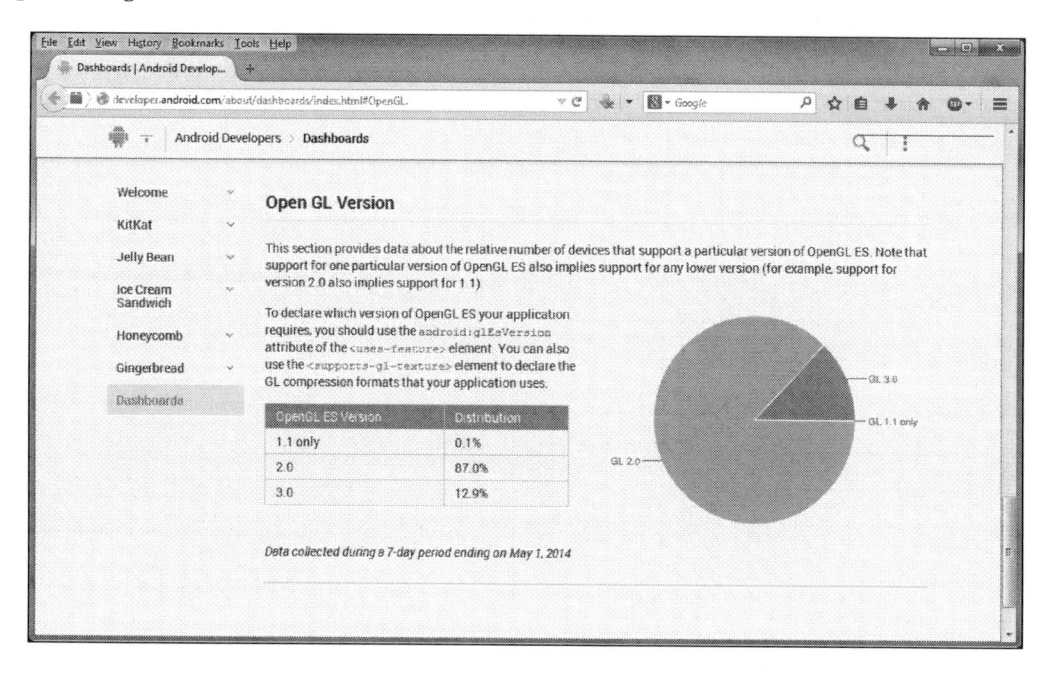

Note that GLES **1.1** is nearly zero. So what's the big deal about GLES **2.0**? A better question to ask would be whether you plan to use shaders in your application. If this is the case, opt for GLES 2.0.

> LibGDX has now removed the support for GLES 1.0, so the default OpenGL version is 2.0.

In any other case, there will be no real benefit except being able to use **Non-Power-Of-Two (NPOT)** textures—arbitrarily sized textures that do not equal to widths or heights representable by the formula 2^n, such as 32 x 32, 512 x 512, and 128 x 1024.

> NPOT textures are not guaranteed to work on all devices. For example, Nexus One ignores NPOT textures. Also, it might cause performance penalties on some hardware, so it is best to avoid using this feature at all. In *Chapter 4, Gathering Resources*, you will learn about a concept called **Texture Atlas**. This will allow you to use arbitrarily sized textures even when you are not using GLES2.

Additionally, on Android, you will have to take care of a manifest file that defines a huge list of parameters to configure the application. If you are not yet familiar with Android's manifest file, read the official documentation at http://developer.android.com/guide/topics/manifest/manifest-intro.html.

The following listing is `AndroidManifest.xml` from `demo-android`:

```xml
<?xml version="1.0" encoding="utf-8"?>
<manifest xmlns:android=
 "http://schemas.android.com/apk/res/android"
    package="com.packtpub.libgdx.demo"
    android:versionCode="1"
    android:versionName="1.0" >
    <uses-sdk android:minSdkVersion="8"
     android:targetSdkVersion="19"/>
    <uses-feature android:glEsVersion="0x00020000"
     android:required="true"/>
    <application
        android:icon="@drawable/ic_launcher"
        android:label="@string/app_name" >
        <activity
            android:name=".MainActivity"
            android:label="@string/app_name"
            android:screenOrientation="landscape"
            android:configChanges="keyboard|keyboardHidden|
             orientation">
            <intent-filter>
                <action android:name="android.intent.action.
                 MAIN" />
                <category android:name="android.
                 intent.category.LAUNCHER"/>
            </intent-filter>
        </activity>
    </application>
</manifest>
```

There will be an error displayed in `android:configChanges` after changing to Android API level 8, as shown in the following screenshot:

`android:configChanges="keyboard|keyboardHidden|orientation|screenSize">`

This is because the value `screenSize` is not supported by the API Level 8. Just remove this value for our project. To know more about this `android:configChanges` element and other elements, visit `http://developer.android.com/guide/topics/manifest/activity-element.html`.

The following short (and incomplete) list is meant to give you a quick idea of what could be defined in the manifest file:

- `minSdkVersion`: This is the minimum API Level required for the application to run. Devices running with lower API Levels will not be able to run this application; if left undeclared, an API Level of `1` is assumed, which might cause your app to crash at runtime when trying to access unavailable APIs.
- `targetSdkVersion`: This is the API Level the application targets. This is used for forward compatibility, where later API Levels can change the behavior of the API that might break old applications. This specification does not prevent the application from running on devices with lower API Levels down to `minSdkVersion`. If left undeclared, its value is set equal to `minSdkVersion`.
- `icon`: This is the application's icon.
- `name`: This is the main class of the application (or the main activity). Note that in terms of LibGDX, this will be the starter class for Android.
- `label`: This is the application's name shown next to the application icon and in the title bar.
- `screenOrientation`: This defines the display orientation of the application. The usual values are `portrait` (tall) and `landscape` (wide). See the documentation for more details.

Another crucial part of the manifest file is the correct definition of the permissions that the application should request when a user wants to install it on a device.

> Make sure that you will never request unnecessary permissions and put as much information as required into the description text of your application. Users are extremely suspicious and justifiably so when it comes to the list of requested permissions. It is not 100 percent clear for which reason an application needs a certain permission.

For an introduction and much more detail on the topic of permissions on Android, refer to the official documentation at `http://developer.android.com/guide/topics/security/permissions.html`.

Now, let's try to run the application on a real, physical device. First, make sure that your Android device is connected via a USB cable and is set up for development. To set up your Android device, follow the instructions at http://developer.android.com/tools/device.html.

Now, right-click on the `demo-android` project in **Project Explorer** in Eclipse and select the **Android Application** option from the **Run As** menu.

The Android application should now be installed and be happily running on your Android device. The following image is of the application running on an HTC Desire HD:

With regards to the Android emulator that comes with the Android SDK, just a few final words, do not use it!

Emulators cannot accurately reflect how a device responds, so instead of using an emulator, it is highly recommended to try and test your applications on as many real devices as you can get your hands on.

Running the demo application in a WebGL-capable web browser

The starter class for the WebGL application is called `GwtLauncher.java`. The following listing is `GwtLauncher.java` from `demo-html`:

```
package com.packtpub.libgdx.demo.client;
import com.packtpub.libgdx.demo.MyDemo;
```

```java
import com.badlogic.gdx.ApplicationListener;
import com.badlogic.gdx.backends.gwt.GwtApplication;
import com.badlogic.gdx.backends.gwt.GwtApplicationConfiguration;

public class GwtLauncher extends GwtApplication {
    @Override
    public GwtApplicationConfiguration getConfig () {
        GwtApplicationConfiguration cfg = new
          GwtApplicationConfiguration(800, 480);
            return cfg;
    }
    @Override
    public ApplicationListener getApplicationListener () {
        return new MyDemo();
    }
}
```

In the preceding code listing, you can see the GwtLauncher class that is inherited from the GwtApplication class. LibGDX encapsulates GWT and only requires you to implement the two abstract methods, getConfig() and getApplicationListener(). The getConfig() method returns an instance of the GwtApplicationConfiguration class. In this case, the window's width and height are directly passed on to its constructor. The getApplicationListener() method returns an instance of a class that implements the ApplicationListener interface, which is the MyDemo class in the preceding code.

Additionally, GWT is organized in so-called modules that bundle together all the configuration settings. In this case, we only have one module called MyDemo.gwt.xml. It defines the source path where GWT should look for Java source files, in this case, com/packtpub/libgdx/demo. These source files will then be cross-compiled by GWT to optimize the JavaScript code that is runnable on all major web browsers.

The following listing is MyDemo.gwt.xml from demo project:

```xml
<?xml version="1.0" encoding="UTF-8"?>
<!DOCTYPE module PUBLIC "-//Google Inc.//DTD Google Web Toolkit
  trunk//EN" "http://google-web-
    toolkit.googlecode.com/svn/trunk/distro-source/core/src/gwt-
      module.dtd">
<module>
   <source path="com/packtpub/libgdx/demo" />
</module>
```

Let's try to run the application now. To do this, right-click on the `demo-html` project in **Project Explorer** in Eclipse and then select the **Web Application** option in the **Run As** menu. A new tab titled **Development Mode** will open at the bottom. Simply do what the description preceding the URL says and double-click on it. Your default browser should launch shortly after this. Then try to load the website that is hosted on your local machine right now. Hence, the URL points to `127.0.0.1`, the infamous IPv4 loopback address that is just another fancy name for this device or computer:

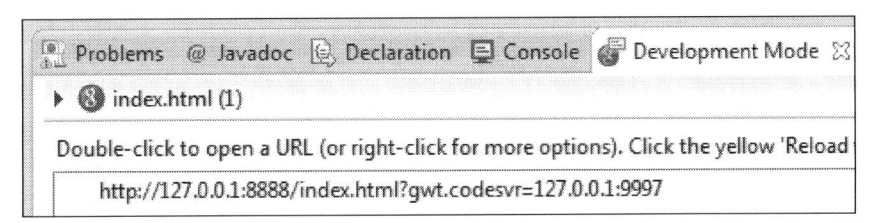

Keep in mind that using the URL suggested by Eclipse will run your WebGL application in debug mode, which is excruciatingly slow for most games. Just remove everything after the question mark in the URL to run your application in normal mode. The resulting URL should look like `http://127.0.0.1:8888/index.html`.

You might be asked to install the **Google Web Toolkit Developer Plugin** for your web browser to use the **Development Mode**, as shown in the following screenshot. You need to install it to develop your local machine.

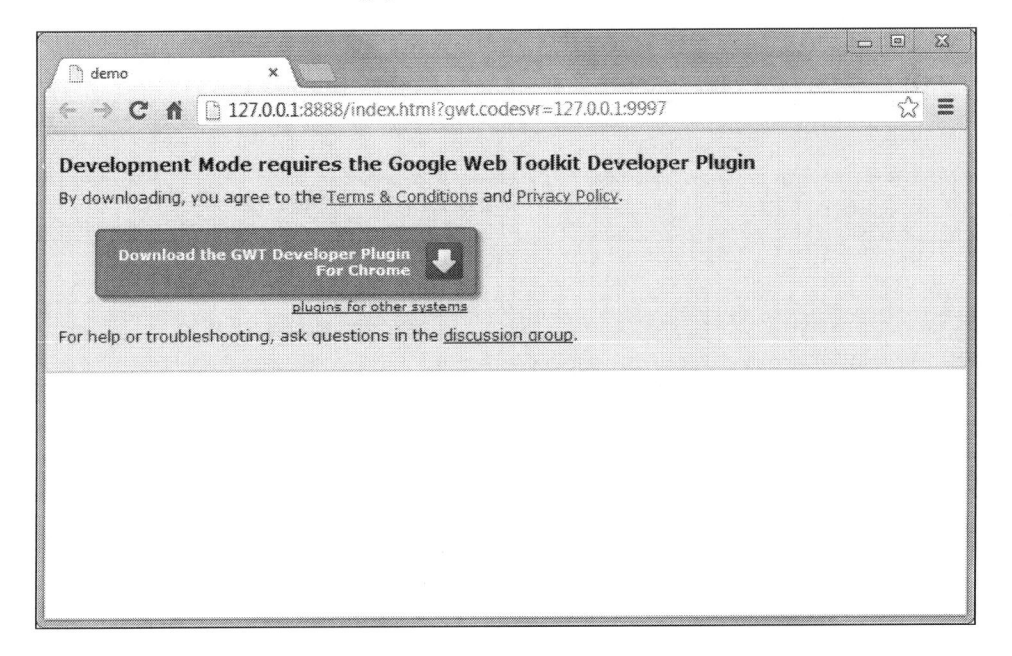

After the plugin has been successfully installed, you will see the following window:

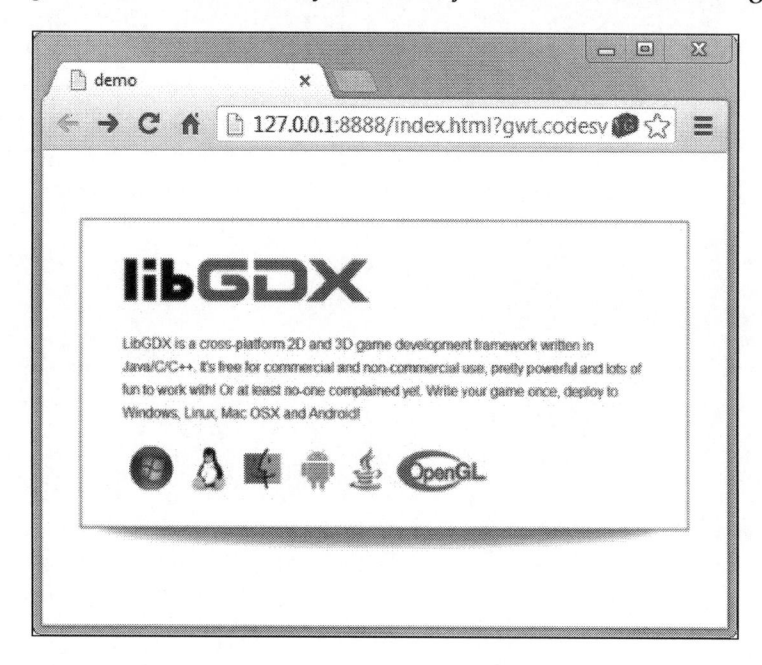

If you want to run this application on a real web server and share it with other users on the Internet, you will have to cross-compile the project first. This is a pretty straightforward process. Simply right-click on the `demo-html` project in **Project Explorer** in Eclipse and then select the **GWT Compile** option from the **Google** menu, as shown here:

A window with the title **GWT Compile** will open. Here, you can choose a log level to narrow down on certain messages such as errors only. Keep the default settings for now and click on **Compile** to begin the cross-compile process, as shown here:

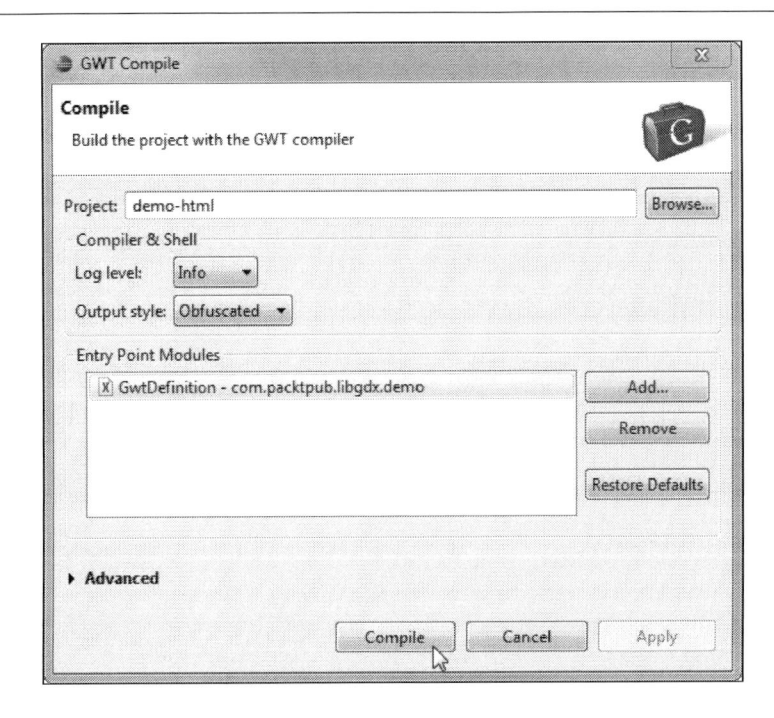

The compilation process is quite lengthy compared to all the other ones shown in this book. It took over two minutes to finish on an Intel Core i7 (3.4GHz) processor. A good moment to exercise your patience!

Once the compilation is finished, go to the war subfolder in the demo-html project, as shown in the following screenshot:

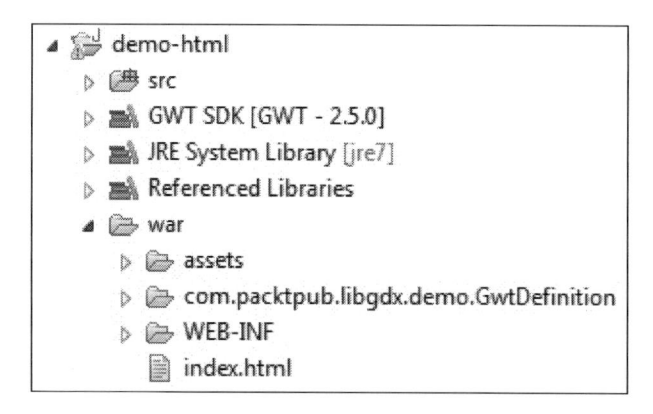

```
▲ 📁 demo-html
  ▷ 📂 src
  ▷ 📚 GWT SDK [GWT - 2.5.0]
  ▷ 📚 JRE System Library [jre7]
  ▷ 📚 Referenced Libraries
  ▲ 📁 war
      ▷ 📁 assets
      ▷ 📁 com.packtpub.libgdx.demo.GwtDefinition
      ▷ 📁 WEB-INF
         📄 index.html
```

You can now upload everything to your web server that is contained in this folder except the WEB-INF folder, which is not needed. Now, you or anyone else can open the URL to your web server and enjoy your LibGDX cross-platform application in a WebGL-capable web browser without having to install any plugin for it to work.

Running the demo application on an iOS device

The starter class for iOS application is RobovmLauncher.java. For Gradle, it is IOSLauncher.java. The following listing is from RobovmLauncher.java in demo-robovm:

```
package com.packtpub.libgdx.demo;

import org.robovm.apple.foundation.NSAutoreleasePool;
import org.robovm.apple.uikit.UIApplication;
import com.badlogic.gdx.backends.iosrobovm.IOSApplication;
import com.badlogic.gdx.backends.iosrobovm.
   IOSApplicationConfiguration;

public class RobovmLauncher extends IOSApplication.Delegate {
   @Override
   protected IOSApplication createApplication() {
      IOSApplicationConfiguration config = new
         IOSApplicationConfiguration();
      config.orientationLandscape = true;
      config.orientationPortrait = false;
```

```
            return new IOSApplication(new MyDemo(), config);
        }

        public static void main(String[] argv) {
            NSAutoreleasePool pool = new NSAutoreleasePool();
            UIApplication.main(argv, null, RobovmLauncher.class);
            pool.close();
        }
    }
```

In the preceding code, you can see the `RobovmLauncher` class that is inherited from the `IOSApplication.Delegate` class. Here is where LibGDX encapsulates tasks and registers handlers to process touch input, and other sensor data, and much more. The instances of `MyDemo` and `IOSApplicationConfiguration` are passed as arguments to the `IOSApplication` function.

In Android, we saw the `AndroidManifest.xml` file that specifies the characteristics, permissions, and other features of our `Demo-Android` app. Similarly, our iOS app has `Info.plist.xml` to hold such details. Before explaining `Info.plist.xml`, let's see the `robovm.properties` and `robovm.xml` file.

The following code is taken from `robovm.properties` file in our `demo-robovm` project:

```
app.version=1.0
app.id=com.packtpub.libgdx.demo
app.mainclass=com.packtpub.libgdx.demo.RobovmLauncher
app.executable=MyDemo
app.build=1
app.name=MyDemo
```

This brief file contains, as the statements indicate, the app version, app ID, main class, executable, build number, and name of app. These values will be used in the `Info.plist.xml` file:

The following listing is taken from `robovm.xml` in our `demo-robovm` project:

```xml
<config>
  <executableName>${app.executable}</executableName>
  <mainClass>${app.mainclass}</mainClass>
  <os>ios</os>
  <arch>thumbv7</arch>
  <target>ios</target>
  <iosInfoPList>Info.plist.xml</iosInfoPList>
  <resources>
    <resource>
      <directory>../android/assets</directory>
```

```xml
      <includes>
        <include>**</include>
      </includes>
      <skipPngCrush>true</skipPngCrush>
    </resource>
    <resource>
        <directory>data</directory>
    </resource>
  </resources>
  <forceLinkClasses>
    <pattern>com.badlogic.gdx.scenes.scene2d.ui.*</pattern>
  </forceLinkClasses>
  <libs>
    <lib>build/libs/ios/libgdx.a</lib>
    <lib>build/libs/ios/libObjectAL.a</lib>
  </libs>
  <frameworks>
    <framework>UIKit</framework>
    <framework>OpenGLES</framework>
    <framework>QuartzCore</framework>
    <framework>CoreGraphics</framework>
    <framework>OpenAL</framework>
    <framework>AudioToolbox</framework>
    <framework>AVFoundation</framework>
  </frameworks>
</config>
```

This file holds the important link: the path to the `assets` folder in the `demo-android` project. Under the `<resource>` key, the path to the Android `assets` folder is set. However, we need iOS-specific icons and splash images, and we don't need to put this in the Android `assets` folder (believe me, you don't want to increase your Android APK size with unwanted data). Instead, we put it in the folder data inside the `demo-robovm` project and include the path under the `<resources>` key in `robovm.xml`.

Now comes the crucial part: the `Info.plist` file. Every iOS app contains the `Info.plist` file and it holds crucial information about the characteristics, permissions, and other features about the app. In our RoboVM version, it is named `Info.plist.xml`. The following code is taken from the `Info.plist.xml` file in our `demo-robovm` project:

```xml
<?xml version="1.0" encoding="UTF-8"?>
<!DOCTYPE plist PUBLIC "-//Apple//DTD PLIST 1.0//EN" "http://www.apple.com/DTDs/PropertyList-1.0.dtd">
<plist version="1.0">
```

```xml
<dict>
    <key>CFBundleDevelopmentRegion</key>
    <string>en</string>
    <key>CFBundleDisplayName</key>
    <string>${app.name}</string>
    <key>CFBundleExecutable</key>
    <string>${app.executable}</string>
    <key>CFBundleIdentifier</key>
    <string>${app.id}</string>
    <key>CFBundleInfoDictionaryVersion</key>
    <string>6.0</string>
    <key>CFBundleName</key>
    <string>${app.name}</string>
    <key>CFBundlePackageType</key>
    <string>APPL</string>
    <key>CFBundleShortVersionString</key>
    <string>${app.version}</string>
    <key>CFBundleSignature</key>
    <string>????</string>
    <key>CFBundleVersion</key>
    <string>${app.build}</string>
    <key>LSRequiresIPhoneOS</key>
    <true/>
    <key>UIStatusBarHidden</key>
    <true/>
    <key>UIViewControllerBasedStatusBarAppearance</key>
    <false />
    <key>UIDeviceFamily</key>
    <array>
        <integer>1</integer>
        <integer>2</integer>
    </array>
    <key>UIRequiredDeviceCapabilities</key>
    <array>
        <string>armv7</string>
    </array>
    <key>UISupportedInterfaceOrientations</key>
    <array>
        <string>UIInterfaceOrientationLandscapeLeft</string>
        <string>UIInterfaceOrientationLandscapeRight</string>
    </array>
    <key>UISupportedInterfaceOrientations~ipad</key>
    <array>
        <string>UIInterfaceOrientationLandscapeLeft</string>
```

```xml
            <string>UIInterfaceOrientationLandscapeRight</string>
        </array>
        <key>CFBundleIcons</key>
        <dict>
            <key>CFBundlePrimaryIcon</key>
            <dict>
                <key>CFBundleIconFiles</key>
                <array>
                    <string>Icon</string>
                    <string>Icon-72</string>
                </array>
            </dict>
        </dict>
    </dict>
</plist>
```

The following short (and incomplete) list will give you a quick idea of what the `Info.plist` keys means:

- `UISupportedInterfaceOrientations`: This key is used to set the allowed device orientations:
    - For iPads, it is `UISupportedInterfaceOrientations~ipad`
    - For iPhones and iPads, the values for these keys are:
        - `UIInterfaceOrientationPortrait`
        - `UIInterfaceOrientationPortraitUpsideDown`
        - `UIInterfaceOrientationLandscapeRight`
        - `UIInterfaceOrientationLandscapeLeft`
- `UIRequiredDeviceCapabilities`: This key lets you declare the hardware or specific capabilities that your app needs in order to run. For example, Wi-Fi, Bluetooth, accelerometer, open GLES 2.0, and so on.
- `CFBundleName`: This is the name of the application as specified in the `robovm.properties` file.
- `CFBundleIdentifier`: This is the unique identifier of the application as specified in the `robovm.properties` file. For our `demo-robovm` project, it is `CFBundleIdentifier com.packtbub.libgdx.demo`.
- `CFBundleIconFiles`: These are the application icons.

For more information on the topic of the `Info.plist` keys, check out the official documentation at `https://developer.apple.com/library/mac/documentation/general/Reference/InfoPlistKeyReference/Articles/iPhoneOSKeys.html#//apple_ref/doc/uid/TP40009252-SW1`.

For more about the device capabilities, check out the official documentation at `https://developer.apple.com/library/mac/documentation/general/Reference/InfoPlistKeyReference/Articles/iPhoneOSKeys.html#//apple_ref/doc/uid/TP40009252-SW3`.

Now, right-click on the `demo-robovm` project in **Project Explorer** in Eclipse and select the **iOS Device App** option in the **Run As** menu.

> Remember that to execute an iOS application, you need a Mac machine.

The iOS application should now be installed as an application icon and should be happily running on your iOS device. The following image is of the application running on an IPad 3:

The demo application – time for code

In this section, we will take a closer look at the actual code of the `demo` project. Thereafter, we will do some simple modifications to the code and also use the debugger.

Inspecting an example code of the demo application

Let's take a first look at the generated code of `MyDemo.java` from the `demo` project.

The following code snippet shows the class definition:

```
public class MyDemo implements ApplicationListener {
  // ...
}
```

As you can see, the `MyDemo` class implements the `ApplicationListener` interface. The `MyDemo` class from Gradle project (`demo-core`) produces a quite different code as follows:

```
public class MyDemo extends ApplicationAdapter {
    //...
}
```

Here, the `ApplicationAdapter` is an abstract class that implements the `ApplicationListener` interface. Before we move on to the implementation details of the interface, we will spend some time on the remaining part of this class.

You will find a definition of the four member variables, each with a class provided by LibGDX:

```
Private OrthographicCamera camera;
Private SpriteBatch batch;
private Texture texture;
private Sprite sprite;
```

Here is a brief explanation of the classes from the preceding code listing to give you the basic background knowledge for the code inspection that will follow shortly.

The camera variable is of the class type `OrthographicCamera`. We will use the orthographic camera to display our 2D scenes. The camera is the player's view of the actual scene in the game, which is defined by a certain width and height (also called viewport).

For more information about projections, check out the great article orthographic versus perspective by Jeff Lamarche at http://iphonedevelopment.blogspot.de/2009/04/opengl-es-from-ground-up-part-3.html.

The `batch` variable is of the class type `SpriteBatch`. This is where you send all your drawing commands to LibGDX. Beyond the ability of this class to draw images, it is also capable of optimizing the drawing performance under certain circumstances.

The `texture` variable is of the class type `Texture`. It holds a reference to the actual image; the texture data that is stored in memory at runtime.

The `sprite` variable is of the class type `Sprite`. It is a complex data type that contains lots of attributes to represent a graphical object that has a position in 2D space, width, and height. It can also be rotated and scaled. Internally, it holds a reference to a `TextureRegion` class that in turn is a means to cut out a certain portion of a texture.

Now that we have a basic knowledge of the involved data types, we can advance to the implementation details of the `ApplicationListener` interface.

In the `MyDemo` class, the only methods containing code are `create()`, `render()`, and `dispose()`. The remaining three methods are left empty, which is just fine.

The create() method

The `create()` method contains the initialization code to prepare the application on startup, as shown in the following code snippet:

```
@Override
public void create() {

    float w = Gdx.graphics.getWidth();
    float h = Gdx.graphics.getHeight();

    camera = new OrthographicCamera(1, h/w);
    batch = new SpriteBatch();

    texture = new Texture(Gdx.files.internal("data/libgdx.png"));
    texture.setFilter(TextureFilter.Linear, TextureFilter.Linear);

    TextureRegion region =
       newTextureRegion(texture, 0, 0, 512, 275);

    sprite = new Sprite(region);
```

```
        sprite.setSize(0.9f, 0.9f *
          sprite.getHeight() / sprite.getWidth());
        sprite.setOrigin(sprite.getWidth()/2,
          sprite.getHeight()/2);
        sprite.setPosition(-sprite.getWidth()/2,
          -sprite.getHeight()/2);
    }
```

At first, the graphics module is queried to return the width and height of the display (for example, a desktop window or the screen of an Android device) and calculate an appropriate width and height for the field of view of the camera. Then, a new instance of `SpriteBatch` is created so that images can be drawn and made visible with the camera. The next step is to load a texture using the files module to get a file handle to `data/libgdx.png`.

> Gradle users will find only two lines of code in the `create()` method and only four lines of code in the `render()` method. The `assets` folder in the `demo-android` project will contain only an image labeled `badlogic.jpg`. Read and understand this code; the complete code is given at the end of this section.

The loaded texture looks like the following screenshot:

As you can see, there is a lot of empty space in this screenshot. In order to be able to use the filled part of this screenshot only, a new instance of `TextureRegion` is created. It references the previously loaded texture that contains the full image and has the additional information to cut all the pixels starting from (0, 0) to (512, 275). These two points describe a rectangle starting at the top-left corner of the image with a width and height of 512 by 275 pixels. Finally, a sprite is created using the information of the previously created texture region. The sprite's size is set to 90 percent of its original size. The sprite's origin is set to half of its width and height to move the origin to its center. Eventually, the position is set to the negative half of the sprite's width and height so that the sprite moves to the center of the scene.

> LibGDX uses a coordinate system that has its origin (0, 0) at the bottom-left corner. This means that the positive *x* axis points to the right-hand side, while the positive *y* axis points upwards.

The render() method

The `render()` method contains the commands to render a scene on screen, as shown here:

```
@Override
public void render() {
    Gdx.gl.glClearColor(1, 1, 1, 1);
    Gdx.gl.glClear(GL20.GL_COLOR_BUFFER_BIT);

    batch.setProjectionMatrix(camera.combined);
    batch.begin();
    sprite.draw(batch);
    batch.end();
}
```

The first two lines call the low-level OpenGL methods to set the clear color to a solid white, and then execute the clear screen command.

Next, the projection matrix of the sprite batch is set to the camera's combined projection and view matrix. You do not have to understand what this means in detail at the moment. It basically just means that every following drawing command will behave according to the rules of an orthographic projection, or simply put, drawing will be done in 2D space using the position and bounds of the given camera.

The `begin()` and `end()` methods will always have to appear in pairs and should not be nested or there will be errors. The actual drawing of the sprite is accomplished by calling the `draw()` method of the sprite to draw and pass the instance of the sprite batch.

The dispose() method

The `dispose()` method is the place where you clean up and free all resources that are still in use by an application, as shown here:

```
@Override
public void dispose() {
    batch.dispose();
    texture.dispose();
}
```

There is an interface called `Disposable` that is implemented by every LibGDX class that allocates resources (that is, memory) and can be easily deallocated by calling the corresponding `dispose` method. In the preceding code, this is done for the sprite batch and the loaded texture.

The following is a complete listing of the `MyDemo.java` source file from the `demo` project:

```
package com.packtpub.libgdx.demo;

import com.badlogic.gdx.ApplicationListener;
import com.badlogic.gdx.Gdx;
import com.badlogic.gdx.Net.HttpRequest;
import com.badlogic.gdx.Net.HttpResponseListener;
import com.badlogic.gdx.graphics.GL20;
import com.badlogic.gdx.graphics.OrthographicCamera;
import com.badlogic.gdx.graphics.Texture;
import com.badlogic.gdx.graphics.Texture.TextureFilter;
import com.badlogic.gdx.graphics.g2d.Sprite;
import com.badlogic.gdx.graphics.g2d.SpriteBatch;
import com.badlogic.gdx.graphics.g2d.TextureRegion;

public class MyDemo implements ApplicationListener {
    private OrthographicCamera camera;
    private SpriteBatch batch;
    private Texture texture;
    private Sprite sprite;

    @Override
    public void create() {

        float w = Gdx.graphics.getWidth();
```

```
        float h = Gdx.graphics.getHeight();

        camera = new OrthographicCamera(1, h/w);
        batch = new SpriteBatch();

        texture = new
          Texture(Gdx.files.internal("data/libgdx.png"));
        texture.setFilter(TextureFilter.Linear,
          TextureFilter.Linear);

        TextureRegion region = new TextureRegion(texture, 0, 0,
          512, 275);

        sprite = new Sprite(region);
        sprite.setSize(0.9f, 0.9f * sprite.getHeight() /
          sprite.getWidth());
        sprite.setOrigin(sprite.getWidth()/2,
          sprite.getHeight()/2);
        sprite.setPosition(-sprite.getWidth()/2, -
          sprite.getHeight()/2);
    }

    @Override
    public void dispose() {
        batch.dispose();
        texture.dispose();
    }

    @Override
    public void render() {
        Gdx.gl.glClearColor(1, 1, 1, 1);
        Gdx.gl.glClear(GL20.GL_COLOR_BUFFER_BIT);

        batch.setProjectionMatrix(camera.combined);
        batch.begin();
        sprite.draw(batch);
        batch.end();
    }

    @Override
    public void resize(int width, int height) {
    }

    @Override
```

```java
        public void pause() {
        }

        @Override
        public void resume() {
        }
}
```

> Gradle users should copy this code to the `MyDemo` class. We need this code to do a simple experimentation with code hot swapping, which is coming in the next section. Although you don't have the `libgdx.png` file, you can use any standard paint tools to create a placeholder image of size 512 x 512, or download the `libgdx.png` file from the example project in the provided code bundle. Then, go to the `assets` directory in the `demo-android` project, create a `data` folder, and save the `libgdx.png` file in it.

Having fun with the debugger and Code Hot Swapping

In this section, we are going to use the debugger to take a look inside the `demo` project at runtime. To do this, we first set a breakpoint where the execution of the application should be halted so that we can easily inspect the current state. Open the `MyDemo`.java source file in Eclipse and set a breakpoint at the line where a new instance of `SpriteBatch` is created, as shown here:

```java
            camera = new OrthographicCamera(1, h/w);
            batch = new SpriteBatch();

            texture = new Texture(Gdx.files.internal("data/libgdx.png"));
            texture.setFilter(TextureFilter.Linear, TextureFilter.Linear);
```

> Double-click on the shaded, empty space at the very left-hand side of the editor window in Eclipse to set or remove already existing breakpoints, which will insert a blue dot to signify the breakpoint, as shown in the preceding screenshot.

Next, right-click on the `demo-desktop` project in **Project Explorer** in Eclipse, and then select the **Java Application** option from the **Debug As** menu, or press the *F11* key on your keyboard. The application should be halted almost directly after the application window becomes visible. Eclipse should have automatically changed to the debugging perspective, which shows lots of extra information about an application running in the debug mode, as shown here:

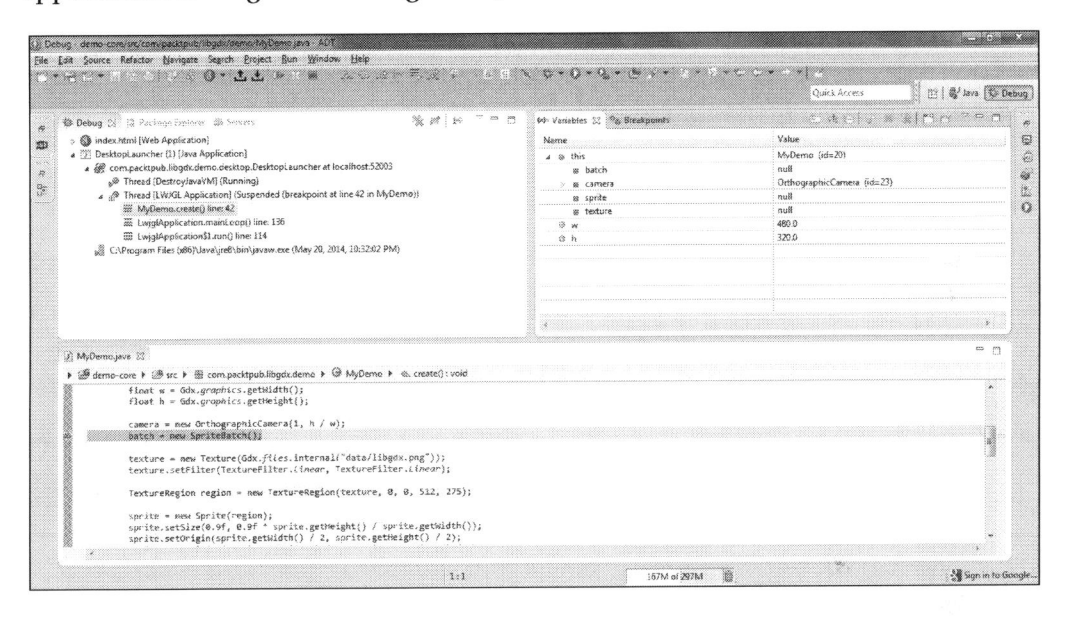

In the **Variables** tab, you can now inspect every variable that is within the current scope of execution, for example, the two floating-point variables, **w** and **h**, have already been set. You can check this by looking for them in the **Variables** tab. The correct values of the variables are displayed as **480.0** for **w** and **320.0** for **h**. To step through, resume or stop the execution of the application; you can go to the **Run** menu and choose the appropriate menu item. Choose to resume the application for now.

Let's try to do code hot swapping now. Make sure that the demo application is currently running and is being executed right now. The following code listing is a modified version of the `render()` method; the modification is highlighted:

```
@Override
public void render() {
    Gdx.gl.glClearColor(1, 1, 1, 1);
    Gdx.gl.glClear(GL20.GL_COLOR_BUFFER_BIT);

    batch.setProjectionMatrix(camera.combined);
```

```
        batch.begin();
        sprite.setRotation(45);
        sprite.draw(batch);
        batch.end();
    }
```

As a result, the following line to your code inside the `MyDemo.java` source file right before `sprite.draw()` is called:

```
    sprite.setRotation(45);
```

It will make the sprite rotate by 45 degrees in a counter-clockwise direction, as shown in the following screenshot. The next step is to save your changes to the source file. What you should see now is that the change you have just made to the code is immediately reflected in the still running application!

For code hot swapping to work, it is necessary that the automatic (re)build feature is enabled. You can quickly check this by going to the **Project** menu and making sure that the menu item **Build Automatically** is checked.

You might already sense the possibilities that this great feature enables a developer to do. Just think of a somewhat more complex scene where you are trying to find the best-looking positions for your objects, or you just want to see how it would look with a couple of different settings. It's a piece of cake with a tool like code hot swapping at your disposal.

Let's take the preceding example a bit further and make the image rotate continuously.

We will need a variable to store the current rotation value. This value is going to be increased over a period of time. To avoid a possible overflow in `rot`, we calculate the remainder of the new rotation value divided by 360 degrees. This can be done in an easy way using the modulo operator (`%`) to wrap around a certain value.

The rotation is calculated in degrees per second. Afterwards, we set the new rotation value of the sprite and draw it while the rotation value is advanced step by step.

The following listing is the modified code for the rotating image:

```java
private float rot;

@Override
public void render() {
    Gdx.gl.glClearColor(1, 1, 1, 1);
    Gdx.gl.glClear(GL20.GL_COLOR_BUFFER_BIT);

    batch.setProjectionMatrix(camera.combined);
    batch.begin();
    final float degreesPerSecond = 10.0f;
    rot = (rot + Gdx.graphics.getDeltaTime() *
       degreesPerSecond) % 360;
    sprite.setRotation(rot);
    sprite.draw(batch);
    batch.end();
}
```

> Note that some changes cannot be hot swapped into a running application, such as changing method names and introducing new variables in class. In order to reflect these changes, you have to rerun the program. However, in such situations, Eclipse will issue a warning when the code cannot be hot swapped.

Now that we have a changing value for the rotation, let's have some more fun with it and turn the continuous rotation effect into a shake effect.

As the sine (or cosine) function has an oscillating behavior, we can make perfect use of it to make the image shake by a certain amount to the left and right. The amount (amplitude) can be increased and decreased by multiplying it with the answer of the sine function.

The following listing is the modified code for the shaking image:

```java
@Override
public void render() {
    Gdx.gl.glClearColor(1, 1, 1, 1);
    Gdx.gl.glClear(GL20.GL_COLOR_BUFFER_BIT);
    batch.setProjectionMatrix(camera.combined);
    batch.begin();
    float degreesPerSecond = 10.0f;
    rot = (rot + Gdx.graphics.getDeltaTime() * degreesPerSecond) % 360;
    final float shakeAmplitudeInDegrees = 5.0f;
    float shake = MathUtils.sin(rot) * shakeAmplitudeInDegrees;
    sprite.setRotation(shake);
    sprite.draw(batch);
    batch.end();
}
```

The following diagram visualizes the effect of both the rotation and the shake:

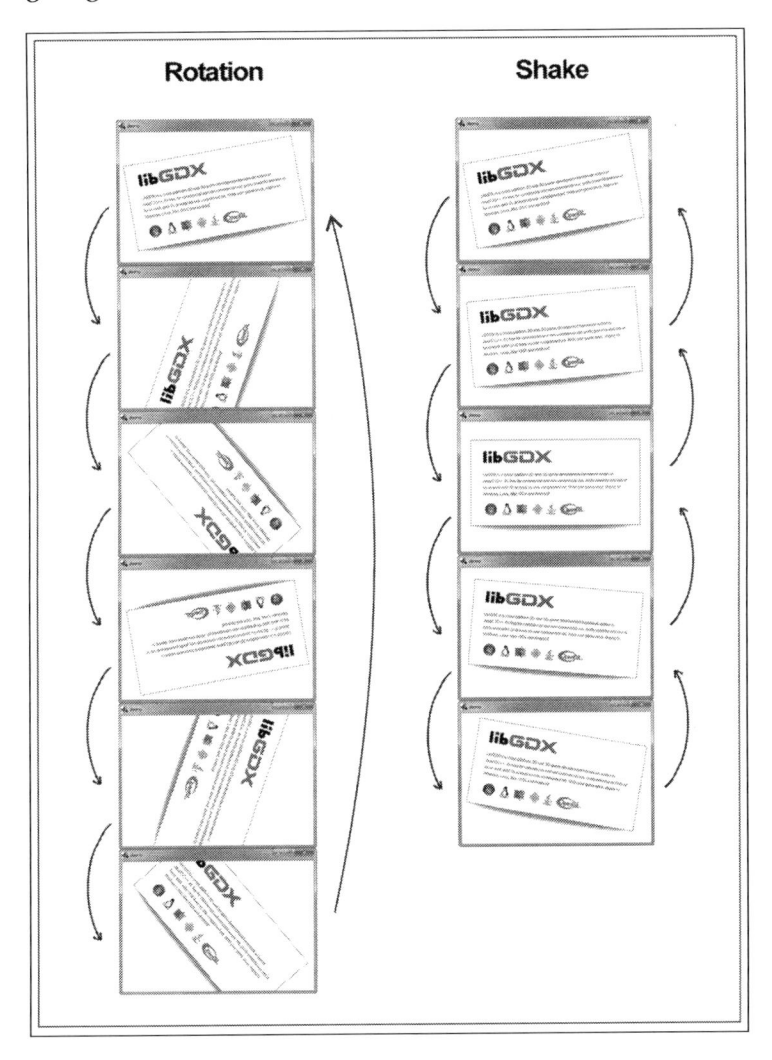

Summary

In this chapter, you learned a lot about LibGDX and how all the projects of an application work together. We covered LibGDX's backends, modules, and starter classes. Additionally, we covered what the application life cycle and corresponding interface are and how they are meant to work. The debugger has been used to inspect the `demo` application at runtime, and furthermore we made use of the JVM Code Hot Swapping feature.

We now know the basics of the LibGDX applications, so we are ready to start developing a real game. We will start at the very beginning of the development cycle step by step. As LibGDX is a framework and not a game engine, we first have to build our own engine. So, we will learn how to create an appropriate program architecture in the next chapter that is suitable to handle our game.

3
Configuring the Game

In this chapter, we will build the game **Canyon Bunny**, which was discussed earlier in *Chapter 1, Introduction to LibGDX and Project Setup*.

In this chapter, we will:

- Create the Canyon Bunny project using the `gdx-setup-ui` tool
- Learn about the game's architecture
- Test your basic code

A **Unified Modeling Language** (**UML**) class diagram will give you the necessary overview of all the new classes that need to be implemented. UML will be explained later in this chapter. When looking from a software engineer's perspective, the architecture and the implementation code shown in this book does not always follow the best design decisions on purpose to keep the examples discussed simple and easy to understand wherever possible. Keep in mind that the primary objective of this book is to teach you how to work with and manage the vast complexity of creating games using LibGDX. The following parts are going to be very code-oriented, so be sure to make use of the class diagram as a point of orientation so that you don't get lost in all these code listings and their corresponding explanations.

By the end, you will have created and tested the base code that serves as the foundation for all the subsequent chapters in which more game features will be added successively.

Setting up the Canyon Bunny project

Download and run the `gdx-setup-ui` tool as you learned in *Chapter 1, Introduction to LibGDX and Project Setup*, and use the following settings:

- **Name**: CanyonBunny
- **Package**: com.packtpub.libgdx.canyonbunny
- **Game class**: CanyonBunnyMain
- **Destination**: C:\libgdx
- **Generate the desktop project**: Select the checkbox
- **Generate the html project**: Select the checkbox
- **Generate the ios project**: Select the checkbox

> Gradle users can also use the preceding configuration to generate the project.

The following is a screenshot of the configuration described:

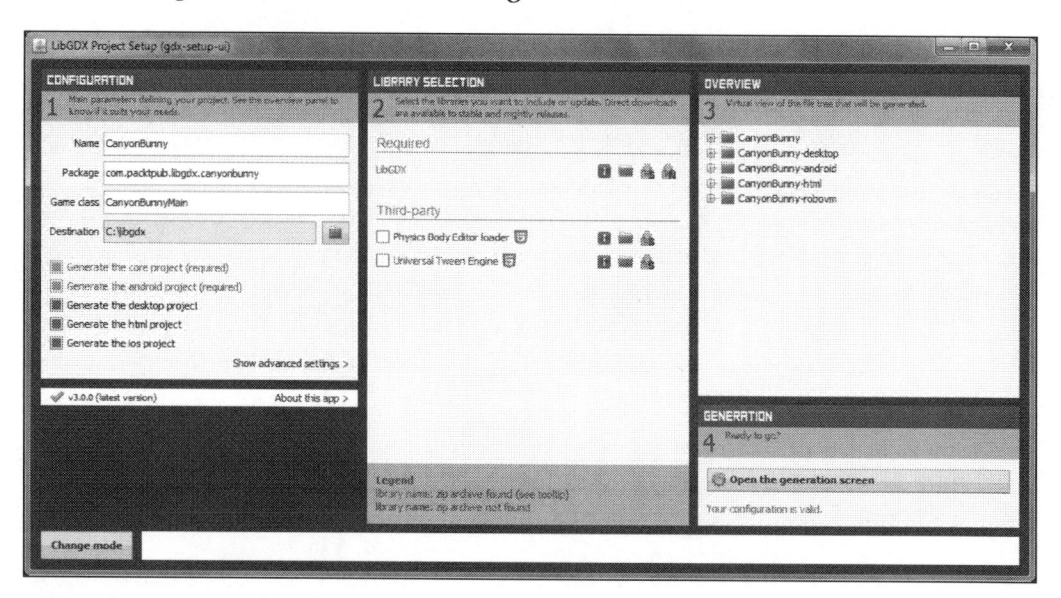

Next, click on **Generate** to generate all the projects. It will take some time to generate the projects. Now that all the projects are generated, you can now import these projects into your workspace.

> Refer to the *Creating a new application* section in *Chapter 1, Introduction to LibGDX and Project Setup*, for more details.

Next, go to the **Project Explorer** window in Eclipse and open the `strings.xml` file under `CanyonBunny-android/res/values/strings.xml`. There is a `name` variable that is used for the application name that users will see on their smartphones. The **Project Explorer** window can be opened by navigating to **Window | Show View | Project Explorer**.

Currently, the line of code should look like this:

```
<string name="app_name">My LibGDX Game</string>
```

Change the name to something more appropriate such as `Canyon Bunny`:

```
<string name="app_name">Canyon Bunny</string>
```

Save and close the `strings.xml` file. Also, in the **Project Explorer** window, remove the following two files and a directory that comes with the generated projects:

- Remove the `CanyonBunnyMain.java` file from the `com.packtpub.libgdx.canyonbunny` package of the `CanyonBunny-core/CanyonBunny` project
- Remove all the images and folders inside the `assets` folder of the `CanyonBunny-android` project

Then, open the starter class for the `CanyonBunny-desktop` project and change the resolution parameters for `width` and `height` to `800 x 480` pixels respectively, as shown here:

```
cfg.width = 800;
cfg.height = 480;
```

Save and close the file to continue. All done! You have finished the project setup for Canyon Bunny.

Configuring the Game

Using a class diagram for Canyon Bunny

We will now take a closer look at the architecture of Canyon Bunny. A so-called class diagram is used to help us visualize and explain the architecture in a standardized and structured form. The class diagram is illustrated as follows:

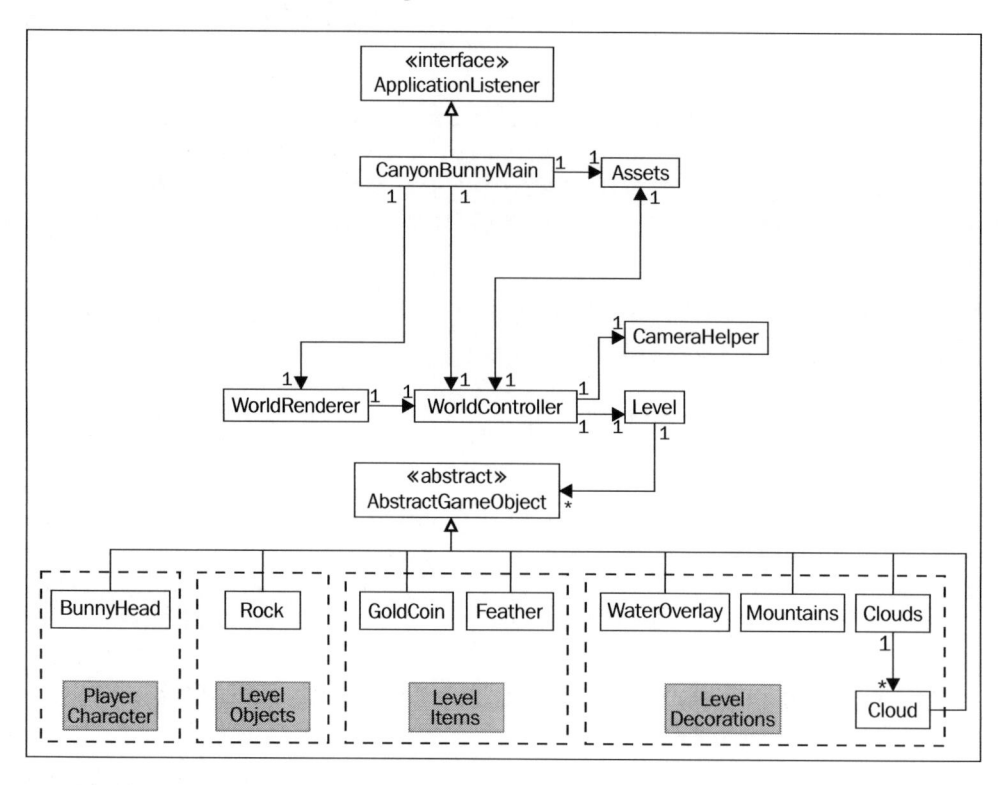

In this class diagram, you will find a lot of classes that will be used in this game. It also shows important information about the kind of classes and how they are interconnected. Firstly, before we continue, don't be scared of all these boxes, lines, and arrows pointing in every direction. If you are not familiar with reading class diagrams or UML in general, take a look at the following section for a quick explanation of what you should know to be able to read it. Otherwise, simply skip to the next paragraph to continue.

Each class is represented in a rectangle. If it is a special kind of class (a stereotype in UML), it is indicated in double angle quotation marks above its name, such as `"abstract"` for an abstract class or `"interface"` for an interface. Lines are used to show the relationship between two classes.

A line without arrows designates a bidirectional relationship between two classes, meaning that they depend on each other in order to work correctly. If there is a line with a filled arrowhead at one end, it means that the class that points to the other class needs it to work properly and not vice versa. On the other hand, if there is a line with an unfilled arrowhead at one end, it always points from an implementing class (specialization in UML) to its super class (generalization in UML), which can either be an interface or an abstract class.

Lastly, there are numbers to describe the multiplicity or, in other words, how many instances of an object will exist from one class in another. The syntax for this is as follows:

- `0..1`: This indicates zero or one instance; the notation `n..m` indicates n to m instances
- `0..*` or `*`: This indicates that there is no limit to the number of instances (including none)
- `1`: This indicates that there is exactly one instance
- `1..*`: This indicates that there is at least one instance, but no limit to the number above this

You should now be able to read the information in the class diagram.

At the top of the class diagram, you will see `CanyonBunnyMain`. It is the starter class of the game and therefore necessarily needs to implement the `ApplicationListener` interface provided by LibGDX. It holds a reference to an `Assets` class that will be used to organize and simplify the way to access the game's assets. There are two more references pointing to `WorldController` and `WorldRenderer`.

The `WorldController` class contains all the game logic to initialize and modify the game world. It also needs access to `CameraHelper`—a helper class for the camera—that, for example, enables it to target and follow any game object; `Level` that holds the level data; and a list of `AbstractGameObject` instances representing any game object that exists in the game world.

The rendering takes place in `WorldRenderer` that apparently also requires it to have access to the list of the `AbstractGameObject` instances. As the game objects need to be created before the process of modification and rendering, `Level` needs access to the list of the `AbstractGameObject` instances as well when a level is loaded from a level file at the beginning of the game.

Configuring the Game

What is still left is the bottom row of classes in the diagram, all of which point to the abstract class: `AbstractGameObject`. They all implement a specialized type of this class, and thus share a common functionality of being a general game object that can be rendered in the game world. Furthermore, these classes have been grouped in this diagram to indicate their purpose in this game. You might want to peek at the end of *Chapter 1, Introduction to LibGDX and Project Setup,* again and take a quick look at the sketch that shows all the relevant game objects in one picture. Here is a brief description of the grouped classes:

- Player character:
  - `BunnyHead`: This represents the character that is controlled by the player
- Level objects:
  - `Rock`: This represents a platform that has an edge at the left- and right-hand side, and a middle part that can be set to an arbitrary length. It is the ground in a level where the player will move on.
- Level items:
  - `GoldCoin`: This represents an item that will increase the player's score when picked up
  - `Feather`: This represents a power-up that will grant the ability to fly to the player's character when picked up
- Level decorations:
  - `WaterOverlay`: This represents an image that is attached to the camera's horizontal position; thus, it is always visible regardless of wherever the camera moves on its x axis
  - `Mountains`: This represents two mountain images moving at different speeds to simulate a parallax optical illusion
  - `Cloud`: This represents one cloud moving slowly to the left-hand side in the sky

These classes will be covered in much more detail from *Chapter 4, Gathering Resources,* to *Chapter 6, Adding the Actors.*

Laying foundations

Let's now move on from theory to practice and get down to the actual implementation details. We will begin with implementing the first basic version of `CanyonBunnyMain`, `WorldController`, and `WorldRenderer`. Additionally, we will use a utility class to store constant values in a new class called `Constants`. It is true that this class does not appear in the class diagram, as it is just there for our convenience to avoid scattering or, even worse, duplicating certain constants all over the source code files. Also, as the stored values in `Constants` are meant to be used in virtually any other class, it would only clutter up the class diagram by drawing one additional line for each class to `Constants`.

> For simplicity, we will use the `Constants` class to store our constant values. Alternatively, game constants could be made data-driven via a settings file. This would avoid the need to recompile your code when a constant is changed.

Implementing the Constants class

Here is the listing of the code for `Constants`:

```
package com.packtpub.libgdx.canyonbunny.util;

public class Constants {
    // Visible game world is 5 meters wide
    public static final float VIEWPORT_WIDTH = 5.0f;

    // Visible game world is 5 meters tall
    public static final float VIEWPORT_HEIGHT = 5.0f;
}
```

First, we need to define the visible world size that can be seen at once when it is not moving around in the game world. In this case, we have chosen a visible world size of five meters in terms of its width and height.

Next, we will create the other three mentioned classes, but will only add the so-called method stubs (empty methods). This way, we can focus on the layout first and gradually implement the code and other new features later, when needed. Hopefully, this approach will give you the best insight into the whole development process from start to finish.

Implementing the CanyonBunnyMain class

The following listing shows the first implementation of `CanyonBunnyMain`:

```
package com.packtpub.libgdx.canyonbunny;

import com.badlogic.gdx.ApplicationListener;
import com.packtpub.libgdx.canyonbunny.game.WorldController;
import com.packtpub.libgdx.canyonbunny.game.WorldRenderer;

public class CanyonBunnyMain implements ApplicationListener {
    private static final String TAG =
    CanyonBunnyMain.class.getName();

    private WorldController worldController;
    private WorldRenderer worldRenderer;

  @Override public void create () { }
  @Override public void render () { }
  @Override public void resize (int width, int height) { }
  @Override public void pause () { }
  @Override public void resume () { }
  @Override public void dispose () { }
}
```

This class implements `ApplicationListener` to become one of LibGDX's starter classes.

A reference each to `WorldController` and `WorldRenderer` enables this class to update and control the game's flow and also to render the game's current state to the screen.

There is a `TAG` variable that holds a unique label derived from the class's name. It will be used for any logging purposes. LibGDX's built-in logging facility requires you to pass in a so-called tag name for every message to be logged. So, to stay consistent in our code, we will simply add a tag variable to each class.

Implementing the WorldController class

The following listing shows the first implementation of `WorldController`:

```
package com.packtpub.libgdx.canyonbunny.game;

public class WorldController {
  private static final String TAG =
    WorldController.class.getName();
  public WorldController () { }

  private void init () { }

  public void update (float deltaTime) { }
}
```

This class has an internal `init()` method that initializes it. Naturally, all the initialization code could also be put into the constructor. However, it appears to be very helpful in many ways when an initialization code is available in a separate method. Whenever we need to reset an object in the game, we do not always want or have to completely rebuild it, thereby saving a lot of performance. Also, this approach can greatly reduce the interruptions by the **Garbage Collector** (**GC**). Instead, we try to actively reuse existing objects, which is always a recommended design goal to maximize performance and minimize memory usage. This is especially true for smartphones such as Android with limited resources.

The `update()` method will contain the game logic and will be called several hundred times per second. It requires a delta time so that it can apply updates to the game world according to the fraction of time that has passed since the last rendered frame.

> The configurations of our starter classes use **vertical synchronization** (**vsync**) that is enabled by default. Using vsync will cap your frame rate and likewise the calls to `update()` at a maximum of 60 frames per second.

Implementing the WorldRenderer class

The following listing shows the first implementation of `WorldRenderer`:

```java
package com.packtpub.libgdx.canyonbunny.game;

import com.badlogic.gdx.graphics.OrthographicCamera;
import com.badlogic.gdx.graphics.g2d.SpriteBatch;
import com.badlogic.gdx.utils.Disposable;
import com.packtpub.libgdx.canyonbunny.util.Constants;

public class WorldRenderer implements Disposable {
  private OrthographicCamera camera;
  private SpriteBatch batch;
  private WorldController worldController;

  public WorldRenderer (WorldController worldController) { }
  private void init () { }

  public void render () { }
  public void resize (int width, int height) { }

  @Override public void dispose () { }
}
```

This class also has an internal `init()` method for its initialization. Furthermore, it contains a `render()` method that will contain the logic to define in which order the game objects are drawn over others. Whenever the screen size is changed, including the event at the start of the program, `resize()` will spring into action and initiate the required steps to accommodate the new situation.

The rendering is accomplished using an orthographic camera that is suitable for two-dimensional projections. Fortunately, LibGDX comes with a ready-to-use `OrthographicCamera` class to simplify our 2D rendering tasks. The `SpriteBatch` class is the actual workhorse that draws all our objects with respect to the camera's current settings (for example, position, zoom, and so on) to the screen. As `SpriteBatch` implements LibGDX's `Disposable` interface, it is advisable to always call its `dispose()` method to free the allocated memory when it is no longer needed. We will do this in `WorldRenderer` by also implementing the `Disposable` interface. This allows us to easily cascade the disposal process when `dispose()` in `CanyonBunnyMain` is called by LibGDX. In this case, we will simply call the `WorldRenderer` class' `dispose()` method, which in turn will call the `SpriteBatch` class' `dispose()` method.

Notice that this class requires a reference to an instance of `WorldController` in its constructor so that it will be accessible later on to render all the game world objects that are managed by the controller.

Putting it all together

We will now begin to fill in the stub methods with some life. The game loop is a good starting point; it is our driving engine that keeps the game world updated and rendered in a continuous way. After this, we will add some sprites and verify that the updating and rendering mechanism is working fine. In order to manipulate the world and game objects, controls are added to receive and react on user input. Finally, the `CameraHelper` class will be implemented to allow us to move around freely in the game world and to select a game object of our choice that the camera is supposed to follow.

> The additions and modifications in code listings will be highlighted.

Building the game loop

The game loop will reside in the `CanyonBunnyMain` class' `render()` method. Before we can add the new code, we have to import the following packages to gain access to some classes that we are going to use:

```
import com.badlogic.gdx.Application;
import com.badlogic.gdx.Gdx;
import com.badlogic.gdx.graphics.GL20;
```

After this, add the following code to `create()`:

```
@Override
public void create () {
  // Set Libgdx log level to DEBUG
  Gdx.app.setLogLevel(Application.LOG_DEBUG);
  // Initialize controller and renderer
  worldController = new WorldController();
  worldRenderer = new WorldRenderer(worldController);
}
```

First, we set the log level of LibGDX's built-in logger to debug the mode in order to print out everything to the console that might be logged during runtime. Do not forget to change the log level to something more appropriate such as `LOG_NONE` or `LOG_INFO` before publishing your game.

After this, we simply create a new instance of `WorldController` and `WorldRenderer` and save them in their respective member variables.

Configuring the Game

To continuously update and render the game world to the screen, add the following code to `render()`:

```
@Override
public void render() {
  // Update game world by the time that has passed
  // since last rendered frame.
  worldController.update(Gdx.graphics.getDeltaTime());
  // Sets the clear screen color to: Cornflower Blue
  Gdx.gl.glClearColor(0x64/255.0f, 0x95/255.0f, 0xed/255.0f,
    0xff/255.0f);
  // Clears the screen
  Gdx.gl.glClear(GL20.GL_COLOR_BUFFER_BIT);

  // Render game world to screen
  worldRenderer.render();
}
```

The game world is incrementally updated using delta times. Luckily, LibGDX already does the math and housekeeping behind this for us, so all we need to do is to query the value by calling `getDeltaTime()` from the `Gdx.graphics` module and passing it to `update()` of `WorldController`. After this, LibGDX is instructed to execute two direct OpenGL calls using the `Gdx.gl` module. The first call `glClearColor()` sets the color white to a light blue color using **red, green, blue, and alpha (RGBA)** values written in a hexadecimal notation. Each color component needs to be expressed as a floating-point value ranging between 0 and 1 with a resolution of 8 bits. This is the reason why we are also dividing each color component by the value of `255.0f` (8 bit = 2^8 = 256 = 0..255 distinct levels per color component).

> Some prefer a hexadecimal notation, while others prefer a decimal notation. Here is an example of setting the same color in a decimal notation if you prefer to do so:
> ```
> Gdx.gl.glClearColor(
>     100/255.0f, 149/255.0f, 237/255.0f, 255/255.0f);
> ```

The second call `glClear()` uses the color white we set before to fill in the screen, and therefore erase all of the screen's previous contents. The last step renders the new frame of the updated game world to the screen.

> You should never reverse the order of code execution, as shown in the preceding listing. For example, you could first try to render and then update the game world. Now, in this case, the displayed game world will always lag one frame behind of its actual state. The change is very subtle and might even go unnoticed. This, of course, depends on many factors. If it is an action game that requires fast reactions, it will probably be much more noticeable as compared to a slow-paced cardboard game with enough pauses to bridge the time gap until the screen eventually shows the true game world state.

Next, add the following code to `resize()`:

```
@Override
public void resize (int width, int height) {
  worldRenderer.resize(width, height);
}
```

Whenever a resize event occurs, the `resize()` method of the `ApplicationListener` interface will be called. As this event is related to rendering, we want it to be handled in `WorldRenderer`; therefore, simply hand over the incoming values to its own `resize()` method.

The same is almost true for the code to be added in `dispose()`:

```
@Override
public void dispose() {
  worldRenderer.dispose();
}
```

Whenever a `dispose` event occurs, it is passed on to the renderer.

There is one more tiny addition to improve the code for execution on Android devices. As you learned in *Chapter 2, Cross-platform Development – Build Once, Deploy Anywhere*, there are system events on Android to pause and resume its applications. In case of an incoming `pause` or `resume` event, we also want the game to either stop or continue updating our game world accordingly. To make this work, we need a new member variable called `paused`. Hence, add the following line of code to the class:

```
private boolean paused;
```

Configuring the Game

Then, modify the `create()` and `render()` methods, as shown in the following code snippet:

```
@Override
public void create () {
    // Set Libgdx log level to DEBUG
    Gdx.app.setLogLevel(Application.LOG_DEBUG);
    // Initialize controller and renderer
    worldController = new WorldController();
    worldRenderer = new WorldRenderer(worldController);
    // Game world is active on start
    paused = false;
}

@Override
public void render () {
    // Do not update game world when paused.
    if (!paused) {
        // Update game world by the time that has passed
        // since last rendered frame.
        worldController.update(Gdx.graphics.getDeltaTime());
    }
    // Sets the clear screen color to: Cornflower Blue
    Gdx.gl.glClearColor(0x64/255.0f, 0x95/255.0f, 0xed/255.0f,
       0xff/255.0f);
    // Clears the screen
    Gdx.gl.glClear(GL20.GL_COLOR_BUFFER_BIT);

    // Render game world to screen
    worldRenderer.render();
}
```

Lastly, add the following code to `pause()` and `resume()` in order to let the game respond to these events by setting `paused` to the correct state:

```
@Override
public void pause () {
    paused = true;
}

@Override
public void resume () {
    paused = false;
}
```

We have now reached a stage in our development process where it is worthwhile to take a quick look at whether everything works as expected. Run the game on a platform of your choice to test it. The following is the screenshot of the game running on Windows:

You should see a window entirely filled with a blue color. Seriously, the result is not very exciting yet, nor does it resemble anything like a game. However, all the work we have done so far gives us a foundation on which we can continue to build our next extensions for the game.

Adding the test sprites

Let's now add some test code to try out the mechanism we built for updating and rendering. We will do this by adding some simple test sprites that are procedurally generated at runtime.

First, add the following imports to `WorldController`:

```
import com.badlogic.gdx.graphics.Pixmap;
import com.badlogic.gdx.graphics.Pixmap.Format;
import com.badlogic.gdx.graphics.Texture;
import com.badlogic.gdx.graphics.g2d.Sprite;
import com.badlogic.gdx.math.MathUtils;
```

Configuring the Game

After this, add the following code:

```java
public Sprite[] testSprites;
public int selectedSprite;

public WorldController () {
  init();
}

private void init () {
  initTestObjects();
}

private void initTestObjects() {
  // Create new array for 5 sprites
  testSprites = new Sprite[5];
  // Create empty POT-sized Pixmap with 8 bit RGBA pixel data
  int width = 32;
  int height = 32;
  Pixmap pixmap = createProceduralPixmap(width, height);
  // Create a new texture from pixmap data
  Texture texture = new Texture(pixmap);
  // Create new sprites using the just created texture
  for (int i = 0; i < testSprites.length; i++) {
    Sprite spr = new Sprite(texture);
    // Define sprite size to be 1m x 1m in game world
    spr.setSize(1, 1);
    // Set origin to sprite's center
    spr.setOrigin(spr.getWidth() / 2.0f, spr.getHeight() / 2.0f);
    // Calculate random position for sprite
    float randomX = MathUtils.random(-2.0f, 2.0f);
    float randomY = MathUtils.random(-2.0f, 2.0f);
    spr.setPosition(randomX, randomY);
    // Put new sprite into array
    testSprites[i] = spr;
  }
  // Set first sprite as selected one
  selectedSprite = 0;
}

private Pixmap createProceduralPixmap (int width, int height) {
  Pixmap pixmap = new Pixmap(width, height, Format.RGBA8888);
  // Fill square with red color at 50% opacity
```

[122]

```
        pixmap.setColor(1, 0, 0, 0.5f);
        pixmap.fill();
        // Draw a yellow-colored X shape on square
        pixmap.setColor(1, 1, 0, 1);
        pixmap.drawLine(0, 0, width, height);
        pixmap.drawLine(width, 0, 0, height);
        // Draw a cyan-colored border around square
        pixmap.setColor(0, 1, 1, 1);
        pixmap.drawRectangle(0, 0, width, height);
        return pixmap;
    }

    public void update (float deltaTime) {
        updateTestObjects(deltaTime);
    }

    private void updateTestObjects(float deltaTime) {
        // Get current rotation from selected sprite
        float rotation = testSprites[selectedSprite].getRotation();
        // Rotate sprite by 90 degrees per second
        rotation += 90 * deltaTime;
        // Wrap around at 360 degrees
        rotation %= 360;
        // Set new rotation value to selected sprite
        testSprites[selectedSprite].setRotation(rotation);
    }
}
```

The new code adds two new member variables, `testSprites` and `selectedSprite`. The first one holds instances of the `Sprite` objects. We chose to add five sprites for our test. The second variable holds the index of the currently selected sprite that is stored in the array. The `Sprite` class can be used to display textures. As we do not have any textures added to our project yet, we will generate one for our test on the fly using the `Pixmap` class. `Pixmap` holds the actual pixel data (in a map of bytes) to represent any image. Its class provides some basic drawing methods that we will use in this code to draw a 32 x 32 pixel-sized transparent red box with a yellow "X" crossing it diagonally and a cyan border. The final pixel data is then put in a new `Texture` object. This object is eventually attached to each new `Sprite` we create so that it will show our handcrafted image when rendered.

The following is an image of the procedurally-generated test sprite:

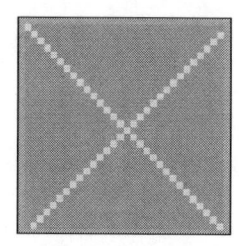

Each sprite's size is set to 1 x 1 meter. Remember that we defined our visible world size to be 5 x 5 meters at the beginning of this chapter. So, these sprites will be exactly one-fifth of the size in our game world. This fact is very important to understand because it is not the dimension of pixels in your image that defines the size of your game objects. Everything needs to be defined in virtual meters that relate to the visible game world.

The origin of the sprite is set to its center point. This allows us to rotate the sprites around itself without an added translation effect. The position is set randomly between two meters in negative and positive directions. Additionally, we set the index to 0 (the first element in the array) for the initially selected sprite. In `updateTestObjects()`, we refer to the selected sprite to rotate it on each update cycle. This allows us to easily see which of the shown sprites is currently the selected one.

All that we have achieved so far is to add the logic to create and modify the game world with its objects, but none of them are rendered to the screen yet. This is what we will change next.

First, add one new line to also import the `Sprite` class in `WorldRenderer`, as follows:

```
import com.badlogic.gdx.graphics.g2d.Sprite;
```

After this, add the following code to `WorldRenderer`:

```
public WorldRenderer (WorldController worldController) {
  this.worldController = worldController;
  init();
}

private void init () {
  batch = new SpriteBatch();
  camera = new OrthographicCamera(Constants.VIEWPORT_WIDTH,
    Constants.VIEWPORT_HEIGHT);
  camera.position.set(0, 0, 0);
  camera.update();
}
```

```
    public void render () {
      renderTestObjects();
    }

    private void renderTestObjects() {
       batch.setProjectionMatrix(camera.combined);
       batch.begin();
       for(Sprite sprite : worldController.testSprites) {
         sprite.draw(batch);
       }
       batch.end();
    }

    public void resize (int width, int height) {
       camera.viewportWidth = (Constants.VIEWPORT_HEIGHT / height) *
         width;
       camera.update();
    }

    @Override
    public void dispose () {
       batch.dispose();
    }
```

The first action in `WorldRenderer` is to store the reference to `WorldController` when it is instantiated. This is necessary for the renderer to access the game objects that are managed by the controller. In `init()`, a new `SpriteBatch` object is created, which will be used for all our rendering tasks. Before we can start to render objects, we need to create a camera and define its viewport properly. The camera's viewport defines the size of the captured game world it is looking at. It works basically the same as a real camera. Obviously, when looking through a camera, you cannot see anything else except the area it is currently pointed at. For example, if you want to see what is to the left of it, you will have to move your camera to the left, which holds true for both real and virtual cameras. We are using the width and height defined in `Constants` to set the viewport.

In the event of a resized displaying area, `resize()` will be called by LibGDX. This is our chance to adapt to the new display dimensions and redefine how the game world should be rendered in this case. The code we added in `resize()` calculates the aspect ratio between our desired visible world height and the currently available display height. The answer is then multiplied with the available display width to find the new viewport width for the camera. The resulting effect of this calculation is that the world's visible height will always be kept to its full extent, while the world's width will scale according to the calculated aspect ratio. It is very important to not forget to call `camera.update()` whenever changes are made to the camera to let them take effect.

The rendering of the game world takes place in the `render()` method. The `SpriteBatch` class offers two methods called `begin()` and `end()`. These methods are used to start and end a new batch of drawing commands. Before any drawing command can be executed, it is mandatory to call `begin()`. In `renderTestObjects()`, we loop through all the sprites by accessing the previously stored reference to `WorldController` and calling the `Sprite` class' `draw()` method to draw it. After all drawing commands have been executed, we end the batch with the corresponding call to `end()`, which is just as mandatory as `begin()`.

All done! You can now run the game to try it out. One of the sprites should be constantly rotating around its center point, which tells us that this must be the currently selected sprite.

Here is a screenshot of the game with the rendered test sprites running on Windows:

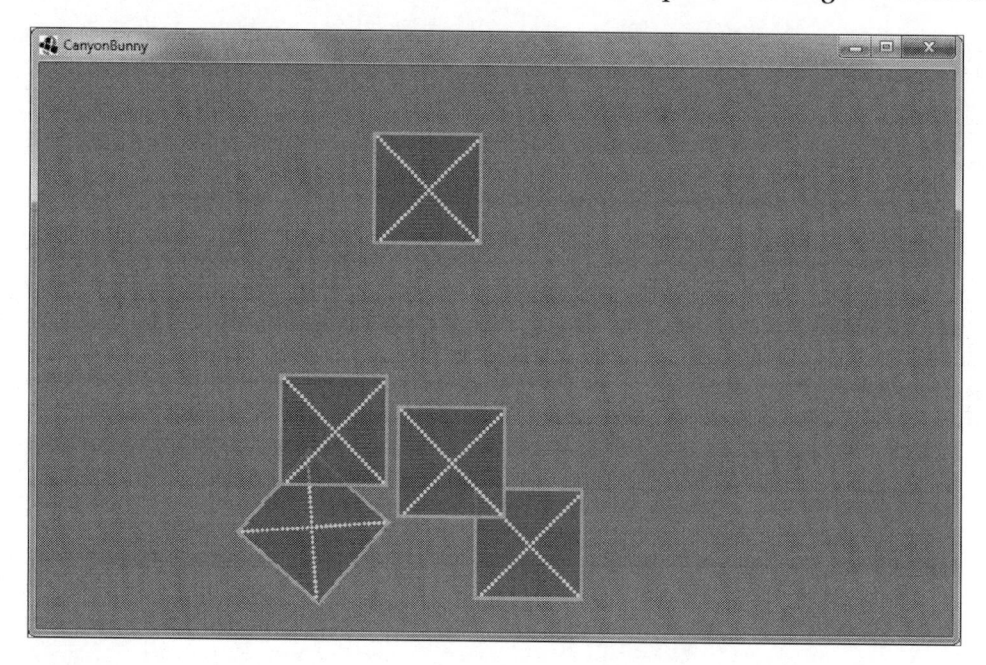

Adding the game world's debug controls

During development, having debug controls built into an application to be able to directly manipulate certain behaviors can be a very powerful feature. Debug controls are what gamers usually call game cheats, although this is a very elastic term. What is certain is that it will make your life as a developer a lot easier and more fun too. Just be sure to remove or disable all debug controls before publishing your game as long as you do not intend them to be available to the user.

There are two ways to handle the input events. We will make use of both of them shortly to demonstrate when and how to use them. The debug controls we are going to implement will allow us to do the following operations:

- Move a selected sprite into any of the four directions (left, right, up, or down)
- Reset the game world to its initial state
- Cycle through the list of sprites to select the other ones

The first of the three requirements is quite different to the other two in respect of continuity. For example, when holding down a key for a move action, you would expect this action to be repeatedly executed while the key is still being pressed. In contrast, the other two actions are characterized by being nonrecurring events. This is because you usually don't want to reset the game or cycle through the list of sprites a hundred times per second when the respective key is pressed and even held for a longer period of time.

Let's begin with the movement of a selected sprite that uses the continuous execution approach. Add the following line of code to `WorldController` to import a new class that holds all the available key constants that are supported by LibGDX:

```
import com.badlogic.gdx.Input.Keys;
```

Then, add the following code:

```
public void update (float deltaTime) {
  handleDebugInput(deltaTime);
  updateTestObjects(deltaTime);
}

private void handleDebugInput (float deltaTime) {
  if (Gdx.app.getType() != ApplicationType.Desktop) return;

  // Selected Sprite Controls
  float sprMoveSpeed = 5 * deltaTime;
  if (Gdx.input.isKeyPressed(Keys.A)) moveSelectedSprite(
    -sprMoveSpeed, 0);
  if (Gdx.input.isKeyPressed(Keys.D))
    moveSelectedSprite(sprMoveSpeed, 0);
  if (Gdx.input.isKeyPressed(Keys.W)) moveSelectedSprite(0,
    sprMoveSpeed);
  if (Gdx.input.isKeyPressed(Keys.S)) moveSelectedSprite(0,
    -sprMoveSpeed);
```

```
    }

    private void moveSelectedSprite (float x, float y) {
        testSprites[selectedSprite].translate(x, y);
    }
```

The new code adds two new methods, `handleDebugInput()` and `moveSelectedSprite()` to the class. The `handleDebugInput()` method is added as the topmost call to ensure that the available user inputs are handled first before other update logic is executed. Otherwise, similar to the order of updating and rendering in the game loop, it might introduce some sort of lagging behind the user input and response to such an event. This method also takes the delta time as an argument.

It is used for the same purpose as it is used in `updateTestObjects()` — to apply incremental updates in relation to the time that has passed since the last frame was rendered. As a measure of precaution, the handling of our debug controls is skipped if the game is not run on a system that is identified as desktop by LibGDX. In this way, if we were to only target Android for our game, we could leave all the code for the debug controls in the game without having to worry about it any time later.

The `Gdx.input` module provides an `isKeyPressed()` method that can be used to find out whether a key is (still) pressed. You have to use LibGDX's `Keys` class for valid constants to receive the correct results. So what we basically did here is ask whether any possible combination of the keys A, D, W, and S is currently pressed. If a condition returns `true`, meaning that the key is really pressed, `moveSelectedSprite()` is called. The method requires two values that indicate the direction and magnitude of the desired motion that is to be applied to the selected sprite. The magnitude here is `sprMoveSpeed` with a constant value of 5 meters multiplied by the delta time, which means that our sprite will effectively be able to move at a speed of 5 meters per second.

You can now start the game at the desktop and try it out. Press any of the keys (A, D, W, or S) to move around the selected sprite in the game world.

The next controls to implement are the keys to reset the game world and to select the next sprite. Once again, add another line of code to `WorldController` to import a new class, as follows:

```
import com.badlogic.gdx.InputAdapter;
```

The `InputAdapter` class is a default implementation of the `InputProcessor` interface that provides various methods to handle input events. We want to use the adapter variant instead of the `InputProcessor`. This is because it is a convenient way of not being forced to implement all the interface methods when you know that you are not going to implement most of them anyway. It would be perfectly valid, of course, to still use the `InputProcessor` interface since it is just a matter of taste. Derive `WorldController` from `InputAdapter` by changing the existing class like this:

```
public class WorldController extends InputAdapter {
  // ...
}
```

Then, add the following code snippet to the existing class:

```
private void init () {
  Gdx.input.setInputProcessor(this);
  initTestObjects();
}
```

The `WorldController` class serves a second purpose from now on by also being an instance of the `InputProcessor` interface that can receive input events. LibGDX needs to be told about where it should send the received input events. This is done by calling `setInputProcessor()` from the `Gdx.Input` module. As `WorldController` is also our `InputProcessor`, we can simply pass it into this method.

Now that LibGDX will send all the input events to our listener, we need to actually implement an event handler for each event we are interested in. In our case, this will only be the event where a key was released. These events are handled in `keyUp()`. Override the adapter's default implementation of this method with the following code:

```
@Override
public boolean keyUp (int keycode) {
  // Reset game world
  if (keycode == Keys.R) {
    init();
    Gdx.app.debug(TAG, "Game world resetted");
  }
  // Select next sprite
  else if (keycode == Keys.SPACE) {
    selectedSprite = (selectedSprite + 1) % testSprites.length;
    Gdx.app.debug(TAG, "Sprite #" + selectedSprite + " selected");
  }
  return false;
}
```

Configuring the Game

The code will check whether `keycode` contains the code for either *R* or the Space bar. If it is *R*, the initialization method `init()` of `WorldController` is called. This results in an internal restart of the game as if the whole game was restarted. If the Space bar was pressed, the index stored in `selectedSprite` is incremented by one. The modulo operator (`%`) that is followed by the size of the array is used to wrap around the incremented value if it exceeds the maximum value allowed.

> This handler method is called only when there is an event. This is the huge difference as compared to the previous way we were handling user input. Both ways are correct, as it only depends on your situation and how you need the input in question to be handled.

You can now start the game and try it out on your desktop. You should be able to reset the game world with the *R* key. The test sprites should be shuffling around on every executed reset action. Selecting another sprite using the Space bar should make the previously selected one stop rotating and in turn, let the newly selected sprite start rotating. You can also use the keys *A*, *D*, *W*, and *S* that will only move the currently selected sprite one at a time.

Adding the CameraHelper class

We now want to implement a helper class called `CameraHelper` that will assist us to manage and manipulate certain parameters of the camera we use to render the game world.

Here is the implementation of `CameraHelper`:

```
package com.packtpub.libgdx.canyonbunny.util;

import com.badlogic.gdx.graphics.OrthographicCamera;
import com.badlogic.gdx.graphics.g2d.Sprite;
import com.badlogic.gdx.math.MathUtils;
import com.badlogic.gdx.math.Vector2;

public class CameraHelper {
  private static final String TAG = CameraHelper.class.getName();

  private final float MAX_ZOOM_IN = 0.25f;
  private final float MAX_ZOOM_OUT = 10.0f;

  private Vector2 position;
  private float zoom;
```

```java
    private Sprite target;

    public CameraHelper () {
      position = new Vector2();
      zoom = 1.0f;
    }

    public void update (float deltaTime) {
      if (!hasTarget()) return;

      position.x = target.getX() + target.getOriginX();
      position.y = target.getY() + target.getOriginY();
    }
    public void setPosition (float x, float y) {
      this.position.set(x, y);
    }
    public Vector2 getPosition () { return position; }

    public void addZoom (float amount) { setZoom(zoom + amount); }
    public void setZoom (float zoom) {
      this.zoom = MathUtils.clamp(zoom, MAX_ZOOM_IN, MAX_ZOOM_OUT);
    }
    public float getZoom () { return zoom; }

    public void setTarget (Sprite target) { this.target = target; }
    public Sprite getTarget () { return target; }
    public boolean hasTarget () { return target != null; }
    public boolean hasTarget (Sprite target) {
      return hasTarget() && this.target.equals(target);
    }

    public void applyTo (OrthographicCamera camera) {
      camera.position.x = position.x;
      camera.position.y = position.y;
      camera.zoom = zoom;
      camera.update();
    }
}
```

Configuring the Game

The helper class stores the current position and zoom value for the camera. Furthermore, it can follow one game object at a time when set as a target by calling `setTarget()`. The target can also be set to `null` to make the camera stop following at all. To find out what the last set target is, you can call `getTarget()`. Usually, you will want to do this for `null` checks or to find out whether the set target is a certain sprite. These checks are wrapped into the `hasTarget()` method and can be used either with or without a sprite argument to find out whether a certain target has been set if any. The `update()` method should be called on every update cycle to let it update the camera position whenever needed. The `applyTo()` method should always be called at the beginning of the rendering of a new frame as it takes care of updating the camera's attributes.

Adding the camera debug controls using CameraHelper

The last step in this chapter will be to add the camera debug controls using the `CameraHelper` class. This will greatly improve your debugging abilities just because you can freely move around the game world, zoom in and out to/from game objects, and follow any game object.

Before we can use `CameraHelper`, we have to import it in `WorldController` as follows:

```
import com.packtpub.libgdx.canyonbunny.util.CameraHelper;
```

After this, add the following code to `WorldController`:

```
public CameraHelper cameraHelper;

private void init () {
  Gdx.input.setInputProcessor(this);
  cameraHelper = new CameraHelper();
  initTestObjects();
}

public void update (float deltaTime) {
  handleDebugInput(deltaTime);
  updateTestObjects(deltaTime);
  cameraHelper.update(deltaTime);
}
```

```java
@Override
public boolean keyUp (int keycode) {
  // Reset game world
  if (keycode == Keys.R) {
    init();
    Gdx.app.debug(TAG, "Game world resetted");
  }
  // Select next sprite
  else if (keycode == Keys.SPACE) {
    selectedSprite = (selectedSprite + 1) % testSprites.length;
    // Update camera's target to follow the currently
    // selected sprite
    if (cameraHelper.hasTarget()) {
      cameraHelper.setTarget(testSprites[selectedSprite]);
    }
    Gdx.app.debug(TAG, "Sprite #" + selectedSprite + "
      selected");
  }
  // Toggle camera follow
  else if (keycode == Keys.ENTER) {
    cameraHelper.setTarget(cameraHelper.hasTarget() ? null :
      testSprites[selectedSprite]);
    Gdx.app.debug(TAG, "Camera follow enabled: " +
      cameraHelper.hasTarget());
  }
  return false;
}
```

The WorldController class now has an instance of CameraHelper that is initialized in init() and appended at the end of update(). Remember to continuously call update() of CameraHelper on every update cycle to ensure that its internal calculations are also performed. In the keyUp() method, we add two new functionalities. The first one is that the target of the camera helper is updated according to a newly selected sprite. Secondly, when the *Enter* key is pressed, the target is toggled on and off. Additionally, add the following code to WorldRenderer:

```java
public void renderTestObjects () {
  worldController.cameraHelper.applyTo(camera);
  batch.setProjectionMatrix(camera.combined);
  batch.begin();
  for(Sprite sprite : worldController.testSprites) {
    sprite.draw(batch);
  }
  batch.end();
}
```

Configuring the Game

The `applyTo()` method should be called on each frame right at the beginning in the `renderTestObjects()` method of `WorldRenderer`. It will take care of correctly setting up the camera object that is passed.

You can now start the game on your desktop and try it out. To enable the camera follow feature, simply press the *Enter* key to toggle the state. A message is also logged to the console that informs you about the current state it is in. When the camera follow feature is enabled, use the *A*, *D*, *W*, and *S* keys to move the selected sprite. However, the difference now is that the camera is following you to every location until the camera follow feature is disabled again.

The last change to the code deals with adding a lot of new keys to control the camera in various ways.

Add the following code to `WorldController`:

```
private void handleDebugInput (float deltaTime) {
  if (Gdx.app.getType() != ApplicationType.Desktop) return;

  // Selected Sprite Controls
  float sprMoveSpeed = 5 * deltaTime;
  if (Gdx.input.isKeyPressed(Keys.A)) moveSelectedSprite(
    -sprMoveSpeed, 0);
  if (Gdx.input.isKeyPressed(Keys.D))
    moveSelectedSprite(sprMoveSpeed, 0);
  if (Gdx.input.isKeyPressed(Keys.W)) moveSelectedSprite(0,
    sprMoveSpeed);
  if (Gdx.input.isKeyPressed(Keys.S)) moveSelectedSprite(0,
    -sprMoveSpeed);

  // Camera Controls (move)
  float camMoveSpeed = 5 * deltaTime;
  float camMoveSpeedAccelerationFactor = 5;
  if (Gdx.input.isKeyPressed(Keys.SHIFT_LEFT)) camMoveSpeed *=
    camMoveSpeedAccelerationFactor;
  if (Gdx.input.isKeyPressed(Keys.LEFT)) moveCamera(-camMoveSpeed,
    0);
  if (Gdx.input.isKeyPressed(Keys.RIGHT)) moveCamera(camMoveSpeed,
    0);
  if (Gdx.input.isKeyPressed(Keys.UP)) moveCamera(0, camMoveSpeed);
  if (Gdx.input.isKeyPressed(Keys.DOWN)) moveCamera(0,
    -camMoveSpeed);
  if (Gdx.input.isKeyPressed(Keys.BACKSPACE))
    cameraHelper.setPosition(0, 0);
```

```
    // Camera Controls (zoom)
    float camZoomSpeed = 1 * deltaTime;
    float camZoomSpeedAccelerationFactor = 5;
    if (Gdx.input.isKeyPressed(Keys.SHIFT_LEFT)) camZoomSpeed *=
      camZoomSpeedAccelerationFactor;
    if (Gdx.input.isKeyPressed(Keys.COMMA))
      cameraHelper.addZoom(camZoomSpeed);
    if (Gdx.input.isKeyPressed(Keys.PERIOD)) cameraHelper.addZoom(
      -camZoomSpeed);
    if (Gdx.input.isKeyPressed(Keys.SLASH)) cameraHelper.setZoom(1);
  }

  private void moveCamera (float x, float y) {
    x += cameraHelper.getPosition().x;
    y += cameraHelper.getPosition().y;
    cameraHelper.setPosition(x, y);
  }
```

There are two new code blocks to control the moving and zooming features of the camera in `handleDebugInput()`. They look and also work similar to the block above them that deals with the controls for the selected sprite. The keys are checked for their state and if pressed, the respective action is taken.

The camera controls to move are as follows:

- The arrow keys left, right, up, and down control the movement of the camera
- The magnitude of motion is set to 500 percent when the *Shift* key is pressed
- Pressing the *Backspace* key resets the camera position to the origin (0, 0) of the game world

The camera controls to zoom are as follows:

- The comma (,) and period (.) keys control the zoom level of the camera
- The magnitude of motion is set to 500 percent when the *Shift* key is pressed
- The forward slash (/) key resets the zoom level to 100 percent (the original position)

The `moveCamera()` method is used to execute relative movements of the camera similar to what `moveSelectedSprite()` is doing by calling sprite's `translate()` method.

Summary

In this chapter, you learned how to set up the Canyon Bunny project. We used an UML class diagram to structure the game into manageable and logical pieces. The first classes were implemented to lay the foundation for later extensions to the game. The discussion about the implementation details took place at a gradual and steady pace so that you could learn from the development process as a whole instead of only talking about accomplished facts.

In the next chapter, we will gather all the resources (assets) needed for Canyon Bunny, including graphics, audio files, and level data. You will also learn how to prepare data for use in our game.

4
Gathering Resources

In this chapter, we are going to gather and prepare the resources for Canyon Bunny to spice up the visual appearance of the game. We will do this using a collection of image files that have been created beforehand. You will learn how to replace the Android default launcher icon that comes with every new Android project. Additionally, you will be introduced to the technique of texture atlases and also learn how to create and use them in conjunction with LibGDX.

You will learn why it is important to keep track of your assets at runtime, and how to make it an almost hassle-free task by delegating most of it to LibGDX. Hassle-free means that you will not have to worry about keeping track when unloading or reloading your assets becomes necessary. Instead, LibGDX only needs to know what assets should be loaded to manage them transparently for you in the background.

Organizing the access to the loaded assets is another important topic. You will learn how to create your own `Assets` class that allows convenient and structured access from anywhere in the game code.

After this, you will put everything together. To verify that the images of the game objects are loaded and work just fine, you will replace the test sprite texture from *Chapter 3, Configuring the Game*, with a random selection of some of the loaded images.

Finally, you will learn how to handle the level data. This will enable you to create your own game world and populate it with game objects to your liking.

To sum up, in this chapter, we will:

- Prepare the resources for Canyon Bunny
- Organize the access to our resources in our code
- Understand the level data
- Run the game to test our resources

Setting up a custom Android application icon

First, we want to replace the default launcher icon that came with the generated Canyon Bunny Android project. There is a special directory called res that resides in the Android CanyonBunny-android project. It contains resource files that are exclusively available to the Android application.

You will see the following four folders starting with drawable in their names:

- drawable-ldpi (low-density screen)
- drawable-mdpi (medium-density screen)
- drawable-hdpi (high-density screen)
- drawable-xdpi (extra high-density screen)

These folders are used by Android to support different screen sizes and resolutions resulting in different screen densities. For the sake of simplicity, we will ignore the whole topic of screen support and create a special common folder called drawable. Android will use the contents from this folder regardless of the screen density detected.

The following screenshot shows the default launcher icon called ic_launcher.png that our application is currently using:

Now, delete all the four files of the default launcher icon from drawable-ldpi, drawable-mdpi, drawable-hdpi, and drawable-xdpi.

The following image is what we want to use for the application icon of Canyon Bunny:

Copy the new `ic_launcher.png` icon to the common `drawable` folder. As we have not changed the icon's name, it will work without any additional changes. Also, do not forget to change the icon's reference in the `AndroidManifest.xml` file if you want to rename it. The corresponding line should look like the following listing:

```
<application
    android:icon="@drawable/ic_launcher"
    ... />
```

The application icon is now replaced with our very own Canyon Bunny application icon. The following screenshot shows the installed application on Google Nexus 4:

Gathering Resources

The support of different screens and resource sizes is a complex topic of its own, which is beyond the scope of this book. For more information, check out the official Android Developer websites at `http://developer.android.com/guide/practices/screens_support.html` and `http://developer.android.com/design/style/iconography.html`.

Setting up a custom iOS application icon

Unlike Android devices, the iOS application icons require specific names and sizes to target specific devices. For example, to target an iPad device, the icon should be named `Icon-72.png` and should be of size `72x72`. If not given, the iOS will scale the available icons to fill in the targeted device. The same concept goes for launch images.

Now, open the `data` folder in our `CanyonBunny-robovm` project. The following is a screenshot of the `data` folder:

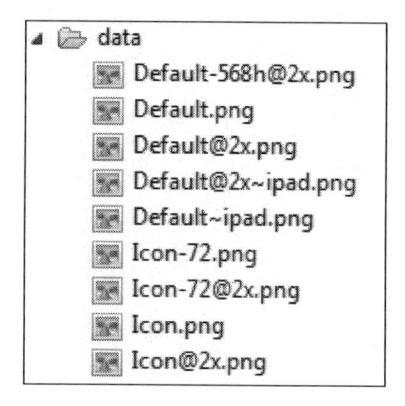

⊿ 📁 data
    🖼 Default-568h@2x.png
    🖼 Default.png
    🖼 Default@2x.png
    🖼 Default@2x~ipad.png
    🖼 Default~ipad.png
    🖼 Icon-72.png
    🖼 Icon-72@2x.png
    🖼 Icon.png
    🖼 Icon@2x.png

Now, delete all the icon images and copy the Canyon Bunny icon to the `data` folder. Also, remove the reference to `Icon-72.png` from the `Info.plist.xml` under `<key>CFBundleIconFiles</key>`, as shown here:

```
<array>
  <string>Icon</string>
</array>
```

If you have more icons to add, then you can also update them in the `Info.plist.xml` file. However, for the launch images, you don't need to add them in the `Info.plist.xml` file as it will be automatically detected by the device based on the name.

> The support for different screens and launch image sizes is a complex topic. For more information, check out the official Apple Developer website at `https://developer.apple.com/library/ios/documentation/userexperience/conceptual/mobilehig/IconMatrix.html#//apple_ref/doc/uid/TP40006556-CH27-SW1`.

Creating the texture atlases

Before we start creating a texture atlas, let's first find out what this technique is actually good for. A texture atlas (also known as a **sprite sheet**) is just an ordinary image file that can be rendered to the screen like any other image. So what makes it so special? It is used as a container image that holds several smaller subimages arranged in such a way that they do not overlap each other and it still fits into the size of the texture atlas. This way, we can greatly reduce the amount of textures that are sent to the graphics processor, which will significantly improve the overall render performance. The texture atlases are especially useful for games where a lot of small and different images are rendered at once. The reason for this is that switching between different textures is a very costly process. Each time you change textures while rendering, new data needs to be sent to the video memory. If you use the same texture for everything, this can be avoided.

The texture atlases will not only increase the frame rate of the game significantly, but will also allow us to use subimages as **Non-Power-Of-Two** (**NPOT**) textures. The reason why our subimages can be of arbitrary size is that the power-of-two rule only applies to textures that are loaded into the video memory. Therefore, when we actually render a subimage, we are still using the texture atlas, which is a power-of-two texture as our pixel source; however, we will only use a certain part of it as our final texture to draw something.

> Due to the default support of OpenGL ES 2.0, LibGDX will support NPOT textures or images; however, it will take more time to render than a POT texture, depending on the underlying hardware. Nevertheless, it is more efficient to store the subimages in a texture atlas, which is treated as a single unit by the graphics hardware. Also, it can be faster to bind one large texture once than to bind many smaller images.

Gathering Resources

Take a look at the following screenshot that shows all the images of our game objects in separate image files:

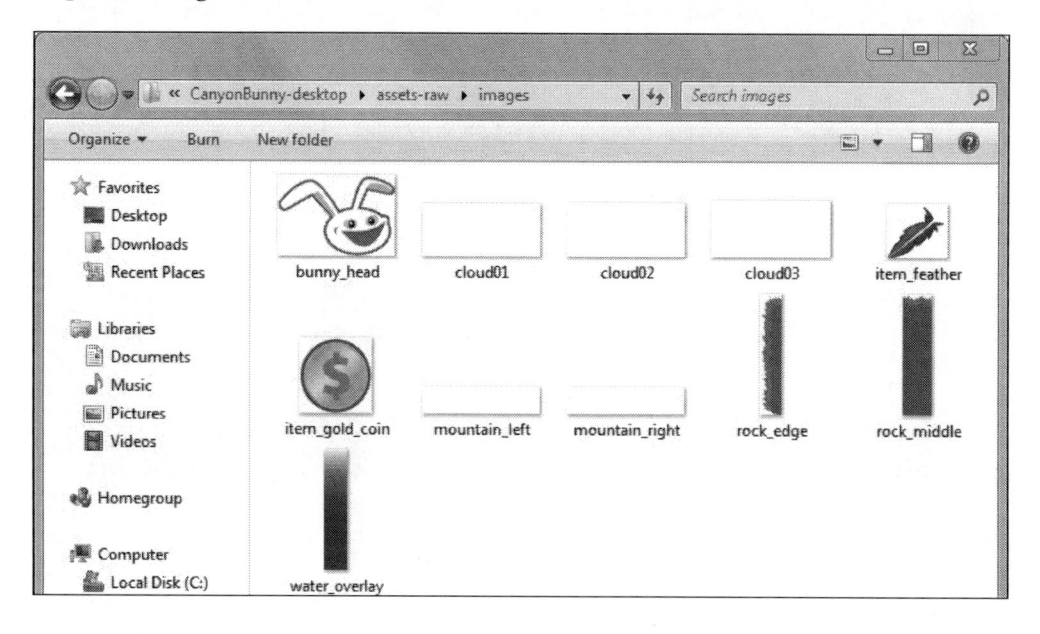

You might wonder why the cloud and mountain images in the preceding screenshot are filled with plain white color. This is because the images contain only white and transparent pixels, so it is indeed hard or rather impossible to make out the actual image information on a white background, as it usually appears in print media. Therefore, all the images of our game objects that follow will be shown with an added gray background to rectify this small display issue. However, the actual image files still remain unchanged, as shown in the preceding screenshot.

LibGDX has a built-in TexturePacker that we will use to automate the process of creating and refreshing the texture atlas for Canyon Bunny. We will put all the game's object images shown in the preceding screenshot into the atlas to get the following result:

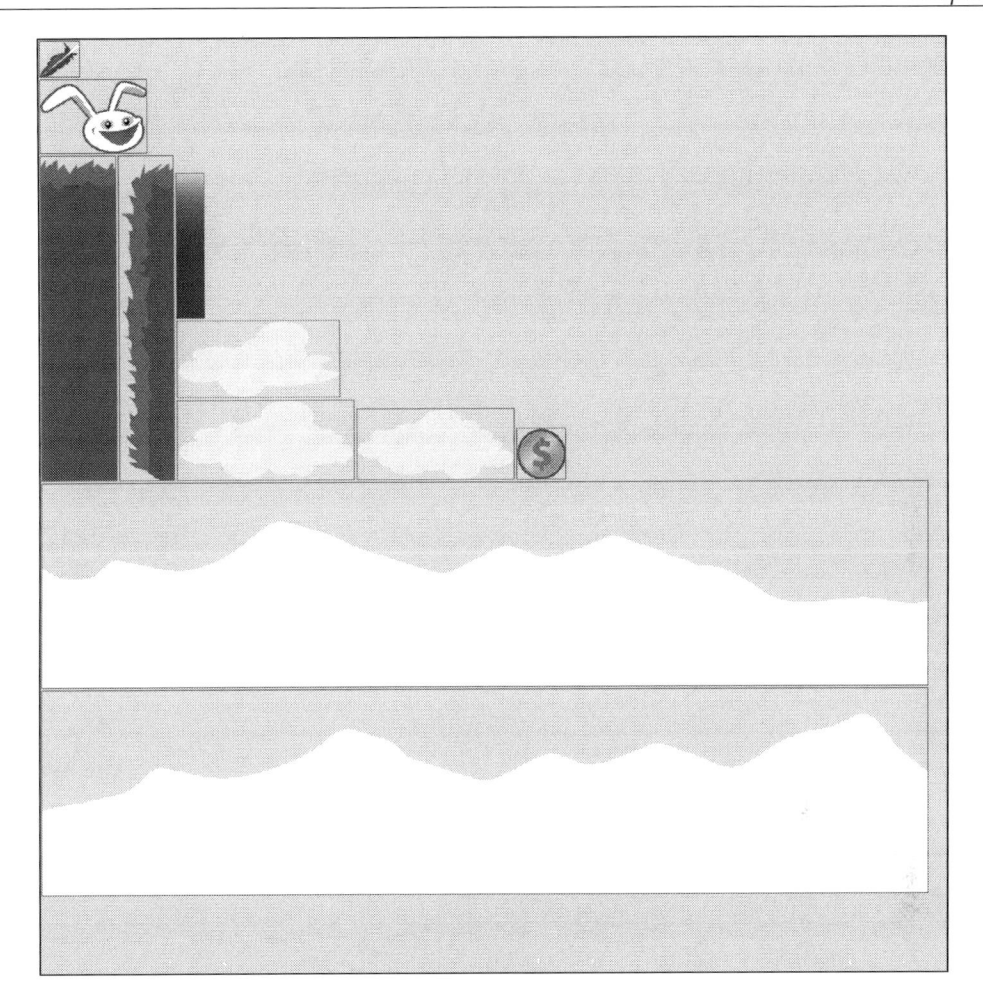

The images have been nicely arranged on the atlas without any overlap. The purple border around each image is a debugging feature of LibGDX's TexturePacker that can be toggled on and off. It can be used to visualize the true size of your subimages, which otherwise can be difficult to see whether the subimages use transparency. Good examples of these are the cloud and mountain images in our texture atlas. Also, when padding is enabled, which is the default by using two pixels for each direction, you would barely see the difference without the enabled debugging lines.

Gathering Resources

> Padding your images inside a texture atlas helps you avoid an issue called texture bleeding (also known as pixel bleeding) while texture filtering and/or mipmapping are enabled.
>
> The texture filter mode can be set to smooth pixels of a texture. This is basically done by looking for the pixel information that is next to the current pixel that is to be smoothened. The problem here is that if there is a pixel of a neighboring subimage, its pixels can also be taken into account, which results in an unwanted effect of pixels bleeding from one subimage to another.

For the TexturePacker, the following preparations need to be done beforehand as it is a so-called extension to LibGDX that is not a part of the core functionality:

1. Go to `C:\libgdx\` and extract `extensions/gdx-tools.jar` from the `libgdx-1.2.0.zip` file you downloaded earlier in *Chapter 1*, *Introduction to LibGDX and Project Setup*.
2. Put the `gdx-tools.jar` file in the `CanyonBunny-desktop/libs` subfolder. Next, the extension has to be added to **Build Path** in Eclipse.
3. In Eclipse, right-click on the `CanyonBunny-desktop` project and navigate to **Build Path** | **Configure Build Path** | **Libraries**.
4. Then, click on the **Add JARs** button, which will open a new window titled **JAR selection** that shows a list of projects.
5. In this list, search for the `CanyonBunny-desktop` project and expand it until you reach the `libs` subfolder.
6. Finally, select the newly added `gdx-tools.jar` extension and confirm each opened window by clicking on their **OK** buttons.

> For Gradle users, adding `gdx-tools` is easy; we just need to add the following highlighted line to the `build.gradle` file in `C:/libgdx`:
>
> ```
> project(":desktop") {
>     ...
>     compile "com.badlogic.gdx:gdx-tools:$gdxVersion"
> ```
>
> Make sure that you are editing under the section `project(":desktop")`. After editing, we need to refresh our dependencies. To do this, right-click on the `CanyonBunny-desktop` project and go to the **Refresh All** option in the **Gradle** menu. Make sure that you are connected to the Internet because Eclipse will download the relevant dependencies.

Chapter 4

We will now add the code to automate the generation process of the texture atlas. Perform the following steps:

1. Create a new folder called `assets-raw` under `CanyonBunny-desktop`. Also, add a subfolder named `assets-raw/images`. This is where we put our image files to be included in the texture atlas.

2. Next, open the starter class for `CanyonBunny-desktop` and add the following two lines of code to import the `TexturePacker` and its `Settings` class:

   ```
   import com.badlogic.gdx.tools.texturepacker.TexturePacker;
   import com.badlogic.gdx.tools.texturepacker.TexturePacker.Settings;
   ```

3. Then, apply the following changes to `Main.java` in the `CanyonBunny-desktop` project:

   ```
   public class Main {
       private static boolean rebuildAtlas = true;
       private static boolean drawDebugOutline = true;

     public static void main(String[] args) {
       if (rebuildAtlas) {
           Settings settings = new Settings();
           settings.maxWidth = 1024;
           settings.maxHeight = 1024;
           settings.duplicatePadding = false;
           settings.debug = drawDebugOutline;
           TexturePacker.process(settings, "assets-raw/images", "../CanyonBunny-android/assets/images", "canyonbunny.pack");
       }

       LwjglApplicationConfiguration cfg = new LwjglApplicationConfiguration();
       cfg.title = "CanyonBunny";
       cfg.width = 800;
       cfg.height = 480;

       new LwjglApplication(new CanyonBunnyMain(), cfg);
     }
   }
   ```

Gathering Resources

The added code provides a convenient way to rebuild the texture atlas every time the game is run on the desktop. The `rebuildAtlas` variable controls whether the atlas is rebuilt on startup or not by setting it to `true` or `false`. Using the `TexturePacker` class to create the texture atlas is pretty straightforward. It contains a static method called `process()` that takes an optional `settings` object to configure the way the texture atlas will be generated as well as the three parameters that are mandatory. The first mandatory parameter is the source folder that contains our image files. The second one is the destination folder where the generated texture atlas should be created. Finally, the third parameter is the name of the description file that is needed to load and use the texture atlas.

The source folder (in our example, `assets-raw/images`) is specified relative to the `desktop` project as the TexturePacker code is executed from here. The destination folder (in our example, `../CanyonBunny-android/assets/images`) is also specified relative to the `desktop` project. However, the resulting texture atlas has to be put into the `assets` folder of the Android project so that it becomes available to all platform-specific projects. The description file (in our example, `canyonbunny.pack`) will be created by `TexturePacker` and will contain all the information about all the subimages, such as their location in the texture atlas, their size, and offsets.

However, for projects generated from Gradle, the project folders will have different names, refer to the `gdx-setup` versus `gdx-setup-ui` section in *Chapter 1, Introduction to LibGDX and Project Setup*. Hence, for targeting the `assets` folder inside the Android project folder in a Gradle-based project, the destination path is `../android/assets/images`.

The `maxWidth` and `maxHeight` variables of the `Settings` instance define the maximum dimensions (in pixels) for the texture atlas. Always make sure that a single subimage does not exceed the maximum size of the atlas either in the width or height or both dimensions. Padding the subimages in the atlas will reduce the available size a little bit more, so make sure to take this factor into account too. The `debug` variable controls whether the debug lines should be added to the atlas or not. We use the `drawDebugOutline` variable to set the value to debug. The static variables `rebuildAtlas` and `drawDebugOutline` are there just for our convenience to make these two behavior controls stand out a bit more because we usually change these variables every now and then while debugging our game.

> If the TexturePacker cannot fit all the subimages into a single texture, it will automatically split them up into several texture atlases. However, there is a chance that the subimages are distributed in an unfavorable way between these atlases if it creates two textures that will be switched between frequently, which in turn could have an impact on render performance.
>
> LibGDX's TexturePacker has a very smart feature to tackle this type of problem. All you need to do is group the subimages in their own subfolder in `assets-raw`. This way TexturePacker will create one image file per subfolder that belongs to the texture atlas. You have to use the full path to the subimage if you want to use this functionality; for example, a subimage `assets-raw/items/gold_coin.png` would be referenced as `items/gold_coin`.

Now you know how to create texture atlases in code. This approach mostly works very well, but it is not very user friendly in terms of seeing the outcome directly when a setting or an image is changed in the atlas. Fortunately, there is already a nice tool called `TexturePacker-GUI` that has been developed by Aurélien Ribon. This tool is directly designed for LibGDX to work with its TexturePacker.

Check out the official project website at `https://code.google.com/p/libgdx-texturepacker-gui/`. You can also find more about the offline TexturePacker at `https://github.com/libgdx/libgdx/wiki/Texture-packer`.

The following screenshot is taken from the project's website that shows the tool in action:

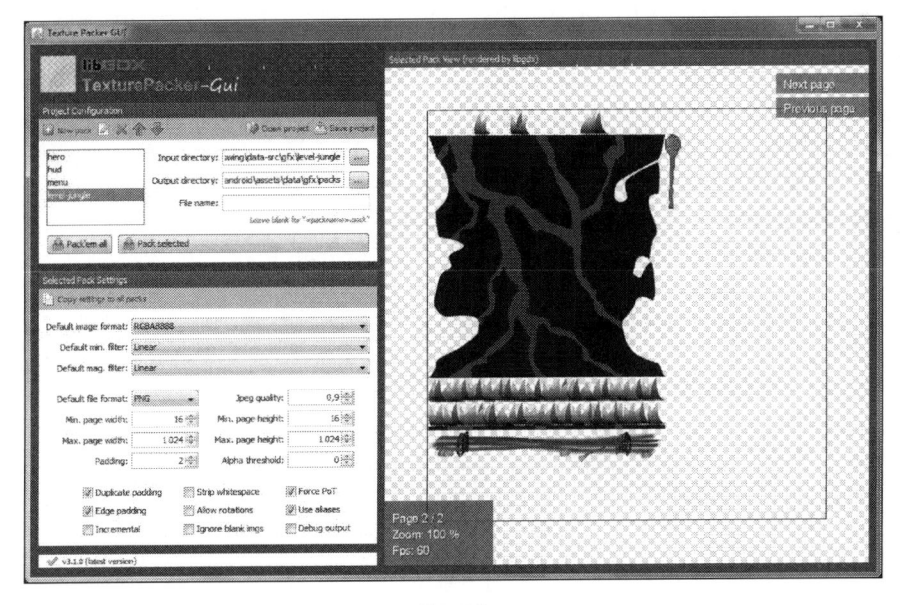

There is also a popular commercial tool called **TexturePacker** to create texture atlases. This tool has been developed by Andreas Löw and is available for all three major platforms. For more information, check out the official website at http://www.codeandweb.com/texturepacker.

Loading and tracking assets

After making our assets, the next step is to allow our game to use them and load the texture atlas. Loading an asset such as a texture can be as simple as the following line of code:

```
Texture texture = new
  Texture(Gdx.files.internal("texture.png"));
```

In the preceding example, we ask LibGDX to get an internal file handle to the `texture.png` file. Invoking an internal file means that LibGDX has to resolve the file's path by scanning the `assets` folder of the game. Then, the handle is passed over as an argument to the constructor of the `Texture` class to instantiate a new object of this type. This `texture` instance can now be directly rendered to the screen with another line of code, as shown in the following listing:

```
batch.draw(texture, x, y);
```

Obviously, working with assets is basically very easy. However, this matter becomes a lot more complicated when we want to use several assets. It gets even worse if we want to run the game on Android. As we have learned in earlier chapters, there are `pause` and `resume` events that might involve a so-called context loss. When a context loss occurs on Android, it means that the operating system has decided to forcefully free the memory that was occupied with your loaded assets. Therefore, directly accessing your assets after a context loss would immediately crash the resumed game. To prevent these crashes, you need to reload your assets before accessing them again. Furthermore, you should always free the memory when your game is no longer using a certain asset by calling its `dispose()` method, as shown in the following listing:

```
texture.dispose();
```

You probably already guessed that this is not going to be much fun as you have to worry about all the housekeeping to load, reload, and unload while using lots of assets, especially as these actions will add up very quickly with each new asset that will be used. This is one of the reasons why LibGDX provides a manager class for this task, which is called `AssetManager`. It allows you to delegate the work of keeping a list of the loaded assets to the manager. The manager is also able to asynchronously load new assets, which simply means that loading is done in the background and therefore does not stop the updating and rendering to the screen. This is a very useful functionality; for example, it allows you to render and update a progress bar that shows the current loading status. Nonetheless, the actual loading of our assets still has to be done on our own. For this reason, we are going to create our own `Assets` class, which will also help us structure our loaded assets in logical units and make them accessible from everywhere in the game code.

Organizing the assets

We will now create our own `Assets` class to organize and structure our assets. First, add a new constant to the `Constants` class that points to the description file of the texture atlas:

```
public class Constants {
    // Visible game world is 5 meters wide
    public static final float VIEWPORT_WIDTH = 5.0f;

    // Visible game world is 5 meters tall
    public static final float VIEWPORT_HEIGHT = 5.0f;
    // Location of description file for texture atlas
    public static final String TEXTURE_ATLAS_OBJECTS =
       "images/canyonbunny.pack";
}
```

Next, create a new file for the `Assets` class and add the following code:

```
package com.packtpub.libgdx.canyonbunny.game;

import com.badlogic.gdx.Gdx;
import com.badlogic.gdx.assets.AssetDescriptor;
import com.badlogic.gdx.assets.AssetErrorListener;
import com.badlogic.gdx.assets.AssetManager;
import com.badlogic.gdx.graphics.g2d.TextureAtlas;
import com.badlogic.gdx.utils.Disposable;
import com.packtpub.libgdx.canyonbunny.util.Constants;

public class Assets implements Disposable, AssetErrorListener {
```

```java
    public static final String TAG = Assets.class.getName();

    public static final Assets instance = new Assets();

    private AssetManager assetManager;

    // singleton: prevent instantiation from other classes
    private Assets () {}

    public void init (AssetManager assetManager) {
        this.assetManager = assetManager;
        // set asset manager error handler
        assetManager.setErrorListener(this);
        // load texture atlas
        assetManager.load(Constants.TEXTURE_ATLAS_OBJECTS,
      TextureAtlas.class);
        // start loading assets and wait until finished
        assetManager.finishLoading();
    Gdx.app.debug(TAG, "# of assets loaded: "
      + assetManager.getAssetNames().size);
    for (String a : assetManager.getAssetNames())
      Gdx.app.debug(TAG, "asset: " + a);
  }

  @Override
  public void dispose () {
    assetManager.dispose();
  }

  @Override
  public void error (String filename, Class type,
    Throwable throwable) {
    Gdx.app.error(TAG, "Couldn't load asset '"
      + filename + "'", (Exception)throwable);
   }

   @Override
   public void error(AssetDescriptor asset, Throwable throwable) {
          Gdx.app.error(TAG, "Couldn't load asset '" +
asset.fileName + "'", (Exception)throwable);

   }
}
```

There is quite a lot going on in the preceding code, so let's break it down. First, notice that this class is using a design pattern called **singleton**. Simply put, a singleton class ensures that only a single instance of it will exist; hence the name singleton. This makes sense here because there is no reason to have multiple instances that point to the same resources. A singleton is implemented by defining a private constructor that prevents other classes from instantiating it. The `instance` variable holds the actual instance of the class. It uses the `public static final` modifiers that allows read-only access and is the one and only way to access this class. The staticness of this class allows us to access it from virtually anywhere in the game code without having to pass over its reference to every method where we will use it.

> A singleton can be implemented to do either lazy or eager initialization. Using lazy initialization means that the instance is created only when it is requested for the very first time. Any subsequent requests will always yield the exact same instance. In contrast, eager initialization means that the instance is directly created on startup.
>
> For more information, refer to the book *Design Patterns: Elements of Reusable Object-Oriented Software*, Erich Gamma, Richard Helm, Ralph Johnson, and John Vlissides, Addison Wesley.

The `init()` method will be called at the very beginning when the game starts. It will initialize the asset manager, which in turn will load all the assets. Loading the assets using the asset manager is simply done by calling its `load()` method. The method takes the path and filename as the first argument and the corresponding class to instantiate as the second argument. The loading process is started by calling `finishLoading()`. This is a blocking method that waits until all the assets are fully loaded. After that, we always print the number of loaded assets and their names to the console to easily check whether it is working the way we expect it to work.

The `Assets` class implements the `Disposable` and `AssetErrorListener` interfaces. As we know that assets should always be unloaded when they are no longer needed, we have implemented the `dispose()` method to delegate these requests to the asset manager. The `error()` method will be called whenever an error has occurred in the asset manager. However, before the asset manager calls our implementation of the interface, it needs to be told about the class that implements the `AssetErrorListener` interface by calling the asset manager's `setErrorListener()` method. We are using the `error()` method to print error logs only to the console. You could add additional code here to handle errors and therefore avoid the game from crashing in this case.

Gathering Resources

The next step is to retrieve our subimages from the loaded texture atlas. In general, this is done by calling the atlas's `findRegion()` method, which takes the asset's name as an argument. The method returns an object of the `AtlasRegion` class that contains information about the subimage found and also some additional information about how it is stored in the atlas.

Now, for example, if we wanted to find a subimage that is stored in `assets/my_image.png`, we will write the following code:

```
atlas.findRegion("my_image");
```

Note that the prefix `assets/` is always omitted just like any file extension, such as `.png`. However, the subfolder needs to be specified. The method will silently return `null` if the lookup fails. Therefore, be sure to double-check your spelling of the filename in this case. One very important fact to know about this method is that the lookup of a subimage is an expensive function call.

> Using `atlas.findRegion()` in `render()` will affect performance; so, it is highly recommended to cache the results after the initial lookup to avoid severe performance issues.

Add the following line of code to `Assets` to import the `AtlasRegion` class:

```
import com.badlogic.gdx.graphics.g2d.TextureAtlas.AtlasRegion;
```

The following is a step-by-step implementation of several smaller inner classes of the `Assets` class. These classes allow us to structure (or group) the subimages in logical units and also to permanently store (that is, cache) the looked up references.

We will begin with the player character and will call its class `AssetBunny`. It contains a member variable called `head` that holds the reference to the texture atlas subimage that originates from the `bunny_head.png` file. The lookup is done inside the constructor of the inner class. The constructor takes a reference of the corresponding atlas in which it will find the atlas region it wants. You can see the bunny head in the following screenshot:

Add the following inner class to the `Assets` class:

```
public class AssetBunny {
    public final AtlasRegion head;

    public AssetBunny (TextureAtlas atlas) {
        head = atlas.findRegion("bunny_head");
    }
}
```

Next is the rock game object that represents the platform in our game world. It consists of two image files: `rock_edge.png` and `rock_middle.png`. Both these following images get their own variable in the inner class called `AssetRock`:

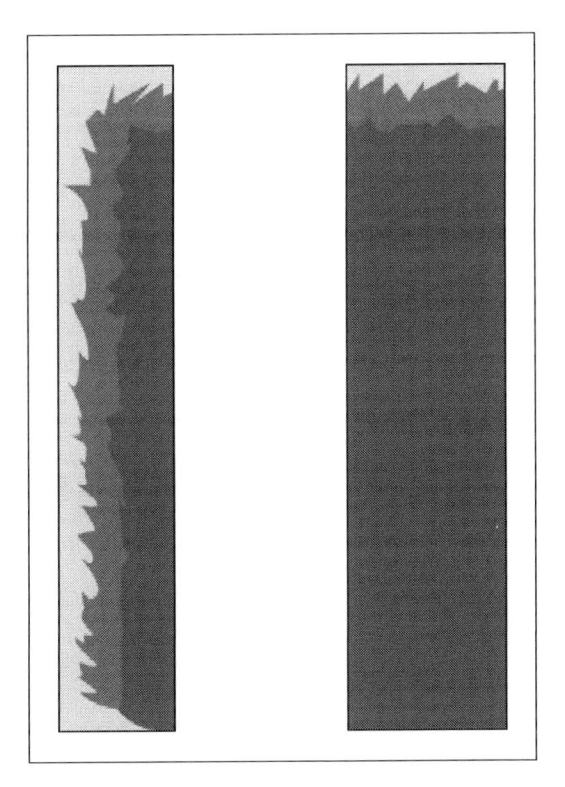

Add the following inner class to the `Assets` class:

```
public class AssetRock {
    public final AtlasRegion edge;
    public final AtlasRegion middle;

    public AssetRock (TextureAtlas atlas) {
```

```
        edge = atlas.findRegion("rock_edge");
        middle = atlas.findRegion("rock_middle");
    }
}
```

Next is the gold coin. Its original filename is `item_gold_coin.png` and its inner class is named `AssetGoldCoin`.

Add the following inner class to the `Assets` class:

```
public class AssetGoldCoin {
    public final AtlasRegion goldCoin;

    public AssetGoldCoin (TextureAtlas atlas) {
        goldCoin = atlas.findRegion("item_gold_coin");
    }
}
```

Next is the feather item. Its original filename is `item_feather.png` and its inner class is named `AssetFeather`.

Add the following inner class to the `Assets` class:

```
public class AssetFeather {
    public final AtlasRegion feather;

    public AssetFeather (TextureAtlas atlas) {
        feather = atlas.findRegion("item_feather");
    }
}
```

Next is the last inner class called `AssetLevelDecoration`. It contains all the decorative images that only add to the look and feel of the level. This collection of assets consists of three differently shaped clouds (cloud01.png, cloud02.png, and cloud03.png), a very wide mountain that spans across two image halves (mountain_left.png and mountain_right.png), and an overlay (water_overlay.png) that will be stretched along the *x* axis to give the illusion of water existing everywhere in the game world.

> The overlay image for the water could have been shrunk down to a total width of one pixel because the content repeats on the *x* axis along which we plan to stretch it anyway. Furthermore, it makes no difference to the render performance how far an image is stretched. However, it is easier to show you an image in a printed book that is wider than one pixel.

Add the following inner class to the `Assets` class:

```
public class AssetLevelDecoration {
    public final AtlasRegion cloud01;
    public final AtlasRegion cloud02;
    public final AtlasRegion cloud03;
    public final AtlasRegion mountainLeft;
    public final AtlasRegion mountainRight;
    public final AtlasRegion waterOverlay;

    public AssetLevelDecoration (TextureAtlas atlas) {
        cloud01 = atlas.findRegion("cloud01");
        cloud02 = atlas.findRegion("cloud02");
        cloud03 = atlas.findRegion("cloud03");
        mountainLeft = atlas.findRegion("mountain_left");
        mountainRight = atlas.findRegion("mountain_right");
        waterOverlay = atlas.findRegion("water_overlay");
    }
}
```

So far, we have established a way to group our assets in logic units, which also cache their references after their initial lookup. What is still missing is the code that uses our new inner classes.

Add the following two imports to the `Assets` class:

```
import com.badlogic.gdx.graphics.Texture;
import com.badlogic.gdx.graphics.Texture.TextureFilter;
```

Gathering Resources

Then, add the following new code to the same class:

```
public AssetBunny bunny;
public AssetRock rock;
public AssetGoldCoin goldCoin;
public AssetFeather feather;
public AssetLevelDecoration levelDecoration;

public void init (AssetManager assetManager) {
    this.assetManager = assetManager;
    // set asset manager error handler
    assetManager.setErrorListener(this);
    // load texture atlas
    assetManager.load(Constants.TEXTURE_ATLAS_OBJECTS,
    TextureAtlas.class);
    // start loading assets and wait until finished
    assetManager.finishLoading();

    Gdx.app.debug(TAG, "# of assets loaded: "
      + assetManager.getAssetNames().size);
    for (String a : assetManager.getAssetNames())
        Gdx.app.debug(TAG, "asset: " + a);
    }

    TextureAtlas atlas =
      assetManager.get(Constants.TEXTURE_ATLAS_OBJECTS);

    // enable texture filtering for pixel smoothing
    for (Texture t : atlas.getTextures()) {
        t.setFilter(TextureFilter.Linear, TextureFilter.Linear);
    }

    // create game resource objects
    bunny = new AssetBunny(atlas);
    rock = new AssetRock(atlas);
    goldCoin = new AssetGoldCoin(atlas);
    feather = new AssetFeather(atlas);
    levelDecoration = new AssetLevelDecoration(atlas);
}
```

Now, the `Assets` class has one member variable for each instance of our inner classes. In the `init()` method, we first retrieve the reference to the loaded texture atlas by calling the `get()` method of the asset manager. Next, we iterate through all textures of the atlas (which currently is just one) and set the texture filter mode to `TextureFilter.Linear`. This will enable smoothing of the pixels when the texture is rendered. The reason why we pass this constant value twice to the method is because the mode has to be set for both cases, minification and magnification, where a rendered texture is either scaled down or up from its original size. The default texture filter mode is set to `TextureFilter.Nearest` for both cases.

The following screenshot is an example to compare the difference between both the modes:

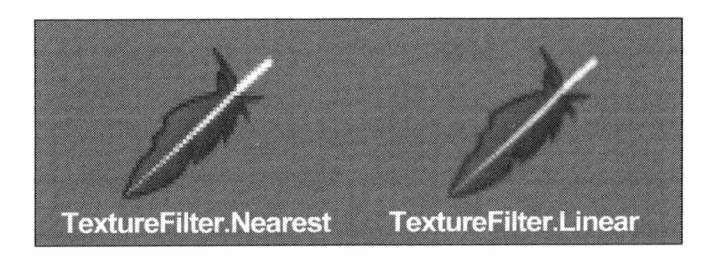

TextureFilter.Nearest   TextureFilter.Linear

Finally, we create each instance of our inner classes and pass them the reference to the texture atlas.

Testing the assets

We are now ready to test our `Assets` class with the rest of the already built game code.

We need to add the following two imports to `CanyonBunnyMain`:

```
import com.badlogic.gdx.assets.AssetManager;
import com.packtpub.libgdx.canyonbunny.game.Assets;
```

After this, we add the calls to load, reload, and unload our assets with the following changes to the code:

```
@Override
public void create () {
  // Set Libgdx log level to DEBUG
  Gdx.app.setLogLevel(Application.LOG_DEBUG);
  // Load assets
  Assets.instance.init(new AssetManager());
```

```
    // Initialize controller and renderer
    worldController = new WorldController();
    worldRenderer = new WorldRenderer(worldController);
}

@Override
public void resume () {
    Assets.instance.init(new AssetManager());
    paused = false;
}

@Override
public void dispose () {
    worldRenderer.dispose();
    Assets.instance.dispose();
}
```

In `create()`, we instantiate a new `AssetManager` object and pass it to the `init()` method of our `Assets` class. Note that we initialized `AssetManager` before `WorldController` is created so that our assets are loaded and ready to be accessed. Remember, an instance of our class does already exist and can be directly accessed through the instance variable. In `resume()`, we actually do the exact same that we did in `create()`; as for Android, the context loss requires all assets to be reloaded when resumed. Finally in `dispose()`, we call the `dispose()` method of our `Assets` class, which in turn delegates this request to its internally stored instance of the asset manager.

The final change will be to replace our test sprites with the ones from the texture atlas. Add the following two imports to `WorldController`:

```
import com.badlogic.gdx.graphics.g2d.TextureRegion;
import com.badlogic.gdx.utils.Array;
```

After this, apply the modifications shown in the following code:

```
private void initTestObjects () {
    // Create new array for 5 sprites
    testSprites = new Sprite[5];
    // Create a list of texture regions
    Array<TextureRegion> regions = new Array<TextureRegion>();
    regions.add(Assets.instance.bunny.head);
    regions.add(Assets.instance.feather.feather);
    regions.add(Assets.instance.goldCoin.goldCoin);
    // Create new sprites using a random texture region
```

```
        for (int i = 0; i < testSprites.length; i++) {
            Sprite spr = new Sprite(regions.random());
            // Define sprite size to be 1m x 1m in game world
            spr.setSize(1, 1);
            // Set origin to sprite's center
            spr.setOrigin(spr.getWidth() / 2.0f,
              spr.getHeight() / 2.0f);
            // Calculate random position for sprite
            float randomX = MathUtils.random(-2.0f, 2.0f);
            float randomY = MathUtils.random(-2.0f, 2.0f);
            spr.setPosition(randomX, randomY);
            // Put new sprite into array
            testSprites[i] = spr;
        }
        // Set first sprite as selected one
        selectedSprite = 0;
    }
```

We are still creating five sprites in `initTestObjects()` as before. The difference is that we are now using the bunny head, feather, and gold coin texture regions. To make our test a little bit more interesting, we create a dynamic array called `regions` that holds all the texture regions we want to use. Then, inside the setup loop, we create a `Sprite` instance with a randomly picked texture region from the dynamic array. This results in a random number of similar looking objects in the test scene.

You can now run the game to test it out. The following is a screenshot that shows a possible outcome due to the randomness that we built in:

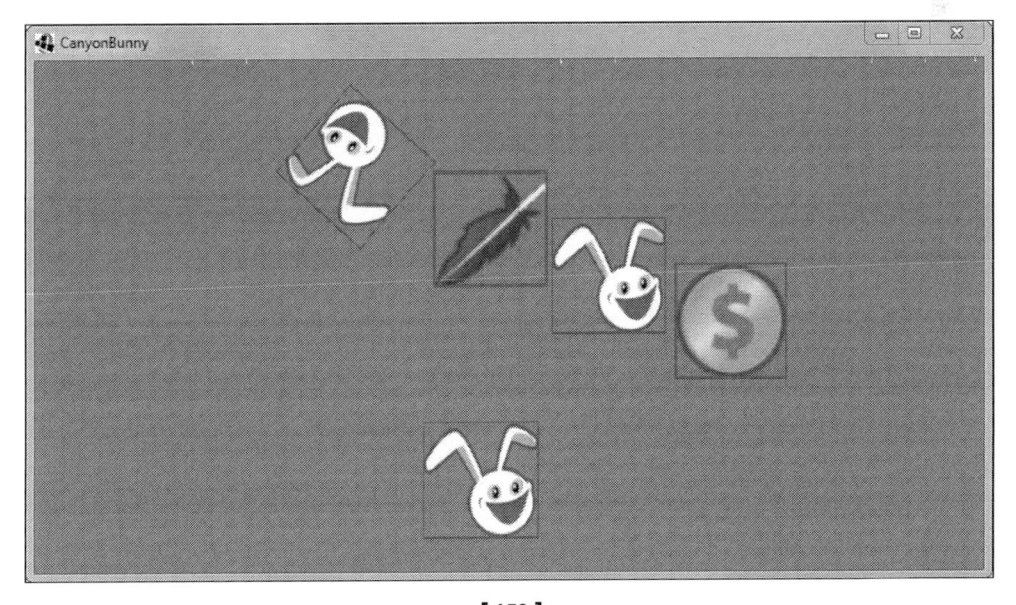

Gathering Resources

As you can see, we left the debug outlines enabled. You can easily disable them by just flipping the `drawDebugOutlines` variable from `true` to `false` in the `Main` class of the `desktop` project. Do not forget to set `rebuildAtlas` to `true` for at least one run of the `desktop` project to refresh the texture atlas.

> Sometimes, your changes to the texture atlas might appear to have no effect at all. If this is the case, Eclipse might not have detected a change to the texture atlas file and therefore did not rebuild the project binaries. A second restart of the game does help from time to time. Alternatively, you can always force Eclipse to rebuild the project by navigating to the **Clean** option in the **Project** menu to clean the project from all compiled files.

The resulting scene should now look similar to the following screenshot:

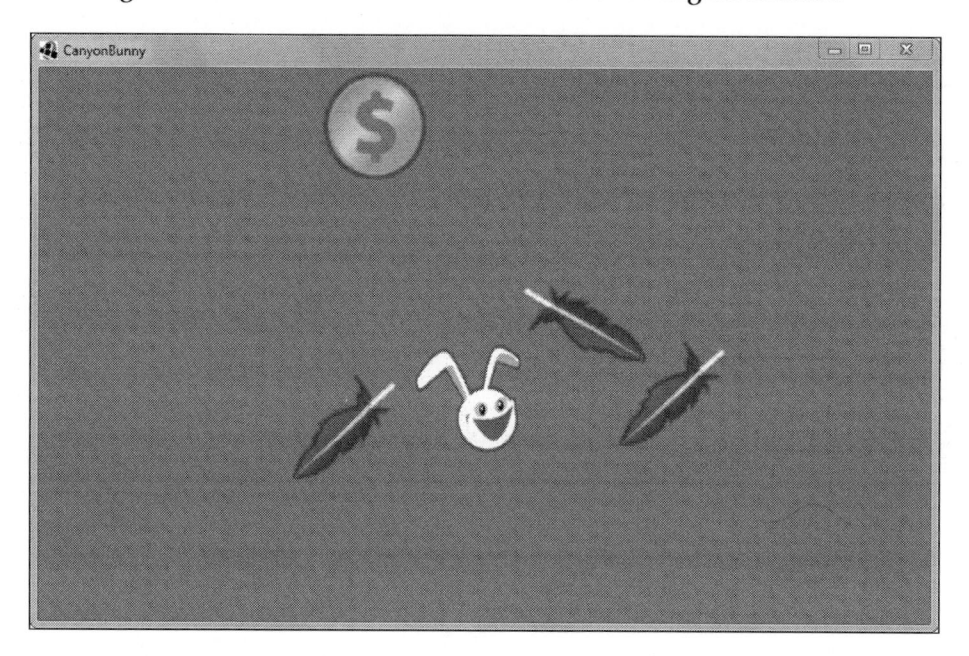

Great! We now have super cool graphics in our game. We can still do all the other things we built earlier, such as moving the camera, selecting an object and moving it, following an object, or zooming in and out.

Handling level data

It's now time to think about how we can handle level data to lay out our levels, put objects into them at certain positions, define a starting position, and so on. This usually implies a lot of work before visible results will appear because creating levels require some kind of a tool to create, modify, save, and load their level data. Furthermore, before we can even load or save levels, we will have to define an appropriate file format to describe the data of a level.

Luckily, there is an easy route as long as we keep our requirements simple enough. We will not have to build our own level editor. Instead, we will use a drawing program such as **GNU Image Manipulation Program (GIMP)** (http://www.gimp.org/) or Paint.NET (http://www.getpaint.net/) to draw an image, where each pixel's color represents an object that is still to be defined. The position of a pixel in this image will also represent the position in our game world. Job done! We just defined our level format in a somewhat creative way by reusing an already existing format and overlaying it with our way of interpreting the content.

The following is a level diagram to give you a better idea of how this works:

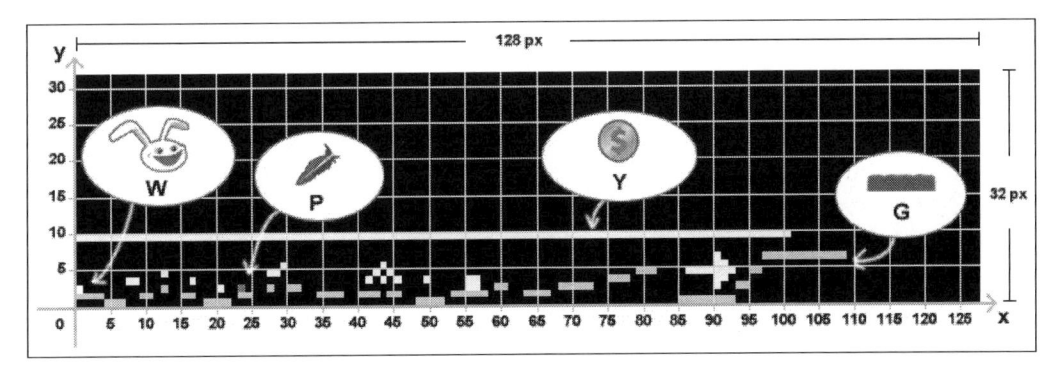

As we are dealing here with an image that is not going to be rendered to the screen, we will not add it to the texture atlas. Therefore, we are bound to the power-of-two rule once again, so be sure to keep this in mind. In the preceding screenshot, the dimension of the level is 128 pixels x 32 pixels in width and height. The diagram has been overlaid with a Cartesian coordinate system for better visibility of the position of a pixel (or object in terms of our future interpretation of this information) inside the level.

Gathering Resources

The following is a list that defines the mapping between pixel colors and game objects:

- **W**: This stands for white and is the starting position of the player (spawn point)
- **P**: This stands for purple and represents the feather
- **Y**: This stands for yellow and represents the gold coin
- **G**: This stands for green and represents the rock

The black background represents empty spaces in the game world.

Create a subfolder in the `assets` folder named `levels` and copy the `level-01.png` level file into it. After this, add a new constant to the `Constants` class:

```
public class Constants {
    // Visible game world is 5 meters wide
    public static final float VIEWPORT_WIDTH = 5.0f;

    // Visible game world is 5 meters tall
    public static final float VIEWPORT_HEIGHT = 5.0f;

    // Location of description file for texture atlas
    public static final String TEXTURE_ATLAS_OBJECTS =
      "images/canyonbunny.pack";

    // Location of image file for level 01
    public static final String LEVEL_01 = "levels/level-01.png";
}
```

This concludes our preparations for the game level. The loading of the level data will be covered in the next chapter.

Summary

In this chapter, you learned how to set a custom Android and iOS app icon for our game. You also learned how to use the texture atlases and why these are useful, and how to load, track, and organize the assets.

We combined our new `Assets` class with the existing game code and verified that we can now use textured objects while the remaining functionalities still work. We covered a brief introduction about handling level data. We also defined our editing tool to be any drawing program and declared certain color values for pixels to represent a specific game object in the game world.

In the next chapter, we will discuss how to create a scene in order to visualize the actual game world. This includes writing a level loader that reads, interprets, and acts on the image data according to the rules we have just defined.

5
Making a Scene

In this chapter, we will make a scene that shows the actual game world of Canyon Bunny. The game world will be composed of several game objects that share common attributes and functionalities. However, the way these objects are rendered to the scene varies from simply drawing its assigned texture to compound rendering using two or more textures.

All the game objects are represented in pixel colors in an image file, the format of which was defined in the last chapter. The next step will be to implement a level loader that is able to parse the level information stored in our level image file `level-01.png`.

After implementing the game objects and the mentioned level loader, we will put the new code into action by adding it to our world controller and renderer, respectively.

The following screenshot illustrates an example scene of what the game will look like at this point:

Making a Scene

As a last addition, we will add a **Graphical User Interface (GUI)** to the scene that overlays the game world. Sometimes, this is also called a **Head-Up Display (HUD)**, but we will use the term GUI here. The GUI will show the player's score, the number of extra lives left, and an FPS counter to measure the performance of the game.

To sum up, in this chapter, we will:

- Create game objects such as rocks, mountains, clouds, and so on
- Implement the level loader
- Implement the game GUI

Creating game objects

Before we start implementing each individual game object, we will create an abstract class called `AbstractGameObject`. It will hold all the common attributes and functionalities that each of our game objects will inherit from.

> You might want to check the Canyon Bunny class diagram in *Chapter 3, Configuring the Game*, again to get an overview of the class hierarchy of the game objects.

Create a new file for the `AbstractGameObject` class and add the following code:

```
package com.packtpub.libgdx.canyonbunny.game.objects;

import com.badlogic.gdx.graphics.g2d.SpriteBatch;
import com.badlogic.gdx.math.Vector2;

public abstract class AbstractGameObject {

    public Vector2 position;
    public Vector2 dimension;
    public Vector2 origin;
    public Vector2 scale;
    public float rotation;

    public AbstractGameObject () {
        position = new Vector2();
        dimension = new Vector2(1, 1);
        origin = new Vector2();
        scale = new Vector2(1, 1);
        rotation = 0;
```

```
    }

    public void update (float deltaTime) {
    }

    public abstract void render (SpriteBatch batch);
}
```

This class is able to store the position, dimension, origin, scale factor, and angle of rotation of a game object. Its methods, `update()` and `render()`, will be called inside our world controller and renderer accordingly. The default implementation to update a game object is currently empty. So, the game objects inheriting from `AbstractGameObject` will do nothing when updated. For rendering, a specific implementation has to be provided for each game object because we defined the `render()` method to be `abstract`.

The rock object

The rock game object basically consists of three distinct parts: a left edge, a middle part, and a right edge. There is one specialty about the middle part: it must be repeatable to be able to create different rocks with arbitrary lengths. Furthermore, the image for the right edge can be easily created by mirroring the image of the left edge. This means that we will need only two textures from our texture atlas to draw a complete rock of any size, as shown in the following screenshot:

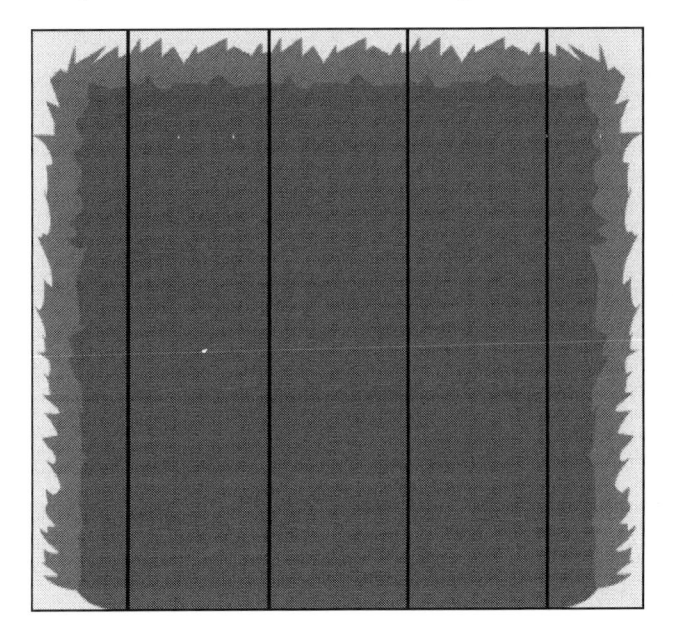

Making a Scene

Create a new file for the `Rock` class and add the following code:

```java
package com.packtpub.libgdx.canyonbunny.game.objects;

import com.badlogic.gdx.graphics.g2d.SpriteBatch;
import com.badlogic.gdx.graphics.g2d.TextureRegion;
import com.packtpub.libgdx.canyonbunny.game.Assets;

public class Rock extends AbstractGameObject {

    private TextureRegion regEdge;
    private TextureRegion regMiddle;

    private int length;

  public Rock () {
    init();
  }

  private void init () {
    dimension.set(1, 1.5f);

    regEdge = Assets.instance.rock.edge;
    regMiddle = Assets.instance.rock.middle;

    // Start length of this rock
    setLength(1);
  }

  public void setLength (int length) {
    this.length = length;
  }

  public void increaseLength (int amount) {
    setLength(length + amount);
  }
}
```

The `Rock` class has two variables, `regEdge` and `regMiddle`, to store the corresponding texture regions for the edge and the middle part of a rock. Additionally, there is a length variable that describes the number of middle parts to use for a rock, or in other words, the resulting length of the rock. In the `init()` method, we set the dimension, the width, and the height of the rock. Remember that these values are given in meters, which relate to our game world. So, in this case, a rock is 1 meter wide and 1.5 meters tall. Next, the texture regions are stored in local variables. Obviously, this is not a necessary step and is really just for our convenience to allow quick and easy changes to the texture regions the code will use to render a specific part. Finally, `setLength()` is called to set the starting length of the rock. The `increaseLength()` method allows you to increase the length of the rock by a given amount. It will come in handy later on when our yet-to-be-implemented level loader eventually creates these rocks.

As `Rock` inherits from `AbstractGameObject`, it is mandatory to also implement its `render()` method. Add the following code to the `Rock` class:

```
@Override
public void render (SpriteBatch batch) {
   TextureRegion reg = null;

   float relX = 0;
   float relY = 0;


   // Draw left edge
   reg = regEdge;
   relX -= dimension.x / 4;
     batch.draw(reg.getTexture(), position.x + relX, position.y +
relY, origin.x, origin.y, dimension.x / 4, dimension.y,
scale.x, scale.y, rotation, reg.getRegionX(), reg.getRegionY(),
reg.getRegionWidth(), reg.getRegionHeight(), false, false);

   // Draw middle
   relX = 0;
   reg = regMiddle;
   for (int i = 0; i < length; i++) {
         batch.draw(reg.getTexture(), position.x + relX, position.y
+  relY, origin.x, origin.y, dimension.x, dimension.y,
scale.x, scale.y, rotation, reg.getRegionX(), reg.getRegionY(),
reg.getRegionWidth(), reg.getRegionHeight(), false, false);
      relX += dimension.x;
   }

   // Draw right edge
```

```
        reg = regEdge;
        batch.draw(reg.getTexture(),position.x + relX, position.y +
relY, origin.x + dimension.x / 8, origin.y, dimension.x / 4,
dimension.y, scale.x, scale.y, rotation, reg.getRegionX(),
reg.getRegionY(), reg.getRegionWidth(), reg.getRegionHeight(),
true, false);
    }
```

Before we continue, let's take a look at the signature of `draw()` from `SpriteBatch` to clear up the more or less convoluted lines of source code that are used to draw the texture regions:

```
public void draw (Texture texture, float x, float y,float originX,
float originY, float width, float height, float scaleX, float
scaleY, float rotation, int srcX, int srcY,
int srcWidth, int srcHeight, boolean flipX, boolean flipY);
```

This method cuts out a rectangle (defined by `srcX`, `srcY`, `srcWidth`, and `srcHeight`) from the texture (here, our texture atlas) and draws it to a given position (x, y). The origin (`originX`, `originY`) defines a relative position to where the rectangle is shifted. The origin (at 0, 0) denotes the bottom-left corner. The width and height define the dimension of the image to be displayed. The scaling factor (`scaleX`, `scaleY`) defines the scale of the rectangle around the origin. The angle of rotation defines the rotation of the rectangle around the origin. The flipping of one or both the axes (`flipX`, `flipY`) means to mirror the corresponding axis of that image.

The rendering of the rock is split up into the following three drawing steps:

1. Draw the left edge at the current position of the rock. A relative x- and y-value, `relX` and `relY`, are also added to the position. These are used to align the left edge to the left-hand side of the object's local *y* axis. The result of doing this is that the following middle parts will now start at 0 on the *x* axis. This makes it much easier to handle the positioning of rocks as each middle part represents one pixel in a level image, while the edges are just cosmetic details.

2. Draw all the middle parts according to the set length of the rock. The drawing starts at 0, which is located directly next to where the left edge ends. Each subsequent middle part is drawn next to the last middle part. This is achieved by adding the middle part's width to the relative position `relX` for each iteration inside the loop.

3. Finally, the mirrored left edge is drawn next to where the last middle part ends. This mirroring is achieved by setting the `flipX` parameter to `true`.

The `reg` variable is used to store the currently selected texture region for each step.

The mountains object

The mountains game object consists of three mountains that each have their own layer. A tinting color and positional offset can be specified for each layer. A single mountain consists of a left and a right image. The ends of both image parts have been carefully crafted so that they can be seamlessly tiled. The following screenshot illustrates this:

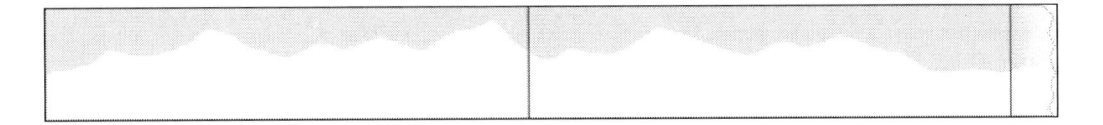

The white color for the mountain images has been chosen on purpose to allow tinting.

Create a new file for the `Mountains` class and add the following code:

```
package com.packtpub.libgdx.canyonbunny.game.objects;

import com.badlogic.gdx.graphics.g2d.SpriteBatch;
import com.badlogic.gdx.graphics.g2d.TextureRegion;
import com.badlogic.gdx.math.MathUtils;
import com.packtpub.libgdx.canyonbunny.game.Assets;

public class Mountains extends AbstractGameObject {

  private TextureRegion regMountainLeft;
  private TextureRegion regMountainRight;

  private int length;

  public Mountains (int length) {
    this.length = length;
    init();
  }

  private void init () {
    dimension.set(10, 2);

    regMountainLeft =
Assets.instance.levelDecoration.mountainLeft;
    regMountainRight =
Assets.instance.levelDecoration.mountainRight;

    // shift mountain and extend length
```

Making a Scene

```
        origin.x = -dimension.x * 2;
        length += dimension.x * 2;
    }

    private void drawMountain (SpriteBatch batch, float offsetX,
float offsetY, float tintColor) {
        TextureRegion reg = null;
        batch.setColor(tintColor, tintColor, tintColor, 1);
        float xRel = dimension.x * offsetX;
        float yRel = dimension.y * offsetY;

        // mountains span the whole level
        int mountainLength = 0;
        mountainLength += MathUtils.ceil(length / (2 * dimension.x));
        mountainLength += MathUtils.ceil(0.5f + offsetX);
        for (int i = 0; i < mountainLength; i++) {
          // mountain left
          reg = regMountainLeft;
          batch.draw(reg.getTexture(), origin.x + xRel, position.y +
origin.y + yRel, origin.x, origin.y, dimension.x, dimension.y,
scale.x, scale.y, rotation, reg.getRegionX(), reg.getRegionY(),
reg.getRegionWidth(), reg.getRegionHeight(), false, false);
          xRel += dimension.x;

          // mountain right
          reg = regMountainRight;
          batch.draw(reg.getTexture(),origin.x + xRel, position.y +
origin.y + yRel, origin.x, origin.y, dimension.x, dimension.y,
scale.x, scale.y, rotation, reg.getRegionX(), reg.getRegionY(),
reg.getRegionWidth(), reg.getRegionHeight(), false, false);
          xRel += dimension.x;
        }
      // reset color to white
      batch.setColor(1, 1, 1, 1);
    }
    @Override
    public void render (SpriteBatch batch) {
        // distant mountains (dark gray)
        drawMountain(batch, 0.5f, 0.5f, 0.5f);
        // distant mountains (gray)
        drawMountain(batch, 0.25f, 0.25f, 0.7f);
        // distant mountains (light gray)
        drawMountain(batch, 0.0f, 0.0f, 0.9f);
    }
}
```

The construction of the `Mountains` class is quite similar to `Rock`. It inherits from `AbstractGameObject` and uses a `length` variable to store the number of times the image needs to be repeated.

The `drawMountain()` method is used to encapsulate the drawing code of a mountain layer so that the task to draw the three layers is greatly simplified. The tinting is achieved by setting the drawing color of `SpriteBatch` to the desired color value using the `setColor()` method. All subsequent draw calls will now produce tinted images. Afterwards, the drawing color is reset to a neutral white color, which simply means that the texture colors will be no longer manipulated. This might cause future calls to `SpriteBatch` to tint irrespective of whatever is drawn next.

The water overlay object

The water overlay game object is very simple compared to the previous game objects. It consists of only one image. This image needs to overlay the ground of the whole level. There are several ways to achieve this. One way would be to span the image from side to side of the camera's viewport and move the overlay together with the camera whenever the camera is moved. This is a good way to create an illusion of water being everywhere in the level. Unfortunately, special care needs to be taken if the camera is also moved in a vertical direction. Another way to implement the image of water everywhere in the level is to just draw a single, horizontally stretched water overlay image from start to end, as shown in the following screenshot. This is exactly what the next code will do.

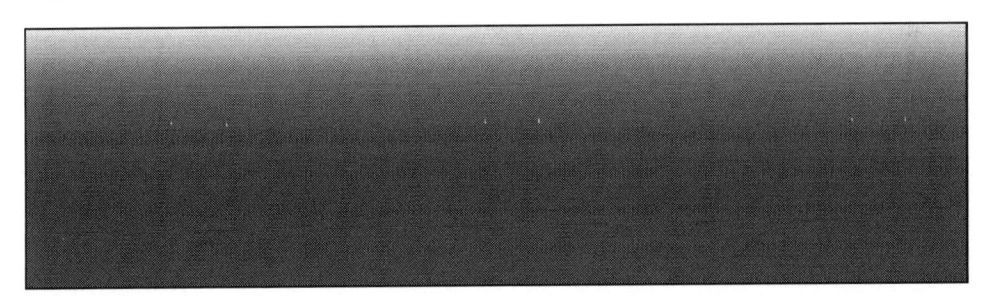

Create a new file for the `WaterOverlay` class and add the following code:

```
package com.packtpub.libgdx.canyonbunny.game.objects;

import com.badlogic.gdx.graphics.g2d.SpriteBatch;
import com.badlogic.gdx.graphics.g2d.TextureRegion;
import com.packtpub.libgdx.canyonbunny.game.Assets;

public class WaterOverlay extends AbstractGameObject {
```

```java
    private TextureRegion regWaterOverlay;
    private float length;

    public WaterOverlay (float length) {
        this.length = length;
        init();
    }

    private void init () {
      dimension.set(length * 10, 3);

      regWaterOverlay =
    Assets.instance.levelDecoration.waterOverlay;

      origin.x = -dimension.x / 2;
    }

    @Override
    public void render (SpriteBatch batch) {
      TextureRegion reg = null;
      reg = regWaterOverlay;
      batch.draw(reg.getTexture(), position.x + origin.x, position.y
    + origin.y, origin.x, origin.y, dimension.x, dimension.y, scale.x,
    scale.y, rotation, reg.getRegionX(), reg.getRegionY(),
    reg.getRegionWidth(), reg.getRegionHeight(), false, false);
    }
}
```

The `WaterOverlay` class is constructed similar to the previous game objects.

The clouds object

The clouds game object consists of a number of clouds. A cloud will use one of the three available cloud images from the texture atlas. The number of clouds depends on the given length that is divided by a constant factor to determine the final distribution of the clouds. The following screenshot illustrates this:

Chapter 5

Create a new file for the Clouds class and add the following code:

```java
package com.packtpub.libgdx.canyonbunny.game.objects;

import com.badlogic.gdx.graphics.g2d.SpriteBatch;
import com.badlogic.gdx.graphics.g2d.TextureRegion;
import com.badlogic.gdx.math.MathUtils;
import com.badlogic.gdx.math.Vector2;
import com.badlogic.gdx.utils.Array;
import com.packtpub.libgdx.canyonbunny.game.Assets;

public class Clouds extends AbstractGameObject {

  private float length;

  private Array<TextureRegion> regClouds;
  private Array<Cloud> clouds;

  private class Cloud extends AbstractGameObject {
    private TextureRegion regCloud;

    public Cloud () {}

    public void setRegion (TextureRegion region) {
      regCloud = region;
    }

    @Override
    public void render (SpriteBatch batch) {
      TextureRegion reg = regCloud;
      batch.draw(reg.getTexture(), position.x + origin.x,
position.y + origin.y, origin.x, origin.y, dimension.x,
dimension.y, scale.x, scale.y, rotation, reg.getRegionX(),
reg.getRegionY(), reg.getRegionWidth(), reg.getRegionHeight(),
false, false);
    }
  }

  public Clouds (float length) {
    this.length = length;
    init();
  }

  private void init () {
```

Making a Scene

```java
      dimension.set(3.0f, 1.5f);
      regClouds = new Array<TextureRegion>();
      regClouds.add(Assets.instance.levelDecoration.cloud01);
      regClouds.add(Assets.instance.levelDecoration.cloud02);
      regClouds.add(Assets.instance.levelDecoration.cloud03);

      int distFac = 5;
      int numClouds = (int)(length / distFac);
      clouds = new Array<Cloud>(2 * numClouds);
      for (int i = 0; i < numClouds; i++) {
        Cloud cloud = spawnCloud();
        cloud.position.x = i * distFac;
        clouds.add(cloud);
      }
  }

  private Cloud spawnCloud () {
    Cloud cloud = new Cloud();
    cloud.dimension.set(dimension);
    // select random cloud image
    cloud.setRegion(regClouds.random());
    // position
    Vector2 pos = new Vector2();
    pos.x = length + 10; // position after end of level
    pos.y += 1.75; // base position
    pos.y += MathUtils.random(0.0f, 0.2f)
          * (MathUtils.randomBoolean() ? 1 : -1); // random
  additional position
    cloud.position.set(pos);
    return cloud;
  }

  @Override
  public void render (SpriteBatch batch) {
    for (Cloud cloud : clouds)
        cloud.render(batch);
  }
}
```

The `Clouds` class is also constructed like the previous game objects. The distribution of the clouds over the level is determined by the given length value and the constant factor `distFact`, which is 5 in this code, meaning that there will be a cloud every five meters.

A single cloud is defined by the `Clouds` inner class `Cloud`, which also inherits from `AbstractGameObject`. So, a `Cloud` object is the actual cloud object, while `Clouds` is the container that maintains a list of all the currently created clouds. A new cloud can be created by simply calling the `spawnCloud()` method of `Clouds`. This will create a new `Cloud` object, assign a random cloud image to it, move it to the end of the level, and randomly shift it up or down a bit. The newly created cloud is also added to the list and returned to the calling method.

Implementing the level loader

We will now implement the level loader that will be able to read and interpret the image data.

> You might want to refer to the handling of level data section in *Chapter 3, Configuring the Game*, where we defined and discussed the level format.

Create a new file for the `Level` class and add the following code:

```
package com.packtpub.libgdx.canyonbunny.game;

import com.badlogic.gdx.Gdx;
import com.badlogic.gdx.graphics.Pixmap;
import com.badlogic.gdx.graphics.g2d.SpriteBatch;
import com.badlogic.gdx.utils.Array;
import com.packtpub.libgdx.canyonbunny.game.objects.AbstractGameObject;
import com.packtpub.libgdx.canyonbunny.game.objects.Clouds;
import com.packtpub.libgdx.canyonbunny.game.objects.Mountains;
import com.packtpub.libgdx.canyonbunny.game.objects.Rock;
import com.packtpub.libgdx.canyonbunny.game.objects.WaterOverlay;

public class Level {
  public static final String TAG = Level.class.getName();

  public enum BLOCK_TYPE {
    EMPTY(0, 0, 0), // black
    ROCK(0, 255, 0), // green
    PLAYER_SPAWNPOINT(255, 255, 255), // white
    ITEM_FEATHER(255, 0, 255), // purple
    ITEM_GOLD_COIN(255, 255, 0); // yellow

    private int color;
```

```
        private BLOCK_TYPE (int r, int g, int b) {
          color = r << 24 | g << 16 | b << 8 | 0xff;
        }

        public boolean sameColor (int color) {
            return this.color == color;
        }

        public int getColor () {
            return color;
        }
    }

    // objects
    public Array<Rock> rocks;

    // decoration
    public Clouds clouds;
    public Mountains mountains;
    public WaterOverlay waterOverlay;

    public Level (String filename) {
      init(filename);
    }

    private void init (String filename) {}
    public void render (SpriteBatch batch) {}
}
```

The `Level` class contains an `enum` data type that we will use to represent our entire game world objects. These objects have a unique RGBA color value that is used to identify them. We will not use the alpha channel and always expect full opacity for our game object color values. As each color component is represented as an 8-bit value, the sum of an RGBA color is 32 bits or 4 bytes. The `int` data type of Java is also defined as a 32-bit value, which makes it the appropriate place to store RGBA color codes in a compact way.

> The compact color value is stored in RGBA format. Also, in the following code, we are going to use bit shift operations. For more information, check out the blog article at http://www.zimnox.com/resources/articles/tutorials/?ar=t002.

Chapter 5

The `sameColor()` method will allow us to easily find out whether two colors are exactly the same by comparing only one value instead of four.

`Level` holds a list of `Rock` instances called `rocks`. There is also a variable to hold an instance of `Clouds`, `Mountains`, and `WaterOverlay`. All these variables are filled in during the level loading process that takes place in the `init()` method.

Add the following code to the still empty `init()` method:

```
private void init (String filename) {
  // objects
  rocks = new Array<Rock>();

  // load image file that represents the level data
  Pixmap pixmap = new Pixmap(Gdx.files.internal(filename));
  // scan pixels from top-left to bottom-right
  int lastPixel = -1;
  for (int pixelY = 0; pixelY < pixmap.getHeight(); pixelY++) {
    for (int pixelX = 0; pixelX < pixmap.getWidth(); pixelX++) {
      AbstractGameObject obj = null;
      float offsetHeight = 0;
      // height grows from bottom to top
      float baseHeight = pixmap.getHeight() - pixelY;
      // get color of current pixel as 32-bit RGBA value
      int currentPixel = pixmap.getPixel(pixelX, pixelY);
      // find matching color value to identify block type at (x,y)
      // point and create the corresponding game object if there is
      // a match

      // empty space
      if (BLOCK_TYPE.EMPTY.sameColor(currentPixel)) {
        // do nothing
      }
      // rock
      else if (BLOCK_TYPE.ROCK.sameColor(currentPixel)) {
        if (lastPixel != currentPixel) {
          obj = new Rock();
          float heightIncreaseFactor = 0.25f;
          offsetHeight = -2.5f;
          obj.position.set(pixelX, baseHeight * obj.dimension.y
 * heightIncreaseFactor + offsetHeight);
          rocks.add((Rock)obj);
        } else {
          rocks.get(rocks.size - 1).increaseLength(1);
```

Making a Scene

```java
            }
          }
          // player spawn point
          else if
              (BLOCK_TYPE.PLAYER_SPAWNPOINT.sameColor(currentPixel)) {
          }
          // feather
          else if (BLOCK_TYPE.ITEM_FEATHER.sameColor(currentPixel)) {
          }
          // gold coin
          else if (BLOCK_TYPE.ITEM_GOLD_COIN.sameColor(currentPixel)) {
          }
          // unknown object/pixel color
          else {
            int r = 0xff & (currentPixel >>> 24); //red color channel
            int g = 0xff & (currentPixel >>> 16); //green color channel
            int b = 0xff & (currentPixel >>> 8);  //blue color channel
            int a = 0xff & currentPixel;   //alpha channel
            Gdx.app.error(TAG, "Unknown object at x<" + pixelX + "> y<"
 + pixelY + ">: r<" + r+ "> g<" + g + "> b<" + b + "> a<" + a + ">");
          }
          lastPixel = currentPixel;
        }
      }

      // decoration
      clouds = new Clouds(pixmap.getWidth());
      clouds.position.set(0, 2);
      mountains = new Mountains(pixmap.getWidth());
      mountains.position.set(-1, -1);
      waterOverlay = new WaterOverlay(pixmap.getWidth());
      waterOverlay.position.set(0, -3.75f);

      // free memory
      pixmap.dispose();
      Gdx.app.debug(TAG, "level '" + filename + "' loaded");
    }
```

This method starts by creating a new and empty list for the rocks. Then, it uses `Gdx.files.internal()` to get a file handle, which in turn is used to create a new `Pixmap` object. It contains the pixel data of the level image that is to be scanned and interpreted.

The scanning is done by looping through each pixel starting from the top-left corner of the image to the bottom-right corner. The `baseHeight` variable is set to the maximum level height minus the current height of the currently scanned pixel, which results in a flipped vertical pixel position. What this basically means is that the game objects will appear at their correct height in the game world, although scanning is done from top to bottom and the game objects grow from the bottom up. The `offsetHeight` variable is used to individually offset an object to correctly fit into the game world. The `currentPixel` variable stores the color value of the currently scanned pixel. Next, this value is compared to each defined color code of a game object until a match has been found. If no color code matches, there will be an error message logged to the console to indicate an implementation error in our game. The error can either mean the use of an undefined color code or that the identification method does not handle this color code. The error message will contain the decoded RGBA values to make troubleshooting a bit less painful.

After the scanning process, there are still some game objects left that need to be initialized. These are the decoration game objects `Clouds`, `Mountains`, and `WaterOverlay`. These are passed over to the width of `Pixmap`, which is the actual length of the level they need to know to work correctly.

Lastly, `Pixmap` is disposed to properly free the occupied memory.

The code part we left out up until now is to look at what happens if there is a matching color code. The current implementation already handles the color code of every game object we want to use, but except for the rock game objects, there is no defined action for these yet. A new rock will be created and added to the list of rocks if the corresponding color code matches. There is also a `lastPixel` variable that stores the last value of `currentPixel` after each iteration inside the loop. This value is used to detect adjacent rock pixels that will increase the length of the last created rock by one, in this case, instead of creating a new one.

Add the following code to the still empty `render()` method:

```
public void render (SpriteBatch batch) {
  // Draw Mountains
  mountains.render(batch);

  // Draw Rocks
  for (Rock rock : rocks)
    rock.render(batch);

  // Draw Water Overlay
  waterOverlay.render(batch);
```

```
    // Draw Clouds
    clouds.render(batch);
}
```

This will finally draw all the elements of a loaded level to create the scene for the game world. The order of the draw calls is important because every subsequent draw call is drawing on top of the scene. The drawing order can be imagined as layers, although there is no real depth or *z* axis like in 3D space.

Nevertheless, if someone were to look at the example scene that is shown at the beginning of this chapter from a 45 degree angled view, it might look like this:

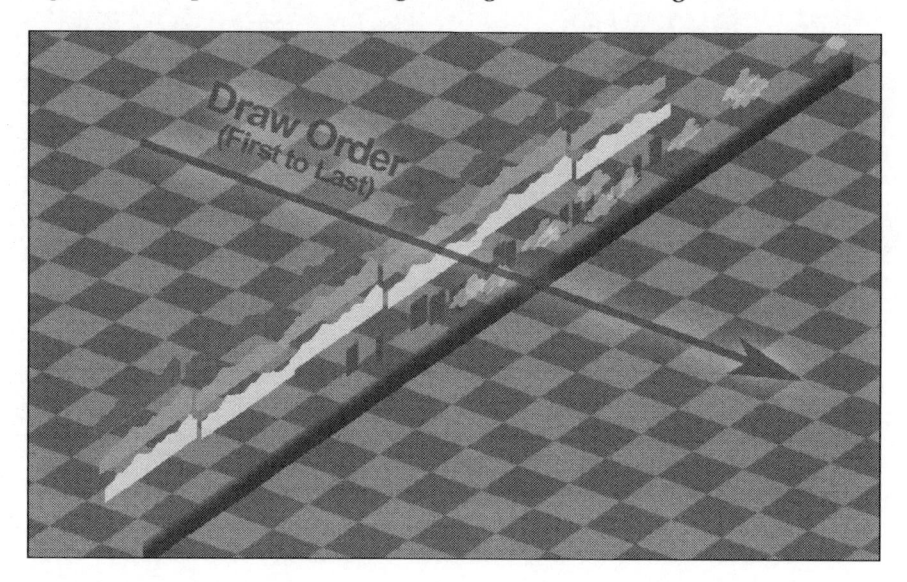

All objects that are drawn first will appear further in the background. Thus, the mountains are further away than the rocks or the stretched water overlay.

Assembling the game world

We will now remove some of the old code that was used to draw test sprites. Additionally, we will add three new constants to define the amount of player lives and the viewport dimension of the GUI camera.

Change the code of the `Constants` class as follows:

```
public class Constants {
  // Visible game world is 5 meters wide
  public static final float VIEWPORT_WIDTH = 5.0f;
```

```
    // Visible game world is 5 meters tall
    public static final float VIEWPORT_HEIGHT = 5.0f;
    // GUI Width
    public static final float VIEWPORT_GUI_WIDTH = 800.0f;
    // GUI Height
    public static final float VIEWPORT_GUI_HEIGHT = 480.0f;
    // Location of description file for texture atlas
    public static final String TEXTURE_ATLAS_OBJECTS =
        "images/canyonbunny.pack";
    // Location of image file for level 01
    public static final String LEVEL_01 = "levels/level-01.png";
    // Amount of extra lives at level start
    public static final int LIVES_START = 3;
}
```

Now, remove these two lines of code in `WorldController`:

```
public Sprite[] testSprites;
public int selectedSprite;
```

Additionally, remove the following methods from `WorldController`:

- `initTestObjects()`
- `updateTestObjects()`
- `moveSelectedSprite()`

Remove the following code in the `handleDebugInput()` method of `WorldController`:

```
// Selected Sprite Controls
float sprMoveSpeed = 5 * deltaTime;
if (Gdx.input.isKeyPressed(Keys.A))
    moveSelectedSprite(-sprMoveSpeed, 0);
if (Gdx.input.isKeyPressed(Keys.D))
    moveSelectedSprite(sprMoveSpeed, 0);
if (Gdx.input.isKeyPressed(Keys.W))
    moveSelectedSprite(0, sprMoveSpeed);
if (Gdx.input.isKeyPressed(Keys.S))
    moveSelectedSprite(0, -sprMoveSpeed);
```

Making a Scene

Next, remove the code below the two comments `Select next sprite` and `Toggle camera follow` in the `keyUp()` method of `WorldController` so that the resulting method looks like this:

```java
@Override
public boolean keyUp (int keycode) {
    // Reset game world
    if (keycode == Keys.R) {
      init();
      Gdx.app.debug(TAG, "Game world resetted");
    }
    return false;
}
```

Add the following two imports to `WorldController`:

```java
import com.packtpub.libgdx.canyonbunny.game.objects.Rock;
import com.packtpub.libgdx.canyonbunny.util.Constants;
```

Next, add the following code to `WorldController`:

```java
public Level level;
public int lives;
public int score;

private void initLevel () {
  score = 0;
  level = new Level(Constants.LEVEL_01);
}
```

Change the code in the `init()` method of `WorldController`:

```java
private void init () {
  Gdx.input.setInputProcessor(this);
  cameraHelper = new CameraHelper();
  lives = Constants.LIVES_START;
  initLevel();
}
```

Finally, remove the call to the deleted `updateTestObjects()` method in `update()`.

We have now removed all of the old code and added level loading to the controller. There are also two variables, `score` and `lives`, that count the player's score and the player's extra lives.

We have to make some minor changes to the `CameraHelper` class in order to make the switch from using `Sprite` objects to `AbstractGameObject`.

Remove the following import line from `CameraHelper`:

```
import com.badlogic.gdx.graphics.g2d.Sprite;
```

Next, add this import line in `CameraHelper`:

```
import com.packtpub.libgdx.canyonbunny.game.objects.
   AbstractGameObject;
```

Now, change the code in `CameraHelper`:

```
private AbstractGameObject target;

public void update (float deltaTime) {
  if (!hasTarget()) return;

  position.x = target.position.x + target.origin.x;
  position.y = target.position.y + target.origin.y;
}

public void setTarget (AbstractGameObject target) {
  this.target = target;
}

public AbstractGameObject getTarget () {
  return target;
}
public boolean hasTarget (AbstractGameObject target) {
  return hasTarget() && this.target.equals(target);
}
```

Next, add the following code in `WorldRenderer`:

```
private void renderWorld (SpriteBatch batch) {
  worldController.cameraHelper.applyTo(camera);
  batch.setProjectionMatrix(camera.combined);
  batch.begin();
  worldController.level.render(batch);
  batch.end();
}
```

Then, remove the `renderTestObjects()` method from `WorldRenderer`.

Lastly, replace the call to the deleted `renderTestObjects()` method with the newly added `renderWorld()` method in `render()`:

```
public void render () {
  renderWorld(batch);
}
```

Now, the world renderer will call the `renderWorld()` method, which in turn calls the `render()` method of `Level` to draw all the game objects of the loaded level.

Implementing the game GUI

In this last part of the chapter, we are going to implement the game's GUI and add it to the scene. The GUI will display the achieved score, extra lives, and an FPS counter.

We will need to load a bitmap font before we are able to write any text output to the screen. Fortunately, LibGDX provides a default font (Arial 15pt) that we can use. Copy the two files `arial-15.fnt` and `arial-15.png` to `CanyonBunny-android/assets/images/`.

This is how LibGDX's default bitmap font looks:

You can also create your own fonts using **Hiero**, a font generator tool provided by LibGDX. Check out the official project website `https://github.com/libgdx/libgdx/wiki/Hiero`. There is also a popular commercial tool called **Glyph Designer**, which is designed specifically for Mac. The official link is `https://71squared.com/en/glyphdesigner`.

Add the following import line to `Assets`:

```
import com.badlogic.gdx.graphics.g2d.BitmapFont;
```

Then, add the following lines of code to `Assets`:

```
public AssetFonts fonts;

public class AssetFonts {
  public final BitmapFont defaultSmall;
  public final BitmapFont defaultNormal;
  public final BitmapFont defaultBig;

  public AssetFonts () {
    // create three fonts using Libgdx's 15px bitmap font
    defaultSmall = new BitmapFont(
        Gdx.files.internal("images/arial-15.fnt"), true);
    defaultNormal = new BitmapFont(
        Gdx.files.internal("images/arial-15.fnt"), true);
    defaultBig = new BitmapFont(
        Gdx.files.internal("images/arial-15.fnt"), true);
    // set font sizes
    defaultSmall.setScale(0.75f);
    defaultNormal.setScale(1.0f);
    defaultBig.setScale(2.0f);
    // enable linear texture filtering for smooth fonts
    defaultSmall.getRegion().getTexture().setFilter(
        TextureFilter.Linear, TextureFilter.Linear);
    defaultNormal.getRegion().getTexture().setFilter(
        TextureFilter.Linear, TextureFilter.Linear);
    defaultBig.getRegion().getTexture().setFilter(
        TextureFilter.Linear, TextureFilter.Linear);
  }
}
public void init (AssetManager assetManager) {
  this.assetManager = assetManager;
  // set asset manager error handler
  assetManager.setErrorListener(this);
  // load texture atlas
  assetManager.load(Constants.TEXTURE_ATLAS_OBJECTS,
                TextureAtlas.class);
  // start loading assets and wait until finished
  assetManager.finishLoading();

  Gdx.app.debug(TAG, "# of assets loaded: "
                + assetManager.getAssetNames().size);
  for (String a : assetManager.getAssetNames())
```

```
            Gdx.app.debug(TAG, "asset: " + a);

        TextureAtlas atlas =
            assetManager.get(Constants.TEXTURE_ATLAS_OBJECTS);

        // enable texture filtering for pixel smoothing
        for (Texture t : atlas.getTextures())
          t.setFilter(TextureFilter.Linear, TextureFilter.Linear);

        // create game resource objects
        fonts = new AssetFonts();
        bunny = new AssetBunny(atlas);
        rock = new AssetRock(atlas);
        goldCoin = new AssetGoldCoin(atlas);
        feather = new AssetFeather(atlas);
        levelDecoration = new AssetLevelDecoration(atlas);
    }

    @Override
    public void dispose () {
      assetManager.dispose();
      fonts.defaultSmall.dispose();
      fonts.defaultNormal.dispose();
      fonts.defaultBig.dispose();
    }
```

The added code includes a new inner class called `AssetFonts` that holds the default bitmap font in three differently configured sizes. The size is configured by scaling the font either up or down. Bitmap fonts must be disposed manually so that the corresponding calls are added to the `dispose()` method.

Chapter 5

We are now ready to begin with the implementation of the game's GUI. It is always good to have an idea of what should be implemented so that we have a picture of what we are aiming for, as shown here:

In the top-left corner, you see an image of the gold coin and the player's current score as text. In the top-right corner, you see three bunny heads that represent the number of extra lives the player has left. Lastly, in the bottom-right corner is a small FPS counter that shows how good or bad the performance of the running game is. The color of the FPS counter will depend on the achieved frames per second.

Add the following import line in `WorldRenderer`:

```
import com.badlogic.gdx.graphics.g2d.BitmapFont;
```

Next, add the following code in `WorldRenderer`:

```
private OrthographicCamera cameraGUI;

private void init () {
  batch = new SpriteBatch();
  camera = new OrthographicCamera(Constants.VIEWPORT_WIDTH,
                                  Constants.VIEWPORT_HEIGHT);
```

```
        camera.position.set(0, 0, 0);
        camera.update();
        cameraGUI = new OrthographicCamera(Constants.VIEWPORT_GUI_WIDTH,
                                Constants.VIEWPORT_GUI_HEIGHT);
        cameraGUI.position.set(0, 0, 0);
        cameraGUI.setToOrtho(true); // flip y-axis
        cameraGUI.update();
    }

    public void resize (int width, int height) {
        camera.viewportWidth = (Constants.VIEWPORT_HEIGHT
                        / (float)height) * (float)width;
        camera.update();
        cameraGUI.viewportHeight = Constants.VIEWPORT_GUI_HEIGHT;
        cameraGUI.viewportWidth = (Constants.VIEWPORT_GUI_HEIGHT
                            / (float)height) * (float)width;
        cameraGUI.position.set(cameraGUI.viewportWidth / 2,
                        cameraGUI.viewportHeight / 2, 0);
        cameraGUI.update();
    }
```

The added code creates a second camera that is specifically set up just to render the game's GUI. The viewport of the GUI camera is defined using a different set of constants that uses much higher values. We have to do this to correctly render the bitmap font that is 15 pixels high. If we were to use the 5 meters x 5 meters viewport, only one-third of the font's glyph would be visible at any time. The rest of the added code does the same as the game camera. Also, this allows us to move the world camera (camera) independently from the GUI (cameraGUI).

The following section describes the implementation of the methods for each GUI element.

The GUI score

The following is a screenshot of the GUI element that shows the player's current score:

Add the following code in `WorldRenderer`:

```
private void renderGuiScore (SpriteBatch batch) {
   float x = -15;
   float y = -15;
   batch.draw(Assets.instance.goldCoin.goldCoin,
       x, y, 50, 50, 100, 100, 0.35f, -0.35f, 0);
   Assets.instance.fonts.defaultBig.draw(batch,
       "" + worldController.score,
       x + 75, y + 37);
}
```

The gold coin image is drawn in the top-left corner of the screen. Next to it, the player's current score is displayed using the big default font.

The GUI extra lives

The following is a screenshot of the GUI element that shows the player's remaining extra lives:

Add the following code in `WorldRenderer`:

```
private void renderGuiExtraLive (SpriteBatch batch) {
   float x = cameraGUI.viewportWidth - 50 -
Constants.LIVES_START * 50;
   float y = -15;
   for (int i = 0; i < Constants.LIVES_START; i++) {
      if (worldController.lives <= i)
         batch.setColor(0.5f, 0.5f, 0.5f, 0.5f);
      batch.draw(Assets.instance.bunny.head,
          x + i * 50, y, 50, 50, 120, 100, 0.35f, -0.35f, 0);
      batch.setColor(1, 1, 1, 1);
   }
}
```

Making a Scene

The three bunny head images that will represent the extra lives of the player are drawn in the top-right corner of the screen. The method starts to draw from left to right. Before a new bunny head is drawn, there is an additional check to find out whether this extra life is used up already. If this is the case, the bunny head is darkened and gets a slightly transparent look by setting the tint color of the sprite batch.

The GUI FPS counter

The following is a screenshot of the GUI element that shows the actual frames per second:

Add the following code in `WorldRenderer`:

```
private void renderGuiFpsCounter (SpriteBatch batch) {
  float x = cameraGUI.viewportWidth - 55;
  float y = cameraGUI.viewportHeight - 15;
  int fps = Gdx.graphics.getFramesPerSecond();
  BitmapFont fpsFont = Assets.instance.fonts.defaultNormal;
  if (fps >= 45) {
    // 45 or more FPS show up in green
    fpsFont.setColor(0, 1, 0, 1);
  } else if (fps >= 30) {
    // 30 or more FPS show up in yellow
    fpsFont.setColor(1, 1, 0, 1);
  } else {
    // less than 30 FPS show up in red
    fpsFont.setColor(1, 0, 0, 1);
  }
  fpsFont.draw(batch, "FPS: " + fps, x, y);
  fpsFont.setColor(1, 1, 1, 1); // white
}
```

An FPS counter that shows the text FPS followed by the current number of frames per second is drawn in the bottom-right corner of the screen. The color of the text depends on the achieved frame rate. If the FPS is 45 or higher, the text will show up in green, indicating a good rendering performance. Otherwise, if there are 30 or more FPS, then the text will show up in yellow, which indicates an average rendering performance. Anything below 30 FPS will show up in red, indicating a really poor rendering performance.

Rendering the GUI

Add the following code in `WorldRenderer`:

```
private void renderGui (SpriteBatch batch) {
  batch.setProjectionMatrix(cameraGUI.combined);
  batch.begin();
  // draw collected gold coins icon + text
  // (anchored to top left edge)
  renderGuiScore(batch);
  // draw extra lives icon + text (anchored to top right edge)
  renderGuiExtraLive(batch);
  // draw FPS text (anchored to bottom right edge)
  renderGuiFpsCounter(batch);
  batch.end();
}
```

Furthermore, change `render()` in `WorldRenderer`:

```
public void render () {
  renderWorld(batch);
  renderGui(batch);
}
```

The implementation of the game's GUI is now finished.

Summary

In this chapter, you learned how to implement your game objects. You also learned how to create compound game objects using several textures. Additionally, the implementation of the level loader was discussed. Afterwards, we assembled the game world using the level loader, which in turn will create all our game objects from now on. You learned how to use bitmap fonts and used LibGDX's built-in font for the game's GUI text. In addition, GUI elements were added to display the game's status, such as the player's current score and extra lives. Remember, we are still using our camera helper class that allows us to easily move around inside our scene. You can also still zoom in and out.

The next chapter will continue to implement the rest of the basic game elements, such as the player character, items, player movement, basic collision detection, and so on.

6
Adding the Actors

In this chapter, we will implement the remaining game objects that represent our actors in the game world. These are the player character bunny head and both the collectible items: the gold coin and the feather power-up. We will complete the level loader by adding support for the actor game objects so that these are handled properly when a level is loaded.

The game will be extended to feature a simple physics simulation that allows any game object to be moved using physical properties, such as velocity, acceleration, and friction. In addition, the game logic will also need to detect collisions of the game objects to trigger certain events. For example, we want the player character to be able to jump, stand, and walk on a rock (platform), collect items by walking over them, and lose a life when it falls into the water. The game logic will also include a check to find out whether the game over condition is met so that the game immediately ends and a **GAME OVER** text message is displayed.

In this chapter, we will:

- Implement our game actors
- Create logic for collision detection
- Finish the GUI

Implementing the actor game objects

The gold coin, feather, and bunny head are some of our game objects. Each of our game objects inherits the `AbstractGameObject` class. The `AbstractGameObject` holds the attributes and functionalities for physics and collision detection.

First, let's make some preparations in `AbstractGameObject` and add a few functionalities for our upcoming physics and collision detection code.

Adding the Actors

Add the following import to `AbstractGameObject`:

```
import com.badlogic.gdx.math.Rectangle;
```

Then, add the following member variables and initialization code to the same class:

```
public Vector2 velocity;
public Vector2 terminalVelocity;
public Vector2 friction;

public Vector2 acceleration;
public Rectangle bounds;

public AbstractGameObject () {
  position = new Vector2();
  dimension = new Vector2(1, 1);
  origin = new Vector2();
  scale = new Vector2(1, 1);
  rotation = 0;
  velocity = new Vector2();
  terminalVelocity = new Vector2(1, 1);
  friction = new Vector2();
  acceleration = new Vector2();
  bounds = new Rectangle();
}
```

The following list contains a brief description of the purpose of each variable:

- `velocity`: This is the object's current speed in m/s.
- `terminalVelocity`: This is the object's positive and negative maximum speed in m/s.
- `friction`: This is an opposing force that slows down the object until its velocity equals zero. This value is given as a coefficient that is dimensionless. A value of zero means no friction, and thus the object's velocity will not decrease.
- `acceleration`: This is the object's constant acceleration in m/s².
- `bounds`: The object's bounding box describes the physical body that will be used for collision detection with other objects. The bounding box can be set to any size and is completely independent of the actual dimension of the object in the game world.

Chapter 6

We will now add simple physics simulation code that makes use of the new physics attributes, namely, `velocity`, `terminalVelocity`, `friction`, and `acceleration`:

1. Add the following import to `AbstractGameObject`:

    ```
    import com.badlogic.gdx.math.MathUtils;
    ```

2. Furthermore, add the following code to the same class:

    ```
    protected void updateMotionX (float deltaTime) {
      if (velocity.x != 0) {
        // Apply friction
        if (velocity.x > 0) {
          velocity.x =
              Math.max(velocity.x - friction.x * deltaTime, 0);
        } else {
          velocity.x =
              Math.min(velocity.x + friction.x * deltaTime, 0);
        }
      }
      // Apply acceleration
      velocity.x += acceleration.x * deltaTime;
      // Make sure the object's velocity does not exceed the
      // positive or negative terminal velocity
      velocity.x = MathUtils.clamp(velocity.x,
          -terminalVelocity.x, terminalVelocity.x);
    }

    protected void updateMotionY (float deltaTime) {
      if (velocity.y != 0) {
        // Apply friction
        if (velocity.y > 0) {
          velocity.y = Math.max(velocity.y - friction.y * deltaTime, 0);
        } else {
          velocity.y = Math.min(velocity.y + friction.y * deltaTime, 0);
        }
      }
      // Apply acceleration
      velocity.y += acceleration.y * deltaTime;
      // Make sure the object's velocity does not exceed the
      // positive or negative terminal velocity
    ```

Adding the Actors

```
        velocity.y = MathUtils.clamp(velocity.y, -
    terminalVelocity.y, terminalVelocity.y);
    }
```

3. Finally, make the following change to the already existing `update()` method:

   ```
   public void update (float deltaTime) {
       updateMotionX(deltaTime);
       updateMotionY(deltaTime);
       // Move to new position
       position.x += velocity.x * deltaTime;
       position.y += velocity.y * deltaTime;
   }
   ```

The two new methods `updateMotionX()` and `updateMotionY()` are called on every update cycle to calculate the next x and y components of the object's velocity in terms of the given delta time. The calculation is done in the following three steps:

1. If the object's velocity is not equal to zero, the object must be in motion. Therefore, friction needs to be applied on the velocity to slow it down. As the property of friction is meant to decrease velocity, the friction coefficient needs to be either subtracted from positive or only added to negative velocity values. The velocity is directly set to zero as soon as the algebraic sign changes to fully stop the ongoing motion using the `Math.max` and `Math.min` functions.
2. Next, acceleration is applied to the current velocity.
3. Finally, it is made sure that the new velocity value will always be inside the range of the positive and negative terminal velocity.

After both the velocity components have been updated, the displacement that simulates the actual motion of an object is done by simply adding the new velocity vector to the position vector that holds the last position.

Creating the gold coin object

The gold coin game object consists of only one image. It is a collectible item, which means that it can be collected by the player's character by simply walking over it. As a result of the gold coin being collected, the object will turn invisible for the rest of the game, as shown here:

Create a new file for the GoldCoin class and add the following code to it:

```java
package com.packtpub.libgdx.canyonbunny.game.objects;

import com.badlogic.gdx.graphics.g2d.SpriteBatch;
import com.badlogic.gdx.graphics.g2d.TextureRegion;
import com.packtpub.libgdx.canyonbunny.game.Assets;

public class GoldCoin extends AbstractGameObject {

  private TextureRegion regGoldCoin;

  public boolean collected;

  public GoldCoin () {
    init();
  }

  private void init () {
    dimension.set(0.5f, 0.5f);

    regGoldCoin = Assets.instance.goldCoin.goldCoin;

    // Set bounding box for collision detection
    bounds.set(0, 0, dimension.x, dimension.y);

    collected = false;
  }

  public void render (SpriteBatch batch) {
    if (collected) return;

    TextureRegion reg = null;
    reg = regGoldCoin;
    batch.draw(reg.getTexture(), position.x, position.y,
origin.x, origin.y, dimension.x, dimension.y, scale.x, scale.y,
rotation, reg.getRegionX(), reg.getRegionY(),
reg.getRegionWidth(), reg.getRegionHeight(), false, false);
  }

  public int getScore() {
    return 100;
  }
}
```

Adding the Actors

The gold coin uses the collected variable to store its current state of visibility. The `render()` method will always check the collected state to decide whether the object should be rendered or not. The `getScore()` method returns the item's score that the player will receive to collect it. The bounding box bounds are set to the exact same size as its dimension inside the game world.

Creating the feather object

The feather game object is very similar to the gold coin. It consists of only one image and is a collectible item that will turn invisible when it is collected by the player's character.

Create a new file for the `Feather` class and add the following code:

```
package com.packtpub.libgdx.canyonbunny.game.objects;

import com.badlogic.gdx.graphics.g2d.SpriteBatch;
import com.badlogic.gdx.graphics.g2d.TextureRegion;
import com.packtpub.libgdx.canyonbunny.game.Assets;

public class Feather extends AbstractGameObject {

  private TextureRegion regFeather;

  public boolean collected;

  public Feather () {
    init();
  }

  private void init () {
    dimension.set(0.5f, 0.5f);

    regFeather = Assets.instance.feather.feather;

    // Set bounding box for collision detection
```

```
      bounds.set(0, 0, dimension.x, dimension.y);

      collected = false;
   }

   public void render (SpriteBatch batch) {
      if (collected) return;

      TextureRegion reg = null;
      reg = regFeather;
      batch.draw(reg.getTexture(), position.x, position.y,
 origin.x, origin.y, dimension.x, dimension.y, scale.x, scale.y,
 rotation, reg.getRegionX(), reg.getRegionY(),
 reg.getRegionWidth(), reg.getRegionHeight(), false, false);
   }

   public int getScore() {
      return 250;
   }
}
```

Obviously, this code is almost similar to the code of the gold coin. The only difference between them is the image used and that the `getScore()` method returns a slightly higher score.

Creating the bunny head object

The bunny head or player's character is the most complex game object that we will create in this project. It consists of only one image, but involves quite a lot of code to enable jumping and falling as well as handling the feather power-up effect.

Create a new file for the `BunnyHead` class and add the following code:

```
package com.packtpub.libgdx.canyonbunny.game.objects;

import com.badlogic.gdx.Gdx;
import com.badlogic.gdx.graphics.g2d.SpriteBatch;
```

Adding the Actors

```java
import com.badlogic.gdx.graphics.g2d.TextureRegion;
import com.packtpub.libgdx.canyonbunny.game.Assets;
import com.packtpub.libgdx.canyonbunny.util.Constants;

public class BunnyHead extends AbstractGameObject {

  public static final String TAG = BunnyHead.class.getName();

  private final float JUMP_TIME_MAX = 0.3f;
  private final float JUMP_TIME_MIN = 0.1f;
  private final float JUMP_TIME_OFFSET_FLYING =
    JUMP_TIME_MAX - 0.018f;

  public enum VIEW_DIRECTION { LEFT, RIGHT }

  public enum JUMP_STATE {
    GROUNDED, FALLING, JUMP_RISING, JUMP_FALLING
  }

  private TextureRegion regHead;

  public VIEW_DIRECTION viewDirection;
  public float timeJumping;
  public JUMP_STATE jumpState;
  public boolean hasFeatherPowerup;
  public float timeLeftFeatherPowerup;

  public BunnyHead () {
    init();
  }

  public void init () {};
  public void setJumping (boolean jumpKeyPressed) {};
  public void setFeatherPowerup (boolean pickedUp) {};
  public boolean hasFeatherPowerup () {};
}
```

Now that we have defined the viewing direction—a state for jumping and another state for the feather power-up—we can go on and fill in the specific implementation details of the still empty methods.

Now, add the following code to the `init()` method:

```
public void init () {
  dimension.set(1, 1);
  regHead = Assets.instance.bunny.head;
  // Center image on game object
  origin.set(dimension.x / 2, dimension.y / 2);
  // Bounding box for collision detection
  bounds.set(0, 0, dimension.x, dimension.y);
  // Set physics values
  terminalVelocity.set(3.0f, 4.0f);
  friction.set(12.0f, 0.0f);
  acceleration.set(0.0f, -25.0f);
  // View direction
  viewDirection = VIEW_DIRECTION.RIGHT;
  // Jump state
  jumpState = JUMP_STATE.FALLING;
  timeJumping = 0;
  // Power-ups
  hasFeatherPowerup = false;
  timeLeftFeatherPowerup = 0;
}
```

The preceding code initializes the bunny head game object by setting its physics values, a starting view direction, and jump state. It also deactivates the feather power-up effect.

Next, add the following code to the `setJumping()` method:

```
public void setJumping (boolean jumpKeyPressed) {
  switch (jumpState) {
    case GROUNDED: // Character is standing on a platform
      if (jumpKeyPressed) {
        // Start counting jump time from the beginning
        timeJumping = 0;
        jumpState = JUMP_STATE.JUMP_RISING;
      }
      break;
    case JUMP_RISING: // Rising in the air
      if (!jumpKeyPressed)
        jumpState = JUMP_STATE.JUMP_FALLING;
      break;
    case FALLING:// Falling down
    case JUMP_FALLING: // Falling down after jump
```

Adding the Actors

```
      if (jumpKeyPressed && hasFeatherPowerup) {
        timeJumping = JUMP_TIME_OFFSET_FLYING;
        jumpState = JUMP_STATE.JUMP_RISING;
      }
      break;
    }
  }
```

The preceding code allows us to make the bunny jump. The state handling in the code will decide whether jumping is currently possible and whether it is a single or a multi jump.

Next, add the following code to the `setFeatherPowerup()` method:

```
  public void setFeatherPowerup (boolean pickedUp) {
    hasFeatherPowerup = pickedUp;
    if (pickedUp) {
      timeLeftFeatherPowerup =
Constants.ITEM_FEATHER_POWERUP_DURATION;
    }
  }

  public boolean hasFeatherPowerup () {
    return hasFeatherPowerup && timeLeftFeatherPowerup > 0;
  }
```

The preceding code allows us to toggle the feather power-up effect via the `setFeatherPowerup()` method. The `hasFeatherPowerup()` method can be used to find out whether the power-up is still active.

Next, add the following code to override the `update()` method:

```
  @Override
  public void update (float deltaTime) {
    super.update(deltaTime);
    if (velocity.x != 0) {
      viewDirection = velocity.x < 0 ? VIEW_DIRECTION.LEFT :
VIEW_DIRECTION.RIGHT;
    }
    if (timeLeftFeatherPowerup > 0) {
      timeLeftFeatherPowerup -= deltaTime;
      if (timeLeftFeatherPowerup < 0) {
        // disable power-up
```

```
          timeLeftFeatherPowerup = 0;
          setFeatherPowerup(false);
        }
      }
    }
```

The preceding code handles the switching of the viewing direction according to the current move direction. Also, the time remaining of the power-up effect is checked. If the time is up, the feather power-up effect is disabled.

Next, add the following code to override the `updateMotionY()` method:

```
    @Override
    protected void updateMotionY (float deltaTime) {
      switch (jumpState) {
        case GROUNDED:
          jumpState = JUMP_STATE.FALLING;
          break;
        case JUMP_RISING:
          // Keep track of jump time
          timeJumping += deltaTime;
          // Jump time left?
          if (timeJumping <= JUMP_TIME_MAX) {
            // Still jumping
            velocity.y = terminalVelocity.y;
          }
          break;
        case FALLING:
          break;
        case JUMP_FALLING:
          // Add delta times to track jump time
          timeJumping += deltaTime;
          // Jump to minimal height if jump key was pressed too short
          if (timeJumping > 0 && timeJumping <= JUMP_TIME_MIN) {
            // Still jumping
            velocity.y = terminalVelocity.y;
          }
      }
      if (jumpState != JUMP_STATE.GROUNDED)
        super.updateMotionY(deltaTime);
    }
```

The preceding code handles the calculations and switching of states that is needed to enable jumping and falling.

Adding the Actors

Next, add the following code to override the `render()` method:

```
@Override
public void render (SpriteBatch batch) {
  TextureRegion reg = null;

  // Set special color when game object has a feather power-up
  if (hasFeatherPowerup) {
  batch.setColor(1.0f, 0.8f, 0.0f, 1.0f);
}
  // Draw image
  reg = regHead;
    batch.draw(reg.getTexture(), position.x, position.y, origin.x,
origin.y, dimension.x, dimension.y, scale.x, scale.y, rotation,
reg.getRegionX(), reg.getRegionY(), reg.getRegionWidth(),
reg.getRegionHeight(), viewDirection == VIEW_DIRECTION.LEFT,
false);

  // Reset color to white
  batch.setColor(1, 1, 1, 1);
}
```

The preceding code handles the drawing of the image for the bunny head game object. The image will be tinted orange if the feather power-up effect is active.

Furthermore, add the following code to `Constants`:

```
// Duration of feather power-up in seconds
public static final float ITEM_FEATHER_POWERUP_DURATION = 9;
```

The viewing direction, `viewDirection`, will change according to the object's velocity as long as it is unequal to zero. It will be set to `VIEW_DIRECTION.LEFT` when the horizontal velocity is negative; otherwise, it will be set to `VIEW_DIRECTION.RIGHT`. This simply means that the player's character will always look in the direction it is moving.

There are four different states to jump, as follows:

- `GROUNDED`: In this state, the player is standing on a platform.
- `FALLING`: In this state, the player is falling down.
- `JUMP_RISING`: In this state, the player has initiated a jump and is still rising. The maximum jump height has not been reached.
- `JUMP_FALLING`: In this state, the player is falling down after a previously initiated jump. This state is reached either by jumping as long as possible or by releasing the jump key earlier than that.

The state to jump is stored in `jumpState`. There is a minimum and maximum jump time defined by the constants `JUMP_TIME_MIN` and `JUMP_TIME_MAX`. These time limits and the jump power affects the resulting possible minimum and maximum jump heights. A minimum jump is enforced on the player whenever the jump key is released before the time defined in `JUMP_TIME_MIN`.

The currently elapsed jump time is accumulated in `timeJumping` and is reset on every new jump. There is a third constant `JUMP_TIME_OFFSET_FLYING` that is used to let the elapsed jump time start at a certain time, which effectively shortens the overall height of such jumps. This is used for the multijump power-up effect of the feather item. It allows the bunny head to fly by rapidly jumping repeatedly. A multijump can only be executed when the bunny head is in midair. A shorter jump time for multijumps makes it more difficult for the player to handle them, which adds a neat detail to the gameplay feeling.

This is all done inside the overridden `updateMotionY()` method. Notice that the original method of `updateMotionY()` from `AbstractGameObject` is also called whenever an actual motion needs to happen, which is always the case when the player is not in the `GROUNDED` jump state.

Adding the Actors

The following diagram visualizes the flow of the preceding method:

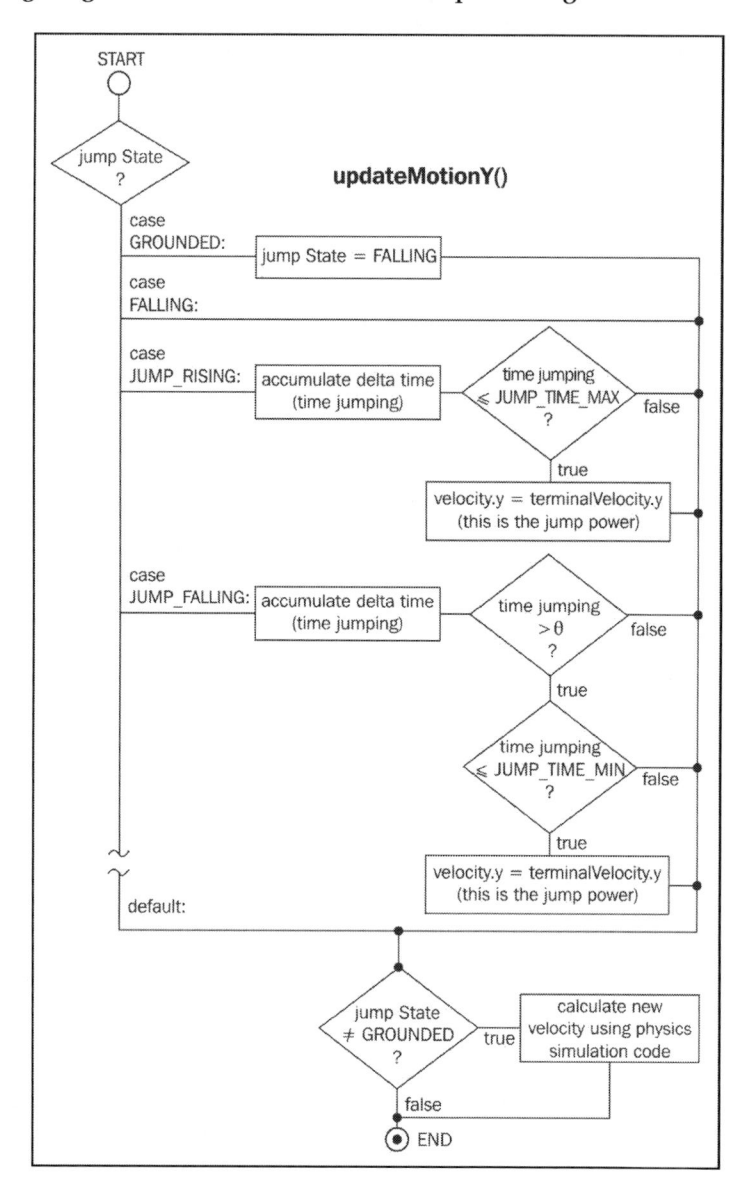

```
                    START
                      ○
                      │
                ┌─ jump State ─┐              updateMotionY()
                │      ?       │
                └──────────────┘
                 case
                 GROUNDED:    ┌──────────────────────┐
                ──────────────│ jump State = FALLING │────────────────┐
                              └──────────────────────┘                │
                 case                                                 │
                 FALLING:                                             │
                ──────────────────────────────────────────────────────┤
                 case         ┌──────────────────┐    ┌─ time jumping ─┐
                 JUMP_RISING: │ accumulate delta │    │  ≤ JUMP_TIME_MAX │ false
                ──────────────│  time            │────│        ?        │──────┤
                              │ (time jumping)   │    └──────────────────┘     │
                              └──────────────────┘         │ true              │
                                                   ┌──────────────────────────┐│
                                                   │ velocity.y = terminalVelocity.y │
                                                   │  (this is the jump power)     │─┤
                                                   └──────────────────────────┘   │
                 case         ┌──────────────────┐    ┌─ time jumping ─┐         │
                 JUMP_FALLING:│ accumulate delta │    │     > 0        │ false   │
                ──────────────│  time            │────│        ?        │────────┤
                              │ (time jumping)   │    └──────────────────┘      │
                              └──────────────────┘         │ true               │
                                                   ┌─ time jumping ─┐           │
                                                   │ ≤ JUMP_TIME_MIN │ false    │
                                                   │        ?        │──────────┤
                                                   └──────────────────┘         │
                                                         │ true                 │
                                                   ┌──────────────────────────┐ │
                                                   │ velocity.y = terminalVelocity.y│
                                                   │  (this is the jump power)   │ │
                                                   └──────────────────────────┘ │
                 default:                                                       │
                ────────────────────────────────────────────────────────────────┤
                                              ┌─ jump State ─┐   ┌──────────────────┐
                                              │  ≠ GROUNDED  │ true│ calculate new  │
                                              │      ?       │────│ velocity using  │
                                              └──────────────┘    │ physics         │
                                                     │ false      │ simulation code │
                                                     │            └──────────────────┘
                                                     ●  END
```

As you can see, the jump state will always change to FALLING whenever it is set to GROUNDED. The reason for this is that we want grounded objects like the player's character to fall down from platforms where they end. There must be a trigger that tests this event so that the jump state will be in fact permanently changed from GROUNDED to FALLING as long as there is a collision detected that resets the jump state back to GROUNDED. Otherwise, the player's character will start to fall down as intended.

A new jump is triggered by calling the `setJumping()` method. A `true` value can be passed as an argument to denote that the jump key has been pressed. So this method checks the current jump state of the bunny and also tests whether the jump key is currently pressed by the player to perform the appropriate actions. These actions can be to start a new jump, cancel an ongoing jump, or allow multijumps with the help of the feather power-up.

The following diagram visualizes the flow of this method:

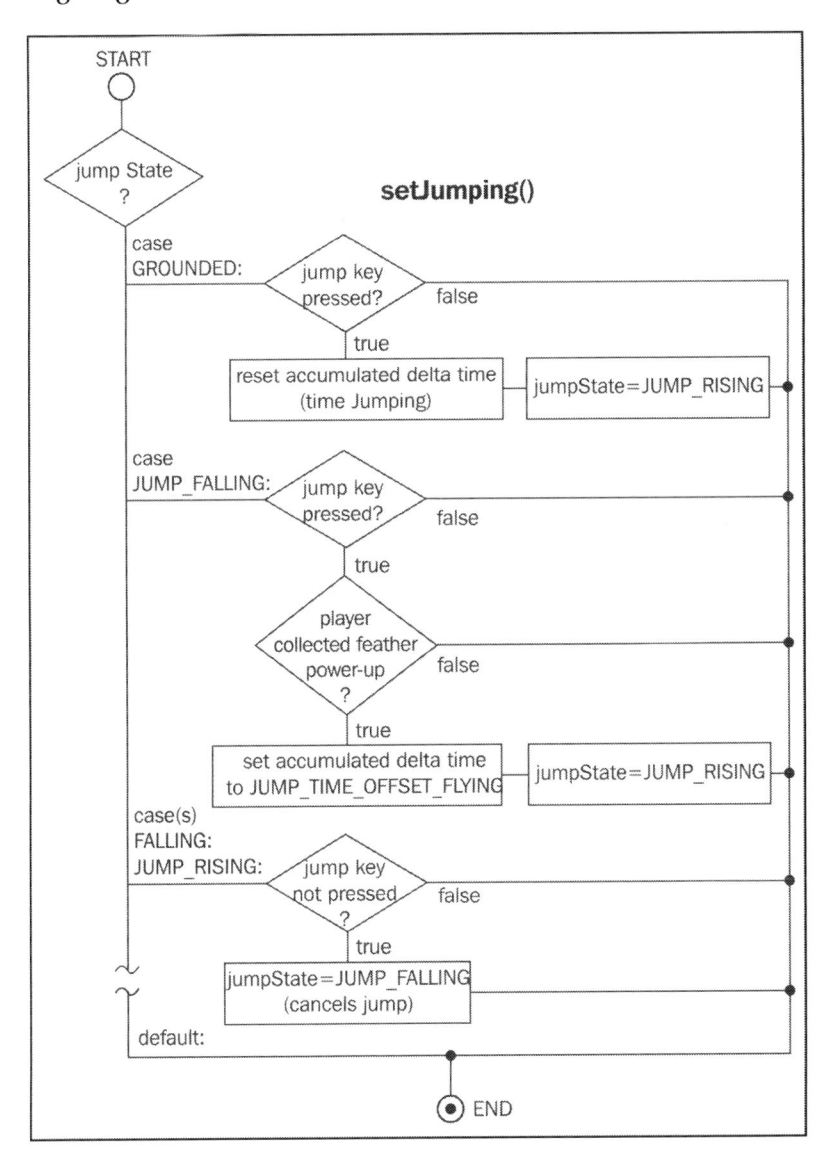

Adding the Actors

The `hasFeatherPowerup` and `timeLeftFeatherPowerup` variables describe whether the player has collected the feather power-up or not and how much time the effect will last. The power-up effect can be enabled and disabled by calling `setFeatherPowerup()`. The `hasFeatherPowerup()` method is used as a combined test to find out whether the power-up has been collected and if the effect is still lasting.

The `render()` method will tint the image of the player character orange if the feather power-up has been collected. The viewing direction `viewDirection` is used to decide whether the image needs to be flipped on the *x* axis.

Updating the rock object

Last but not least, change the `setLength()` method of `Rock` to the following listings:

```
public void setLength (int length) {
  this.length = length;
  // Update bounding box for collision detection
  bounds.set(0, 0, dimension.x * length, dimension.y);
}
```

This will make sure that the size of the bounding box is adjusted whenever the length of a rock is changed.

Completing the level loader

Now that we have implemented all the game objects of Canyon Bunny, we can complete the level loader.

First, add the following import lines to `Level`:

```
import com.packtpub.libgdx.canyonbunny.game.objects.BunnyHead;
import com.packtpub.libgdx.canyonbunny.game.objects.Feather;
import com.packtpub.libgdx.canyonbunny.game.objects.GoldCoin;
```

Additionally, add these three member variables to the same class:

```
public BunnyHead bunnyHead;
public Array<GoldCoin> goldcoins;
public Array<Feather> feathers;
```

Chapter 6

After this, modify the `init()` and `render()` methods:

```java
private void init (String filename) {
  // player character
  bunnyHead = null;
  // objects
  rocks = new Array<Rock>();
  goldcoins = new Array<GoldCoin>();
  feathers = new Array<Feather>();
  // load image file that represents the level data
  Pixmap pixmap = new Pixmap(Gdx.files.internal(filename));
  // scan pixels from top-left to bottom-right
  int lastPixel = -1;
  for (int pixelY = 0; pixelY < pixmap.getHeight(); pixelY++) {
      for (int pixelX = 0; pixelX < pixmap.getWidth(); pixelX++) {
    ...
      // rock
      else if (BLOCK_TYPE.ROCK.sameColor(currentPixel)) {
        ...
      }
      // player spawn point
      else if
      (BLOCK_TYPE.PLAYER_SPAWNPOINT.sameColor(currentPixel)) {
        obj = new BunnyHead();
        offsetHeight = -3.0f;
        obj.position.set(pixelX,baseHeight * obj.dimension.y + offsetHeight);
        bunnyHead = (BunnyHead)obj;
      }
      // feather
      else if(BLOCK_TYPE.ITEM_FEATHER.sameColor(currentPixel)) {
        obj = new Feather();
        offsetHeight = -1.5f;
        obj.position.set(pixelX,baseHeight * obj.dimension.y + offsetHeight);
        feathers.add((Feather)obj);
      }
      // gold coin
      else if
      (BLOCK_TYPE.ITEM_GOLD_COIN.sameColor(currentPixel)) {
        obj = new GoldCoin();
        offsetHeight = -1.5f;
        obj.position.set(pixelX,baseHeight * obj.dimension.y + offsetHeight);
```

Adding the Actors

```
            goldcoins.add((GoldCoin)obj);
        }
        // unknown object/pixel color
        else {
            ...
        }
        lastPixel = currentPixel;
    }
  }
  ...
}
```

This code adds the actors to the level loading process in the `init()` method. Next, make the following changes to the `render()` method:

```
public void render (SpriteBatch batch) {
    // Draw Mountains
    mountains.render(batch);
    // Draw Rocks
    for (Rock rock : rocks)
        rock.render(batch);
    // Draw Gold Coins
    for (GoldCoin goldCoin : goldcoins)
        goldCoin.render(batch);
    // Draw Feathers
    for (Feather feather : feathers)
        feather.render(batch);
    // Draw Player Character
    bunnyHead.render(batch);
    // Draw Water Overlay
    waterOverlay.render(batch);
    // Draw Clouds
    clouds.render(batch);
}
```

Then, add the following lines to `Level`:

```
public void update (float deltaTime) {
  bunnyHead.update(deltaTime);
  for(Rock rock : rocks)
    rock.update(deltaTime);
  for(GoldCoin goldCoin : goldcoins)
    goldCoin.update(deltaTime);
  for(Feather feather : feathers)
```

```
    feather.update(deltaTime);
  clouds.update(deltaTime);
}
```

We added the new actors to the `render()` method and created a new `update()` method so that we can collectively update all the game world objects in a level in one call.

Finally, modify the `update()` method of `WorldController` as the following listings:

```
public void update (float deltaTime) {
  handleDebugInput(deltaTime);
  level.update(deltaTime);
  cameraHelper.update(deltaTime);
}
```

These changes makes sure that all the game objects contained within the level will be updated when the `update()` method of `WorldController` is called.

Adding the game logic

The next step will be to add the game logic that constitutes the rules of our game world. However, the game logic will need to be able to detect the so-called collisions between two game objects before it can handle all of our events, such as walking over an item to collect it. So, we will implement a very basic collision detection method that tests two overlapping rectangles. If an overlap is detected, it means that there is also a collision between these two tested objects. So, we can bind a certain action to this event in the game logic to handle collisions as required.

Adding collision detection

Here, we add the code to check the collision of the bunny head with each actor game object, the gold coin, feather, and the rock.

First, add the following import lines to `WorldController`:

```
import com.badlogic.gdx.math.Rectangle;
import com.packtpub.libgdx.canyonbunny.game.objects.BunnyHead;
import com.packtpub.libgdx.canyonbunny.game.objects.BunnyHead
  .JUMP_STATE;
import com.packtpub.libgdx.canyonbunny.game.objects.Feather;
import com.packtpub.libgdx.canyonbunny.game.objects.GoldCoin;
import com.packtpub.libgdx.canyonbunny.game.objects.Rock;
```

Adding the Actors

After that, add the following code to the same class:

```java
// Rectangles for collision detection
private Rectangle r1 = new Rectangle();
private Rectangle r2 = new Rectangle();

private void onCollisionBunnyHeadWithRock(Rock rock) {};
private void onCollisionBunnyWithGoldCoin(GoldCoin goldcoin) {};
private void onCollisionBunnyWithFeather(Feather feather) {};

private void testCollisions () {
  r1.set(level.bunnyHead.position.x, level.bunnyHead.position.y,
level.bunnyHead.bounds.width, level.bunnyHead.bounds.height);

  // Test collision: Bunny Head <-> Rocks
  for (Rock rock : level.rocks) {
    r2.set(rock.position.x, rock.position.y, rock.bounds.width,
rock.bounds.height);
    if (!r1.overlaps(r2)) continue;
    onCollisionBunnyHeadWithRock(rock);
    // IMPORTANT: must do all collisions for valid
    // edge testing on rocks.
  }

  // Test collision: Bunny Head <-> Gold Coins
  for (GoldCoin goldcoin : level.goldcoins) {
    if (goldcoin.collected) continue;
    r2.set(goldcoin.position.x, goldcoin.position.y,
goldcoin.bounds.width, goldcoin.bounds.height);
    if (!r1.overlaps(r2)) continue;
    onCollisionBunnyWithGoldCoin(goldcoin);
    break;
  }

  // Test collision: Bunny Head <-> Feathers
  for (Feather feather : level.feathers) {
    if (feather.collected) continue;
    r2.set(feather.position.x, feather.position.y,
feather.bounds.width, feather.bounds.height);
    if (!r1.overlaps(r2)) continue;
    onCollisionBunnyWithFeather(feather);
    break;
  }
}
```

This code adds a new method called `testCollisions()` that iterates through all the game objects and tests whether there is a collision between the bunny head and another game object. This particular test is subdivided into three separate methods called `onCollisionBunnyHeadWithRock()`, `onCollisionBunnyWithGoldCoin()`, and `onCollisionBunnyWithFeather()`, which are still empty.

Next, fill in the `onCollisionBunnyHeadWithRock()` method with the following code:

```
private void onCollisionBunnyHeadWithRock (Rock rock) {
  BunnyHead bunnyHead = level.bunnyHead;
  float heightDifference = Math.abs(bunnyHead.position.y
 - ( rock.position.y + rock.bounds.height));
  if (heightDifference > 0.25f) {
    boolean hitRightEdge = bunnyHead.position.x > (
rock.position.x + rock.bounds.width / 2.0f);
    if (hitRightEdge) {
      bunnyHead.position.x = rock.position.x + rock.bounds.width;
    } else {
      bunnyHead.position.x = rock.position.x -
bunnyHead.bounds.width;
    }
    return;
  }

  switch (bunnyHead.jumpState) {
    case GROUNDED:
      break;
    case FALLING:
    case JUMP_FALLING:
      bunnyHead.position.y = rock.position.y +
bunnyHead.bounds.height  + bunnyHead.origin.y;
      bunnyHead.jumpState = JUMP_STATE.GROUNDED;
      break;
    case JUMP_RISING:
      bunnyHead.position.y = rock.position.y +
bunnyHead.bounds.height + bunnyHead.origin.y;
    break;
  }
}
```

This code handles collisions between the bunny head game object and a rock game object and is called when a collision is detected. Then, the bunny head game object is moved accordingly to prevent it from falling through our platforms—the rock game objects.

Adding the Actors

Next, fill in the `onCollisionBunnyWithGoldCoin()` method with the following code:

```
private void onCollisionBunnyWithGoldCoin (GoldCoin goldcoin) {
  goldcoin.collected = true;
  score += goldcoin.getScore();
  Gdx.app.log(TAG, "Gold coin collected");
}
```

This code handles collisions between the bunny head game object and a gold coin game object. It simply flags the gold coin as being collected so that it will disappear. Furthermore, the player's score increases by the value the gold coin game object returns from its `getScore()` method.

Finally, fill in the `onCollisionBunnyWithFeather()` method with the following code:

```
private void onCollisionBunnyWithFeather (Feather feather) {
  feather.collected = true;
  score += feather.getScore();
  level.bunnyHead.setFeatherPowerup(true);
  Gdx.app.log(TAG, "Feather collected");
}
```

This code handles collisions between the bunny head game object and a feather game object. The handling of this collision is similar to the `onCollisionBunnyWithGoldCoin()` method, but it also activates or refreshes the power-up effect for the bunny head.

Now, let's make one more modification to the `update()` method of `WorldController`:

```
public void update (float deltaTime) {
  handleDebugInput(deltaTime);
  level.update(deltaTime);
  testCollisions();
  cameraHelper.update(deltaTime);
}
```

You can now run the game to verify that the level loading and collision detection works. Within a very short time span, you should see that the player's character falls down a bit and then stops on top of the rock underneath it. The following is a screenshot of this scene:

Chapter 6

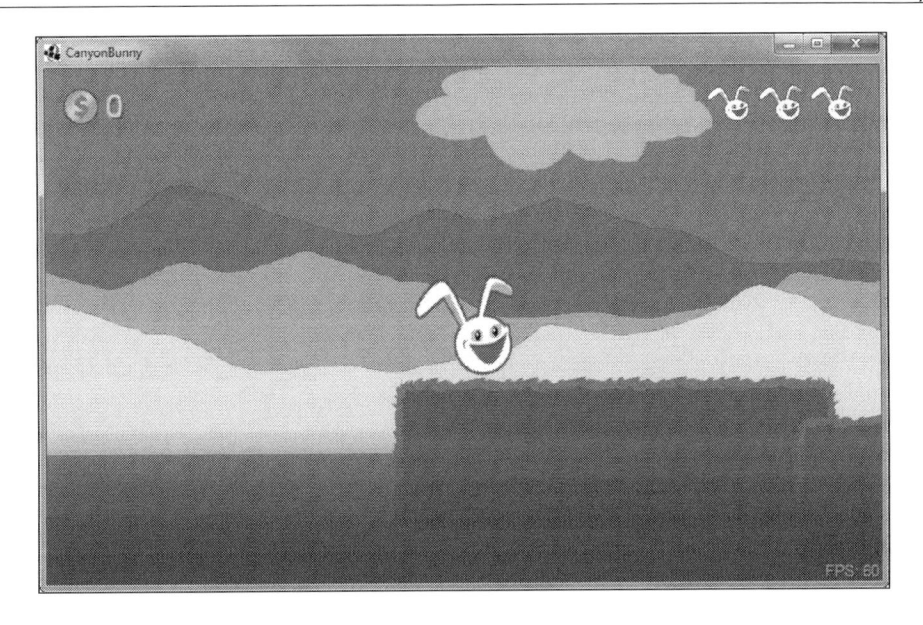

You can still use all the keys (left/right/up/down arrows, comma, dot, and so on) to control the camera, so, now is a good opportunity to just fly around a bit in the game world to verify that all the game objects appear at their correct locations.

The following screenshot shows where the camera has been zoomed out a bit to view all the new game objects at once:

Adding the Actors

We will now add a toggle key to choose whether the arrow keys should control the player character or the camera. The camera should follow the player's character while being in the player control mode. Otherwise, the camera can be freely moved around. We will also add another key to let the player character jump.

Let's begin with the camera that is set to follow the player character at the start of the level. Add the highlighted line of code to the `initLevel()` method of `WorldController`:

```
private void initLevel () {
  score = 0;
  level = new Level(Constants.LEVEL_01);
  cameraHelper.setTarget(level.bunnyHead);
}
```

Next, change the `handleDebugInput()` and `keyUp()` methods of `WorldController`:

```
private void handleDebugInput (float deltaTime) {
  if (Gdx.app.getType() != ApplicationType.Desktop) return;

  if (!cameraHelper.hasTarget(level.bunnyHead)) {
    // Camera Controls (move)
    float camMoveSpeed = 5 * deltaTime;
    float camMoveSpeedAccelerationFactor = 5;
    if (Gdx.input.isKeyPressed(Keys.SHIFT_LEFT)) camMoveSpeed *= camMoveSpeedAccelerationFactor;
    if (Gdx.input.isKeyPressed(Keys.LEFT)) moveCamera(-camMoveSpeed, 0);
    if (Gdx.input.isKeyPressed(Keys.RIGHT)) moveCamera(camMoveSpeed, 0);
    if (Gdx.input.isKeyPressed(Keys.UP)) moveCamera(0, camMoveSpeed);
    if (Gdx.input.isKeyPressed(Keys.DOWN)) moveCamera(0, -camMoveSpeed);
    if (Gdx.input.isKeyPressed(Keys.BACKSPACE)) cameraHelper.setPosition(0, 0);
  }

  // Camera Controls (zoom)
  ...
}

@Override
public boolean keyUp (int keycode) {
  // Reset game world
```

```
    if (keycode == Keys.R) {
      init();
      Gdx.app.debug(TAG, "Game world resetted");
    }
    // Toggle camera follow
    else if (keycode == Keys.ENTER) {
      cameraHelper.setTarget(cameraHelper.hasTarget()
? null: level.bunnyHead);
      Gdx.app.debug(TAG, "Camera follow enabled: "
+ cameraHelper.hasTarget());
    }
    return false;
}
```

Now, we can use the *Enter* key to toggle between the player and camera controls. What is still missing is the code that handles the input for the player's character.

Add the following lines of code to `WorldController`:

```
private void handleInputGame (float deltaTime) {
  if (cameraHelper.hasTarget(level.bunnyHead)) {
    // Player Movement
    if (Gdx.input.isKeyPressed(Keys.LEFT)) {
      level.bunnyHead.velocity.x =
-level.bunnyHead.terminalVelocity.x;
    } else if (Gdx.input.isKeyPressed(Keys.RIGHT)) {
      level.bunnyHead.velocity.x =
level.bunnyHead.terminalVelocity.x;
    } else {
      // Execute auto-forward movement on non-desktop platform
      if (Gdx.app.getType() != ApplicationType.Desktop) {
        level.bunnyHead.velocity.x =
        level.bunnyHead.terminalVelocity.x;
      }
    }

    // Bunny Jump
    if (Gdx.input.isTouched() ||
Gdx.input.isKeyPressed(Keys.SPACE)) {
      level.bunnyHead.setJumping(true);
    } else {
      level.bunnyHead.setJumping(false);
    }
  }
}
```

Adding the Actors

After this, simply call the new method in the `update()` method of `WorldController`:

```
public void update (float deltaTime) {
  handleDebugInput(deltaTime);
  handleInputGame(deltaTime);
  level.update(deltaTime);
  testCollisions();
  cameraHelper.update(deltaTime);
}
```

The player is now controllable using the left and right arrow keys to move in the corresponding direction. We also add an autoforward moving behavior if the game is run on a non-desktop platform such as Android. Pressing either the Space bar key or touching the display of your smartphone will trigger the player character to jump. You can now run the game once again and try to pick up the first items as well as try to carefully jump from rock to rock without falling from the edge. Moreover, you might want to check what happens when you fall down. Obviously, nothing will happen in this case as we have not added any game logic yet to handle it properly. We also want to make the camera stop following the player's character too far down the level to make it more clear to the player that the level ends at the height of the water and to avoid a graphical glitch.

> In a later chapter, we will take a closer look at a full-blown physics engine called Box2D that implements all the necessary features to detect a collision. However, we will not revise our implementation by replacing it with Box2D's one because Canyon Bunny does not use physically accurate movements to make the game feel right. Trying to make real-world physics simulations do unrealistic physics can be a very hard and tedious task.

Losing lives, game over, and fixing the camera

Whenever the player falls into the water, it will cost one extra life. The game will be over as soon as there are no extra lives left and the player falls into the water once again. There will be a short delay of three seconds between the game over message and a complete restart of the game.

Add the following lines to `Constants`:

```
// Delay after game over
public static final float TIME_DELAY_GAME_OVER = 3;
```

Next, add the following lines to `WorldController`:

```
private float timeLeftGameOverDelay;

public boolean isGameOver () {
  return lives < 0;
}

public boolean isPlayerInWater () {
  return level.bunnyHead.position.y < -5;
}
```

In `isPlayerInWater()`, we test the bunny head's vertical position to find out whether it fell down into the water. As the water is placed at the bottom edge of the screen (y = 0), we simply need to look for a value smaller than this. In our example, we use -5 instead of 0 to also add a little delay in time. This is because travelling all the way down to the vertical position of -5 simply takes longer than it would do if we were using 0. The resulting effect is that the game will enforce a little pause on the player after each lost life.

After this, make the following modifications to `init()` and `update()` in `WorldController`:

```
private void init () {
  Gdx.input.setInputProcessor(this);
  cameraHelper = new CameraHelper();
  lives = Constants.LIVES_START;
  timeLeftGameOverDelay = 0;
  initLevel();
}

public void update (float deltaTime) {
  handleDebugInput(deltaTime);
  if (isGameOver()) {
    timeLeftGameOverDelay -= deltaTime;
    if (timeLeftGameOverDelay < 0) init();
  } else {
    handleInputGame(deltaTime);
  }
  level.update(deltaTime);
  testCollisions();
  cameraHelper.update(deltaTime);
  if (!isGameOver() && isPlayerInWater()) {
```

Adding the Actors

```
      lives--;
      if (isGameOver())
        timeLeftGameOverDelay = Constants.TIME_DELAY_GAME_OVER;
      else
        initLevel();
  }
}
```

The player's character will now lose extra lives when falling down into the water. You can verify this by checking the top-right corner of the game screen. Each missing extra life will turn into a transparent bunny head icon. The game over delay and the restart of the game after that are also working now.

There is still one small modification needed to fix the camera follow behavior.

Change the `update()` method of `CameraHelper` as follows:

```
public void update (float deltaTime) {
  if (!hasTarget()) return;

  position.x = target.position.x + target.origin.x;
  position.y = target.position.y + target.origin.y;

  // Prevent camera from moving down too far
  position.y = Math.max(-1f, position.y);
}
```

Adding the game over text and the feather icon to the GUI

Here, we add the game over text and the feather icon to our game.

Add the following method to `WorldRenderer`:

```
private void renderGuiGameOverMessage (SpriteBatch batch) {
  float x = cameraGUI.viewportWidth / 2;
  float y = cameraGUI.viewportHeight / 2;
  if (worldController.isGameOver()) {
    BitmapFont fontGameOver = Assets.instance.fonts.defaultBig;
    fontGameOver.setColor(1, 0.75f, 0.25f, 1);
    fontGameOver.drawMultiLine(batch, "GAME OVER", x, y, 0,
BitmapFont.HAlignment.CENTER);
    fontGameOver.setColor(1, 1, 1, 1);
  }
}
```

This method calculates the center of the GUI camera's viewport. The text is rendered using the big font from our assets. Its color is changed using the `setColor()` method of `BitmapFont`. The game over text is drawn using the `drawMultiLine()` method of `BitmapFont`, which takes a reference to `SpriteBatch`, the actual text to be displayed, a 2D position, a horizontal offset, and a constant for horizontal text alignment.

> We could have used `draw()` instead of `drawMultiLine()`; however, `draw()` does not provide the horizontal text alignment parameter that we need to center the text around its 2D position. The text might contain newlines (\n) to display multiline text, which we do not use in the preceding code.

We are using the `BitmapFont.HAlignment.CENTER` constant to tell `BitmapFont` that we want it to draw the given text horizontally centered to the given position. The text message **GAME OVER** will only be visible if the `isGameOver()` method of `WorldController` returns `true`.

The following is the screenshot of a case where all the extra lives were used up until the game was over:

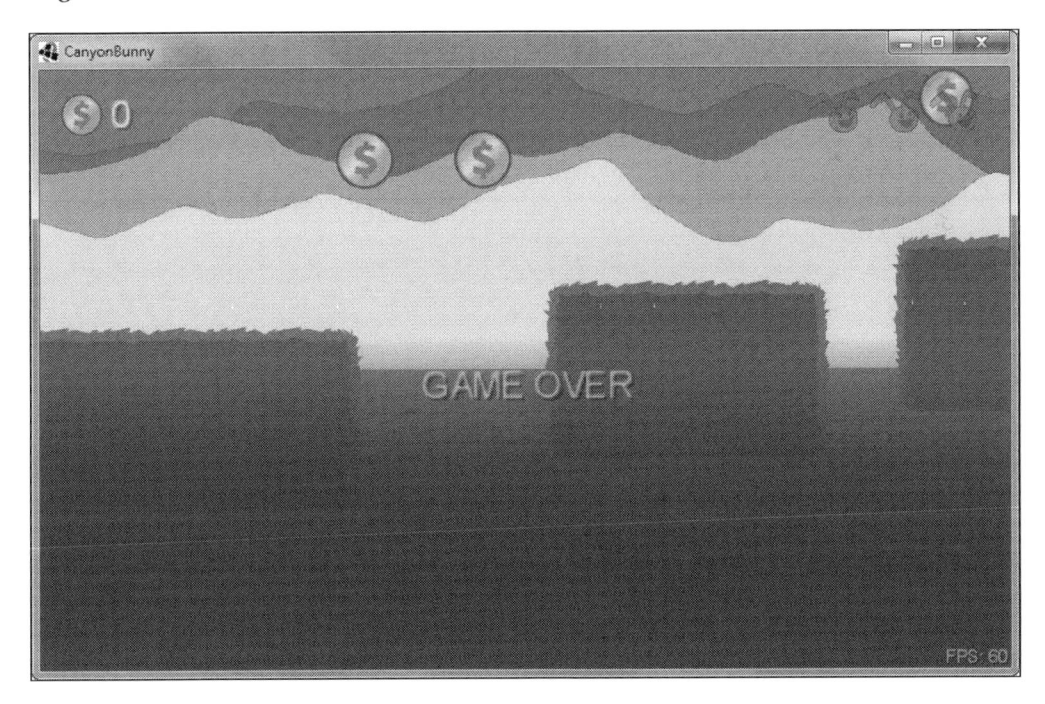

Adding the Actors

Now, add the following method to `WorldRenderer`:

```
private void renderGuiFeatherPowerup (SpriteBatch batch) {
  float x = -15;
  float y = 30;
  float timeLeftFeatherPowerup =
 worldController.level.bunnyHead.timeLeftFeatherPowerup;
  if (timeLeftFeatherPowerup > 0) {
    // Start icon fade in/out if the left power-up time
    // is less than 4 seconds. The fade interval is set
    // to 5 changes per second.
    if (timeLeftFeatherPowerup < 4) {
      if (((int)(timeLeftFeatherPowerup * 5) % 2) != 0) {
        batch.setColor(1, 1, 1, 0.5f);
      }
    }
    batch.draw(Assets.instance.feather.feather,
 x, y, 50, 50, 100, 100, 0.35f, -0.35f, 0);
    batch.setColor(1, 1, 1, 1);
    Assets.instance.fonts.defaultSmall.draw(batch,
 "" + (int)timeLeftFeatherPowerup, x + 60, y + 57);
  }
}
```

This method first checks whether there is still time left for the feather power-up effect to end. Only if this is the case, a feather icon is drawn in the top-left corner under the gold coin icon. A small number is drawn next to it that displays the rounded time that is still left until the effect vanishes. There is also some extra code that makes the feather icon fade back and forth when there are less than four seconds of the power-up effect to last.

The following screenshot shows an example of when the feather power-up has been picked up and has 6 seconds left:

You can see this from the little number shown next to the feather icon in the top-left corner of the game screen.

As the final step for this chapter, both the new GUI render methods need to be added to the `renderGui()` method of `WorldRenderer`:

```
private void renderGui (SpriteBatch batch) {
   batch.setProjectionMatrix(cameraGUI.combined);
   batch.begin();

   // draw collected gold coins icon + text
   // (anchored to top left edge)
   renderGuiScore(batch);
   // draw collected feather icon (anchored to top left edge)
   renderGuiFeatherPowerup(batch);
   // draw extra lives icon + text (anchored to top right edge)
   renderGuiExtraLive(batch);
   // draw FPS text (anchored to bottom right edge)
   renderGuiFpsCounter(batch);
```

Adding the Actors

```
    // draw game over text
    renderGuiGameOverMessage(batch);

    batch.end();
}
```

Summary

In this chapter, you learned how to implement the player's character, platforms, and collectible items in conjunction with a basic yet functional physics simulation and collision detection code. Nonetheless, it should be mentioned that the physics simulation as well as the collision detection code both have their limitations. However, as long as our original requirements of the game do not change, we will be just fine.

Furthermore, we completed the level loader and discussed how jumps for our player's character work. Two conditions to lose extra lives and reaching game over were added. The camera's position has been constrained in a way that it will never follow the player's character below the height of the water. Finally, we added a **GAME OVER** text message so that the player receives a visual feedback that all lives have been used up. The feather power-up also gives visual feedback when collected and active by displaying a feather icon with a nice little countdown timer that shows the remaining time for the effect to last.

This concludes the basic implementation of the Canyon Bunny game, which also means that we have now implemented all the features that we had originally defined in our outline back in *Chapter 1, Introduction to LibGDX and Project Setup*.

In the next chapter, we will create a menu system to enrich the overall game experience.

7
Menus and Options

In this chapter, we will create a menu for Canyon Bunny. There will be two buttons for the player to choose from. One of the buttons is **Play**, which will start a new game. The other button will show an options menu that contains a few changeable settings, such as sound and music volumes. All the settings will be stored to and loaded from a Preferences file to make them permanent.

It is essential to have some sort of mechanism to manage multiple screens if we want to allow the player to switch between them. LibGDX provides a Game class, which already supports such basic screen management.

You will also learn how to use LibGDX's scene graph called **Scene2D** to create and organize complex menu structures as well as how to handle events such as pressed buttons.

In this chapter, we will cover the following topics:

- Create and organize complex menu structures using Scene2D UI
- Store and load the game preferences

Managing multiple screens

We will now make some minor changes to our current class diagram to reflect the support for multiple screens that we want to add to our game.

> You might want to take a peek at the previous class diagram of Canyon Bunny for a quick refresher. See *Chapter 3, Configuring the Game*, for the diagram.

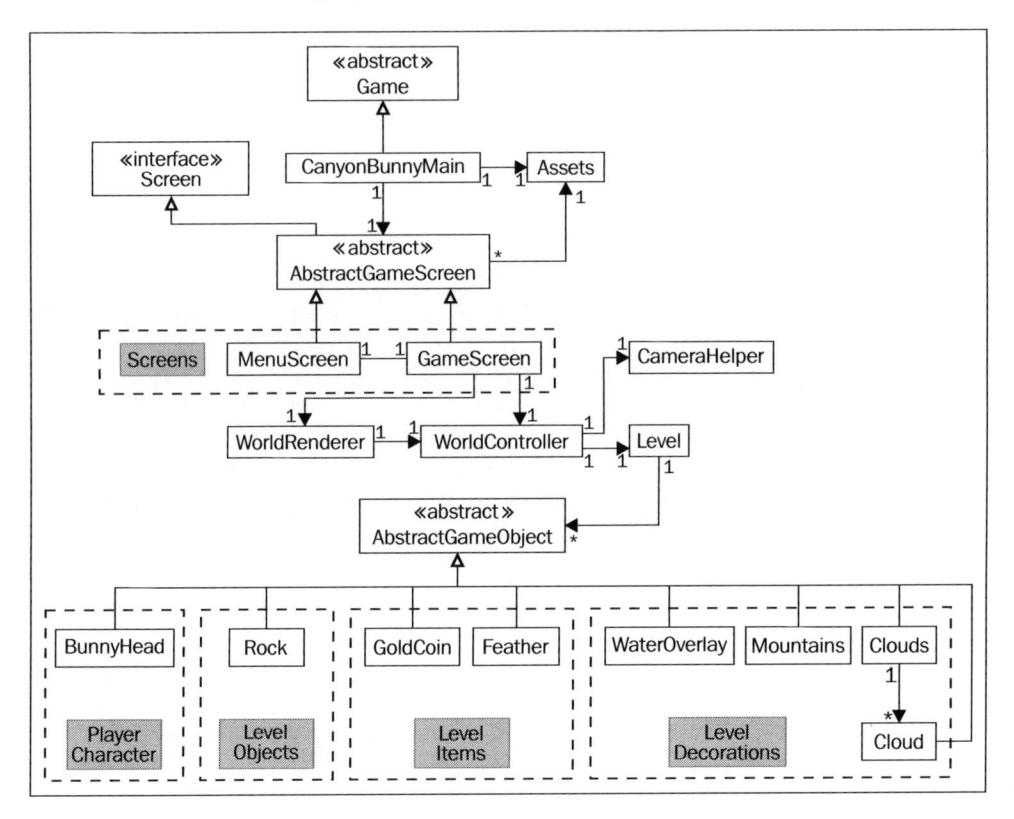

Take a look at the following updated class diagram:

What has been changed here is that `CanyonBunnyMain` no longer implements the `ApplicationListener` interface that is used by LibGDX to control the flow of the application. Instead, `CanyonBunnyMain` now extends LibGDX's `Game` class, which in turn implements the `ApplicationListener` interface. The `Game` class provides a `setScreen()` method. Calling this method allows us to change the current screen to another one.

Every screen that we want to have in our game is encapsulated in a separate class and ends with `*Screen`. This is just a naming convention in this project and you are free to do it differently, of course. There are also three new classes shown in the preceding diagram, which are `AbstractGameScreen`, `MenuScreen`, and `GameScreen`. The menu and the game screen classes extend `AbstractGameScreen` so that we can easily define the common actions that we want to be executed for all our screens. Additionally, `AbstractGameScreen` implements LibGDX's `Screen` interface, which introduces the `show()` and `hide()` method for each screen. These methods will be called by `Game` and will take the place of `create()` and `dispose()`, so we will have to move our existing code accordingly.

The preceding diagram also shows that `WorldController` and `WorldRenderer` are no longer directly used by `CanyonBunnyMain`. Instead, `GameScreen` will be using them from now on as we will move all the game world-specific code from `CanyonBunnyMain` to `GameScreen`.

Create a new file for the `AbstractGameScreen` class and add the following code:

```
package com.packtpub.libgdx.canyonbunny.screens;

import com.badlogic.gdx.Game;
import com.badlogic.gdx.Screen;
import com.badlogic.gdx.assets.AssetManager;
import com.packtpub.libgdx.canyonbunny.game.Assets;

public abstract class AbstractGameScreen implements Screen {
  protected Game game;

  public AbstractGameScreen (Game game) {
    this.game = game;
  }

  public abstract void render (float deltaTime);
  public abstract void resize (int width, int height);
  public abstract void show ();
  public abstract void hide ();
  public abstract void pause ();

  public void resume () {
    Assets.instance.init(new AssetManager());
  }

  public void dispose () {
    Assets.instance.dispose();
  }
}
```

Each screen will take a reference to the instance of `Game`. This is necessary because each screen needs to call the `setScreen()` method of the `Game` class. Apart from this, we have added two lines of code that will make sure that the game's assets will be correctly loaded and disposed as LibGDX sees fit.

Menus and Options

Next, we will implement two new screen classes. Create a new file for the `MenuScreen` class and add the following code:

```
package com.packtpub.libgdx.canyonbunny.screens;

import com.badlogic.gdx.Game;
import com.badlogic.gdx.Gdx;
import com.badlogic.gdx.graphics.GL20;

public class MenuScreen extends AbstractGameScreen {
  private static final String TAG = MenuScreen.class.getName();

  public MenuScreen (Game game) {
    super(game);
  }

  @Override
  public void render (float deltaTime) {
    Gdx.gl.glClearColor(0.0f, 0.0f, 0.0f, 1.0f);
Gdx.gl.glClear(GL20.GL_COLOR_BUFFER_BIT);
    if(Gdx.input.isTouched())
      game.setScreen(new GameScreen(game));
  }

  @Override public void resize (int width, int height) { }
  @Override public void show () { }
  @Override public void hide () { }
  @Override public void pause () { }
}
```

This is still a very rough implementation of the menu screen, but it will serve us well for the moment. The `render()` method takes care of only two things. It constantly clears the screen by filling it with a solid black color and checks whether the screen has been touched, which also includes mouse clicks if the game is running on a desktop. As soon as a touch has been detected, the screen will be switched from the menu screen to the game screen that shows our actual game world.

Next, create a new file for the `GameScreen` class and add the following code:

```
package com.packtpub.libgdx.canyonbunny.screens;

import com.badlogic.gdx.Game;
import com.badlogic.gdx.Gdx;
import com.badlogic.gdx.graphics.GL20;
```

```java
import com.packtpub.libgdx.canyonbunny.game.WorldController;
import com.packtpub.libgdx.canyonbunny.game.WorldRenderer;

public class GameScreen extends AbstractGameScreen {
  private static final String TAG = GameScreen.class.getName();

  private WorldController worldController;
  private WorldRenderer worldRenderer;

  private boolean paused;

  public GameScreen (Game game) {
    super(game);
  }

  @Override
  public void render (float deltaTime) {
    // Do not update game world when paused.
    if (!paused) {
      // Update game world by the time that has passed
      // since last rendered frame.
      worldController.update(deltaTime);
    }
    // Sets the clear screen color to: Cornflower Blue
    Gdx.gl.glClearColor(0x64 / 255.0f, 0x95 / 255.0f,0xed / 255.0f, 0xff / 255.0f);
    // Clears the screen
    Gdx.gl.glClear(GL20.GL_COLOR_BUFFER_BIT);
    // Render game world to screen
    worldRenderer.render();
  }
  @Override
  public void resize (int width, int height) {
    worldRenderer.resize(width, height);
  }

  @Override
  public void show () {
    worldController = new WorldController(game);
    worldRenderer = new WorldRenderer(worldController);
    Gdx.input.setCatchBackKey(true);
  }

  @Override
```

```
  public void hide () {
    worldRenderer.dispose();
    Gdx.input.setCatchBackKey(false);
  }

  @Override
  public void pause () {
    paused = true;
  }

  @Override
  public void resume () {
    super.resume();
    // Only called on Android!
    paused = false;
  }
}
```

You should recognize most of the preceding code as it is merely a duplicate of the current `CanyonBunnyMain` class. However, some small changes have been made. First of all, the code that was in the `create()` and `dispose()` methods of `CanyonBunnyMain` have been moved over to the `show()` and `hide()` methods, respectively, in order to accommodate the `Screen` interface. Furthermore, catching Android's back key will be enabled when the game screen is shown and disabled again when the screen is hidden. This allows us to handle this event and execute a custom action (here, switch back to the menu screen) in place of the system's default action, which is to terminate the running application.

Now, let's fix `CanyonBunnyMain`. For clarity and brevity, we will just replace the whole class as most of its code has to be removed anyway.

Replace the current content of `CanyonBunnyMain` with the following code:

```
package com.packtpub.libgdx.canyonbunny;

import com.badlogic.gdx.Application;
import com.badlogic.gdx.Game;
import com.badlogic.gdx.Gdx;
import com.badlogic.gdx.assets.AssetManager;
import com.packtpub.libgdx.canyonbunny.game.Assets;
import com.packtpub.libgdx.canyonbunny.screens.MenuScreen;

public class CanyonBunnyMain extends Game {
```

```
    @Override
    public void create () {
      // Set Libgdx log level
      Gdx.app.setLogLevel(Application.LOG_DEBUG);
      // Load assets
      Assets.instance.init(new AssetManager());
      // Start game at menu screen
      setScreen(new MenuScreen(this));
    }
}
```

Our platform-independent entry point of the game has obviously become quite simple. Basically, CanyonBunnyMain has been reduced to only contain the create() method, which almost looks the same as before. What has changed inside this method is that after setting the log level and loading our assets, LibGDX is instructed through a call of the setScreen() method by the Game class to change the current screen. As we want the game to start with the menu screen, we simply pass a new instance of MenuScreen.

One last change is required to finish our preparations for multiple screen management. The WorldController class holds our game logic and needs to initiate a switch back to the menu whenever the player has lost the game or if either the *Esc* key or the back button is pressed.

Add the following two import lines to WorldController:

```
import com.badlogic.gdx.Game;
import com.packtpub.libgdx.canyonbunny.screens.MenuScreen;
```

After that, add the following code:

```
    private Game game;

    private void backToMenu () {
      // switch to menu screen
      game.setScreen(new MenuScreen(game));
    }
```

This allows us to save a reference to the game instance, which will enable us to switch to another screen. Additionally, a convenient method called backToMenu() has also been added that will switch to the menu screen when called.

Menus and Options

After this, make the following changes to `WorldController`:

```
public WorldController (Game game) {
  this.game = game;
  init();
}
public void update (float deltaTime) {
  handleDebugInput(deltaTime);
  if (isGameOver()) {
    timeLeftGameOverDelay -= deltaTime;
    if (timeLeftGameOverDelay < 0) backToMenu();
  } else {
    handleInputGame(deltaTime);
  }
  level.update(deltaTime);
  ...
}
@Override
public boolean keyUp (int keycode) {
  ...
  // Toggle camera follow
  else if (keycode == Keys.ENTER) {
    ...
  }
  // Back to Menu
  else if (keycode == Keys.ESCAPE || keycode == Keys.BACK) {
    backToMenu();
  }
  return false;
}
```

The constructor has been extended by taking a reference of the game instance as an argument, which is then stored for later reference when we need to switch the screen. In the `update()` method, a call to `backToMenu()` is initiated as soon as the game-over-delay timer runs out of time instead of restarting the game in the game world as was the case before. As mentioned earlier, we want to handle Android's back key as well as the *Esc* key on the desktop ourselves, which is now done inside the `keyUp()` method.

You can now run the game and verify that you can switch back and forth between `MenuScreen` and `GameScreen`. Touch the black screen of the menu and try to get back to it by hitting either the *Esc* key or the back button, respectively. Losing all lives while still in the game screen should yield the same result and bring you back to the menu screen too.

Exploring Scene2D UI, TableLayout, and skins

LibGDX comes with a great feature set to easily create scene graphs. A scene graph is a hierarchically organized structure of objects similar to files and folders on a hard disk. In LibGDX, such objects are called actors. Actors can be nested to create logical groups. Grouping actors is a very useful feature, as modifications applied to a parent actor will also affect its child actors. Furthermore, each actor has its own local coordinate system, which makes it very easy to define relative offsets inside a group of actors, including position, angle of rotation, and scale.

Scene2D supports hit detection of rotated and scaled actors. LibGDX's flexible event system allows you to handle and route inputs as needed so that the parent actors can intercept inputs before they reach the child actors. Finally, the built-in action system can be used to easily manipulate actors over a period of time, creating complex effects that can execute in sequence, parallel, or in a combination of both. All this described functionality is encapsulated in the Stage class, which contains the hierarchy and distributes user-generated events. Actors can be added to and removed from it at any time. The Stage class and the Actor class both contain an act() method, which takes a delta time as its argument to do a time-based action. Calling act() on a Stage instance will cause a call of act() on every actor in the scene graph. The act() methods of Stage and Actor are basically what we already know as the update() methods, only using a different name. For more information on Scene2D, check out the official documentation at https://github.com/libgdx/libgdx/wiki/Scene2d/.

Until now, we have not used any of Scene2D's functionality in our game. Naturally, we could have implemented the game world, including its game objects, with Scene2D. However, always keep in mind that using a scene graph comes with a certain amount of overhead. LibGDX tries its best to keep the overhead at a bare minimum, such as skipping complex calculations of transformation matrices if objects do not need to be rotated or scaled. So, it really depends on what your requirements are.

As the user interface of the menu that we are going to create is rather complex, we want to make use of LibGDX's scene graph for this task. More precisely, we will use Scene2D UI. This is another implementation in LibGDX that builds on top of Scene2D and extends its functionality by providing a rich set of common and ready-to-use UI elements. In LibGDX, these UI elements are called **widgets**.

Menus and Options

All the widgets currently available in Scene2D UI are `Button`, `ButtonGroup`, `CheckBox`, `Dialog`, `Image`, `ImageButton`, `Label`, `List`, `ScrollPane`, `SelectBox`, `Slider`, `SplitPane`, `Stack`, `Window`, `TextButton`, `TextField`, `TextArea`, `Touchpad`, and `Tree`.

Scene2D UI also supports the easy creation of new custom widgets. We will discuss a selected number of widgets as we implement them in our menu. For a complete list and description of each widget, check out the official documentation at https://github.com/libgdx/libgdx/wiki/Scene2d.ui.

In addition to Scene2D UI, LibGDX also incorporates a separate project called `TableLayout`. The `TableLayout` object makes it very easy to create and maintain dynamic (read: resolution-independent) layouts using tables. It also provides an intuitive API. A `Table` class provides access to the functionality of `TableLayout`, which is also implemented as a widget, and therefore integrates seamlessly into the concept of Scene2D UI. It is highly recommended to check out the official documentation at https://github.com/EsotericSoftware/tablelayout/.

One more important feature of Scene2D UI is the support of skins. A skin is a collection of resources used to style and display UI widgets, for example, resources can be texture regions, fonts, and colors. Typically, a skin uses texture regions that come from a texture atlas. The style definition of each widget is stored in a separate file that uses the JSON file format. For more information, check out the official documentation at https://github.com/libgdx/libgdx/wiki/Skin/.

Using LibGDX's scene graph for the menu UI

We are now going to create the scene of the menu screen. The scene will feature a background image that fills the whole screen. There will be logos in the top-left and bottom-left corner of the screen and two clickable buttons anchored in the bottom-right corner that will trigger either a play or an options action. A gold coin and a huge image of the bunny head are also added to the scene.

The following is a screenshot of how the finished menu screen will look:

However, before we start to create this scene, we have to do some preparations in advance. First of all, we need to add new images to our project and also make a small change to the automatic texture packing process so that we have a texture atlas for our UI.

Add a new subfolder in `CanyonBunny-desktop/assets-raw/` called `images-ui` and copy all the new images into this directory. After this, make the following change to `Main.java`:

```
if (rebuildAtlas) {
    Settings settings = new Settings();
    settings.maxWidth = 1024;
    settings.maxHeight = 1024;
    settings.debug = drawDebugOutline;
    TexturePacker.process(settings, "assets-raw/images",
            "../CanyonBunny-android/assets/images",
"canyonbunny.pack");
    TexturePacker.process(settings, "assets-raw/images-ui",
            "../CanyonBunny-android/assets/images",
"canyonbunny-ui.pack");
}
```

Menus and Options

> You will need to set `rebuildAtlas` to `true` at least once and run the game on the desktop to let TexturePacker create the required texture atlas.

Gradle users must remember that your project folder is named `android` inside the project root `C:/libgdx`. Hence, here you should put the destination path `../android/assets/images` in both the `TexturePacker.process()` functions.

The texture atlas for our UI will then be created in `CanyonBunny-android/assets/images/` called `canyonbunny-ui`.

The resulting texture atlas for our UI should look like the following screenshot:

Next, we will create a suitable JSON file to define the skin of our menu widgets.

Create a new file in `CanyonBunny-android/assets/images/` called `canyonbunny-ui.json` and add the following lines:

```
{
com.badlogic.gdx.scenes.scene2d.ui.Button$ButtonStyle: {
  play: { down: play-dn, up: play-up },
  options: { down: options-dn, up: options-up }
},
com.badlogic.gdx.scenes.scene2d.ui.Image: {
  background: { drawable: background },
  logo: { drawable: logo },
  info: { drawable: info },
  coins: { drawable: coins },
  bunny: { drawable: bunny },
},
}
```

> On running the `CanyonBunny-html` project, it will show a json parsing error while parsing the `CanyonBunny-ui.json` file. This is because of GWT reflection. GWT does not provide reflection in the same way as Java. Hence, extra steps are required to make reflection available in the GWT project.
>
> Open the `GwtDefinition.gwt.xml` file in your `CanyonBunny-html` project and update it with the following code:
>
> ```
> <module>
> ...
> <extend-configuration-property
> name="gdx.reflect.include"
>         value="com.badlogic.gdx.scenes.scene2d.ui"
> />
> <extend-configuration-property
> name="gdx.reflect.include"
>         value="com.badlogic.gdx.utils" />
> </module>
> ```
>
> The preceding code will enable the gwt reflection for the packages `com.badlogic.gdx.scenes.scene2d.ui` and `com.badlogic.gdx.utils`, which is required to parse Scene2D UI elements. Make sure that you add `extend-configuration-property` below `set-configuration-property`. To find out more about LibGDX reflection, visit https://github.com/libgdx/libgdx/wiki/Reflection.

Menus and Options

This definition file describes the type of widget to be used by specifying its completely qualified name. Inside the block of a widget definition, you can freely choose a name. Here we use play, options, background, and so on for our names. These names are then followed by a colon, which is in turn followed by a comma-separated list of attributes enclosed in curly brackets that correspond exactly to the field names of the widget's class. For example, the `Image` widget has a field called `drawable`. Some widgets have an inner class, which is denoted in the JSON file by appending a dollar sign followed by the name of the style class. These style classes contain widget-specific fields. We are using such a definition type for the **Play** and **Options** buttons. Both these buttons have a down and up image assigned in their `Button` widget.

Lastly, add the following lines of code to `Constants` to finish our preparations:

```
public static final String TEXTURE_ATLAS_UI =
    "images/canyonbunny-ui.pack";
public static final String TEXTURE_ATLAS_LIBGDX_UI =
    "images/uiskin.atlas";
// Location of description file for skins
public static final String SKIN_LIBGDX_UI =
    "images/uiskin.json";
public static final String SKIN_CANYONBUNNY_UI =
    "images/canyonbunny-ui.json";
```

The `uiskin.atlas` and `uiskin.json` will be downloaded later in this chapter.

Building the scene for the menu screen

We will now begin with the actual implementation of the scene for the menu screen. First, take a look at the following diagram that shows the hierarchy of the UI scene graph that we are going to build step-by-step:

Chapter 7

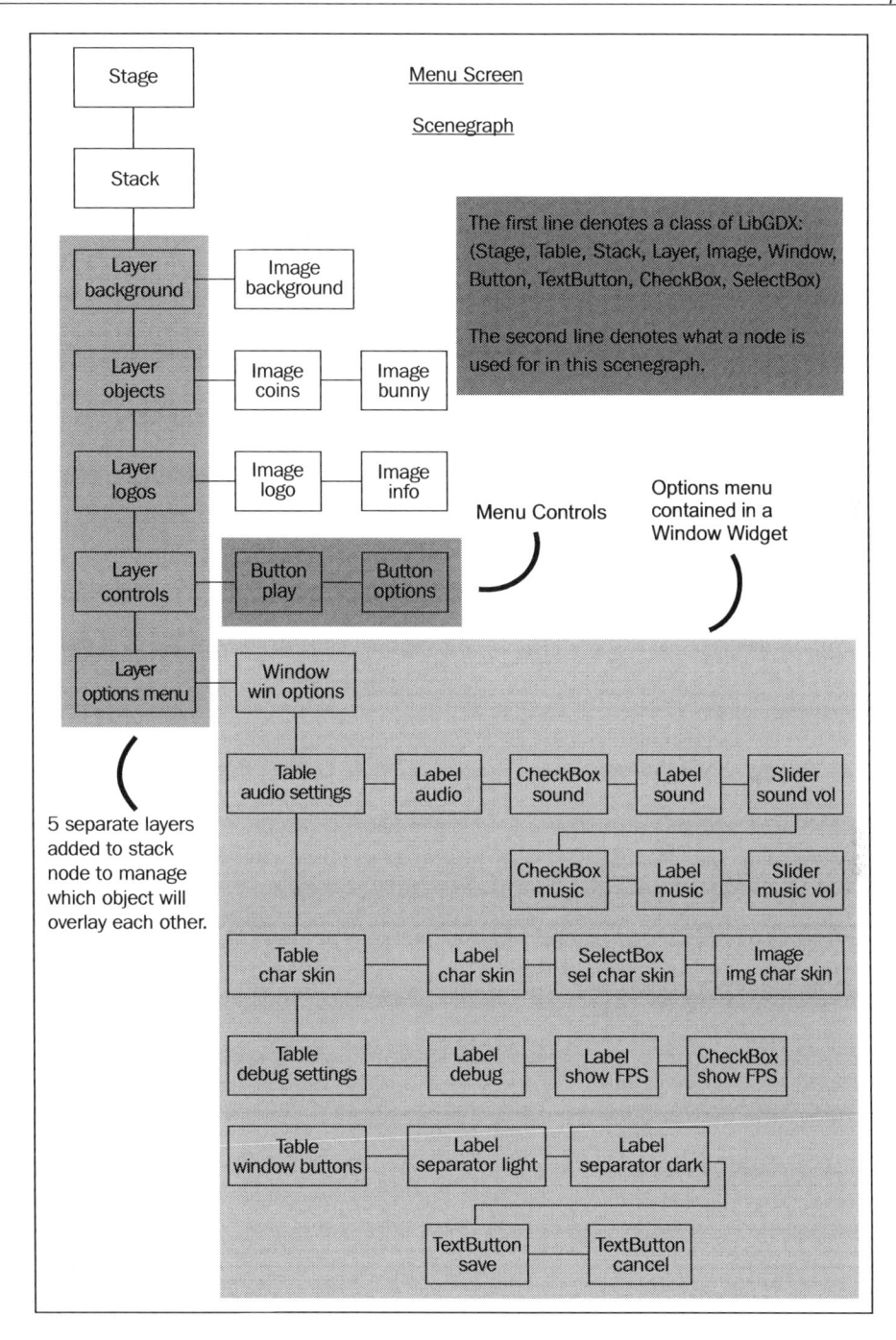

Menu Screen Scenegraph

The first line denotes a class of LibGDX: (Stage, Table, Stack, Layer, Image, Window, Button, TextButton, CheckBox, SelectBox)

The second line denotes what a node is used for in this scenegraph.

5 separate layers added to stack node to manage which object will overlay each other.

Menu Controls: Button play, Button options

Options menu contained in a Window Widget

- Stage
  - Stack
    - Layer background
      - Image background
    - Layer objects
      - Image coins
      - Image bunny
    - Layer logos
      - Image logo
      - Image info
    - Layer controls
      - Button play
      - Button options
    - Layer options menu
      - Window win options
        - Table audio settings
          - Label audio
          - CheckBox sound
          - Label sound
          - Slider sound vol
          - CheckBox music
          - Label music
          - Slider music vol
        - Table char skin
          - Label char skin
          - SelectBox sel char skin
          - Image img char skin
        - Table debug settings
          - Label debug
          - Label show FPS
          - CheckBox show FPS
        - Table window buttons
          - Label separator light
          - Label separator dark
          - TextButton save
          - TextButton cancel

[241]

Menus and Options

The scene graph starts with an empty `Stage`. Then, the first child actor added to the stage is a `Stack` widget. The `Stack` widget allows you to add actors that can overlay other actors. We will make use of this ability to create several layers. Each layer uses a `Table` widget as its parent actor. Using stacked tables enables us to lay out actors in an easy and logical way.

In the first step, we will add the basic structure of our stacked layers and some skeleton methods, which we are going to fill in the subsequent steps.

Add the following import lines to `MenuScreen`:

```
import com.badlogic.gdx.graphics.Color;
import com.badlogic.gdx.graphics.g2d.TextureAtlas;
import com.badlogic.gdx.scenes.scene2d.Stage;
import com.badlogic.gdx.scenes.scene2d.Actor;
import com.badlogic.gdx.scenes.scene2d.ui.Button;
import com.badlogic.gdx.scenes.scene2d.ui.CheckBox;
import com.badlogic.gdx.scenes.scene2d.ui.Image;
import com.badlogic.gdx.scenes.scene2d.ui.Label;
import com.badlogic.gdx.scenes.scene2d.ui.Label.LabelStyle;
import com.badlogic.gdx.scenes.scene2d.ui.SelectBox;
import com.badlogic.gdx.scenes.scene2d.ui.Skin;
import com.badlogic.gdx.scenes.scene2d.ui.Slider;
import com.badlogic.gdx.scenes.scene2d.ui.Stack;
import com.badlogic.gdx.scenes.scene2d.ui.Table;
import com.badlogic.gdx.scenes.scene2d.ui.TextButton;
import com.badlogic.gdx.scenes.scene2d.ui.Window;
import com.badlogic.gdx.scenes.scene2d.utils.ChangeListener;
import com.packtpub.libgdx.canyonbunny.game.Assets;
import com.packtpub.libgdx.canyonbunny.util.Constants;
```

After this, add the following lines of code to the same class:

```
private Stage stage;
private Skin skinCanyonBunny;
// menu
private Image imgBackground;
private Image imgLogo;
private Image imgInfo;
private Image imgCoins;
private Image imgBunny;
private Button btnMenuPlay;
private Button btnMenuOptions;
// options
```

```
    private Window winOptions;
    private TextButton btnWinOptSave;
    private TextButton btnWinOptCancel;
    private CheckBox chkSound;
    private Slider sldSound;
    private CheckBox chkMusic;
    private Slider sldMusic;
    private SelectBox<CharacterSkin> selCharSkin;
    private Image imgCharSkin;
    private CheckBox chkShowFpsCounter;

    // debug
    private final float DEBUG_REBUILD_INTERVAL = 5.0f;
    private boolean debugEnabled = false;
    private float debugRebuildStage;
```

We added new variables to store an instance of Stage called stage, an instance of Skin called skinCanyonBunny, and some more variables for the widgets of the menu screen and the **Options** window.

Next, add the following code to the same class:

```
    private void rebuildStage () {
      skinCanyonBunny = new Skin(
          Gdx.files.internal(Constants.SKIN_CANYONBUNNY_UI),
          new TextureAtlas(Constants.TEXTURE_ATLAS_UI));

      // build all layers
      Table layerBackground = buildBackgroundLayer();
      Table layerObjects = buildObjectsLayer();
      Table layerLogos = buildLogosLayer();
      Table layerControls = buildControlsLayer();
      Table layerOptionsWindow = buildOptionsWindowLayer();

      // assemble stage for menu screen
      stage.clear();
      Stack stack = new Stack();
      stage.addActor(stack);
      stack.setSize(Constants.VIEWPORT_GUI_WIDTH,
  Constants.VIEWPORT_GUI_HEIGHT);
      stack.add(layerBackground);
      stack.add(layerObjects);
      stack.add(layerLogos);
```

Menus and Options

```
    stack.add(layerControls);
    stage.addActor(layerOptionsWindow);
}
```

In `rebuildStage()`, we build everything that will make up the final scene of our menu screen. This method is implemented in a way so that it can be called in a repeated manner, hence the name `rebuildStage`. While we are implementing each of the layers, you might want to try and modify the code in each step to get a better understanding of how `TableLayout` behaves in certain situations.

Next, add the following code to the same class:

```
private Table buildBackgroundLayer () {
  Table layer = new Table();
  return layer;
}
private Table buildObjectsLayer () {
  Table layer = new Table();
  return layer;
}
private Table buildLogosLayer () {
  Table layer = new Table();
  return layer;
}
private Table buildControlsLayer () {
  Table layer = new Table();
  return layer;
}
private Table buildOptionsWindowLayer () {
  Table layer = new Table();
  return layer;
}
```

We have added five new methods that contain dummy implementations for now. These will be used to build each layer of the menu.

Next, make the following changes to the same class:

```
@Override
public void resize (int width, int height) {
  stage.getViewport().update(width, height, true);
}

@Override
public void hide () {
```

```
    stage.dispose();
    skinCanyonBunny.dispose();
}

@Override
public void show () {
stage = new Stage(new StretchViewport(Constants.VIEWPORT_GUI_WIDTH,
Constants.VIEWPORT_GUI_HEIGHT));
    Gdx.input.setInputProcessor(stage);
    rebuildStage();
}
```

The `show()` method is called when the screen is shown. It initializes the stage, sets it as LibGDX's current input processor so that the stage will receive all the future inputs, and finally, the stage is rebuilt by calling `rebuildStage()`. The `hide()` method will free the allocated resources when the screen is hidden. The `resize()` method sets the viewport size of the stage.

Lastly, make the following changes to the `render()` method in the same class:

```
@Override
public void render (float deltaTime) {
    Gdx.gl.glClearColor(0.0f, 0.0f, 0.0f, 1.0f);
    Gdx.gl.glClear(GL20.GL_COLOR_BUFFER_BIT);

    if (debugEnabled) {
        debugRebuildStage -= deltaTime;
        if (debugRebuildStage <= 0) {
            debugRebuildStage = DEBUG_REBUILD_INTERVAL;
            rebuildStage();
        }
    }
    stage.act(deltaTime);
    stage.draw();
    Table.drawDebug(stage);
}
```

The code in `render()` that would switch to the game screen when the screen is touched was replaced by calls to update and render the stage. The statement `Table.drawDebug()` is a debugging feature of `TableLayout`, which enables you to draw debug visuals in a scene. Additionally, you need to specify which `Table` widgets should draw debug lines by calling their `debug()` method.

Menus and Options

> This hint might sound trivial, but this is such a big time saver that it is definitely worth pointing it out.
>
> The code you just added to `MenuScreen` contains some additional debug code that will call `rebuildStage()` in periodic intervals defined in seconds by `DEBUG_REBUILD_INTERVAL`. You can enable periodic refreshing by simply setting `debugEnabled` to `true`. This will give you live updates at runtime, assuming that you are running the game in debug mode on the desktop, and will allow you to take advantage of JVM's awesome Code Hot Swapping feature.

Adding the background layer

Make the following changes in `MenuScreen` to add the background layer:

```
private Table buildBackgroundLayer () {
  Table layer = new Table();
  // + Background
  imgBackground = new Image(skinCanyonBunny, "background");
  layer.add(imgBackground);
  return layer;
}
```

There will now be a background image drawn to the scene of the menu screen. The image is referenced using the background name that we defined earlier in our skin file (`canyonbunny-ui.json`). If you change the size of the screen, the stage will adjust accordingly along with the background layer and its `Image` widget.

Adding the objects layer

Make the following changes in `MenuScreen` to add the objects layer:

```
private Table buildObjectsLayer () {
  Table layer = new Table();
  // + Coins
  imgCoins = new Image(skinCanyonBunny, "coins");
  layer.addActor(imgCoins);
  imgCoins.setPosition(135, 80);
  // + Bunny
  imgBunny = new Image(skinCanyonBunny, "bunny");
  layer.addActor(imgBunny);
  imgBunny.setPosition(355, 40);
  return layer;
}
```

Chapter 7

There will now be an image of some coins and another image of a huge bunny head, which are both drawn on top of the background layer. The positions of each actor are explicitly set to certain coordinates by calling `setPosition()` on each actor.

Adding the logos layer

Make the following changes in `MenuScreen` to add the logos layer:

```
private Table buildLogosLayer () {
  Table layer = new Table();
  layer.left().top();
  // + Game Logo
  imgLogo = new Image(skinCanyonBunny, "logo");
  layer.add(imgLogo);
  layer.row().expandY();
  // + Info Logos
  imgInfo = new Image(skinCanyonBunny, "info");
  layer.add(imgInfo).bottom();
  if (debugEnabled) layer.debug();
  return layer;
}
```

The logos layer is anchored in the top-left corner of the screen. After this, an image logo is added to the table followed by a call of the `row()` and `expandY()` methods. Every time you call `add()` on a `Table` widget, `TableLayout` will add a new column, which means the widget grows in a horizontal direction. So, if you want to start a new row, you can tell `TableLayout` about this by calling `row()`. The `expandY()` method expands the empty space in a vertical direction. The expansion is done by shifting the widgets to the bounds of the cell.

After this, more image information is added to the table, which is literally pushed down to the bottom edge due to the call of `expandY()`.

Lastly, there is a call to `layer.debug()`, which is the way to tell `TableLayout` the object it should draw debug visuals for.

Adding the controls layer

Make the following changes in `MenuScreen` to add the controls layer:

```
private Table buildControlsLayer () {
  Table layer = new Table();
  layer.right().bottom();
```

```
  // + Play Button
  btnMenuPlay = new Button(skinCanyonBunny, "play");
  layer.add(btnMenuPlay);
  btnMenuPlay.addListener(new ChangeListener() {
    @Override
    public void changed (ChangeEvent event, Actor actor) {
      onPlayClicked();
    }
  });
  layer.row();
  // + Options Button
  btnMenuOptions = new Button(skinCanyonBunny, "options");
  layer.add(btnMenuOptions);
  btnMenuOptions.addListener(new ChangeListener() {
    @Override
    public void changed (ChangeEvent event, Actor actor) {
      onOptionsClicked();
    }
  });
  if (debugEnabled) layer.debug();
  return layer;
}
```

After this, add the following lines of code to the same class:

```
private void onPlayClicked () {
  game.setScreen(new GameScreen(game));
}

private void onOptionsClicked () { }
```

The controls layer is anchored in the bottom-right corner of the screen. A new button widget is added using the `Play` style. Next, a new `ChangeListener` is added to this button to define the action to be executed when the button is clicked on.

> We are using `ChangeListener` to register new handlers for our button widgets. This is the recommended way of implementing handlers for widgets as most of them will fire `ChangeEvent` when changes occur. We could also use `ClickListener` to accomplish the detection of clicks on button widgets, but doing so has a major drawback. The `ClickListener` method reacts on the input events received by a widget, but does not know anything about widgets and their properties. Therefore, if a widget is set to be disabled, clicking on events will still be detected and handled by the listener.

After this, a new row is started in which the second button widget is added using the **Options** style. Each event handler calls a separate method to make it easier for us to maintain the code of the layer and the code to handle events. The `onPlayClicked()` method will switch to the game screen, while the `onOptionsClicked()` method is intentionally left empty for the moment.

Adding the Options window layer

The **Options** window layer is going to be a lot more complex in comparison to all the other layers that we have implemented so far. There are also some further preparations required before we can continue to implement this layer.

Here is a screenshot to give you a better idea of how the finished **Options** window will look:

The **Options** window will be a small box that shows a title bar with text on it and has some empty space to hold additional widgets. It can be dragged on the title bar to move it around in the scene. There will be a checkbox to enable and disable the **Sound** and **Music** effects as well as a slider to adjust the volume, respectively. A character skin can be chosen from a drop-down list. The current selection is shown next to it in a small preview image. The preview image is updated whenever a new selection in the drop-down list has been made to reflect the change. Lastly, there is another checkbox that toggles to check whether the FPS counter will be displayed on the game screen.

The menu controls, that is, the **Play** and **Options** buttons, will disappear when the **Options** window is shown. To close the **Options** window, the player has to choose between saving and canceling any changes that have been made in the window. When the **Options** window is hidden, the menu controls will appear again.

Usually, we would have to draw all of these textures that you see in the preceding screenshot to use all of the shown widgets. Luckily, we can take a shortcut here by taking a texture atlas, a suitable skin file, and a font definition file for the text to be displayed in these widgets from LibGDX's test repository. It contains much more than we need, so you might also want to take a closer look at the skin file to find out how certain widgets need to be defined that are not covered here.

You will need the following files from LibGDX's test repository to put them into `CanyonBunny-android/assets/images/`:

- `uiskin.png`
- `uiskin.atlas`
- `uiskin.json`
- `default.fnt`

Alternatively, you can download these files from the code bundle of *Chapter 7, Menus and Options*, and place them at `CanyonBunny-android/assets/images/`.

This is how the image of the file `uiskin.png` should look:

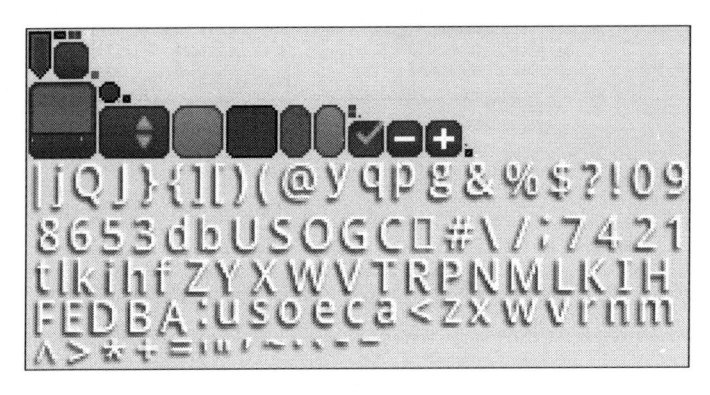

There are two more actions that we will do in advance before we go back to implementing the actual layer for the **Options** menu.

The first action is to create a new class that abstracts the process of loading and saving all of our game settings.

Create a new file called `GamePreferences` and add the following lines of code:

```
package com.packtpub.libgdx.canyonbunny.util;

import com.badlogic.gdx.Gdx;
import com.badlogic.gdx.Preferences;
import com.badlogic.gdx.math.MathUtils;

public class GamePreferences {
  public static final String TAG =
GamePreferences.class.getName();

  public static final GamePreferences instance =
new GamePreferences();

  public boolean sound;
  public boolean music;
  public float volSound;
  public float volMusic;
  public int charSkin;
  public boolean showFpsCounter;

  private Preferences prefs;

  // singleton: prevent instantiation from other classes
  private GamePreferences () {
    prefs = Gdx.app.getPreferences(Constants.PREFERENCES);
  }

  public void load () { }
  public void save () { }
}
```

This class is implemented as a singleton so we can call its `load()` and `save()` methods from virtually anywhere inside our project. The settings will be loaded from and saved to a preferences file defined in `Constants.PREFERENCES`.

Next, add the following code to the `load()` method of the same class:

```
public void load () {
  sound = prefs.getBoolean("sound", true);
  music = prefs.getBoolean("music", true);
  volSound = MathUtils.clamp(prefs.getFloat("volSound", 0.5f),
    0.0f, 1.0f);
```

Menus and Options

```
        volMusic = MathUtils.clamp(prefs.getFloat("volMusic", 0.5f),
           0.0f, 1.0f);
        charSkin = MathUtils.clamp(prefs.getInteger("charSkin", 0),
           0, 2);
        showFpsCounter = prefs.getBoolean("showFpsCounter", false);
    }
```

The `load()` method will always try its best to find a suitable and, more importantly, valid value. This is achieved by supplying default values to the getter methods of the `Preferences` class. For example, the call `getFloat("volSound", 0.5f)` will return a value of `0.5f` if there is no value found for the key named `volSound`. Before the value of the sound volume is finally stored, it is also passed to the `clamp()` utility method to ensure that the value is within the allowed range of values, which is `0.0f` and `1.0f` here.

Next, add the following code to the `save()` method of the same class:

```
    public void save () {
        prefs.putBoolean("sound", sound);
        prefs.putBoolean("music", music);
        prefs.putFloat("volSound", volSound);
        prefs.putFloat("volMusic", volMusic);
        prefs.putInteger("charSkin", charSkin);
        prefs.putBoolean("showFpsCounter", showFpsCounter);
        prefs.flush();
    }
```

The `save()` method is pretty straightforward as it just takes the current values of its public variables and puts them into the map of the preferences file. Finally, `flush()` is called on the preferences file to actually write the changed values into the file.

The second action is to create another class that abstracts all selectable character skins. Create a new file called `CharacterSkin` and add the following lines of code:

```
    package com.packtpub.libgdx.canyonbunny.util;

    import com.badlogic.gdx.graphics.Color;

    public enum CharacterSkin {
        WHITE("White", 1.0f, 1.0f, 1.0f),
        GRAY("Gray", 0.7f, 0.7f, 0.7f),
        BROWN("Brown", 0.7f, 0.5f, 0.3f);

        private String name;
        private Color color = new Color();
```

[252]

```
  private CharacterSkin (String name, float r, float g, float b) {
    this.name = name;
    color.set(r, g, b, 1.0f);
  }

  @Override
  public String toString () {
    return name;
  }

  public Color getColor () {
    return color;
  }
}
```

This class contains three distinct character skins, namely, White, Gray, and Brown. All character skins are defined using a name that is used for display and RGB color values to describe a color that will be used to tint the image of the character player.

Building the Options window

Make the following changes in MenuScreen to add the **Options** window layer:

```
import com.packtpub.libgdx.canyonbunny.util.CharacterSkin;
import com.packtpub.libgdx.canyonbunny.util.GamePreferences;

private Skin skinLibgdx;

private void loadSettings() {
  GamePreferences prefs = GamePreferences.instance;
  prefs.load();
  chkSound.setChecked(prefs.sound);
  sldSound.setValue(prefs.volSound);
  chkMusic.setChecked(prefs.music);
  sldMusic.setValue(prefs.volMusic);
  selCharSkin.setSelectedIndex(prefs.charSkin);
  onCharSkinSelected(prefs.charSkin);
  chkShowFpsCounter.setChecked(prefs.showFpsCounter);
}

private void saveSettings() {
  GamePreferences prefs = GamePreferences.instance;
```

Menus and Options

```java
    prefs.sound = chkSound.isChecked();
    prefs.volSound = sldSound.getValue();
    prefs.music = chkMusic.isChecked();
    prefs.volMusic = sldMusic.getValue();
    prefs.charSkin = selCharSkin.getSelectedIndex();
    prefs.showFpsCounter = chkShowFpsCounter.isChecked();
    prefs.save();
}

private void onCharSkinSelected(int index) {
    CharacterSkin skin = CharacterSkin.values()[index];
    imgCharSkin.setColor(skin.getColor());
}

private void onSaveClicked() {
    saveSettings();
    onCancelClicked();
}

private void onCancelClicked() {
    btnMenuPlay.setVisible(true);
    btnMenuOptions.setVisible(true);
    winOptions.setVisible(false);
}
```

The `loadSettings()` and `saveSettings()` methods are used to translate back and forth between the values stored in the widgets and the instance of the `GamePreferences` class. The methods starting with `on` in their name contain code that we want to be executed at certain events. The `onCharSkinSelected()` method will update the preview image. The `onSaveClicked()` method saves the current settings of the **Options** window and swaps the **Options** window for the menu controls. The `onCancelClicked()` method only swaps the widgets, which also means that any changed settings will be discarded. The visibility of the menu controls and the **Options** window is simply toggled by calling `setVisible()` on the respective widgets.

Next, make the following changes to the same class:

```java
private void rebuildStage() {
    skinCanyonBunny = new Skin(
      Gdx.files.internal(Constants.SKIN_CANYONBUNNY_UI),
  new TextureAtlas(Constants.TEXTURE_ATLAS_UI));
    skinLibgdx = new Skin
(Gdx.files.internal(Constants.SKIN_LIBGDX_UI),
  new TextureAtlas(Constants.TEXTURE_ATLAS_LIBGDX_UI));
```

```
    // build all layers
    ...
}

@Override
public void hide() {
  stage.dispose();
  skinCanyonBunny.dispose();
  skinLibgdx.dispose();
}
```

These changes enable us to use and add widgets defined in the LibGDX skin. As the creation of all the widgets for the **Options** menu involves quite a lot of code, we split it up into four separate build methods.

Now, add the `buildOptWinAudioSettings()` method to the same class:

```
private Table buildOptWinAudioSettings () {
  Table tbl = new Table();
  // + Title: "Audio"
  tbl.pad(10, 10, 0, 10);
  tbl.add(new Label("Audio", skinLibgdx, "default-font",
Color.ORANGE)).colspan(3);
  tbl.row();
  tbl.columnDefaults(0).padRight(10);
  tbl.columnDefaults(1).padRight(10);
  // + Checkbox, "Sound" label, sound volume slider
  chkSound = new CheckBox("", skinLibgdx);
  tbl.add(chkSound);
  tbl.add(new Label("Sound", skinLibgdx));
  sldSound = new Slider(0.0f, 1.0f, 0.1f, false, skinLibgdx);
  tbl.add(sldSound);
  tbl.row();
  // + Checkbox, "Music" label, music volume slider
  chkMusic = new CheckBox("", skinLibgdx);
  tbl.add(chkMusic);
  tbl.add(new Label("Music", skinLibgdx));
  sldMusic = new Slider(0.0f, 1.0f, 0.1f, false, skinLibgdx);
  tbl.add(sldMusic);
  tbl.row();
  return tbl;
}
```

Menus and Options

This method builds a table containing the audio settings. First, a label showing the text `Audio` in an orange color is added. Then, a checkbox (another label showing the text `Sound`) and a slider are added in the next row for the sound settings. This is also done for the music settings in the same way.

Next, add the `buildOptWinSkinSelection()` method to the same class:

```
private Table buildOptWinSkinSelection () {
  Table tbl = new Table();
  // + Title: "Character Skin"
  tbl.pad(10, 10, 0, 10);
  tbl.add(new Label("Character Skin", skinLibgdx,
  "default-font", Color.ORANGE)).colspan(2);
  tbl.row();
  // + Drop down box filled with skin items
    selCharSkin = new SelectBox<CharacterSkin>(skinLibgdx);

selCharSkin.setItems(CharacterSkin.values());

    selCharSkin.addListener(new ChangeListener() {
        @Override
        public void changed(ChangeEvent event, Actor actor) {
            onCharSkinSelected(((SelectBox<CharacterSkin>)
actor).getSelectedIndex());
        }
    });
  tbl.add(selCharSkin).width(120).padRight(20);
  // + Skin preview image
  imgCharSkin = new Image(Assets.instance.bunny.head);
  tbl.add(imgCharSkin).width(50).height(50);
  return tbl;
}
```

This method builds a table that contains the character skin selection via a drop-down box and a preview image next to it. A `ChangeListener` method is added to the drop-down widget `selCharSkin` so that the setting and preview image is updated by calling `onCharSkinSelected()` whenever a new selection occurs.

[256]

> Observe the highlighted code. This code will work in Android, iOS, and desktop, but might not work in an HTML project and will show `ArrayStoreException`. This is due to the GWT reflection. Alternately, we can substitute this part with the following code:
>
> ```
> Array<CharacterSkin> items = new
> Array<CharacterSkin>();
> CharacterSkin[] arr = CharacterSkin.values();
> for (int i = 0; i < arr.length; i++) {
>     items.add(arr[i]);
> }
> selCharSkin.setItems(items);
> ```

Next, add the `buildOptWinDebug()` method to the same class:

```
private Table buildOptWinDebug () {
  Table tbl = new Table();
  // + Title: "Debug"
  tbl.pad(10, 10, 0, 10);
  tbl.add(new Label("Debug", skinLibgdx, "default-font",
Color.RED)).colspan(3);
  tbl.row();
  tbl.columnDefaults(0).padRight(10);
  tbl.columnDefaults(1).padRight(10);
  // + Checkbox, "Show FPS Counter" label
  chkShowFpsCounter = new CheckBox("", skinLibgdx);
  tbl.add(new Label("Show FPS Counter", skinLibgdx));
  tbl.add(chkShowFpsCounter);
  tbl.row();
  return tbl;
}
```

This method builds a table that contains the debug settings. At the moment, we only have one checkbox here that allows the player to toggle and checks whether the FPS Counter is shown or not.

Next, add the `buildOptWinButtons()` method to the same class:

```
private Table buildOptWinButtons () {
  Table tbl = new Table();
  // + Separator
  Label lbl = null;
  lbl = new Label("", skinLibgdx);
```

Menus and Options

```
        lbl.setColor(0.75f, 0.75f, 0.75f, 1);
        lbl.setStyle(new LabelStyle(lbl.getStyle()));
        lbl.getStyle().background = skinLibgdx.newDrawable("white");
        tbl.add(lbl).colspan(2).height(1).width(220).pad(0, 0, 0, 1);
        tbl.row();
        lbl = new Label("", skinLibgdx);
        lbl.setColor(0.5f, 0.5f, 0.5f, 1);
        lbl.setStyle(new LabelStyle(lbl.getStyle()));
        lbl.getStyle().background = skinLibgdx.newDrawable("white");
        tbl.add(lbl).colspan(2).height(1).width(220).pad(0, 1, 5, 0);
        tbl.row();
        // + Save Button with event handler
        btnWinOptSave = new TextButton("Save", skinLibgdx);
        tbl.add(btnWinOptSave).padRight(30);
        btnWinOptSave.addListener(new ChangeListener() {
          @Override
          public void changed (ChangeEvent event, Actor actor) {
            onSaveClicked();
          }
        });
        // + Cancel Button with event handler
        btnWinOptCancel = new TextButton("Cancel", skinLibgdx);
        tbl.add(btnWinOptCancel);
        btnWinOptCancel.addListener(new ChangeListener() {
          @Override
          public void changed (ChangeEvent event, Actor actor) {
            onCancelClicked();
          }
        });
        return tbl;
    }
```

This method builds a table that contains a separator, and the **Save** and **Cancel** buttons at the bottom of the **Options** window. The **Save** and **Cancel** buttons use `ChangeListener`, which will call the `onSaveClicked()` and `onCancelClicked()` methods, respectively, whenever a click is detected.

Next, make the following changes to the `buildOptionsWindowLayer()` method:

```
    private Table buildOptionsWindowLayer() {
      winOptions = new Window("Options", skinLibgdx);
      // + Audio Settings: Sound/Music CheckBox and Volume Slider
      winOptions.add(buildOptWinAudioSettings()).row();
      // + Character Skin: Selection Box (White, Gray, Brown)
```

```
    winOptions.add(buildOptWinSkinSelection()).row();
    // + Debug: Show FPS Counter
    winOptions.add(buildOptWinDebug()).row();
    // + Separator and Buttons (Save, Cancel)
    winOptions.add(buildOptWinButtons()).pad(10, 0, 10, 0);

    // Make options window slightly transparent
    winOptions.setColor(1, 1, 1, 0.8f);
    // Hide options window by default
    winOptions.setVisible(false);
    if (debugEnabled) winOptions.debug();
    // Let TableLayout recalculate widget sizes and positions
    winOptions.pack();
    // Move options window to bottom right corner
    winOptions.setPosition
(Constants.VIEWPORT_GUI_WIDTH - winOptions.getWidth() - 50,
       50);
    return winOptions;
}
```

This method contains the code that initializes the **Options** window. It builds each part of the menu using the `build` methods that we just implemented before this one. The **Options** window is set to an opacity value of 80 percent. This makes the window appear slightly transparent, which adds a nice visual detail to it. The call of the `pack()` method of the `Window` widget makes sure that `TableLayout` recalculates the widget sizes and positions them so that all added widgets will correctly fit into the window. After this, the window is moved to the bottom-right corner of the screen.

Last but not least, make the following changes to the `onOptionsClicked()` method:

```
    private void onOptionsClicked() {
      loadSettings();
      btnMenuPlay.setVisible(false);
      btnMenuOptions.setVisible(false);
      winOptions.setVisible(true);
    }
```

Finally, the added code allows the **Options** window to be opened. The settings are loaded before the **Options** window is shown so that the widgets will always be correctly initialized.

Menus and Options

Here is a screenshot of the final **Options** window, menu screen, and the opened **Options** window:

The thin pixel lines that are drawn all over the widgets are the enabled debug visuals of `TableLayout`.

The **Options** window is now fully functional. It shows up when the **Options** button is clicked and hides when the **Save** or **Cancel** button is clicked. The settings are only applied and saved with a click on the **Save** button.

Using the game settings

A lot of work went into the creation of our menu screen and also into the **Options** window in order to allow the change of certain game settings. What is still missing is the actual usage of the set values in our game. Luckily, this can be achieved very easily now with just a couple of additional lines of code.

Add the following import line to `GameScreen`:

```
import com.packtpub.libgdx.canyonbunny.util.GamePreferences;
```

After this, make the following changes to the same class:

```
@Override
public void show () {
  GamePreferences.instance.load();
  worldController = new WorldController(game);
  worldRenderer = new WorldRenderer(worldController);
  Gdx.input.setCatchBackKey(true);
}
```

The added code ensures that the game screen will always work with the latest game settings. Next, add the following import lines to `BunnyHead`:

```
import com.packtpub.libgdx.canyonbunny.util.CharacterSkin;
import com.packtpub.libgdx.canyonbunny.util.GamePreferences;
```

After this, make the following change to the same class:

```
@Override
public void render (SpriteBatch batch) {
  TextureRegion reg = null;

  // Apply Skin Color
  batch.setColor(
    CharacterSkin.values()[GamePreferences.instance.charSkin]
  .getColor());

  // Set special color when game object has a feather power-up
  if (hasFeatherPowerup)
    batch.setColor(1.0f, 0.8f, 0.0f, 1.0f);

  // Draw image
  reg = regHead;
  batch.draw(reg.getTexture(),
    position.x, position.y,
    origin.x, origin.y,
    dimension.x, dimension.y,
    scale.x, scale.y,
    rotation,
    reg.getRegionX(), reg.getRegionY(),
    reg.getRegionWidth(), reg.getRegionHeight(),
    viewDirection == VIEW_DIRECTION.LEFT, false);

  // Reset color to white
  batch.setColor(1, 1, 1, 1);
}
```

Menus and Options

This will apply the correct skin color by tinting the image of the bunny head. Next, add the following import line to `WorldRenderer`:

```
import com.packtpub.libgdx.canyonbunny.util.GamePreferences;
```

After this, make the following change to the same class:

```
private void renderGui (SpriteBatch batch) {
  batch.setProjectionMatrix(cameraGUI.combined);
  batch.begin();

  // draw collected gold coins icon + text
  // (anchored to top left edge)
  renderGuiScore(batch);
  // draw collected feather icon (anchored to top left edge)
  renderGuiFeatherPowerup(batch);
  // draw extra lives icon + text (anchored to top right edge)
  renderGuiExtraLive(batch);
  // draw FPS text (anchored to bottom right edge)
  if (GamePreferences.instance.showFpsCounter)
    renderGuiFpsCounter(batch);
  // draw game over text
  renderGuiGameOverMessage(batch);

  batch.end();
}
```

This change will make the FPS counter appear only if the checkbox has been ticked in the **Options** window. Otherwise, the FPS counter will not be drawn to the scene.

Summary

In this chapter, you learned how to manage multiple screens and how to switch between them. We discussed what a scene graph is and how it basically works in LibGDX in conjunction with Scene2D UI, `TableLayout`, and skins to create complex user interfaces like the one we have now implemented in Canyon Bunny. You also learned how input events for widgets can be handled.

In the next chapter, you will learn how to enhance the visual appearance of the game. Among others, we will use particle effects and interpolation algorithms to achieve special effects.

8
Special Effects

In this chapter, you will learn to add special effects to Canyon Bunny using LibGDX's particle system, and learn about linear interpolation, and several other ways to enhance the visual appearance of the game. You will also design a custom particle effect in a graphical editor, which will serve as *dust*. This dust effect will be shown whenever the player character is running on rocks. You will be introduced to the concept of linear interpolation, using examples of smoothing the camera's movement while it is following a set target, as well as letting the rocks slowly bob up and down on the water.

In addition to this, you will implement a parallax scrolling effect for the displayed mountains in the background. The clouds will continuously move at random speeds from the right to the left of the level. The game's GUI will also be enhanced by adding some subtle effects for events where the player has lost a life or when the game score has increased.

In this chapter, you will learn to:

- Create complex effects using LibGDX's particle editor
- Add a dust particle to our bunny
- Smooth the movement of clouds and rocks using the **linear interpolation (Lerp)** operation
- Add some animations to show changes in the score and life of the player

Special Effects

Creating complex effects with particle systems

A particle system is a great way to simulate complex effects such as fire, smoke, explosions, and so on. Basically, a particle system consists of a number of images that are rendered using either a normal (alpha masked) mode, or an additive blending mode to create interesting results.

Take a look at the following screenshot to see the difference between normal and additive blending modes:

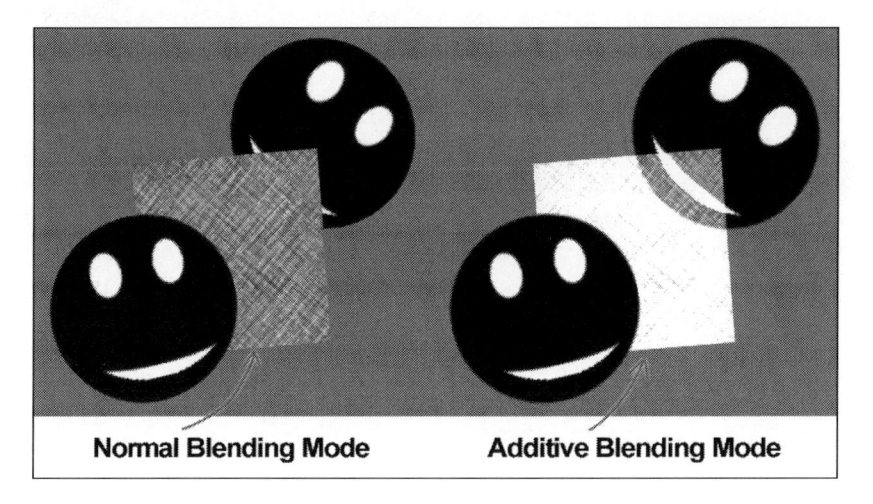

LibGDX provides a sophisticated particle system through its `ParticleEffect` class. It's merely a container that allows you to easily work with your final effects on a high level, such as setting the position or triggering or cancelling the designed particle effect.

The following is a brief description of the most important methods of `ParticleEffect`:

- `start()`: This starts the animation of the particle effect
- `reset()`: This resets and restarts the animation of the particle effect
- `update()`: This must be called to let the particle effect act in accordance to time
- `draw()`: This renders the particle effect at its current position
- `allowCompletion()`: This allows emitters to stop smoothly even if particle effects are set to play continuously

- `setDuration()`: This sets the overall duration the particle effect will run
- `setPosition()`: This sets the position to where it will be drawn
- `setFlip()`: This sets the horizontal and vertical flip modes
- `save()`: This saves a particle effect with all its settings to a file
- `load()`: This loads a particle effect with all its settings from a saved file
- `dispose()`: This frees all the resources allocated by the particle effect

Using an instance of `ParticleEffect` alone will not yield anything visible on the screen yet. This is because particles are represented as images and this class does not have such a reference to an image. Instead, an instance of the `ParticleEmitter` class is required, which among other attributes can take a reference to an image for the particles to be rendered. An emitter manages particles that use the same image. The particles of an emitter also share the same specific behavior, which is usually given in ranged values. These ranged values define the range to generate random values for each spawned particle, which will make the resulting effect look much more natural. If needed, several emitters can be added to a single effect in order to create more complex particle effects that use multiple images and collective behavior.

The following code is an example of how to create a particle effect with one emitter:

```
ParticleEffect effect = new ParticleEffect();
ParticleEmitter emitter = new ParticleEmitter();
effect.getEmitters().add(emitter);
emitter.setAdditive(true);
emitter.getDelay().setActive(true);
emitter.getDelay().setLow(0.5f);
// ... more code for emitter initialization ...
```

While there is absolutely nothing wrong with this approach in general, it is not recommended to initialize particle emitters in code. Emitters contain roughly 20 attributes that can be played with, so it is quite obvious at this point that this approach will lead very quickly to a lot of code snippets that are hard to understand and maintain. A much cleaner and fun solution is to use LibGDX's graphical particle editor in order to create new particle effects or modify the existing ones. The editor features a live preview of the current settings of the particle effect, which simplifies the design phase a lot. The preview gives direct feedback on the final result of the particle effect as well as how changed attributes alter the effect.

You can download and run the latest editor by entering `http://wiki.libgdx.googlecode.com/git/jws/particle-editor.jnlp` in your browser.

Special Effects

To know more about running the editor, check out this wiki article at
`https://github.com/libgdx/libgdx/wiki/2D-Particle-Editor`.

The following screenshot shows the **Particle Editor** window right after it was started:

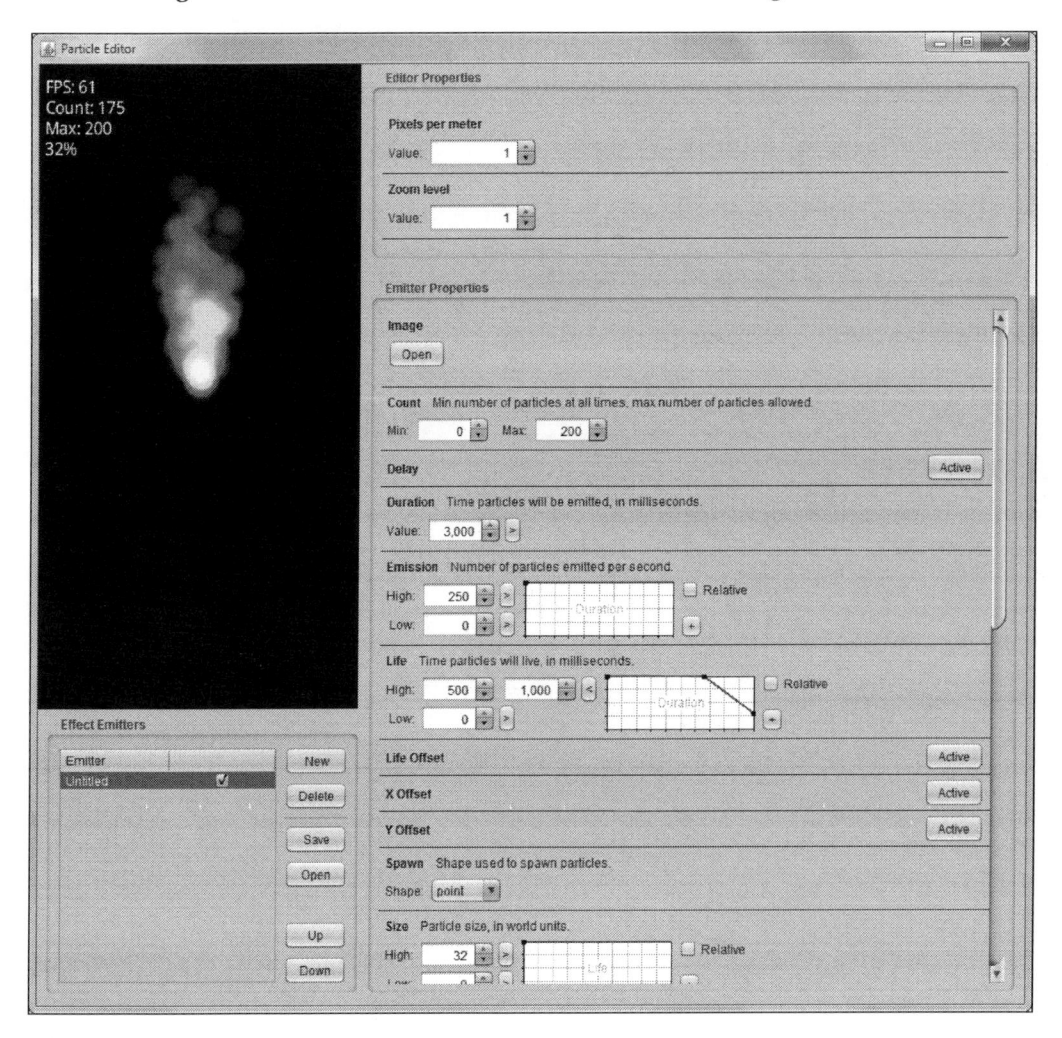

The live preview is located in the top-left corner and shows the current particle effect as well as some runtime information as follows:

- **FPS**: This gives the frames per second achieved
- **Count**: This gives the current number of particles in use

- **Max**: This gives the maximum number of simultaneously existing particles allowed
- **Percentage**: This gives the progress between the start (0 seconds) and the end (**Duration**)

The particle effect in the live preview can be moved around by clicking-and-dragging it with the mouse. This is a pretty neat feature not only because it allows adjustments to the effect's starting position, but also because it can be used to quickly check out how the effect behaves under non-stationary circumstances.

The bottom-left corner holds the already mentioned list of particle emitters. Emitters can be given a name, but this is completely optional. The checkmark next to an emitter's name toggles its visibility. However, take note that this is just an editor-only setting to make the editing of complex effects with many emitters a bit easier. The state of the visibility checkmark is also not going to be saved to the particle effect file. The order of emitters can be changed using the **Up** and **Down** buttons to the right of the emitters list. The rendering of the emitters list runs from the top to the bottom. This means that the last emitter in the list is also going to be the last, and therefore the most rendered emitter. New emitters can be added by clicking on the **New** button. Similarly, a click on the **Delete** button will remove the currently selected emitter from the emitters list.

The right-hand side of the particle editor is split into two framed parts that contain two types of properties. The upper one is labeled **Editor Properties**, which controls how the live preview is rendered. The **Pixels** per meter setting defines the dimensions just like we did for our game screen camera. The **Zoom** level setting is used to scale things either up or down depending on what can be seen in the live preview.

The last and biggest portion of the particle editor is contained in the frame labeled **Emitter Properties**. It controls everything about how the particles of an emitter look and how they will behave over a period of time.

Here is a list of all the available properties and their meanings:

- **Image**: This is the image file that graphically represents the particle.
- **Count**: This is the minimum number of particles that will always exist at the start and the maximum number of particles that are allowed to exist at once. Keep in mind that the maximum value also affects the amount of preallocated memory.
- **Delay**: The emitter will pause for the given amount of time in milliseconds before it starts to emit particles. This setting must be activated in order to take effect.

- **Duration**: This is the amount of time in milliseconds during which particles will be emitted.
- **Emission**: This is the number of emitted particles per second.
- **Life**: This is the amount of time in milliseconds until a particle is destroyed.
- **Life Offset**: This is the amount of time in milliseconds that is used up of the particle's lifetime. This can be used, for example, to let a particle start at the middle of its life. All interim changes that would have normally been applied will be precalculated and set as the particle's starting state, such as the current displacement, the angle of rotation, and any change of color. This setting must be activated in order to take effect.
- **X Offset**: This is the horizontal displacement in world units of the particle from its emitter's position. This setting must be activated in order to take effect.
- **Y Offset**: This is the vertical displacement in world units of the particle from its emitter's position. This setting must be activated in order to take effect.
- **Spawn**: This defines the shape used to spawn particles. The available shapes are point, line, square, and ellipse. By default, it is point.
- **Size**: This is the particle's size in world units.
- **Velocity**: This is the particle's speed in world units per second. This setting must be activated in order to take effect.
- **Angle**: This is the particle's emission angle in degrees. This setting must be activated in order to take effect.
- **Rotation**: This is the particle's local rotation angle in degrees. This setting must be activated in order to take effect.
- **Wind**: This is the horizontal force applied to the particle in world units per second. This setting must be activated in order to take effect.
- **Gravity**: This is the vertical force applied to the particle in world units per second. This setting must be activated in order to take effect.
- **Tint**: This multiplies the colors of the particle's image with the set color. Therefore, using a monochrome-colored image is advisable for best tint results.
- **Transparency**: This is the particle's alpha or transparency value. This allows the particle to be anything between fully opaque and fully translucent. Moreover, multiple changes during a particle's life allows the fade-in and fade-out effects.

- **Options**: This contains the following five additional checkmarks to configure the emitter's behavior:
    - **Additive**: This option, if checked, will enable the additive blending mode.
    - **Attached**: This option, if checked, will allow the existing particles to follow the movement of its emitter.
    - **Continuous**: This option, if checked, will restart the emitter after its duration of time is over. Emitters that are not set to be continuous will only show up once at the beginning.
    - **Aligned**: This option, if checked, will add the particle's emission angle to its local rotation. This will turn the particle's image face in the same direction as it is moving.
    - **Behind**: This option, if checked, will set the corresponding marker flag to `true`. Otherwise, it is set to `false`. This is just a marker flag that can be queried by calling `isBehind()` to decide whether the emitter should be rendered behind or in front of something else.

Some of the emitter's properties contain charts. The x axis in a chart always represents the lifetime of a particle, while the y axis represents the percentage of each emitter property's actual value. A click on the chart adds a new node. Double-clicking on a node removes it again. Clicking-and-dragging a node moves it inside the chart.

The following screenshot shows a portion of the emitter properties:

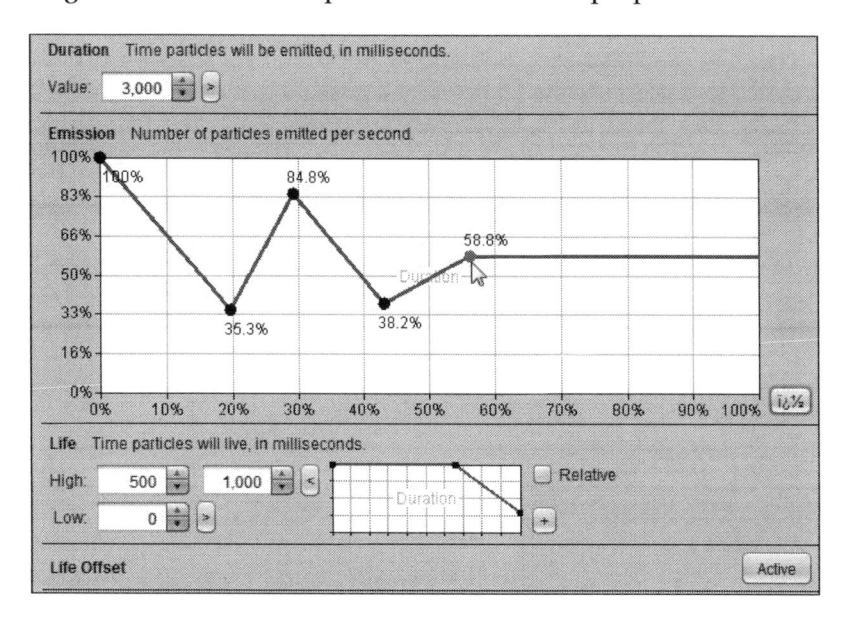

Special Effects

A chart can be expanded by clicking on the small **+** button next to it. The chart has a **High** and **Low** value, which defines the absolute values of 100 percent and 0 percent on the *y* axis in the chart. Most value fields have a **>** button next to them. Clicking on this button shows a second value field, which changes the single value to a ranged value. A ranged value has a minimum and a maximum value from which a random value is picked for each particle.

Adding a dust particle effect to the player character

We now want to create a dust particle effect that will appear whenever the player character runs on rocks. This effect will stop as soon as the player stops moving or if the player is no longer grounded on a platform.

First, we will need to design a custom particle effect that looks like dust. The following screenshot is an example of what we are aiming for:

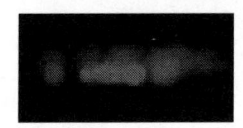

Open the particle editor to begin with the default fire particle effect and apply the following modifications to the editor and emitter properties:

- In **Pixels per meter**, enter 200 for **Value**
- In **Size**, enter 0.75 for **High**, enter 0 for **Low**, and enter (0,0), (67,28), (100,0) for **Chart**
- In **Velocity**, enter 1 to 5 for **High**, enter -1 to -5 for **Low**, and enter (0,50) for **Chart**
- In **Duration**, enter 100 for **Value**
- In **Emission**, enter 200 for **High**, enter 0 for **Low**, and enter (0,100) for **Chart**
- In **Life**, enter 250 to 500 for **High**, enter 0 for **Low**, and enter (0,100) for **Chart**
- In **Angle**, enter 0 for **High**, enter 0 for **Low**, and enter (0,100) for **Chart**
- In **Gravity**, enter 5 for **High**, enter -1 for **Low**, and enter (0,0), (67,28), (100,0) for **Chart**
- In **Tint**, enter 107 for **R**, enter 107 for **G**, and enter 107 for **B**

- In **Transparency**, enter (0,100) (100,0) for **Chart**
- In **Options**, select off for **Additive** and select **on** for **Continuous**

Next, click on the **Save** button to save the file and then place it at `CanyonBunny-android/assets/particles`.

> There is no official file extension for particle effects in LibGDX. Nonetheless, it does not do any harm to make things explicit and name files after their intended purpose. As `sfx` is a well-known abbreviation for sound effect, it makes sense to follow this scheme and adapt it to the particle effect; hence, the file extension used in this book is `.pfx`.

There is one more preparation required before we can start to implement the dust particle effect in Canyon Bunny. As you already know, particle effects are made out of images and so is our dust particle effect. You might have noticed that we skipped over that part to select a proper (another) image file for the dust particle in the editor. This is perfectly fine as we did not start from scratch, but instead used the already existing particle image from the default fire particle effect. Its file is called `particle.png` and can be found in the `assets` folder of the GDX tools. You can also download it from LibGDX's repository at https://raw.githubusercontent.com/libgdx/libgdx/master/tests/gdx-tests-android/assets/data/particle.png.

The `particle.png` image basically contains just a small, white circle that smoothly fades out from the center. The image should look like this:

Place the `particle.png` file in `CanyonBunny-android/assets/particles/` folder.

Next, add the following two import lines to the `BunnyHead` class:

```
import com.badlogic.gdx.Gdx;
import com.badlogic.gdx.graphics.g2d.ParticleEffect;
```

After this, add the following new line to the same class:

```
public ParticleEffect dustParticles = new ParticleEffect();
```

Special Effects

This is the variable where we are going to hold a reference to our loaded and ready-to-fire dust particle effect. Next, make the following modifications to the same class:

```
public void init () {
  ...
  // Power-ups
hasFeatherPowerup = false;
timeLeftFeatherPowerup = 0;

  // Particles
dustParticles.load(Gdx.files.internal("particles/dust.pfx"),
Gdx.files.internal("particles"));
}
@Override
public void update (float deltaTime) {
super.update(deltaTime);
  ...
dustParticles.update(deltaTime);
}

@Override
public void render (SpriteBatch batch) {
TextureRegionreg = null;

  // Draw Particles
dustParticles.draw(batch);

  // Apply Skin Color
  ...
}
```

As you can see, only a few changes were required to implement the dust particle effect in the game. The particle effect is loaded in `init()` and is continuously updated and rendered in `update()` and `render()`, respectively. However, calling `draw()` on a particle effect does not mean that it is always going to be rendered.

The particle effect needs to be triggered first to start playing. Furthermore, if it is a continuous particle effect, it also needs to be stopped explicitly to become invisible again.

To take care of this, make the following changes to the code in `updateMotionY()`:

```
@Override
protected void updateMotionY (float deltaTime) {
switch (jumpState) {
case GROUNDED:
jumpState = JUMP_STATE.FALLING;
if (velocity.x != 0) {
dustParticles.setPosition(position.x + dimension.x / 2,
position.y);
dustParticles.start();
    }
break;
    ...
  }
if (jumpState != JUMP_STATE.GROUNDED) {
**dustParticles.allowCompletion();**
super.updateMotionY(deltaTime);
   }
}
```

Here is a screenshot of the result in the game:

Special Effects

Moving the clouds

Our next enhancement will be to make clouds, which are just sitting in the air and move to the left. The idea here is to simulate some kind of wind property in the game world, while each cloud will also move at slightly different speeds to make their movement look more natural. In addition to this, there needs to be a condition to let more clouds appear at the right end of the level. Otherwise, the game will run out of clouds at some point. We could just take the easy route here and spawn a huge number, say 1000 clouds, but this is not very clever performance-wise, and this also does not tackle our original problem, that is, the game will run out of clouds at some point. So, a better approach to solve our problem is to keep the maximum number of existing cloud objects to a minimum.

Make the following changes to the `Clouds` class:

```java
private Cloud spawnCloud () {
  Cloud cloud = new Cloud();
  cloud.dimension.set(dimension);
  // select random cloud image
  cloud.setRegion(regClouds.random());
  // position
  Vector2 pos = new Vector2();
  pos.x = length + 10; // position after end of level
  pos.y += 1.75; // base position
  // random additional position
  pos.y += MathUtils.random(0.0f, 0.2f)
  * (MathUtils.randomBoolean() ? 1 : -1);
  cloud.position.set(pos);
  // speed
  Vector2 speed = new Vector2();
  speed.x += 0.5f; // base speed
  // random additional speed
  speed.x += MathUtils.random(0.0f, 0.75f);
  cloud.terminalVelocity.set(speed);
  speed.x *= -1; // move left
  cloud.velocity.set(speed);
  return cloud;
}
```

Next, add the following lines of code to the same class:

```java
@Override
public void update (float deltaTime) {
  for (int i = clouds.size - 1; i >= 0; i--) {
    Cloud cloud = clouds.get(i);
```

```
        cloud.update(deltaTime);
        if (cloud.position.x< -10) {
            // cloud moved outside of world.
            // destroy and spawn new cloud at end of level.
        clouds.removeIndex(i);
        clouds.add(spawnCloud());
        }
    }
}
```

The `spawnCloud()` method will now create a new cloud that also makes use of our simple physics simulation code we implemented earlier. The `update()` method iterates through all existing clouds, which in turn calls the `update()` method to let the physics move them. Afterwards, the cloud's new position is checked to see whether it has moved off screen. If a cloud fulfills this condition, it is removed from the list of current clouds and a new one is added and positioned at the right end of the level.

> The list of clouds in `update()` is iterated in reverse on purpose to avoid a so-called mutating list. Normally, you should never modify the list you are currently iterating over. However, when iterating backwards from the last to the first element, the removal of an object, like in our case, will only happen to elements that have already been processed.

Smoothing with linear interpolation (Lerp)

Lerp is a method to find unknown values between two known points. The unknown values are approximated through Lerp by connecting these two known points with a straight line.

Lerp operations can also be used to smoothen movements. We will show this using an example in which we will smoothen the camera's target-following feature as well as use it to make the rocks move up and down slightly to simulate them floating on the water. First, add the following line to the `CameraHelper` class:

```
private final float FOLLOW_SPEED = 4.0f;
```

Special Effects

After this, make the following modifications to the same class:

```
public void update (float deltaTime) {
if (!hasTarget()) return;

position.lerp(target.position, FOLLOW_SPEED * deltaTime);
   // Prevent camera from moving down too far
position.y = Math.max(-1f, position.y);
}
```

Luckily, LibGDX already provides a `lerp()` method in its `Vector2` class that makes Lerp operations easy to execute. What happens here is that we call `lerp()` on the camera's current position vector: a 2D coordinate, and pass it in a target position as well as a so-called alpha value. This alpha value describes the ratio between the current and the target positions. Remember that Lerp is virtually connecting the current and the target positions with a straight line and the alpha value determines the point on this very line. If the alpha value is equal to 0.5, it means that the new position is exactly in the middle of both the current and the target positions.

As these Lerp operations are executed inside `update()`, we expect very small increments in movement. The value of `deltaTime` is usually something around 0.016 seconds (16 milliseconds or 1.6 percent if interpreted in the context of a Lerp operation). We actually just use the `deltaTime` variable to make the Lerp operation time-dependent. It is a common misconception that the usage of `deltaTime` here means that the interpolated movement will happen in one second. Instead, the movement will start fast and slow down over time as the distance between the current and the target positions becomes smaller and smaller. This is why we also use a speed factor `FOLLOW_SPEED` that needs to be multiplied with `deltaTime` to speed things up a bit.

Letting the rocks float on the water

We will almost follow the same procedure here using Lerp operations to smoothly move all the rocks up and down to create the illusion of rocks floating on the water.

Add the following two import lines to the `Rock` class:

```
import com.badlogic.gdx.math.MathUtils;
import com.badlogic.gdx.math.Vector2;
```

After this, add the following lines of code to the same class:

```
private final float FLOAT_CYCLE_TIME = 2.0f;
private final float FLOAT_AMPLITUDE = 0.25f;
```

```
private float floatCycleTimeLeft;
private boolean floatingDownwards;
private Vector2 floatTargetPosition;
```

Next, make the following modifications to the same class:

```
private void init () {
dimension.set(1, 1.5f);

regEdge = Assets.instance.rock.edge;
regMiddle = Assets.instance.rock.middle;

  // Start length of this rock
setLength(1);

floatingDownwards = false;
floatCycleTimeLeft = MathUtils.random(0,
FLOAT_CYCLE_TIME / 2);
floatTargetPosition = null;
}
```

These changes make sure that the floating mechanism is correctly initialized. The starting value for the float direction is set to up; the cycle time is randomly picked between 0 and half of the maximum float cycle time. Using a random cycle time gives the floating effect a more natural look because every rock seems to move just on its own. The floatTargetPosition variable is used to store the next target position, as shown here:

```
@Override
public void update (float deltaTime) {
super.update(deltaTime);

floatCycleTimeLeft -= deltaTime;
if (floatTargetPosition == null)
floatTargetPosition = new Vector2(position);

if (floatCycleTimeLeft<= 0) {
  floatCycleTimeLeft = FLOAT_CYCLE_TIME;
  floatingDownwards = !floatingDownwards;
  floatTargetPosition.y += FLOAT_AMPLITUDE
* (floatingDownwards ? -1 : 1);
  }
position.lerp(floatTargetPosition, deltaTime);
}
```

Adding parallax scrolling to the mountains in the background

Parallax scrolling is a special scrolling technique that creates the illusion of depth in a 2D scene. Therefore, the objects in the background move slower than the objects in the foreground when the camera moves by.

We will now implement a parallax scrolling effect for the mountains in the background of the game screen.

Add the following import line to the `Mountains` class:

```
import com.badlogic.gdx.math.Vector2;
```

After this, add the following lines of code to the same class:

```
public void updateScrollPosition (Vector2 camPosition) {
position.set(camPosition.x, position.y);
}
```

Next, make the following changes to the same class:

```
private void drawMountain (SpriteBatch batch, float offsetX, float
offsetY, float tintColor, float parallaxSpeedX) {
TextureRegion reg = null;
batch.setColor(tintColor, tintColor, tintColor, 1);
floatxRel = dimension.x * offsetX;
floatyRel = dimension.y * offsetY;

  // mountains span the whole level
int mountainLength = 0;
mountainLength += MathUtils.ceil(
length / (2 * dimension.x) * (1 - parallaxSpeedX));
mountainLength += MathUtils.ceil(0.5f + offsetX);
for (int i = 0; i<mountainLength; i++) {
    // mountain left
reg = regMountainLeft;
batch.draw(reg.getTexture(),
origin.x + xRel + position.x * parallaxSpeedX,
origin.y + yRel + position.y,
origin.x, origin.y,
dimension.x, dimension.y,
scale.x, scale.y,
rotation,
reg.getRegionX(), reg.getRegionY(),
reg.getRegionWidth(), reg.getRegionHeight(),
false, false);
```

```
            xRel += dimension.x;
                // mountain right
            reg = regMountainRight;
            batch.draw(reg.getTexture(),
            origin.x + xRel + position.x * parallaxSpeedX,
            origin.y + yRel + position.y,
            origin.x, origin.y,
            dimension.x, dimension.y,
            scale.x, scale.y,
            rotation,
            reg.getRegionX(), reg.getRegionY(),
            reg.getRegionWidth(), reg.getRegionHeight(),
            false, false);
            xRel += dimension.x;
              }
              // reset color to white
            batch.setColor(1, 1, 1, 1);
            }
            @Override
            public void render (SpriteBatch batch) {
              // 80% distant mountains (dark gray)
            drawMountain(batch, 0.5f, 0.5f, 0.5f, 0.8f);
              // 50% distant mountains (gray)
            drawMountain(batch, 0.25f, 0.25f, 0.7f, 0.5f);
              // 30% distant mountains (light gray)
            drawMountain(batch, 0.0f, 0.0f, 0.9f, 0.3f);
            }
```

We have added a fifth parameter to `drawMountain()` that ranges between `0.0` and `1.0` and describes the distance and its scrolling speed. The scrolling depends on the camera's current position, which is then multiplied with the distance factor. This is the reason why we have also added a new method called `updateScrollPosition()`, which needs to be called in every update cycle where the camera can move.

Make the following changes to the `WorldController` class:

```
            public void update (float deltaTime) {
            handleDebugInput(deltaTime);
            if (isGameOver()) {
            timeLeftGameOverDelay -= deltaTime;
            if (timeLeftGameOverDelay< 0) backToMenu();
              } else {
            handleInputGame(deltaTime);
              }
            level.update(deltaTime);
```

```
    testCollisions();
    cameraHelper.update(deltaTime);
    if (!isGameOver() &&isPlayerInWater()) {
    lives--;
    if (isGameOver())
    timeLeftGameOverDelay = Constants.TIME_DELAY_GAME_OVER;
    else
    initLevel();
      }
    level.mountains.updateScrollPosition
    (cameraHelper.getPosition());
    }
```

All three mountain layers will now scroll at different speeds: 30 percent, 50 percent, and 80 percent.

Enhancing the game screen's GUI

The last part of this chapter is dedicated to two enhancements of the game screen's GUI. Firstly, we will add a small animation that gives visual feedback to the player when a life is lost. Secondly, a counting-up animation for the player's score will be implemented.

Event – player lost a life

We want to play a small animation in the event when the player has just lost a life. The extra lives are shown as bunny heads in the top-right corner of the game screen. These icons become dark one after another as soon as another life has been lost. The animation we are aiming for is a temporary bunny head icon on top of the just lost extra life. The temporary icon is going to be scaled up, rotated, and will have a slightly red tint.

The following screenshot is an example of the animation:

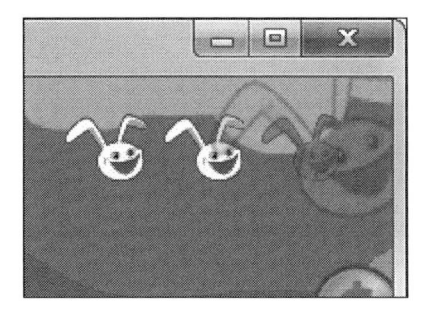

Add the following line to the `WorldController` class:

```
public float livesVisual;
```

After this, make the following changes to the same class:

```
private void init () {
Gdx.input.setInputProcessor(this);
cameraHelper = new CameraHelper();
lives = Constants.LIVES_START;
livesVisual = lives;
timeLeftGameOverDelay = 0;
initLevel();
}

public void update (float deltaTime) {
handleDebugInput(deltaTime);
if (isGameOver()) {
timeLeftGameOverDelay -= deltaTime;
if (timeLeftGameOverDelay< 0) backToMenu();
  } else {
handleInputGame(deltaTime);
  }
level.update(deltaTime);
testCollisions();
cameraHelper.update(deltaTime);
if (!isGameOver() &&isPlayerInWater()) {
lives--;
if (isGameOver())
timeLeftGameOverDelay = Constants.TIME_DELAY_GAME_OVER;
else
initLevel();
```

Special Effects

```
    }
    level.mountains.updateScrollPosition
    (cameraHelper.getPosition());
    if (livesVisual> lives)
    livesVisual = Math.max(lives, livesVisual - 1 * deltaTime);
    }
```

We have introduced a new variable `livesVisual` that will contain pretty much the same information as lives. However, `livesVisual` will only decrease slowly over time whenever the lives are decreased. This enables us to play an animation as long as `livesVisual` has not yet reached the current value of lives.

Additionally, add the following import line to the `WorldRenderer` class:

```
import com.badlogic.gdx.math.MathUtils;
```

Next, make the following changes to the same class:

```
        private void renderGuiExtraLive (SpriteBatch batch) {
        float x = cameraGUI.viewportWidth - 50
        Constants.LIVES_START * 50;
        float y = -15;
        for (int i = 0; i<Constants.LIVES_START; i++) {
        if (worldController.lives<= i)
        batch.setColor(0.5f, 0.5f, 0.5f, 0.5f);
        batch.draw(Assets.instance.bunny.head,
        x + i * 50, y, 50, 50, 120, 100, 0.35f, -0.35f, 0);
        batch.setColor(1, 1, 1, 1);
        }
        if (worldController.lives>= 0
        &&worldController.livesVisual>worldController.lives) {
        int i = worldController.lives;
        float alphaColor = Math.max(0, worldController.livesVisual
         - worldController.lives - 0.5f);
        float alphaScale = 0.35f * (2 + worldController.lives
         - worldController.livesVisual) * 2;
        float alphaRotate = -45 * alphaColor;
        batch.setColor(1.0f, 0.7f, 0.7f, alphaColor);
        batch.draw(Assets.instance.bunny.head,
         x + i * 50, y, 50, 50, 120, 100, alphaScale, -alphaScale,
        alphaRotate);
        batch.setColor(1, 1, 1, 1);
            }
        }
```

The added code will draw a temporary bunny head icon that is changed in its alpha color, scale, and rotation over time to create the animation. The progress of the animation is controlled by the current value in `livesVisual`.

Event – score increased

Every time the player collects an item, a reward is given that is added to the overall game score. The current score and a gold coin icon are shown in the top-left corner of the game screen. We want to add two subtle effects that begin to play when an increased score is detected. Firstly, we want the score to slowly add up to the new score. Secondly, the gold coin icon will shake a bit while the score is still adding up.

Here is a screenshot of the combined animation in five steps where some items have been collected:

Special Effects

Add the following line to the `WorldController` class:

```
public float scoreVisual;
```

Next, make the following changes to the same class:

```
private void initLevel () {
score = 0;
scoreVisual = score;
level = new Level(Constants.LEVEL_01);
cameraHelper.setTarget(level.bunnyHead);
}
public void update (float deltaTime) {
  ...
level.mountains.updateScrollPosition
(cameraHelper.getPosition());
if (livesVisual> lives)
livesVisual = Math.max(lives, livesVisual - 1 * deltaTime);
if (scoreVisual< score)
scoreVisual = Math.min(score, scoreVisual
+ 250 * deltaTime);
}
```

We introduced the new variable `scoreVisual`, which serves the same purpose as `livesVisual` does to control the progress of the score animation.

Additionally, make the following changes to the `WorldRenderer` class:

```
private void renderGuiScore (SpriteBatch batch) {
float x = -15;
float y = -15;
float offsetX = 50;
float offsetY = 50;
if (worldController.scoreVisual<worldController.score) {
long shakeAlpha = System.currentTimeMillis() % 360;
float shakeDist = 1.5f;
offsetX += MathUtils.sinDeg(shakeAlpha * 2.2f) * shakeDist;
offsetY += MathUtils.sinDeg(shakeAlpha * 2.9f) * shakeDist;
  }
batch.draw(Assets.instance.goldCoin.goldCoin, x, y, offsetX,
offsetY, 100, 100, 0.35f, -0.35f, 0);
Assets.instance.fonts.defaultBig.draw(batch,
 "" + (int)worldController.scoreVisual,
 x + 75, y + 37);
}
```

The value in `scoreVisual` is cast to an integer value to cut off the fraction. The resulting intermediate value will be the score that is shown in the GUI for the counting-up animation. To let the coin icon shake, we use a sine function with different factors as input angles to find the offset for the temporary displacement of the icon.

Summary

In this chapter, we used a variety of approaches to add our special effects, which let the game become more and more alive. You learned about particle systems and how they work in LibGDX. Particle effects can be easily designed using the powerful particle editor, and it is recommended to use this instead of working them out in code. You learned how a finished particle effect can be incorporated and controlled in our existing game. You also learned how to achieve a wind effect using our simple physics simulation to animate the clouds in the game world with just a few changes. An introduction to Lerp was provided and how it can be applied to create smooth movements for the game's camera and rocks that now appear to float on the water. Also, parallax scrolling was added to the mountains in the background to increase the game immersion even further. As a final touch, the game screen's GUI was enhanced with subtle effects.

In the next chapter, we will enhance the multiple screens management that was introduced in *Chapter 7, Menus and Options*. Therefore, we will implement a flexible system to easily create smoothly animated screen transitions that will upgrade the screen switching.

9
Screen Transitions

In this chapter, you will learn about screen transitions, a technique to create a smooth user experience, while switching from one screen to another over a certain period of time. You will be introduced to a technique known as **Render to Texture** (**RTT**) that allows easy composition of two individually rendered screens. Normally, transition effects make use of linear and nonlinear interpolation to create interesting and natural-looking results. LibGDX provides a class that implements a wide variety of common interpolation algorithms, which are suitable not only for transition effects but also for any values that should follow a certain behavior over time.

Moreover, in *Chapter 7, Menus and Options*, you learned how to create and manage several screens that can be shown and hidden using LibGDX's Game class. We will expand on this idea in this chapter by adding a feature to use transition effects for switching our screens. With reference to our game, Canyon Bunny, we are going to implement three distinct transition effects: fade, slide, and slice.

Adding the screen transition capability

We need to use an interface that all our screen transitions will implement. This will allow us to easily add new transition effects later on a modular basis.

Create a new file for the ScreenTransition interface and add the following code:

```
package com.packtpub.libgdx.canyonbunny.screens.transitions;

import com.badlogic.gdx.graphics.Texture;
import com.badlogic.gdx.graphics.g2d.SpriteBatch;

public interface ScreenTransition {
  public float getDuration ();
```

```
    public void render (SpriteBatch batch, Texture currScreen,
Texture nextScreen, float alpha);
}
```

The preceding interface allows us to query the duration of a transition effect and enables us to let it render its effect using two supplied textures that contain the images of the current and the next screens. In addition to this, the alpha value is used to describe the current state of progress of the transition effect that is to be rendered. Using an alpha value of 0.0, for example, will render the effect at the very beginning while a value of say, 0.25, will render it when the effect has progressed to 25 percent.

You might wonder why the `render()` method takes two instances of `Texture` instead of `AbstractGameScreen`. This is because, in general, a transition effect should not depend on the contents of the screens that it is working with. Therefore, both the screens, the current and the next one, need to be transformed into two self-contained units. This can be achieved by rendering each screen to its own in-memory texture. This technique is also known as RTT.

OpenGL has a feature called **Framebuffer Objects (FBO)** that allows this kind of offscreen rendering to textures present in memory. FBOs can be used by instantiating new objects of LibGDX's `Framebuffer` class.

The following is an example of how FBOs should be used in general:

```
// ...
Framebuffer fbo;
fbo = new Framebuffer(Format.RGB888, width, height, false);
fbo.begin(); // set render target to FBO's texture buffer
Gdx.gl.glClearColor(0.0f, 0.0f, 0.0f, 1.0f); // solid black
Gdx.gl.glClear(GL20.GL_COLOR_BUFFER_BIT); // clear FBO
batch.draw(someTextureRegion, 0, 0); // draw (to FBO)
fbo.end(); // revert render target back to normal
// retrieve result
Texture fboTexture = fbo.getColorBufferTexture();
// ...
```

A new FBO is initialized by passing in a format, a width and a height, and a flag indicating whether an attached depth buffer is needed. The passed format and dimensions are used to initialize the FBO's texture that will serve as its render target. The flag for the depth buffer, also referred to as the Z-buffer, enables the sorting of pixels in a three-dimensional space. Since we are creating a game in a two-dimensional space and also have taken care of the rendering order by ourselves, there is no need to enable this buffer, which would just waste precious memory.

As you can see in the preceding code example, rendering to an FBO is just a matter of calling its `begin()` method to temporarily redirect all subsequent draw calls to the FBO's texture buffer. The rendering to an FBO must always be finished by calling its `end()` method. Afterwards, the resulting texture can be retrieved by simply calling the `getColorBufferTexture()` method.

> In order to work with FBOs, your device needs GLES 2.0 hardware support. For simplicity, we assume full hardware support for GLES 2.0 in this book.

We will now make some mandatory changes to our platform-specific projects wherever needed to enable the OpenGL ES 2.0 mode so that we can use FBOs.

For the Android platform, make the following changes to the `AndroidManifest.xml` file of the `CanyonBunny-android` project:

```xml
<?xml version="1.0" encoding="utf-8"?>
<manifest
    xmlns:android="http://schemas.android.com/apk/res/android"
    package="com.packtpub.libgdx.canyonbunny"
    android:versionCode="1"
    android:versionName="1.0" >

    <uses-sdk android:minSdkVersion="8" android:targetSdkVersion="19" />
    <uses-feature android:glEsVersion="0x00020000"
    android:required="true" />
    ...
</manifest>
```

The `android:glEsVersion` value is used to specify the OpenGL ES version required by the app. To specify OpenGL ES version 2.0, you would set the value as `0x00020000`.

For the iOS platform, make the following changes to the `Info.plist.xml` file of the `CanyonBunny-robovm/CanyonBunny-ios` project:

```xml
<?xml version="1.0" encoding="UTF-8"?>
<!DOCTYPE plist PUBLIC "-//Apple//DTD PLIST 1.0//EN" "http://www.apple.com/DTDs/PropertyList-1.0.dtd">
<plist version="1.0">
<dict>
    ...
    <key>UIRequiredDeviceCapabilities</key>
    <array>
```

Screen Transitions

```xml
    <string>armv7</string>
    <string>opengles-2</string>
  </array>
  ...
</dict>
</plist>
```

> For the desktop and HTML5 project, no extra modifications need to be made as both of them by default use OpenGL ES 2.0 mode.

In *Chapter 7, Menus and Options*, you learned about LibGDX's `Game` class and used it to manage and switch back and forth between screens. We are now going to build a new class that expands on the idea of the `Game` class to support screen switching as well as an optional screen transition.

Create a new file for the `DirectedGame` class and add the following code:

```java
package com.packtpub.libgdx.canyonbunny.screens;

import com.badlogic.gdx.ApplicationListener;
import com.badlogic.gdx.Gdx;
import com.badlogic.gdx.graphics.Pixmap.Format;
import com.badlogic.gdx.graphics.g2d.SpriteBatch;
import com.badlogic.gdx.graphics.glutils.FrameBuffer;
import com.packtpub.libgdx.canyonbunny.screens.transitions
    .ScreenTransition;

public abstract class DirectedGame implements ApplicationListener
{
  private boolean init;
  private AbstractGameScreen currScreen;
  private AbstractGameScreen nextScreen;
  private FrameBuffer currFbo;
  private FrameBuffer nextFbo;
  private SpriteBatch batch;
  private float t;
  private ScreenTransition screenTransition;

  public void setScreen (AbstractGameScreen screen) {
    setScreen(screen, null);
  }
```

```
    public void setScreen (AbstractGameScreen screen,
       ScreenTransition screenTransition) {
      int w = Gdx.graphics.getWidth();
      int h = Gdx.graphics.getHeight();
      if (!init) {
        currFbo = new FrameBuffer(Format.RGB888, w, h, false);
        nextFbo = new FrameBuffer(Format.RGB888, w, h, false);
        batch = new SpriteBatch();
        init = true;
      }
      // start new transition
      nextScreen = screen;
      nextScreen.show(); // activate next screen
      nextScreen.resize(w, h);
      nextScreen.render(0); // let screen update() once
      if (currScreen != null) currScreen.pause();
      nextScreen.pause();
      Gdx.input.setInputProcessor(null); // disable input
      this.screenTransition = screenTransition;
      t = 0;
    }
  }
```

This new class is meant to work in a similar way to LibGDX's Game class. Therefore, DirectedGame implements the same interface (ApplicationListener) with its corresponding methods as well as the setScreen() method, which we are already using to switch our screens. Actually, there are two variants of this method in this new class: one that allows changing to a new screen with a transition effect and one without any effect similar to the original screen.

The setScreen() method, which takes an instance of ScreenTransition, initializes two FBOs for the current and the next screens on its first call. Then, a new transition is started by storing the next-to-be screen in nextScreen, which in turn is activated and initialized so that it becomes renderable.

Next, add the following code to the same class to implement the render() method of the ApplicationListener interface:

```
    @Override
    public void render () {
      // get delta time and ensure an upper limit of one 60th second
      float deltaTime = Math.min(Gdx.graphics.getDeltaTime(),
1.0f / 60.0f);
      if (nextScreen == null) {
        // no ongoing transition
```

```
          if (currScreen != null) currScreen.render(deltaTime);
        } else {
          // ongoing transition
          float duration = 0;
          if (screenTransition != null)
            duration = screenTransition.getDuration();
          // update progress of ongoing transition
          t = Math.min(t + deltaTime, duration);
          if (screenTransition == null || t >= duration) {
            //no transition effect set or transition has just finished
            if (currScreen != null) currScreen.hide();
            nextScreen.resume();
            // enable input for next screen
            Gdx.input.setInputProcessor(
                nextScreen.getInputProcessor());
            // switch screens
            currScreen = nextScreen;
            nextScreen = null;
            screenTransition = null;
          } else {
            // render screens to FBOs
            currFbo.begin();
            if (currScreen != null) currScreen.render(deltaTime);
            currFbo.end();
            nextFbo.begin();
            nextScreen.render(deltaTime);
            nextFbo.end();
            // render transition effect to screen
            float alpha = t / duration;
            screenTransition.render(batch,
  currFbo.getColorBufferTexture(), nextFbo.getColorBufferTexture(),
  alpha);
          }
        }
    }
```

Notice the call to the next screen's `render()` method to which the delta time of 0 is passed. This allows the next screen to update its internal state once for initialization purposes. After this, both screens are paused so that they do not make any progress in time as long as the transition effect is not finished. Also, the input processor is set to `null` to avoid any interference from a potential user input during a running transition. The desired transition effect, if any, is stored in `screenTransition` for future reference. Finally, the `t` variable is used to keep a track of the effect's elapsed time and always needs to be reset to 0 to let new transitions start from the beginning.

There are basically two ways in which the `render()` method works. In the first case, it will simply call the `render()` method of the currently set screen. This holds true as long as no next screen is set, which implicates no ongoing transition effect. Otherwise, it is assumed that there is an ongoing transition. In this case, `t` is increased by the current delta time to let the transition effect progress correctly in time. After this, the current and next screens are rendered to their designated FBOs. Then, the resulting two textures are eventually passed on to the transition effect's `render()` method to do something fancy with it. Finally, the screens are switched and the input processor is reactivated as soon as the value of `t` has reached the transition effect's duration. Also, `nextScreen` is set back to `null` so that the first way of rendering is used again.

> The delta time in the `render()` method of our new `DirectedGame` class is constrained to a maximum value of one-sixth of a second to ensure semifixed time steps in all our screens. We will use this from now on to avoid potential time-related problems that may arise from using variable time steps, which we used before.
>
> For a thorough explanation about various time stepping strategies, check out the following article on Glen Fiedler's blog http://gafferongames.com/game-physics/fix-your-timestep/.

After this, add the following code to the same class to implement the remaining parts of the `ApplicationListener` interface:

```
@Override
public void resize (int width, int height) {
   if (currScreen != null) currScreen.resize(width, height);
   if (nextScreen != null) nextScreen.resize(width, height);
}

@Override
public void pause () {
   if (currScreen != null) currScreen.pause();
}

@Override
public void resume () {
   if (currScreen != null) currScreen.resume();
}

@Override
public void dispose () {
```

Screen Transitions

```
      if (currScreen != null) currScreen.hide();
      if (nextScreen != null) nextScreen.hide();
      if (init) {
        currFbo.dispose();
        currScreen = null;
        nextFbo.dispose();
        nextScreen = null;
        batch.dispose();
        init = false;
      }
    }
```

The preceding code ensures that the current and the next screens will be informed about the occurring events and that the screens, the sprite batch, and the FBOs will be correctly disposed off when they are no longer needed.

As a last step, we now want to rewire some parts of Canyon Bunny to use the added screen transition capability, which we just implemented. Therefore, we are going to make some minor modifications in those places where we are still using LibGDX's `Game` class and replace it with our own class, `DirectedGame`.

Add the following import line to `AbstractGameScreen`:

```
    import com.badlogic.gdx.InputProcessor;
```

After this, add the following line to the same class:

```
    public abstract InputProcessor getInputProcessor ();
```

Next, make the following changes to the same class:

```
    protected DirectedGame game;
       public AbstractGameScreen (DirectedGame game) {
      this.game = game;
    }
```

These changes introduce a new method called `getInputProcessor()`, which also needs to be implemented in `MenuScreen` and `GameScreen`. This is necessary to allow `DirectedGame` to route and control the flow of input processing as needed. As mentioned earlier, this will avoid any interference with the user input during a running transition.

Now, add the following import line to `CanyonBunnyMain`:

```
    import com.packtpub.libgdx.canyonbunny.screens.DirectedGame;
```

After this, make the following changes to the same class:

```
public class CanyonBunnyMain extends DirectedGame {
   ...
}
```

Next, we are going to move on to MenuScreen. Make the following changes to this class:

```
public MenuScreen (DirectedGame game) {
   super(game);
}
```

After this, add the following code to the same class:

```
import com.badlogic.gdx.InputProcessor;

@Override
public InputProcessor getInputProcessor () {
   return stage;
}
```

Finally, remove the line that sets the input processor in show() so that it now looks as follows:

```
@Override
public void show () {
stage = new Stage(new StretchViewport(Constants.VIEWPORT_GUI_WIDTH,
Constants.VIEWPORT_GUI_HEIGHT));
   rebuildStage();
}
```

Next, we are going to move on to GameScreen. Make the following changes to this class:

```
public GameScreen (DirectedGame game) {
   super(game);
}
```

After this, add the following code to the same class:

```
import com.badlogic.gdx.InputProcessor;

@Override
public InputProcessor getInputProcessor () {
   return worldController;
}
```

Lastly, we are going to move on to `WorldController`. Add the following import line to this class:

```
import com.packtpub.libgdx.canyonbunny.screens.DirectedGame;
```

After this, make the following changes to the same class:

```
private DirectedGame game;

public WorldController (DirectedGame game) {
  this.game = game;
  init();
}
```

Finally, remove the line that sets the input processor in `init()` so that it now looks like this:

```
private void init () {
  cameraHelper = new CameraHelper();
  lives = Constants.LIVES_START;
  livesVisual = lives;
  timeLeftGameOverDelay = 0;
  initLevel();
}
```

Admittedly, the game code has been subjected to a number of small but important changes, which has led us to having a generic way of handling any kind of screen transition. You might want to test run the game so as to verify that screen switching is still working the same as before.

Implementing the transition effects

Now that we have established a generic way to describe and use screen transitions, we can now start to implement the transition effects that we want. However, let's take a quick look at interpolation first as this will greatly improve the overall look and feel of our transition effects.

Knowing about interpolation algorithms

In *Chapter 8, Special Effects*, we have already seen an interpolation algorithm called Lerp, which stands for Linear Interpolation. As the name implies, it calculates its interpolated values in an equal stepping from start to end. This works very well for any kind of constant movement. However, if we want to create more complex effects such as acceleration, deceleration, or maybe even both in a combination, we will need to use formulas that express these progressions as nonlinear curves.

Chapter 9

Luckily, LibGDX provides an `Interpolation` class that already implements many useful linear and nonlinear interpolation algorithms so that we can happily skip the math involved and just use it.

Take a look at the following diagram that shows individual graphs of each available interpolation algorithm:

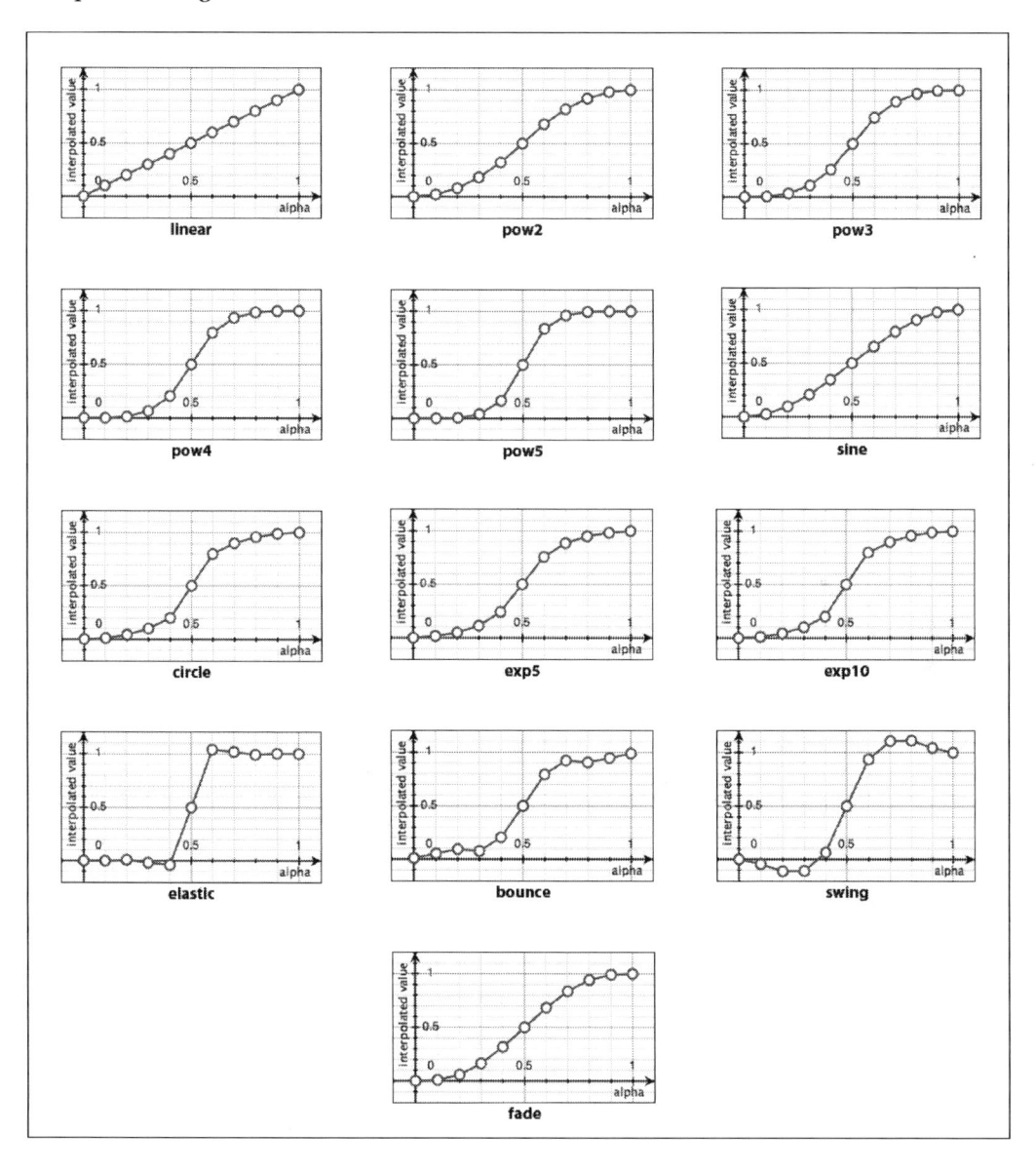

In Layman's terms, what can be seen in each graph is a kind of lookup table. The function of one of these algorithms takes the `alpha` value (*x* axis) as its input and outputs the corresponding interpolated value (*y* axis). The actual output simply depends on the algorithm's curve and what `alpha` value is used. The label below each graph also denotes the name of the method, which you will find in `Interpolation`. Also, note that each algorithm reverses its effect at an `alpha` value of `0.5`. There are variants of each method for an algorithm in case you may want to apply a certain effect on the first half (`alpha` from `0.0` to `0.5`) or on the second one (`alpha` from `0.5` to `1.0`) only. This can be achieved using the `In` or `Out` suffix, respectively, such as `fadeIn`, `pow4In`, and `swingOut`.

The basic usage of `Interpolation` looks as follows:

```
float alpha = 0.25f;
float interpolatedValue = Interpolation.elastic.apply(alpha);
```

This code example finds the interpolated value (*y* axis) for a given `alpha` value (*x* axis) of `0.25` using the elastic algorithm. Remember, the `alpha` value can also be interpreted as progress (here, 25 percent) of the overall effect.

With this in mind, we will now start to implement three distinct effects, namely fade, slide, and slice.

Creating a fade transition effect

We will now create a fade transition effect that we will use to switch from the menu screen to the game screen. In this effect, the next screen overlays the current screen while gradually increasing the next screen's opacity. The opacity will start at 0 percent (fully translucent) and end at 100 percent (fully opaque).

The following sequence of screenshots shows this effect:

Now, create a new file for the `ScreenTransitionFade` class and add the following code:

```java
package com.packtpub.libgdx.canyonbunny.screens.transitions;

import com.badlogic.gdx.Gdx;

import com.badlogic.gdx.graphics.GL20;
import com.badlogic.gdx.graphics.Texture;
import com.badlogic.gdx.graphics.g2d.SpriteBatch;
import com.badlogic.gdx.math.Interpolation;

public class ScreenTransitionFade implements ScreenTransition {
    private static final ScreenTransitionFade instance =
        new ScreenTransitionFade();

    private float duration;

    public static ScreenTransitionFade init (float duration) {
        instance.duration = duration;
        return instance;
    }

    @Override
    public float getDuration () {
        return duration;
    }

    @Override
    public void render (SpriteBatch batch, Texture currScreen,
        Texture nextScreen, float alpha) {
        float w = currScreen.getWidth();
        float h = currScreen.getHeight();
        alpha = Interpolation.fade.apply(alpha);

        Gdx.gl.glClearColor(0.0f, 0.0f, 0.0f, 1.0f);
        Gdx.gl.glClear(GL20.GL_COLOR_BUFFER_BIT);

        batch.begin();
        batch.setColor(1, 1, 1, 1);
        batch.draw(currScreen, 0, 0, 0, 0, w, h, 1, 1, 0, 0, 0,
            currScreen.getWidth(), currScreen.getHeight(),
            false, true);
```

```
        batch.setColor(1, 1, 1, alpha);
        batch.draw(nextScreen, 0, 0, 0, 0, w, h, 1, 1, 0, 0, 0,
            nextScreen.getWidth(), nextScreen.getHeight(),
            false, true);
        batch.end();
    }
}
```

First of all, notice how we were able to tuck away the render logic of our new transition effect in such a nice and compact manner. The `ScreenTransitionFade` class is built as a singleton so that it can be easily accessed from anywhere in the code without having to create and keep multiple instances of it. The `init()` method should be called before it is used. It takes one argument to define the duration of the effect. The `render()` method uses both the supplied textures to create the desired effect. It is achieved by first clearing the screen, followed by drawing the current screen's texture, and lastly by drawing the next screen's texture on top of the other. However, prior to the `draw` call of the next screen, we also change the drawing color. It is set to full white, and the `alpha` channel, which controls the opacity for each of the following `draw` calls, is set to `alpha`. The `alpha` variable contains the interpolated value where we have chosen to use the fade algorithm.

Finally, let the menu screen use the fade transition effect when the player clicks on the **Play** button. Add the following import lines to the `MenuScreen` class:

```
import com.packtpub.libgdx.canyonbunny.screens.transitions
    .ScreenTransition;
import com.packtpub.libgdx.canyonbunny.screens.transitions
    .ScreenTransitionFade;
```

After this, make the following changes to the same class:

```
private void onPlayClicked () {
    ScreenTransition transition = ScreenTransitionFade.init(0.75f);
    game.setScreen(new GameScreen(game), transition);
}
```

With these changes, the transition from the menu screen to the game screen will last for 0.75 seconds or 750 milliseconds until finished. You can start the game now and watch the transition live in action. Change the transition's duration to either slow down or speed up the effect.

Creating a slide transition effect

We will now create a slide transition effect that we will use to switch from the game screen to the menu screen. In this effect, the next screen slides in from the top edge and moves downwards until it is entirely visible.

The following sequence of screenshots illustrates this effect:

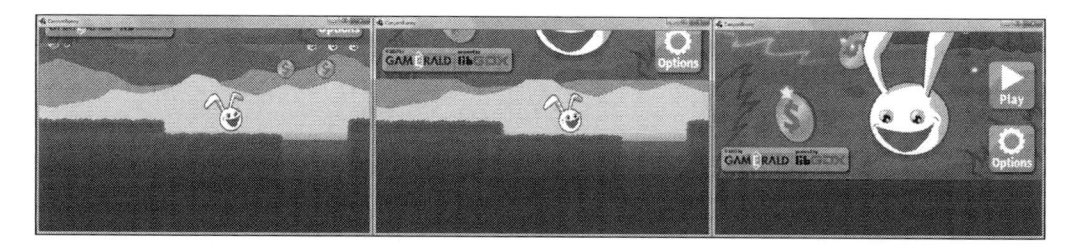

Now, create a new file for the `ScreenTransitionSlide` class and add the following code:

```
package com.packtpub.libgdx.canyonbunny.screens.transitions;

import com.badlogic.gdx.Gdx;

import com.badlogic.gdx.graphics.GL20;
import com.badlogic.gdx.graphics.Texture;
import com.badlogic.gdx.graphics.g2d.SpriteBatch;
import com.badlogic.gdx.math.Interpolation;

public class ScreenTransitionSlide implements ScreenTransition {
  public static final int LEFT = 1;
  public static final int RIGHT = 2;
  public static final int UP = 3;
  public static final int DOWN = 4;

  private static final ScreenTransitionSlide instance =
new ScreenTransitionSlide();

  private float duration;
  private int direction;
  private boolean slideOut;
  private Interpolation easing;

  public static ScreenTransitionSlide init (float duration,
int direction, boolean slideOut, Interpolation easing) {
```

```
            instance.duration = duration;
            instance.direction = direction;
            instance.slideOut = slideOut;
            instance.easing = easing;
            return instance;
        }
        @Override
        public float getDuration () {
            return duration;
        }
    }
```

The second transition effect is implemented in the same way as we did for "fade" as a singleton class. As you will see in a moment, this class is a little bit heavier because it not only allows sliding in another screen from the top edge, but also allows you to slide out the current screen to define the direction of movement. The `init()` method allows you to specify all these settings and also takes an interpolation algorithm that should be used.

Next, add the following code to the same class to implement the `render()` method of the `ScreenTransition` interface:

```
        @Override
        public void render (SpriteBatch batch, Texture currScreen,
            Texture nextScreen, float alpha) {
          float w = currScreen.getWidth();
          float h = currScreen.getHeight();
          float x = 0;
          float y = 0;
          if (easing != null) alpha = easing.apply(alpha);

          // calculate position offset
          switch (direction) {
          case LEFT:
            x = -w * alpha;
            if (!slideOut) x += w;
            break;
          case RIGHT:
            x = w * alpha;
            if (!slideOut) x -= w;
            break;
          case UP:
            y = h * alpha;
            if (!slideOut) y -= h;
```

```
      break;
    case DOWN:
      y = -h * alpha;
      if (!slideOut) y += h;
      break;
    }
    // drawing order depends on slide type ('in' or 'out')
    Texture texBottom = slideOut ? nextScreen : currScreen;
    Texture texTop = slideOut ? currScreen : nextScreen;

    // finally, draw both screens
    Gdx.gl.glClearColor(0.0f, 0.0f, 0.0f, 1.0f);

    Gdx.gl.glClear(GL20.GL_COLOR_BUFFER_BIT);

    batch.begin();
    batch.draw(texBottom, 0, 0, 0, 0, w, h, 1, 1, 0, 0, 0,
        currScreen.getWidth(), currScreen.getHeight(),
false, true);
    batch.draw(texTop, x, y, 0, 0, w, h, 1, 1, 0, 0, 0,
nextScreen.getWidth(), nextScreen.getHeight(),
false, true);
    batch.end();
  }
```

The render() method of this transition effect calculates the drawing order and position offsets for the current and the next screens using the direction, slideOut, and alpha variables. The value in alpha might be altered before it is used for calculations if an interpolation algorithm is set.

Finally, let the game screen use the slide transition effect when it wants to go back to the menu screen. Add the following import lines to the WorldController class:

```
import com.badlogic.gdx.math.Interpolation;
import com.packtpub.libgdx.canyonbunny.screens.transitions
    .ScreenTransition;
import com.packtpub.libgdx.canyonbunny.screens.transitions
    .ScreenTransitionSlide;
```

After this, make the following changes to the same class:

```
    private void backToMenu () {
      // switch to menu screen
      ScreenTransition transition = ScreenTransitionSlide.init(0.75f,
```

```
            ScreenTransitionSlide.DOWN, false, Interpolation.bounceOut);
      game.setScreen(new MenuScreen(game), transition);
}
```

It is highly recommended to take some time and play around with the constants for UP, DOWN, LEFT, and RIGHT, as well as to try different combinations of interpolation algorithms either doing a slide-in or slide-out movement.

Creating a slice transition effect

We will now create a slice transition effect that we will use at the start of the game. As you will see in a moment, we can also start a transition without a current screen to another (first) one, which is exactly what we are going to do when the game starts. In this effect, the next screen is cut in a number of vertical slices. These slices are then vertically moved off the screen to their respective starting positions. The starting position alternates between the top and bottom edges. Finally, each slice is moved in and over the current screen until it is entirely visible.

The following sequence of screenshots illustrates this effect:

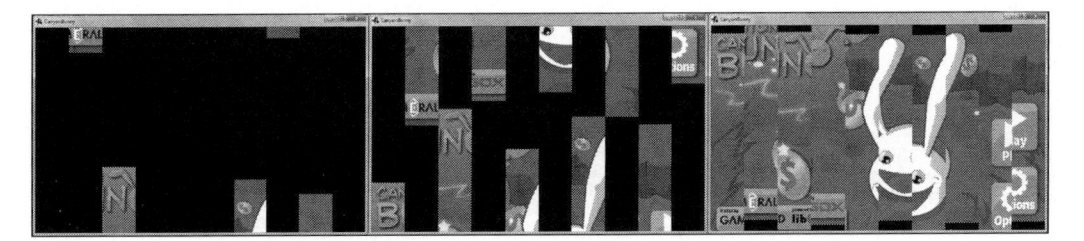

Now, create a new file for the ScreenTransitionSlice class and add the following code:

```
package com.packtpub.libgdx.canyonbunny.screens.transitions;

import com.badlogic.gdx.Gdx;
import com.badlogic.gdx.graphics.GL20;
import com.badlogic.gdx.graphics.Texture;
import com.badlogic.gdx.graphics.g2d.SpriteBatch;
import com.badlogic.gdx.math.Interpolation;
import com.badlogic.gdx.utils.Array;

public class ScreenTransitionSlice implements ScreenTransition {
    public static final int UP = 1;
    public static final int DOWN = 2;
```

```
  public static final int UP_DOWN = 3;

  private static final ScreenTransitionSlice instance =
new ScreenTransitionSlice();

  private float duration;
  private int direction;
  private Interpolation easing;
  private Array<Integer> sliceIndex = new Array<Integer>();
  public static ScreenTransitionSlice init (float duration,
int direction, int numSlices, Interpolation easing) {
    instance.duration = duration;
    instance.direction = direction;
    instance.easing = easing;
    // create shuffled list of slice indices which determines
    // the order of slice animation
    instance.sliceIndex.clear();
    for (int i = 0; i < numSlices; i++)
      instance.sliceIndex.add(i);
    instance.sliceIndex.shuffle();
    return instance;
  }

  @Override
  public float getDuration () {
    return duration;
  }

  @Override
  public void render (SpriteBatch batch, Texture currScreen,
      Texture nextScreen, float alpha) {
    float w = currScreen.getWidth();
    float h = currScreen.getHeight();
    float x = 0;
    float y = 0;
    int sliceWidth = (int)(w / sliceIndex.size);

    Gdx.gl.glClearColor(0.0f, 0.0f, 0.0f, 1.0f);
    Gdx.gl.glClear(GL20.GL_COLOR_BUFFER_BIT);
    batch.begin();
    batch.draw(currScreen, 0, 0, 0, 0, w, h, 1, 1, 0, 0, 0,
currScreen.getWidth(), currScreen.getHeight(),
false, true);
    if (easing != null) alpha = easing.apply(alpha);
```

```
      for (int i = 0; i < sliceIndex.size; i++) {
        // current slice/column
        x = i * sliceWidth;
        // vertical displacement using randomized
        // list of slice indices
        float offsetY = h * (1 + sliceIndex.get(i)
                            / (float)sliceIndex.size);
        switch (direction) {
        case UP:
          y = -offsetY + offsetY * alpha;
          break;
        case DOWN:
          y = offsetY - offsetY * alpha;
          break;
        case UP_DOWN:
          if (i % 2 == 0) {
            y = -offsetY + offsetY * alpha;
          } else {
            y = offsetY - offsetY * alpha;
          }
          break;
        }
        batch.draw(nextScreen, x, y, 0, 0, sliceWidth, h, 1, 1, 0,
            i * sliceWidth, 0, sliceWidth, nextScreen.getHeight(),
            false, true);
      }
    batch.end();
  }
}
```

The effect builds a random list of indices for each slice. The randomization is used to create a small vertical displacement for the slices so that they arrive at their target location at different times.

Finally, let the main class of Canyon Bunny use the slice transition effect when the game is started. Add the following import lines to the CanyonBunnyMain class:

```
import com.badlogic.gdx.math.Interpolation;
import com.packtpub.libgdx.canyonbunny.screens.transitions
    .ScreenTransition;
import com.packtpub.libgdx.canyonbunny.screens.transitions
    .ScreenTransitionSlice;
```

After this, make the following changes to the same class:

```
@Override
public void create () {
  // Set Libgdx log level
  Gdx.app.setLogLevel(Application.LOG_DEBUG);

  // Load assets
  Assets.instance.init(new AssetManager());

  // Start game at menu screen
    ScreenTransition transition = ScreenTransitionSlice.init(2,
ScreenTransitionSlice.UP_DOWN, 10, Interpolation.pow5Out);
    setScreen(new MenuScreen(this), transition);
}
```

Summary

In this chapter, you learned how to manage screen transitions in a generic way by separating the implementation details of the transition effects from the actual screens that should be rendered. You learned about OpenGL's FBOs, which allow you to render multiple screens to in-memory textures (RTT). Then, with the knowledge gained on how to use FBOs, we created a screen transition system that can apply any kind of transition effect while being completely independent of the screen's contents. We used LibGDX's Interpolation class, which comes with a pool of 13 ready-to-use interpolation algorithms. Finally, we discussed and implemented the three transition effects.

In the next chapter, you will learn how to create sound effects using several sound generators. Furthermore, we will add background music and create an audio manager using the LibGDX Audio API to easily manage music and sound effects in the game.

10
Managing the Music and Sound Effects

In this chapter, you will learn how to manage your music and sound effects. LibGDX provides you with four interfaces to handle different types of audio data. The first two interfaces that we will discuss are targeted at playing back prerecorded audio files. The two remaining interfaces give us even more low-level access to the audio device. They can be used to record and play back raw samples of audio data, which is a so-called **Pulse Code Modulation** (**PCM**) encoded audio signal. Next, we will take a look at the great world of sound generators. These tools are extremely handy as they allow you to quickly create new sound effects in a short period of time.

Lastly, looping background music and some sound effects for certain in-game events will be added to Canyon Bunny. The game's audio settings can be changed in the options menu of the menu screen through two new checkboxes and sliders for music and sound effects.

Playing back the music and sound effects

LibGDX provides cross-platform audio playback for prerecorded audio files of the following three supported file formats:

- `.wav` (RIFF WAVE)
- `.mp3` (MPEG-2 Audio Layer III)
- `.ogg` (Ogg Vorbis)

> However, Ogg support is not available for the robovm version because iOS doesn't support it.

There are two interfaces, namely `Music` and `Sound`. They serve two different use cases of playing back audio files. In terms of LibGDX, sounds are audio files that usually play no longer than one second; think of laser or machine gun sounds. Audio files used as `Sound` objects are loaded and decoded so that they can be directly sent to the audio device. Obviously, the decoded audio data kept in memory can heavily increase the overall memory usage. On the contrary, audio files are used as the `Music` objects are streamed, which means that only the necessary portion of it is decoded and held in memory. Therefore, the `Music` objects should be used for playing long audio files, such as background music.

> The `Music` objects may require more CPU cycles because the streamed audio data needs to be decoded before it can be sent to the audio device. This is not the case with the `Sound` objects because they are already decoded upon loading. So, it is simply a trade-off between performance and memory usage.

The next sections will give you an overview of LibGDX's `Sound` and `Music` interfaces.

Exploring the Sound interface

The `Sound` interface is suitable for playing back short audio files. New sound instances can be requested from LibGDX's `Gdx.audio` module using the `newSound()` method as follows:

```
Sound sound = Gdx.audio.newSound(
  Gdx.files.internal("sound.wav"));
```

This line of code will allocate new memory for the decoded audio data of the `sound.wav` file. The `Sound` interface also makes use of the `Disposable` interface, which implicates that the allocated resources need to be disposed manually using the respective `dispose()` method when a sound instance is no longer needed, as shown in the following code snippet:

```
sound.dispose(); // free allocated memory
```

Calling the `play()` method of a sound instance will start the playback of its audio data and will return an ID that is associated with the sound that is being played. A sound ID can be used to refer to a specific playing sound. This allows you to control sounds at a later time, such as stopping the playback and changing the volume, pitch, and pan.

> LibGDX will silently ignore any requests to a referred sound if that sound is no longer playing.

There are several overloaded methods to start playing a sound for a single time or in an endless loop. Optionally, values for the sound's volume, pitch, and pan can also be passed as shown here:

```
long play();
long play(float volume);
long play(float volume, float pitch, float pan);
long loop();
long loop(float volume);
long loop(float volume, float pitch, float pan);
```

The value for volume ranges between 0.0 and 1.0, where higher values result in louder audio signals. Sounds can be pitched up and down resulting in lower or higher frequency audio signals, respectively. A pitch value of 1.0 will play the sound at its normal speed. Pitch values above 1.0 will let the sound play faster, while values below 1.0 will result in slower playback. A pan value of 0.0 will play the sound equally loud on the left and right audio channels, which is also referred to as the center. Negative pan values will play the sound only on the left audio channel whereas positive pan values will achieve the opposite.

Consider a scenario where we have two sounds, one for a cat and the other for a dog. Both sounds will be loaded in LibGDX as separate sound instances that can be used to play back several copies of them in parallel. To stop all playing copies of a (cat or dog) sound instance, the stop() method can be called. Alternatively, a sound ID can be passed to the stop() method to stop a specific copy of the (cat or dog) sound instance only, as shown here:

```
void stop();
void stop(long soundId);
```

Sounds that are currently playing can be modified using their sound ID and one of the following methods:

```
void setVolume(long soundId, float volume);
void setPan(long soundId, float pan, float volume);
void setPitch(long soundId, float pitch);
void setLooping(long soundId, boolean looping);
```

Exploring the Music interface

The `Music` interface is suitable for playing back long audio files and is designed in a very similar way when compared with the `Sound` interface. Therefore, new music instances can also be requested from LibGDX's `Gdx.audio` module; however, the method is called `newMusic()`, as shown here:

```
Music music = Gdx.audio.newMusic(Gdx.files.internal("music.mp3"));
```

The `Music` interface also makes use of the `Disposable` interface. The music instances that are no longer needed should always be disposed to free the allocated memory as follows:

```
music.dispose(); // free allocated memory
```

Apart from this, the interface provides the expected method to control music playback as follows:

```
void play();
void pause();
void stop();
```

Additionally, there are some methods to modify the music being played, as shown in the following listing:

```
void setPan(float pan, float volume);
void setVolume(float volume);
void setLooping(boolean isLooping);
```

At times, it might be useful to query the music for its state, such as its current position (in milliseconds) and whether it is still playing or not, as follows:

```
boolean isPlaying();
float getPosition();
```

Accessing the audio device directly

In addition to the `Music` and `Sound` interfaces, LibGDX also provides you with two more low-level audio interfaces, `AudioDevice` and `AudioRecorder`, that enable direct access to the audio device. They can be used for recording and playback of raw samples of audio data. These samples are stored as a PCM-encoded audio signal.

> These direct access features are currently unavailable in HTML5/GWT applications.

Exploring the AudioDevice interface

The `AudioDevice` interface allows you to send PCM-encoded audio samples directly to the audio device. For this to work, a new audio device can be requested using LibGDX's `Gdx.audio` module and called by its `newAudioDevice()` method as follows:

```
AudioDevice audioDevice =
Gdx.audio.newAudioDevice(44100, false);
```

The preceding line of code allocates a new instance of an audio device with a sample rate of 44.1 kHz in stereo mode. Requested instances of `AudioDevice` need to be disposed using the `dispose()` method when they are no longer needed in order to avoid memory leaks, as follows:

```
audioDevice.dispose(); // free allocated memory
```

New audio data can be sent to an audio device either using an array of floats or an array of 16-bit signed shorts, as shown here:

```
void writeSamples(float[] samples, int offset, int numSamples);
void writeSamples(short[] samples, int offset, int numSamples);
```

The `offset` (start) and `numSamples` (length) parameters are used to define the range of samples that will be sent to the audio device.

> Using an audio device with stereo mode enabled implies that the number of samples needs to be doubled as there are two separate audio channels to be fed with the audio data. Stereo samples are interleaved, starting with the left channel followed by the right channel; for example, to create a sound that will last for exactly one second at a sample rate of 44.1 kHz will require a total number of 44,100 samples in mono mode and 88,200 samples in stereo mode.

Exploring the AudioRecorder interface

The `AudioRecorder` interface allows you to record samples in a 16-bit PCM format using a connected microphone. New instances of `AudioRecorder` can be requested using LibGDX's `Gdx.audio` module and by calling its `newAudioRecorder()` method as follows:

```
AudioRecorder audioRecordedr =
Gdx.audio.newAudioRecorder(44100, false);
```

Basically, `AudioRecorder` works nearly the same as `AudioDevice` except that it captures samples. As always, the unused instances need to be disposed in order to avoid memory leaks, as shown here:

```
audioRecorder.dispose(); // free allocated memory
```

To record samples with the audio recorder, all that is needed is an array into which the captured samples will be stored:

```
void read(short[] samples, int offset, int numSamples);
```

The `offset` (start) and `numSamples` (length) parameters are used to define which samples in the `samples` target array will be overwritten with new data.

Using sound generators

Until now, you learned about direct access to the audio device in LibGDX, and you now know how to write audio samples to it. Sure enough, you could now (try to) write your own sound generator class from here and feed one of LibGDX's audio device instances with the resulting audio samples. However, audio programming is beyond the scope of this book, and it is also a very advanced topic even for seasoned programmers.

A viable solution to get hold of some nice sound effects is to use one of the existing sound generators, which are free and open source. One of these sound generators is **sfxr**, which was originally developed by Tomas "DrPetter" Pettersson in 2007. Over the time, several sfxr variants, such as **bfxr**, **cfxr**, and **as3sfxr**, have emerged.

The sfxr generator

The sfxr sound generator quickly became widespread among independent game developers everywhere because it simplified the creation of new sounds just by clicking on the **RANDOMIZE** button. Naturally, all other parameters used to create a sound are tweakable to allow fine-tuning. Also, simple means are provided to get the basic sound effects into games through presets as buttons to the left of the program GUI, such as **PICKUP/COIN**, **LASER/SHOOT**, **EXPLOSION**, **POWERUP**, **HIT/HURT**, **JUMP**, and **BLIP/SELECT**, as shown in the following screenshot. If you like a generated sound effect, you can export it to a `.wav` file to be used in your game.

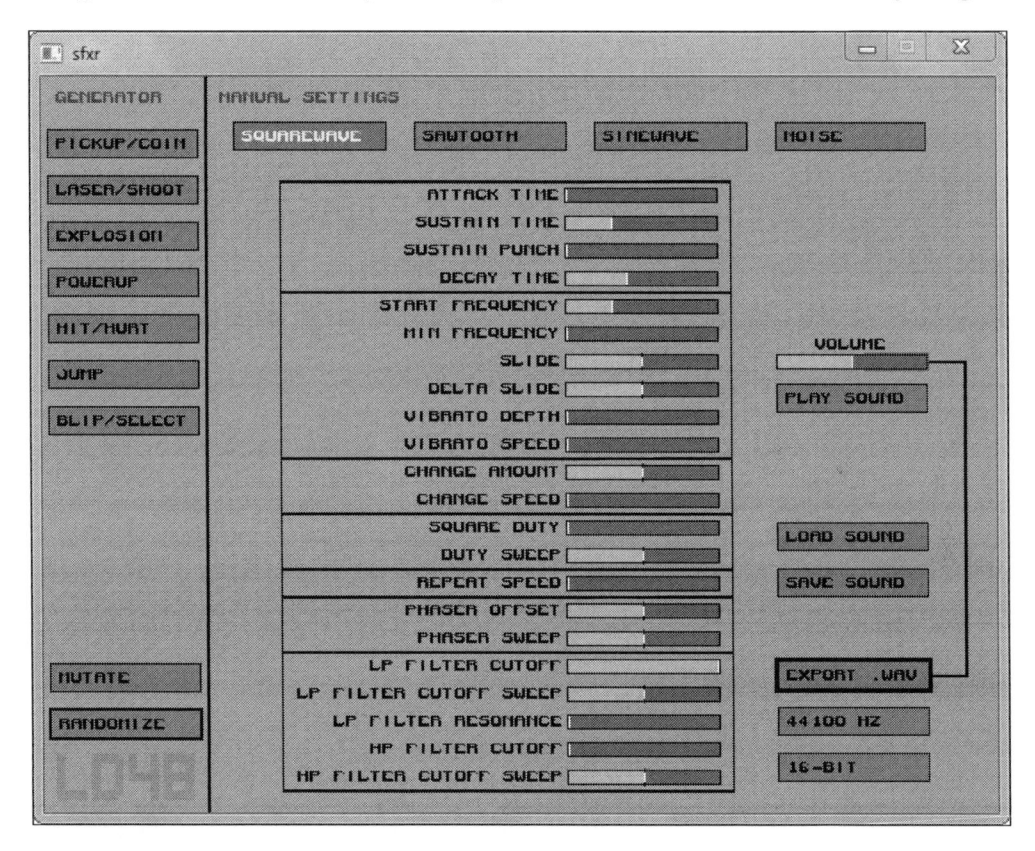

The official source code repository of sfxr can be found at `https://code.google.com/p/sfxr/`.

A web version is also available at `http://www.superflashbros.net/as3sfxr/`.

Managing the Music and Sound Effects

The cfxr generator

The cfxr sound generator was originally developed by Joachim Bengtsson in 2008. It is based on sfxr and was ported to Mac OS as a native Cocoa application, and hence the name cfxr (Cocoa sfxr). A history list was added with the possibility to rate each generated sound effect by the user. This also allows you to easily flip through a couple of sounds and jump back to previous ones if needed. The following screenshot shows the interface of the cfxr generator:

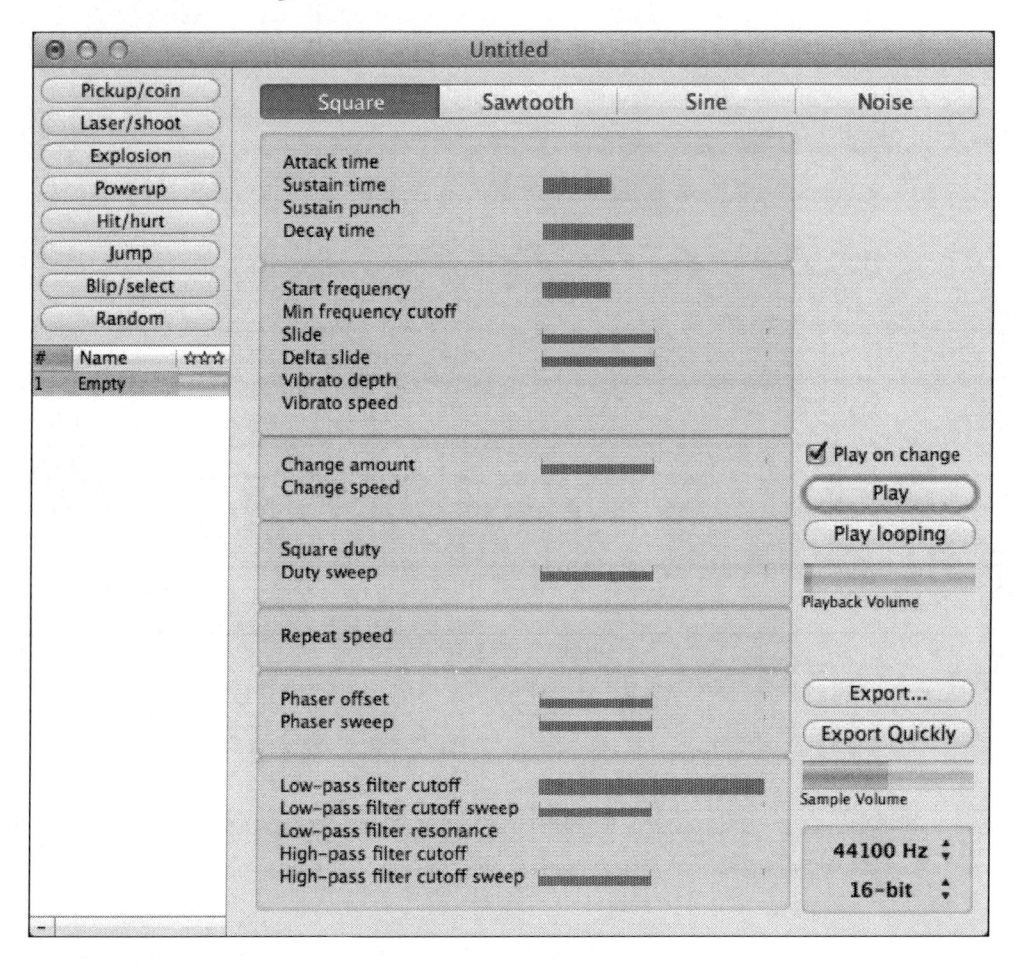

The official source code repository of cfxr can be found at `https://github.com/nevyn/cfxr/`.

The bfxr generator

This sound generator was originally developed by Stephen "Increpare" Lavelle. It appears to be the most advanced version of that time. Some additional waveforms as well as a mixer have been added to create more complex sounds. The created sounds can be saved to and loaded from files, which is a useful feature that is available in neither sfxr nor cfxr. Additionally, the lock symbol next to each parameter can be used to avoid any further changes to them while using the **Randomize** and **Mutation** buttons, as shown in the following screenshot:

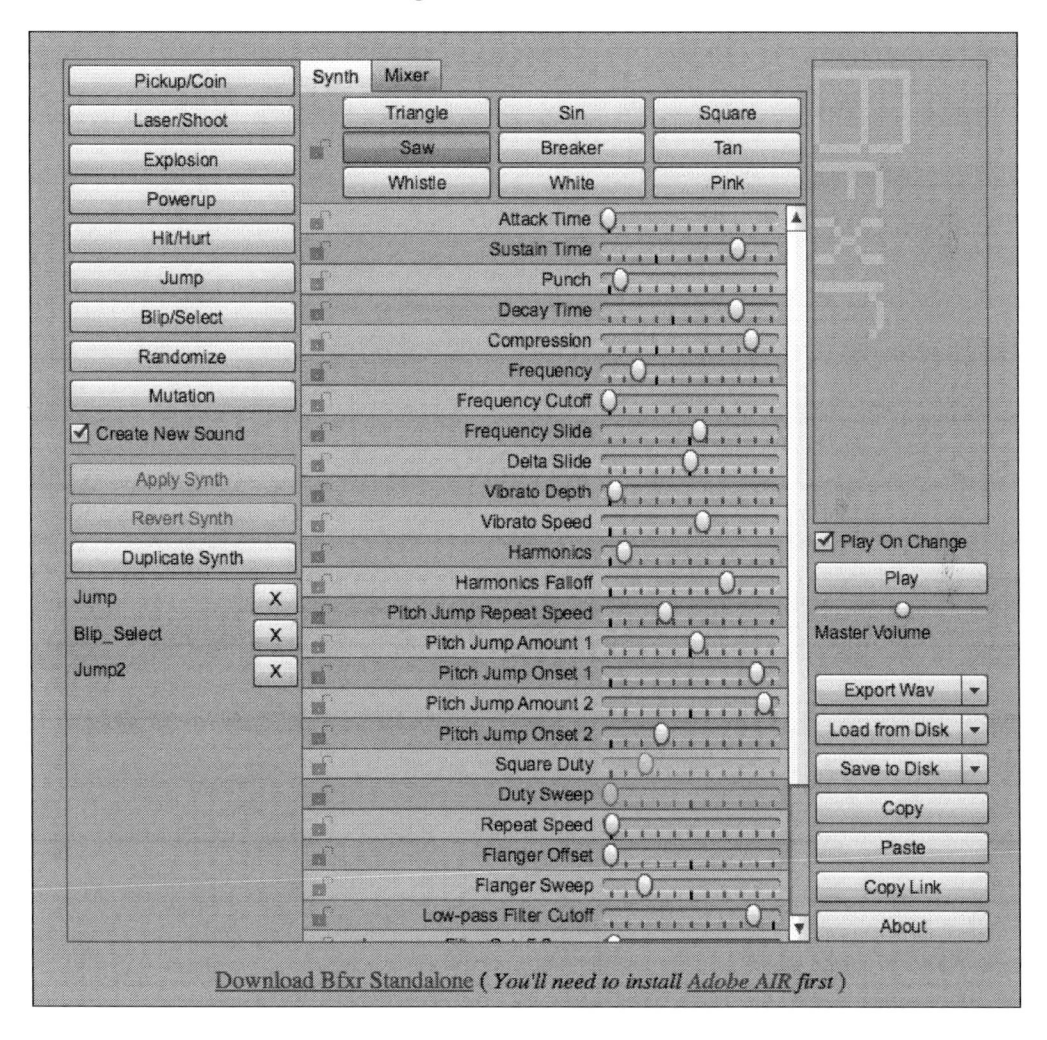

The official source code repository of bfxr can be found at `https://github.com/increpare/bfxr/`.

Adding music and sounds to Canyon Bunny

Let's now add some music and sound effects to our game. First, we need to know what audio files are needed and then copy them to our `assets` folder.

> All assets shown and discussed in this book, including any other project files, are provided in the code bundle, which can be downloaded from the Packt Publishing website.

The next two tables contain descriptions of each audio file and their function in Canyon Bunny.

For sounds (generated with bfxr), refer to the following table:

Filename	Event
`jump.wav`	When the player jumps
`jump_with_feather.wav`	When the player jumps in mid-air (requires an active feather power-up)
`pickup_coin.wav`	When the player picks up a gold coin
`pickup_feather.wav`	When the player picks up a feather power-up
`live_lost.wav`	When the player loses a life (for example, the player falls down into the water)

For music (provided by Klaus "keith303" Spang), refer to the following table:

Filename	Event
`keith303_-_brand_new_highscore.mp3`	When the application starts (indefinitely looping background music)

Now, add all these files to `CanyonBunny-android/assets/`. Split up the audio files by placing them either in the `music` or `sound` subfolder. The following screenshot shows how the final structure of your `assets` folder should look:

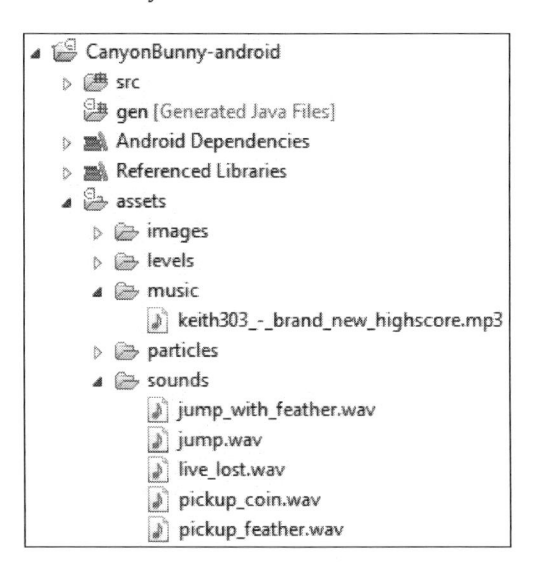

```
CanyonBunny-android
├── src
├── gen [Generated Java Files]
├── Android Dependencies
├── Referenced Libraries
└── assets
    ├── images
    ├── levels
    ├── music
    │   └── keith303_-_brand_new_highscore.mp3
    ├── particles
    └── sounds
        ├── jump_with_feather.wav
        ├── jump.wav
        ├── live_lost.wav
        ├── pickup_coin.wav
        └── pickup_feather.wav
```

After this, we need to update our `Assets` class in order to make the audio files accessible in the same way as the rest of our assets. We will also use `AssetManager` to let LibGDX handle the loading and unloading processes of the music and sound files.

Add the following two import lines to the `Assets` class:

```
import com.badlogic.gdx.audio.Music;
import com.badlogic.gdx.audio.Sound;
```

Then, add the following code to the same class:

```
public AssetSounds sounds;
public AssetMusic music;

public class AssetSounds {
  public final Sound jump;
  public final Sound jumpWithFeather;
  public final Sound pickupCoin;
  public final Sound pickupFeather;
  public final Sound liveLost;
  public AssetSounds (AssetManager am) {
    jump = am.get("sounds/jump.wav", Sound.class);
```

Managing the Music and Sound Effects

```java
    jumpWithFeather = am.get("sounds/jump_with_feather.wav",
Sound.class);
    pickupCoin = am.get("sounds/pickup_coin.wav", Sound.class);
    pickupFeather = am.get("sounds/pickup_feather.wav",
Sound.class);
    liveLost = am.get("sounds/live_lost.wav", Sound.class);
  }
}
public class AssetMusic {
  public final Music song01;
  public AssetMusic (AssetManager am) {
    song01 = am.get("music/keith303_-_brand_new_highscore.mp3",
Music.class);
  }
}
```

This adds the two new inner classes, `AssetSounds` and `AssetMusic`, which will hold the loaded instances of the music and sound effects. Next, make the following changes to the same class:

```java
public void init (AssetManager assetManager) {
  this.assetManager = assetManager;
  // set asset manager error handler
  assetManager.setErrorListener(this);
  // load texture atlas
  assetManager.load(Constants.TEXTURE_ATLAS_OBJECTS,
TextureAtlas.class);
  // load sounds
  assetManager.load("sounds/jump.wav", Sound.class);
  assetManager.load("sounds/jump_with_feather.wav", Sound.class);
  assetManager.load("sounds/pickup_coin.wav", Sound.class);
  assetManager.load("sounds/pickup_feather.wav", Sound.class);
  assetManager.load("sounds/live_lost.wav", Sound.class);
  // load music
  assetManager.load("music/keith303_-_brand_new_highscore.mp3",
Music.class);
  // start loading assets and wait until finished
  assetManager.finishLoading();
  Gdx.app.debug(TAG, "# of assets loaded: "
 + assetManager.getAssetNames().size);
  for (String a : assetManager.getAssetNames())
  Gdx.app.debug(TAG, "asset: " + a);

  TextureAtlas atlas =
assetManager.get(Constants.TEXTURE_ATLAS_OBJECTS);
```

```
    // enable texture filtering for pixel smoothing
    for (Texture t : atlas.getTextures())
        t.setFilter(TextureFilter.Linear, TextureFilter.Linear);

    // create game resource objects
    fonts = new AssetFonts();
    bunny = new AssetBunny(atlas);
    rock = new AssetRock(atlas);
    goldCoin = new AssetGoldCoin(atlas);
    feather = new AssetFeather(atlas);
    levelDecoration = new AssetLevelDecoration(atlas);
    sounds = new AssetSounds(assetManager);
    music = new AssetMusic(assetManager);
}
```

These changes tell the asset manager to load and manage every audio file that we want to use in the game. We are now all set to play back our audio files. However, the game should also respect the current audio settings that are available in the **Options** menu of the menu screen, as shown in the following screenshot:

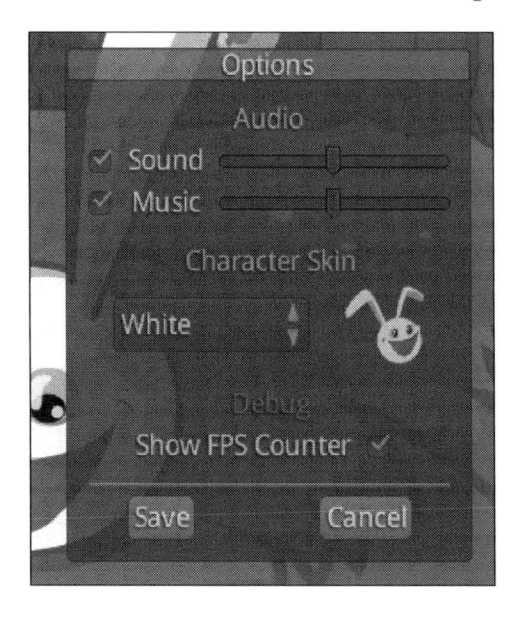

Managing the Music and Sound Effects

At this point, it would seem logical to just call `play()` on the sound and music instances in the game code where needed. However, this approach poses an issue in terms of clean code with regard to the game settings as the current game settings need to be checked every time an audio file is played. So, it would be ideal to have an audio manager as a centralized point of control over the game's audio playback. Since LibGDX does not provide an audio manager, we will build one of our own.

Create a new file for the `AudioManager` class and add the following code:

```
package com.packtpub.libgdx.canyonbunny.util;

import com.badlogic.gdx.audio.Music;
import com.badlogic.gdx.audio.Sound;

public class AudioManager {
  public static final AudioManager instance = new AudioManager();

  private Music playingMusic;

  // singleton: prevent instantiation from other classes
  private AudioManager () { }

  public void play (Sound sound) {
    play(sound, 1);
  }

  public void play (Sound sound, float volume) {
    play(sound, volume, 1);
  }

  public void play (Sound sound, float volume, float pitch) {
    play(sound, volume, pitch, 0);
  }

  public void play (Sound sound, float volume, float pitch,
 float pan) {
      if (!GamePreferences.instance.sound) return;
      sound.play(GamePreferences.instance.volSound * volume,
 pitch, pan);
    }
}
```

The `AudioManager` class is a singleton class so that we can access it from anywhere in the code. It features a couple of overloaded `play()` methods just like the original `Sound` and `Music` interfaces. The advantage of overloading these methods is that you can make some parameters optional. The methods in this class check against the values in `GamePreferences`, which holds the currently loaded audio settings among others. If the checkbox for sounds is not selected in the **Options** menu, `GamePreferences.instance.sound` will return `false`, and therefore any call of `AudioManager` class's `play()` will be aborted before the actual `play()` call of a sound is executed.

Next, add the following code to the same class:

```
public void play (Music music) {
  stopMusic();
  playingMusic = music;
  if (GamePreferences.instance.music) {
    music.setLooping(true);
    music.setVolume(GamePreferences.instance.volMusic);
    music.play();
  }
}

  public void stopMusic () {
    if (playingMusic != null) playingMusic.stop();
  }

public void onSettingsUpdated () {
  if (playingMusic == null) return;
  playingMusic.setVolume(GamePreferences.instance.volMusic);
  if (GamePreferences.instance.music) {
    if (!playingMusic.isPlaying()) playingMusic.play();
  } else {
    playingMusic.pause();
  }
}
```

This code adds another overloaded `play()` method, which takes an instance of `Music` that will be played. If music is already playing, it is stopped first. Then, new music is initialized for playback and started if `Music` is enabled in the game settings. The `onSettingsUpdated()` method is used to allow the **Options** menu to inform `AudioManager` when settings have changed to execute appropriate actions, such as setting a new music volume.

Managing the Music and Sound Effects

Now, let's connect the audio manager with the **Options** menu in the menu screen and the rest of the game.

Add the following import line to `MenuScreen`:

```
import com.packtpub.libgdx.canyonbunny.util.AudioManager;
```

Next, make the following changes to the same class:

```
private void onSaveClicked () {
  saveSettings();
  onCancelClicked();
  AudioManager.instance.onSettingsUpdated();
}

private void onCancelClicked () {
  btnMenuPlay.setVisible(true);
  btnMenuOptions.setVisible(true);
  winOptions.setVisible(false);
  AudioManager.instance.onSettingsUpdated();
}
```

These changes make sure that when the **Options** menu is closed, the audio manager will start or stop the music depending on the current audio settings.

Next, add the following import lines to the `CanyonBunnyMain` class:

```
import com.packtpub.libgdx.canyonbunny.util.AudioManager;
import com.packtpub.libgdx.canyonbunny.util.GamePreferences;
```

After this, make the following changes to the same class:

```
@Override
public void create () {
  // Set Libgdx log level
  Gdx.app.setLogLevel(Application.LOG_DEBUG);

  // Load assets
  Assets.instance.init(new AssetManager());

  // Load preferences for audio settings and start playing music
  GamePreferences.instance.load();
  AudioManager.instance.play(Assets.instance.music.song01);

  // Start game at menu screen
```

```
    ScreenTransition transition = ScreenTransitionSlice.init(2,
ScreenTransitionSlice.UP_DOWN, 10, Interpolation.pow5Out);
    setScreen(new MenuScreen(this), transition);
}
```

These changes will make sure that after the assets and game preferences have been loaded, the music starts playing. This is done using the `play()` method of `AudioManager`, which takes care of checking the current audio settings, setting the correct music volume, and potentially starting the playback of the music file.

> LibGDX automatically handles the task of pausing and resuming for any instances of playing music. Therefore, no extra code is required to handle these cases in the game code.

Next, add the following import line to the `WorldController` class:

```
import com.packtpub.libgdx.canyonbunny.util.AudioManager;
```

After this, make the following changes to the same class:

```
public void update (float deltaTime) {
  handleDebugInput(deltaTime);
  if (isGameOver()) {
    timeLeftGameOverDelay -= deltaTime;
    if (timeLeftGameOverDelay < 0) backToMenu();
  } else {
    handleInputGame(deltaTime);
  }
  level.update(deltaTime);
  testCollisions();
  cameraHelper.update(deltaTime);
  if (!isGameOver() && isPlayerInWater()) {
    AudioManager.instance.play(Assets.instance.sounds.liveLost);
    lives--;
    if (isGameOver())
    timeLeftGameOverDelay = Constants.TIME_DELAY_GAME_OVER;
    else
    initLevel();
  }
  level.mountains.updateScrollPosition(
    cameraHelper.getPosition());
  if (livesVisual > lives)
  livesVisual = Math.max(lives, livesVisual - 1 * deltaTime);
  if (scoreVisual < score)
```

Managing the Music and Sound Effects

```
      scoreVisual = Math.min(score, scoreVisual +250 * deltaTime);
  }

  private void onCollisionBunnyWithGoldCoin (GoldCoin goldcoin) {
    goldcoin.collected = true;
    AudioManager.instance.play(Assets.instance.sounds.pickupCoin);
    score += goldcoin.getScore();
    Gdx.app.log(TAG, "Gold coin collected");
  }

  private void onCollisionBunnyWithFeather (Feather feather) {
    feather.collected = true;
    AudioManager.instance.play(Assets.instance.sounds.pickupFeather);
    score += feather.getScore();
    level.bunnyHead.setFeatherPowerup(true);
    Gdx.app.log(TAG, "Feather collected");
  }
```

These changes add the code to trigger the sound effects for the `Life Lost`, `Picked up Gold Coin`, and `Picked up Feather` events at the right time.

Next, add the following two import lines to the `BunnyHead` class:

```
import com.badlogic.gdx.math.MathUtils;
import com.packtpub.libgdx.canyonbunny.util.AudioManager;
```

After this, make the following changes to the same class:

```
public void setJumping (boolean jumpKeyPressed) {
  switch (jumpState) {
    case GROUNDED: // Character is standing on a platform
    if (jumpKeyPressed) {
      AudioManager.instance.play(Assets.instance.sounds.jump);
      // Start counting jump time from the beginning
      timeJumping = 0;
      jumpState = JUMP_STATE.JUMP_RISING;
    }
    break;
    case JUMP_RISING: // Rising in the air
    if (!jumpKeyPressed) {
      jumpState = JUMP_STATE.JUMP_FALLING;
    }
    break;
    case FALLING:// Falling down
```

```
    case JUMP_FALLING: // Falling down after jump
    if (jumpKeyPressed && hasFeatherPowerup) {
      AudioManager.instance.play(
        Assets.instance.sounds.jumpWithFeather, 1,
MathUtils.random(1.0f, 1.1f));
      timeJumping = JUMP_TIME_OFFSET_FLYING;
      jumpState = JUMP_STATE.JUMP_RISING;
    }
    break;
  }
}
```

The changes in the code for `BunnyHead` trigger the sound effects for the `jumped` and `jumped-in-mid-air` events at the right time. The `jumpWithFeather` sound is played using a different `play()` method of the `AudioManager` class. It is also provided with a random pitch value in the range from 1.0 to 1.1, which adds a little change in the frequency, rendering the rapidly repeated sound effect more interesting.

These were the last changes and thus we conclude this chapter about working with audio in LibGDX and how to use it in Canyon Bunny.

> Currently, sound pitching does not work in the GWT backend that is used in LibGDX to support the WebGL target platform. The sound will just play at its normal rate if pitching is used.

Summary

In this chapter, you learned how to use LibGDX's four audio interfaces, `Sound`, `Music`, `AudioDevice`, and `AudioRecorder`, and about their specific use cases. We took a look at the freely available and open source sound generators and used one of them to create sound effects that can be used in Canyon Bunny. We also added background music to the game and understood that LibGDX takes care of when a music instance being played needs to be paused and resumed in terms of the life cycle in a LibGDX application. A manager class called `AudioManager` was created to gain centralized control over any audio-related actions. Finally, playing music and sounds turned out to be a very straightforward process in conjunction with the use of our audio manager. We had to add just a few new lines of code to trigger the music and sound effects at the right time for each event.

In the next chapter, we will look at some advanced programming techniques. This includes using a physics engine suitable for two-dimensional game objects, creating a shader program to apply a simple monochrome filter effect, and querying the accelerometer hardware to implement an alternative input method.

11
Advanced Programming Techniques

In this chapter, we will take a look at Box2D—a physics engine to simulate realistic-looking physics of the objects in 2D space. After we cover the basics of how to use Box2D, we will move on and create a little physics simulation that is going to be triggered at the end of the level. For this to work, we will also need to add a new level object that represents the level's end.

Next, we will look at the topic of shader programs. Shaders, in general, are simple programs that are executed on the **Graphics Processing Unit (GPU)**. We will create our own shader program consisting of a vertex and a fragment shader to achieve a simple monochrome filter effect.

Physics engines, such as Box2D and programming shaders, are very complex topics. Each deserves at least one book on their own to get hold of their gist. Nonetheless, this chapter is meant to give you the first push in the right direction on how to approach these broad topics.

Today's smartphones have an integrated accelerometer. This can be used to detect the spatial position of the device, which is delivered by the accelerometer as one value for each of the three axes. We will query the accelerometer hardware and use the read values to translate them into the player movement in Canyon Bunny.

In this chapter, we will cover the following topics:

- 2D physics using Box2D
- Shader programs
- Use accelerometer as an alternate input method to move the bunny head

Advanced Programming Techniques

Simulating physics with Box2D

Box2D was created by Erin Catto and is an open source physics engine to simulate rigid bodies in 2D space. It is written in a platform-independent C++ code that has encouraged ports to several frameworks, game engines, and programming languages in general.

You should check out at least one of these popular games if you have never seen Box2D in action before: *Angry Birds*, *Limbo*, *Tiny Wings*, and *Crayon Physics Deluxe*.

LibGDX integrates Box2D, which is similar to other frameworks, through a thin wrapper API that is congruent with Box2D's original API. This approach makes it pleasantly easy to transfer existing knowledge about Box2D by following tutorials and examples that are not based on LibGDX, and of course, using the official Box2D manual.

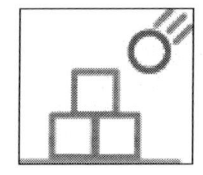

For more information, you can check out the official website of Box2D at `http://www.box2d.org/`.

Also check out the LibGDX's Box2D wiki at `https://github.com/libgdx/libgdx/wiki/Box2d/`.

For Box2D tutorials, you can check out the following websites:

- C++ (`http://www.iforce2d.net/b2dtut/`)
- Objective-C (`http://www.raywenderlich.com/28602/intro-to-box2d-with-cocos2d-2-x-tutorial-bouncing-balls`)
- Flash (`http://www.emanueleferonato.com/category/box2d/`)
- JavaScript (`http://blog.sethladd.com/2011/09/box2d-collision-damage-for-javascript.html`)

Exploring the concepts of Box2D

We will now shed some light on the basic ideas behind Box2D, and find out how it allows us to define virtual worlds that can be used to simulate believable physics with rigid bodies.

Understanding the rigid bodies

First of all, let's clarify what this seemingly mysterious term rigid body means. A body, in the sense of physics, is just a collection of matter with some attributes assigned to it, such as its position and orientation. It is what we usually call an object in our real world. Now, a so-called rigid body describes an idealized body that is assumed to be solid and thus incapable of being deformed by the exerting forces. From now on, we will use the shorter term, body, for brevity since Box2D has only the support for rigid bodies anyway.

> LibGDX also integrates a second open source physics engine named **Bullet**. In contrast to Box2D, which is limited to 2D space and rigid body support only, Bullet features a full-fledged 3D physics simulation as well as support for both rigid and soft bodies. However, we will solely focus on Box2D in this chapter as 3D physics is an even more advanced topic.

In addition to the (2D) position and orientation attributes, a body also has the following features:

- A mass given in kilograms
- A velocity (directed speed) given in meters per second (m/s)
- An angular velocity (rotational speed) given in radian per second (rad/s).

Choosing the body types

There are three different body types to choose from. They are as follows:

- **Static**: This is a stationary body. It does not collide with other static or kinematic bodies. It is useful for floors, walls, non-moving platforms, and so on.
- **Kinematic**: This is a movable body. The position can be manually updated or changed according to its velocity, which is the preferred and more reliable method. Kinematic bodies do not collide with other static or kinematic bodies. They are useful for moving platforms (for example, elevators), reflecting dynamic bodies, and so on.

- **Dynamic**: This is a movable body. The position can be manually updated or changed according to forces, which is the preferred and more reliable method. Dynamic bodies can collide with all body types. It is useful for players, enemies, items, and so on.

> In a real-world scenario, humans and other movable items are always dynamic, and they collide with others. However, the ones that do not move such as trees, house, floor, and so on are classified as static; they won't go toward the dynamic objects but the dynamic objects can come and collide with them. Kinematic objects are those that don't respond to force; they would move in a predefined path according to a set velocity. An elevator would be a good example.

Using shapes

Shapes describe the 2D objects in a geometrical way using radiuses for circles, widths and heights for rectangles, or a certain number of points (also vertices) for more complex shapes using polygons. So, these shapes define areas that can be tested for collisions with other shapes later on. For more information about creating polygon shapes, see the Box2D manual, *4.4 Polygon Shapes*.

Using fixtures

A fixture uses exactly one shape to which it adds material properties, such as density, friction, and restitution. The shape defined in a fixture is then attached to a body by adding the fixture to it. So, it plays an important role in how bodies interact with each other. For more information about using fixtures, see the Box2D manual, *6.2 Fixture Creation*.

Simulating physics in the world

The world is the virtual sandbox inside which the physics simulation takes place. Each body, including its fixture and shape, needs to be inserted into the world to be included in the simulation.

Box2D is a very feature-rich engine and thus contains a lot more features, such as **Constraints**, **Joints**, **Sensors**, and **Contact Listener** just to name a few, but which are not in the scope of this chapter.

For more in-depth information, consult the official manual of Box2D at http://www.box2d.org/manual.pdf.

Physics body editor

The creation of bodies for images with complex shapes can be a very time-consuming task. The Physics Body Editor, created by Aurélien Ribon, lets you build bodies in a graphical editor and comes with many useful features, such as decomposition of concave shapes into convex polygons, tracing outlines of images, and a built-in collision tester.

Check out the official project website at https://code.google.com/p/box2d-editor/. A screenshot from the project's website that shows the editor in action is as follows:

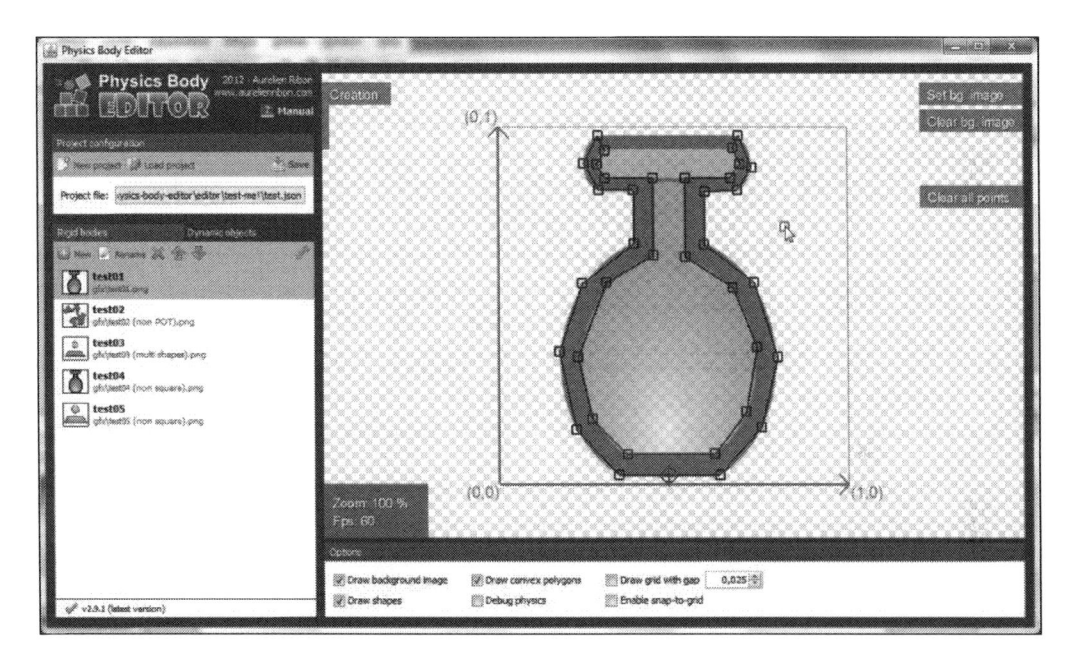

Adding Box2D

From LibGDX 1.0.0 onward, Box2D is separated from gdx.jar and moved to a new extension. However, if you are using the Gradle-based setup tool, you can simply check the **Box2D** box and generate your project.

Advanced Programming Techniques

Adding Box2D dependency in Gradle

Wait a minute, we have not yet added Box2D at project creation, and so now we have to add it manually. Everything in a Gradle-based project is managed by `build.gradle` in the project root. Go to the `C:/libgdx` folder and open the `build.gradle` file with a text editor such as Notepad or WordPad.

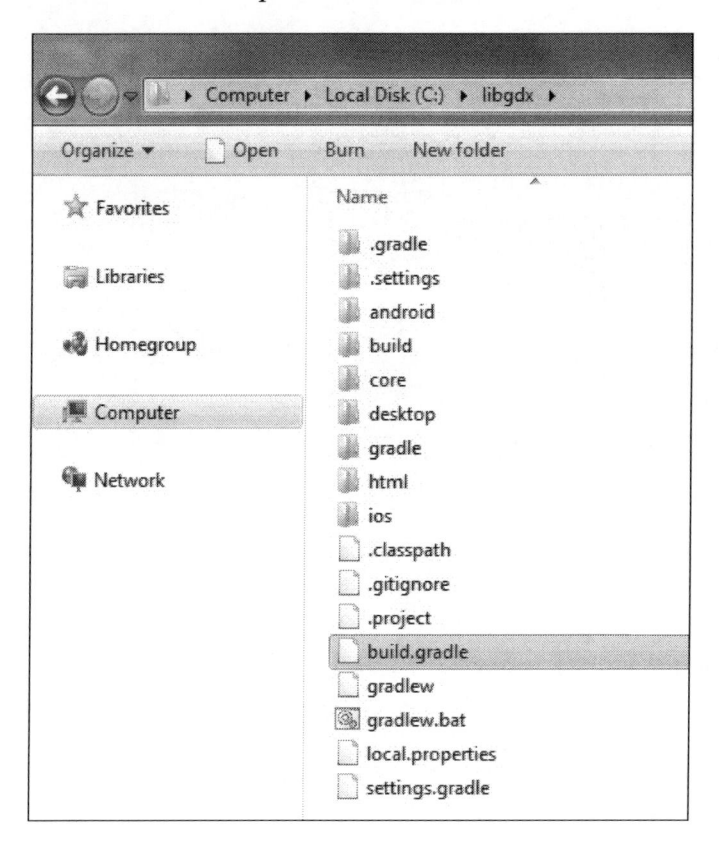

Next, add the lines of code, given in the following section, to the `build.gradle` to add Box2D dependency to our project:

- To add the desktop dependency, use this:
  ```
  project(":desktop") {
  apply plugin: "java"

  dependencies {
  compile project(":core")
  compile "com.badlogicgames.gdx:gdx-backend-lwjgl:$gdxVersion"
  ```

```
compile "com.badlogicgames.gdx:gdx-
platform:$gdxVersion:natives-desktop"
compile "com.badlogicgames.gdx:gdx-box2d-
platform:$gdxVersion:natives-desktop"
compile "com.badlogicgames.gdx:gdx-tools:$gdxVersion"
    }
}
```

- To add the Android dependency, use this:

```
project(":android") {
apply plugin: "android"
configurations { natives }
dependencies {
compile project(":core")
compile "com.badlogicgames.gdx:gdx-backend-
android:$gdxVersion"
natives "com.badlogicgames.gdx:gdx-
platform:$gdxVersion:natives-armeabi"
natives "com.badlogicgames.gdx:gdx-
platform:$gdxVersion:natives-armeabi-v7a"
natives "com.badlogicgames.gdx:gdx-
platform:$gdxVersion:natives-x86"
compile "com.badlogicgames.gdx:gdx-box2d:$gdxVersion"
natives "com.badlogicgames.gdx:gdx-box2d-
platform:$gdxVersion:natives-armeabi"
natives "com.badlogicgames.gdx:gdx-box2d-
platform:$gdxVersion:natives-armeabi-v7a"
natives "com.badlogicgames.gdx:gdx-box2d-
platform:$gdxVersion:natives-x86"
    }
}
```

- To add the iOS dependency, use this:

```
project(":ios") {
apply plugin: "java"
apply plugin: "robovm"

configurations { natives }

dependencies {
compile project(":core")
compile "org.robovm:robovm-rt:${roboVMVersion}"
compile "org.robovm:robovm-cocoatouch:${roboVMVersion}"
compile "com.badlogicgames.gdx:gdx-backend-robovm:$gdxVersion"
```

```
        natives "com.badlogicgames.gdx:gdx-
        platform:$gdxVersion:natives-ios"
        natives "com.badlogicgames.gdx:gdx-box2d-
        platform:$gdxVersion:natives-ios"
            }
        }
```

- To add the HTML dependency, use this:
  ```
  project(":html") {
  apply plugin: "gwt"
  apply plugin: "war"
  dependencies {
  compile project(":core")
  compile "com.badlogicgames.gdx:gdx-backend-gwt:$gdxVersion"
  compile "com.badlogicgames.gdx:gdx:$gdxVersion:sources"
  compile "com.badlogicgames.gdx:gdx-backend-
  gwt:$gdxVersion:sources"
  compile "com.badlogicgames.gdx:gdx-box2d:$gdxVersion:sources"
  compile "com.badlogicgames.gdx:gdx-box2d-
  gwt:$gdxVersion:sources"
      }
  }
  ```

- To add the core dependency, use this:
  ```
  project(":core") {
  apply plugin: "java"
  dependencies {
  compile "com.badlogicgames.gdx:gdx:$gdxVersion"
  compile "com.badlogicgames.gdx:gdx-box2d:$gdxVersion"
      }
  }
  ```

Now, refresh all dependencies. To do this, select all the five projects in the package explorer and then right-click on the **Refresh Dependencies** option in the **Gradle** menu.

For non-Gradle users

Now for the folks who used the old LibGDX project generation method (gdx-setup-ui.jar), you have to copy the JAR files into the libs folder in the respective projects and add them to build path. The JAR files can be found in libgdx-1.2.0, downloaded earlier in *Chapter 1, Introduction to LibGDX and Project Setup*. To do this, follow these steps:

1. Copy gdx-box2d.jar to the CanyonBunny project.
2. Copy gdx-box2d-native.jar to the CanyonBunny-desktop project.
3. Copy libgdx-box2d.so from armeabi, armeabi-v7a, and x86 to the corresponding subfolders inside the libs folder in the CanyonBunny-android project.
4. Copy gdx-box2d-gwt.jar and gdx-box2d-gwt-sources.jar to the lib subfolder under the war folder in the CanyonBunny-html project folder.
5. You will also need to add `<inherits name='com.badlogic.gdx.physics.box2d.box2d-gwt' />` to your GwtDefinition.gwt.xml file.
6. Copy libgdx-box2d.a to the libs/ios folder in the CanyonBunny-robovm project, and update the robovm.xml file as follows:

   ```
   <libs>
   <lib>libs/ios/libgdx.a</lib>
   <lib>libs/ios/libObjectAL.a</lib>
   <lib>libs/ios/libgdx-box2d.a</lib>
   </libs>
   ```

7. Now to add the JAR files to build the path, simply right-click on the newly added JAR files in each project and go to the **Add to build path** option in the **Build Path** menu.

Now, it's all set. Let's check the weather for raining carrots.

Advanced Programming Techniques

Preparing Canyon Bunny for raining carrots

What, raining carrots? Absolutely! We are going to add two new game objects to Canyon Bunny. One will act as the end point or goal of a level, while the other is a regular carrot that we will use later in our physics simulation. To be able to place the goal game object in our level, we will also have to make some minor changes to the level image and level loader.

So, a screenshot to give you a better impression of what we are aiming for, while we are working on it step by step, is as follows:

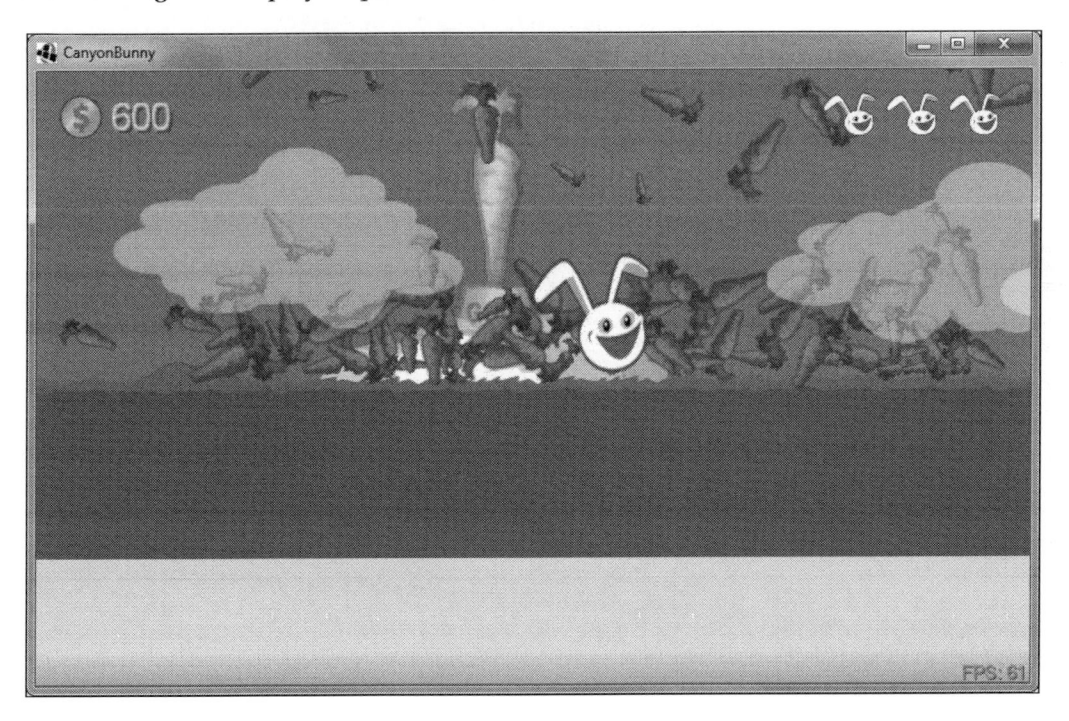

In the preceding screenshot, you can see the running physics simulation of raining carrots, which is kicked off as soon as the player character passes the goal (golden carrot statue). Lots of carrots will fall down from the sky, nicely bounce off the ground, and eventually pile up on each other.

Adding the new assets

Firstly, copy the two new images `carrot.png` and `goal.png` to `CanyonBunny-desktop/assets-raw/images/`. Also, do not forget to rebuild your texture atlas. After this, let's add them to our global assets class for easier access.

Add the following lines to the inner class `AssetLevelDecoration` of the `Assets` class:

```
public final AtlasRegion carrot;
public final AtlasRegion goal;
```

Next, make the following changes to the same (inner) class so that the new images will become available for later use:

```
public AssetLevelDecoration (TextureAtlas atlas) {
waterOverlay = atlas.findRegion("water_overlay");
carrot = atlas.findRegion("carrot");
goal = atlas.findRegion("goal");
}
```

Adding the carrot game object

The carrot is just a normal game object like any other, as shown here, that we have created for Canyon Bunny so far:

Create a new file for the `Carrot` class and add the following code:

```
package com.packtpub.libgdx.canyonbunny.game.objects;

import com.badlogic.gdx.graphics.g2d.SpriteBatch;
import com.badlogic.gdx.graphics.g2d.TextureRegion;
import com.packtpub.libgdx.canyonbunny.game.Assets;

public class Carrot extends AbstractGameObject {
private TextureRegion regCarrot;

public Carrot () {
init();
    }

private void init () {
```

Advanced Programming Techniques

```
    dimension.set(0.25f, 0.5f);

    regCarrot = Assets.instance.levelDecoration.carrot;

        // Set bounding box for collision detection
    bounds.set(0, 0, dimension.x, dimension.y);
    origin.set(dimension.x / 2, dimension.y / 2);
    }
    public void render (SpriteBatch batch) {
    TextureRegion reg = null;

    reg = regCarrot;
    batch.draw(reg.getTexture(), position.x - origin.x,
    position.y - origin.y, origin.x, origin.y, dimension.x,
    dimension.y, scale.x, scale.y, rotation, reg.getRegionX(),
    reg.getRegionY(), reg.getRegionWidth(),
    reg.getRegionHeight(), false, false);
    }
}
```

Adding the goal game object

The following goal game object will be used to mark the end of a level:

Create a new file for the `Goal` class and add the following code:

```java
package com.packtpub.libgdx.canyonbunny.game.objects;

import com.badlogic.gdx.graphics.g2d.SpriteBatch;
import com.badlogic.gdx.graphics.g2d.TextureRegion;
import com.packtpub.libgdx.canyonbunny.game.Assets;

public class Goal extends AbstractGameObject {
private TextureRegion regGoal;

public Goal () {
init();
  }

private void init () {
dimension.set(3.0f, 3.0f);
regGoal = Assets.instance.levelDecoration.goal;

    // Set bounding box for collision detection
bounds.set(1, Float.MIN_VALUE, 10, Float.MAX_VALUE);
origin.set(dimension.x / 2.0f, 0.0f);
  }

public void render (SpriteBatch batch) {
TextureRegion reg = null;

reg = regGoal;
batch.draw(reg.getTexture(), position.x - origin.x,
position.y - origin.y, origin.x, origin.y, dimension.x,
dimension.y, scale.x, scale.y, rotation,
reg.getRegionX(), reg.getRegionY(),
reg.getRegionWidth(), reg.getRegionHeight(),
false, false);
  }
}
```

There is one specialty about this game object that is important enough to be mentioned. We have set the bounds of the goal to values that make it almost infinitely tall in relation to other objects in the game world. This ensures that the player character will always collide with the goal and trigger the corresponding event.

Extending the level

The next step is to include the goal game object in the level image. Remember that each pixel color represents a certain game object in the world of Canyon Bunny. For the goal game object, we choose red as the pixel color (R=255, G=0, B=0).

Add the new red pixel marked as **Goal** to the level image. Use the following screenshot for reference:

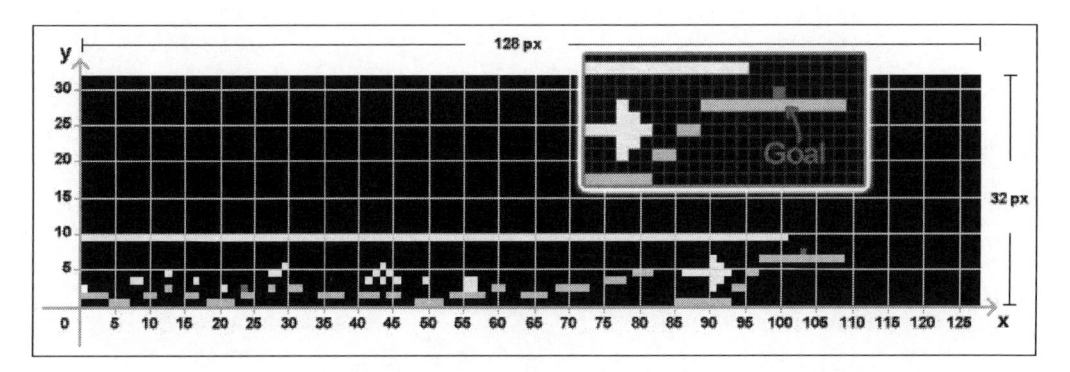

Obviously, the goal should be placed at the far right-hand side to make it harder to reach for the player. In our example level, this is the elongated platform right after the arrow that is made out of gold coins.

Now, we need to tell the level loader about the new pixel and game object to let it handle correctly.

Add the following import lines to the Level class:

```
import com.packtpub.libgdx.canyonbunny.game.objects.Carrot;
import com.packtpub.libgdx.canyonbunny.game.objects.Goal;
```

After this, add the following code to the same class:

```
public Array<Carrot> carrots;
public Goal goal;
```

Furthermore, add the following constant to the BLOCK_TYPE enumeration that defines the goal's red pixel color:

```
GOAL(255, 0, 0), // red
```

Chapter 11

Next, make the following changes to the init() method in which we want to initialize a new array for the carrot game objects, and create a new goal game object if the corresponding pixel color was found in the level image:

```
private void init (String filename) {

  // objects
rocks = new Array<Rock>();
goldcoins = new Array<GoldCoin>();
feathers = new Array<Feather>();
carrots = new Array<Carrot>();

  // load image file that represents the level data
Pixmap pixmap = new Pixmap(Gdx.files.internal(filename));
  // scan pixels from top-left to bottom-right
int lastPixel = -1;
for (int pixelY = 0; pixelY<pixmap.getHeight(); pixelY++) {
for (int pixelX = 0; pixelX<pixmap.getWidth(); pixelX++) {

      // gold coin
else if
      (BLOCK_TYPE.ITEM_GOLD_COIN.sameColor(currentPixel)) {
            ...
        }
      // goal
else if (BLOCK_TYPE.GOAL.sameColor(currentPixel)) {
obj = new Goal();
offsetHeight = -7.0f;
obj.position.set(pixelX, baseHeight + offsetHeight);
goal = (Goal)obj;
        }
      // unknown object/pixel color
else {

        }
lastPixel = currentPixel;
      }
    }
  }
```

[343]

Advanced Programming Techniques

Finally, make the following changes to the `update()` and `render()` methods in the same class to let each carrot update correctly as well as render the goal and the carrot game objects in the right order on the screen, as follows:

```
public void update (float deltaTime) {
  // Feathers
for (Feather feather : feathers)
feather.update(deltaTime);
for (Carrot carrot : carrots)
carrot. Update(deltaTime);
  // Clouds
clouds.update(deltaTime);
  }

public void render (SpriteBatch batch) {
  // Draw Mountains
mountains.render(batch);
  // Draw Goal
goal.render(batch);
  // Draw Rocks
for (Rock rock : rocks)
rock.render(batch);

for (Feather feather : feathers)
feather.render(batch);
  // Draw Carrots
for (Carrot carrot : carrots)
carrot.render(batch);
  // Draw Player Character
bunnyHead.render(batch);
  }
```

You may want to run the game now and verify that the goal game object is visible at the end of the level. However, nothing will happen when the player character passes it. We will address the implementation details for the event handling and physics simulation next.

Letting it rain carrots

We will now focus on the implementation details, where we actually make use of Box2D in Canyon Bunny. Remember that we have created our own simple physics simulation for the game objects before. We do not want to replace this implementation but in fact allow the use of either one of them as it suits our needs. In other words, we want to keep the existing implementation that is doing collision detection and physics for the game objects, and just add a coexisting alternative that uses Box2D.

Add the following import line to the `AbstractGameObject` class:

```
import com.badlogic.gdx.physics.box2d.Body;
```

After this, add the following line to the same class:

```
public Body body;
```

The (rigid) `Body` class directly relates to what we have discussed at the beginning of this chapter. Next, make the following changes to the `update()` method in the same class:

```
public void update (float deltaTime) {
if (body == null) {
updateMotionX(deltaTime);
updateMotionY(deltaTime);

    // Move to the new position
position.x += velocity.x * deltaTime;
position.y += velocity.y * deltaTime;
    } else {
position.set(body.getPosition());
rotation = body.getAngle() * MathUtils.radiansToDegrees;
    }
  }
```

The idea here is that each game object will be using our simple physics as long as there is no Box2D body defined in the body variable. Otherwise, the current position and angle of rotation is simply taken from the body and applied to the game object to reflect the state of Box2D's calculations. In conclusion, this means that we have given full control to Box2D over the movement parameters for these game objects.

Advanced Programming Techniques

Next, add the following import lines to the `WorldController` class:

```
import com.badlogic.gdx.math.MathUtils;
import com.badlogic.gdx.math.Vector2;
import com.badlogic.gdx.physics.box2d.Body;
import com.badlogic.gdx.physics.box2d.BodyDef;
import com.badlogic.gdx.physics.box2d.BodyDef.BodyType;
import com.badlogic.gdx.physics.box2d.FixtureDef;
import com.badlogic.gdx.physics.box2d.PolygonShape;
import com.badlogic.gdx.physics.box2d.World;
import com.packtpub.libgdx.canyonbunny.game.objects.Carrot;
```

Then, add the following lines of code to the same class:

```
private boolean goalReached;
public World b2world;

private void initPhysics () {
if (b2world != null) b2world.dispose();
  b2world = new World(new Vector2(0, -9.81f), true);
  // Rocks
  Vector2 origin = new Vector2();
for (Rock rock : level.rocks) {
BodyDef bodyDef = new BodyDef();
bodyDef.type = BodyType.KinematicBody;
bodyDef.position.set(rock.position);
    Body body = b2world.createBody(bodyDef);
rock.body = body;
PolygonShape polygonShape = new PolygonShape();
origin.x = rock.bounds.width / 2.0f;
origin.y = rock.bounds.height / 2.0f;
polygonShape.setAsBox(rock.bounds.width / 2.0f,
rock.bounds.height / 2.0f, origin, 0);
FixtureDef fixtureDef = new FixtureDef();
fixtureDef.shape = polygonShape;
body.createFixture(fixtureDef);
polygonShape.dispose();
    }
  }
```

The `goalReached` variable is used to keep track of the game's state whether or not the player has already managed to reach the goal. The `World` class directly relates to the description at the beginning of this chapter. In the `initPhysics()` method, we create a new instance of `World`, and store it in the `b2world` variable for later reference. The constructor of `World` takes an instance of `Vector2` for the world's simulated gravity, and a second parameter that controls the weather bodies in Box2D can become inactive. Usually, this flag should be enabled to reduce the CPU load and in particular to preserve some battery power on mobile devices. In our case, we create a world with gravity, pulling down objects at 9.81 meters per second squared, which is the same acceleration that we experience on earth.

> Remember to always call the `dispose()` method of World when it is no longer needed. This is also true for all the Box2D shape classes, for example, `PolygonShape` and `CircleShape`.

After the Box2D world is created, we loop through the level's list of rocks, and create the corresponding Box2D bodies that are mapped to the same position and size as defined in the loaded level. Thus, both worlds, the Box2D one and our level, will start in a synchronized model state for each rock. Creating bodies for the rocks is a necessary step because Box2D will have to take each rock into account in its calculations. Otherwise, the carrot game objects will fall through everything in the level because there simply is nothing to collide with from Box2D's point of view.

Box2D requires you to use separate definition classes to create new instances of `Body` and `Fixture`, which are named `BodyDef` and `FixtureDef`, respectively. The instance in the `bodyDef` variable is configured to describe a kinematic body type whose initial position is set to the same position as the rock instance. After this, we call the `createBody()` method of `b2world` and pass in the body definition to create and add the new body at once. The method returns the reference of the newly created body, which is then stored in the rock instance to activate the Box2D physics handling, according to the changes we just made in our `update()` method of `AbstractGameObject`.

The created body also needs a shape to allow interaction with other bodies. So, we create a shape using the `PolygonShape` class and call its `setAsBox()` helper method to define a rectangle. Shapes cannot be directly attached to bodies; thus, we create a new instance of the `Fixture` class, bind our shape to it, and eventually attach the fixture to the body of the rock by calling the `createFixture()` method of the `body` instance. Now, the shape is no longer needed as its information has been processed in the new fixture. This is why we can safely call the `dispose()` method on the shape to free the memory that was allocated by this shape.

Advanced Programming Techniques

A screenshot of Box2D's view of the rock bodies is as follows:

The thin blue lines forming a rectangle visualizes how (the shape) and where (the position) Box2D sees each rock. These lines have been rendered with the help of Box2D's `Box2DDebugRenderer` class. Let's add this feature to the game code so that it can be quickly enabled when needed.

Add the following import line to the `WorldRenderer` class:

```
import com.badlogic.gdx.physics.box2d.Box2DDebugRenderer;
```

After this, add the following lines of code to the same class:

```
private static final boolean DEBUG_DRAW_BOX2D_WORLD = false;
private Box2DDebugRenderer b2debugRenderer;
```

Then, make the following changes to the same class:

```
private void init () {
batch = new SpriteBatch();
camera = new OrthographicCamera(Constants.VIEWPORT_WIDTH,
Constants.VIEWPORT_HEIGHT);
camera.position.set(0, 0, 0);
camera.update();
cameraGUI = new OrthographicCamera(Constants.VIEWPORT_GUI_WIDTH,
Constants.VIEWPORT_GUI_HEIGHT);
cameraGUI.position.set(0, 0, 0);
cameraGUI.setToOrtho(true);
   // flip y-axis
cameraGUI.update();
```

```
    b2debugRenderer = new Box2DDebugRenderer();
}

private void renderWorld (SpriteBatch batch) {
worldController.cameraHelper.applyTo(camera);
batch.setProjectionMatrix(camera.combined);
batch.begin();
worldController.level.render(batch);
batch.end();
if (DEBUG_DRAW_BOX2D_WORLD) {
b2debugRenderer.render(worldController.b2world,
camera.combined);
    }
}
```

Now, we can easily toggle the debug view for Box2D, by setting DEBUG_DRAW_BOX2D_WORLD to true or false.

Next, add the following lines of code to the Constants class:

```
// Number of carrots to spawn
public static final int CARROTS_SPAWN_MAX = 100;

// Spawn radius for carrots
public static final float CARROTS_SPAWN_RADIUS = 3.5f;

// Delay after game finished
public static final float TIME_DELAY_GAME_FINISHED = 6;
```

We will use these new constants to control the number of carrots to spawn and the delay time before the game switches back to the menu screen after the goal was reached by the player. In this particular case, we use a value of 100 carrots and a delay of 6 seconds.

Next, add the following lines of code to the WorldController class:

```
private void spawnCarrots (Vector2 pos, int numCarrots,
float radius) {
float carrotShapeScale = 0.5f;
   // create carrots with box2d body and fixture
for (int i = 0; i<numCarrots; i++) {
   Carrot carrot = new Carrot();
   // calculate random spawn position, rotation, and scale
float x = MathUtils.random(-radius, radius);
```

```
        float y = MathUtils.random(5.0f, 15.0f);
        float rotation = MathUtils.random(0.0f, 360.0f)
            * MathUtils.degreesToRadians;
        float carrotScale = MathUtils.random(0.5f, 1.5f);
        carrot.scale.set(carrotScale, carrotScale);
            // create box2d body for carrot with start position
            // and angle of rotation
        BodyDef bodyDef = new BodyDef();
        bodyDef.position.set(pos);
        bodyDef.position.add(x, y);
        bodyDef.angle = rotation;
            Body body = b2world.createBody(bodyDef);
        body.setType(BodyType.DynamicBody);
        carrot.body = body;
            // create rectangular shape for carrot to allow
            // interactions (collisions) with other objects
        PolygonShape polygonShape = new PolygonShape();
        float halfWidth = carrot.bounds.width / 2.0f * carrotScale;
        float halfHeight = carrot.bounds.height /2.0f * carrotScale;
        polygonShape.setAsBox(halfWidth * carrotShapeScale,
        halfHeight * carrotShapeScale);
            // set physics attributes
        FixtureDef fixtureDef = new FixtureDef();
        fixtureDef.shape = polygonShape;
        fixtureDef.density = 50;
        fixtureDef.restitution = 0.5f;
        fixtureDef.friction = 0.5f;
        body.createFixture(fixtureDef);
        polygonShape.dispose();
            // finally, add new carrot to list for updating/rendering
        level.carrots.add(carrot);
        }
    }
```

The spawnCarrots() method contains the logic to create a variable number (numCarrots) of the new carrot game objects at a specific location (pos) in the game world. Inside the loop, a new carrot game object is created for which random values are calculated for the starting position (x, y), angle of rotation (rotation), and scale (carrotScale). The location that is passed in the pos variable is used as the center spawn point. The third parameter, radius, is used to distribute the carrots around the center spawn point of the horizontal starting position. The vertical starting position is randomly chosen in the range between 5 and 15 to ensure that the carrots will always spawn outside the game camera's view.

Also, this range helps to create a more rain-like effect by distributing the carrots in a column full of carrots, so that they will hit the ground at different points in time. The random rotation values are chosen within a range of a full circle (0 to 360 degrees), which simply means that any angle of rotation can occur. The random scale values are chosen within the range of half below or above the carrot's original size, which gives the overall effect a more natural touch as carrots are not of the same size in real life either.

Similar to what we did for the rock game object, a Box2D body, fixture, and shape must be created for each carrot game object. It should be noted once more that the reference of a Box2D body is stored in the `body` variable of the carrot instance to activate the Box2D update mechanism for the game object. Also, notice that the fixture is set to have a density of 50, which affects the object's calculated mass data, and thus controls whether it is a light or a heavy object. Furthermore, `restitution` is set to 0.5, which means that the carrots will be half-elastic to allow some rebound to happen until it comes to rest eventually. A `friction` value of 0.5 lets the carrots skid down on each other. Using a value of 1 or higher for `friction` will make the object look sticky when it gets in contact with other objects.

As a last tweak, each Box2D shape is shrunk to half the size (`carrotShapeScale = 0.5f`) of the carrot game object to eliminate small gaps between the adjacent carrots. Finally, each new carrot with its corresponding Box2D body is added to the level's list of carrots for updating and rendering.

Next, add the following lines of code to the `WorldController` class:

```
private void onCollisionBunnyWithGoal () {
goalReached = true;
timeLeftGameOverDelay = Constants.TIME_DELAY_GAME_FINISHED;
   Vector2 centerPosBunnyHead =
     new Vector2(level.bunnyHead.position);
centerPosBunnyHead.x + = level.bunnyHead.bounds.width;
spawnCarrots(centerPosBunnyHead, Constants.CARROTS_SPAWN_MAX,
Constants.CARROTS_SPAWN_RADIUS);
}
```

This new method will handle the event when the player passes the goal-level object. The `goalReached` flag is set to `true`, which will be used to avoid unnecessary collision tests and start the countdown that will switch back to the menu screen. The countdown starts at the value that is taken from the new constant `TIME_DELAY_GAME_FINISHED`. Then, the `spawnCarrots()` method is called with the player's current position, the number of carrots, and the spawn radius.

Advanced Programming Techniques

> In this project, we check collision with the nearest object using the basic rectangle overlapping algorithm; however, LibGDX also provides a callback interface for detecting collisions. The callback approach will be helpful in a game with many rigid bodies at motion.
>
> An excellent article on contact listeners can be found at http://sysmagazine.com/posts/162079/.

Now, make the following changes to the `WorldController` class:

```
private void initLevel () {
score = 0;
scoreVisual = score;
goalReached = false;
level = new Level(Constants.LEVEL_01);
cameraHelper.setTarget(level.bunnyHead);
initPhysics();
}

private void testCollisions (float deltaTIme) {
r1.set(level.bunnyHead.position.x, level.bunnyHead.position.y,
level.bunnyHead.bounds.width, level.bunnyHead.bounds.height);

  // Test collision: Bunny Head <-> Rocks
  ...

  // Test collision: Bunny Head <-> Gold Coins
  ...

  // Test collision: Bunny Head <-> Feathers
  ...
  // Test collision: Bunny Head <-> Goal
if (!goalReached) {
r2.set(level.goal.bounds);
    r2.x += level.goal.position.x;
    r2.y += level.goal.position.y;
if (r1.overlaps(r2)) onCollisionBunnyWithGoal();
    }
}

public void update (float deltaTime) {
handleDebugInput(deltaTime);
```

```
        if (isGameOver() || goalReached) {
        timeLeftGameOverDelay-= deltaTime;
        if (timeLeftGameOverDelay< 0) backToMenu();
            } else {
        handleInputGame(deltaTime);
            }
        level.update(deltaTime);
        testCollisions();
        b2world.step(deltaTime, 8, 3);
        cameraHelper.update(deltaTime);
           }
```

At the end of the `initLevel()` method, right after the level is loaded, we will call the `initPhysics()` method. It is important to do it in this particular order because `initPhysics()` works with the list of rocks of the loaded level. The `testCollisions()` method is extended by another check that will call the `onCollisionBunnyWithGoal()` method as soon as it detects a collision between the player and the goal game objects.

In the `update()` method, we added the `goalReached` flag as an alternative condition to the `isGameover()` condition. So, from now on, a delayed switchback to the menu screen will be executed, if either condition is met.

Lastly, the Box2D world instance stored in `b2world` needs to be updated just like the rest of the game to make any progress. This is done by calling its `step()` method and passing in the delta time. The last two parameters denote the number of iterations that Box2D is allowed to execute for its velocity and position calculations. Using higher values for these parameters may increase the precision of the simulation as well as the computational workload. However, Box2D is not going to always use up the maximum number of iterations if it decides that the errors in the simulation are small enough to go unnoticed.

> Box2D suggests an iteration count of 8 for velocities and 3 for positions. See 2.4 *Simulating the World (of Box2D)* in the official manual.

There are only two more, but not less important, changes to fully complete our new game feature.

Advanced Programming Techniques

Make the following changes to the `Rock` class:

```
@Override
public void update (float deltaTime) {
super.update(deltaTime);

floatCycleTimeLeft -= deltaTime;
if (floatCycleTimeLeft<= 0) {
floatCycleTimeLeft = FLOAT_CYCLE_TIME;
floatingDownwards = !floatingDownwards;
body.setLinearVelocity(0, FLOAT_AMPLITUDE
 * (floatingDownwards ? -1 : 1));
  } else {
body.setLinearVelocity(body.getLinearVelocity().scl(0.98f));

  }
}
```

These changes represent an almost direct translation from our own physics simulation to Box2D's one for the rocks' floating-on-water effect. It is crucial to understand why we have to change this part or else you will probably spend a lot of time hunting down nasty problems in conjunction with Box2D.

In our previous implementation, the rocks' movement was achieved by directly modifying its position vector. Since the rocks are now controlled by Box2D, we would have to change the position of the rock's body using the `setTransform()` method instead. Usually, this is a really bad idea as it can confuse Box2D when a manual change of a body position results in two or more overlapping shapes. These overlapping shapes, then, can cause quite unpredictable effects such as extreme accelerations or a disruption of resting objects. So, additional care needs to be taken if the position and/or angle of the rotation of a body are set directly.

As you can see in the preceding changed code, we are actually not using `setTransform()` but `setLinearVelocity()`. So, the general rule to avoid the mentioned problems is to tell Box2D about the physical cause to get the desired effect. This means that we have to express changes in the world through forces, which in turn are translated into velocities.

After all this, the last modification is to free the allocated memory when appropriate.

Add the following import line to the `WorldController` class:

```
import com.badlogic.gdx.utils.Disposable;
```

Next, let the same class implement the `Disposable` interface as follows:

```
public class WorldController extends InputAdapter
implements Disposable {
...
}
```

Then, add the following lines of code to the same class:

```
@Override
public void dispose () {
if (b2world != null) b2world.dispose();
}
```

Finally, make the following changes to the `GameScreen` class:

```
@Override
public void hide () {
worldController.dispose();
worldRenderer.dispose();
Gdx.input.setCatchBackKey(false);
}
```

Memory that is allocated by a Box2D's world instance is now going to be freed correctly when it is no longer needed.

Now, run the game and finish the level by passing the goal to marvel at the awesome rain of carrots. A screenshot of what you should see is as follows:

Advanced Programming Techniques

The preceding screenshot shows the spawned carrots that have already come to rest as well as the debug overlay drawn by the Box2D debug renderer. If you take a closer look at the shape location of each carrot, you will probably come to the conclusion that it must be misaligned, though the simulation appears to be perfectly fine.

Fortunately, there is no real issue at all because it is just an illusion due to the transparent area and the green leaves of the carrot. An isolated view that only shows a couple of carrots and two debug boxes is shown in the following screenshot:

The inner box is still drawn using the Box2D debug render. The outer box, however, is the real border of the image used for the carrot game object. You can try this yourself by enabling the debug outline for TexturePacker and rebuilding the texture atlas afterwards.

Working with shaders in LibGDX

Let's now turn our attention to the topic of shaders. This is a feature that is available in OpenGL (ES) 2.0 and above as it makes use of the so-called **Programmable Pipeline**. Shaders are usually small programs, which allow us to take over control of certain stages in the rendering process to define the way a scene should be rendered by the graphics processor. In consequence, shaders are an important building block in today's computer graphics and are also an extremely powerful tool to create all sorts of (special) effects that would be very hard to realize otherwise. For the sake of simplicity, we will only discuss vertex and fragment shaders here.

> Fragment shaders are also called pixel shaders. Unfortunately, this is a bit misleading as this type of shader actually operates on fragments instead of pixels.

Consider the following list of reasons as to why shaders are generally useful and highly recommended to be in the toolkit of every (graphics) programmer:

- Programmability of the GPU rendering pipeline via shaders to create arbitrary complex effects. This means a high degree of flexibility for all sorts of special effects expressible through mathematical formulas.
- Shaders are run on the GPU, which saves the CPU time that can be spent on other tasks, such as doing physics and general game logic.
- Heavy mathematical computations are usually done faster on GPUs than on CPUs.
- GPUs are able to parallelize the processing of vertices and fragments.

Vertex shaders operate on each vertex given to the GPU. A vertex is a point in 3D space with attributes, such as a position, a color, and texture coordinates. These values can then be manipulated through the shader to achieve effects, for example, the deformation of an object. The output for each vertex computed by the vertex shader is then passed along in the rendering pipeline as the input for the next rendering stage.

Fragment shaders compute the color of a pixel for each fragment. For this, many factors may be taken into account to simulate different kinds of materials. Some of them are values for lighting, translucency, shadows, and so on.

Advanced Programming Techniques

The combination of a vertex and a fragment shader is called a shader program. Shaders are usually written in an API-specific, high-level language, such as **OpenGL Shading Language (GLSL)** for OpenGL, which uses C-like code syntax. Take a look at the last two pages of the OpenGL ES 2.0 Reference Card at `http://www.khronos.org/opengles/sdk/docs/reference_cards/OpenGL-ES-2_0-Reference-card.pdf`.

This should give a quick overview of the available feature set in GLSL. For more details about the specifications of OpenGL (ES) 2.0, GLSL, as well as the Programmable Pipeline, check out the official website of the Khronos Group at `http://www.khronos.org/opengles/2_X/`.

Also, the following list contains some links to the GLSL tutorials and websites with collections of shader examples ranging from beginners to experts:

- `https://github.com/mattdesl/lwjgl-basics/wiki/Shaders`
- `http://www.lighthouse3d.com/tutorials/glsl-tutorial/`
- `http://glslsandbox.com/`
- `https://www.shadertoy.com/`

Creating a monochrome filter shader program

We now want to create a new pair of vertex and fragment shaders to form a shader program. Its purpose will be to act as a color filter that renders everything it has applied to in a beautiful grayscale.

Let's start with the vertex shader. Create a new subdirectory in `CanyonBunny-android/assets` named `shaders`. Then, create a new file `monochrome.vs` in the `shaders` directory, and add the following code:

```
attribute vec4 a_position;
attribute vec4 a_color;
attribute vec2 a_texCoord0;
varying vec4 v_color;
varying vec2 v_texCoords;
uniform mat4 u_projTrans;

void main() {
v_color = a_color;
v_texCoords = a_texCoord0;
gl_Position = u_projTrans * a_position;
}
```

The first six lines in the vertex shader declare the variables of different data types using the so-called storage qualifiers in terms of GLSL. The data `typesvec2` and `vec4` stand for the float vectors with two and four components, respectively, while `mat4` stands for a square matrix of order four of floats. The `attribute` qualifier is only available in the vertex shader and denotes the inputs that are passed from the vertex arrays sent by the application. As mentioned before, these inputs are the position, color, and texture coordinates of one vertex at a time. The `varying` qualifier denotes the variables that are readable and writeable in the context of the vertex shader but read only to the fragment shader. Thus, the variables using this qualifier allow the transfer of additional information from the vertex shader to the fragment shader. Last but not least, the `uniform` qualifier denotes the variables that are known to be constant during multiple executions of the shader in the same draw call. The variable `u_projTrans` is automatically set to the combined projection-model view matrix by the LibGDX's `Spritebatch` class.

The next step is the declaration of the `main()` function. It is the entry point of the shader where the execution begins. In this vertex shader, we pass the input values of the color and texture coordinates via varying variables to the fragment shader for later use. The variable `gl_Position` is a predefined GLSL output variable (refer to GLES2 Reference Card) that holds the projected position vector and is computed by the multiplication of the combined projection-model view matrix (`u_projTrans`) and the position vector (`a_position`) of the current vertex.

Next, create another new file `monochrome.fs` in the `shaders` directory and add the following code:

```
#ifdef GL_ES
precision mediump float;
#endif
varying vec4 v_color;
varying vec2 v_texCoords;
uniform sampler2D u_texture;
uniform float u_amount;

void main() {
vec4 color = v_color * texture2D(u_texture, v_texCoords);
float grayscale = dot(color.rgb, vec3(0.222, 0.707, 0.071));
color.rgb = mix(color.rgb, vec3(grayscale), u_amount);
gl_FragColor = color;
}
```

Advanced Programming Techniques

In the first three lines, we use a GLSL macro to set precision of the float values to medium for devices that use OpenGL ES. In the next lines, you may have already recognized our two varying variables that we pass from within our vertex shader to this one.

> Be sure to always match the name and data type of each varying variable passed from a vertex shader to the corresponding fragment shader.

The data type sampler2D stands for a two-dimensional texture. The `u_amount` variable is meant to be set by the application code to control the amount of grayscale that should be applied. The first line inside the `main()` function of the fragment shader computes a combined color value between the original vertex color and the color value of the texture referenced in `u_texture` using the coordinates passed in `v_texCoords`. Now, to find an appropriate grayscale value, we compute the dot product of our color vector and another vector containing varying color weights that match best with the sensitivity of a typical human eyesight as suggested in *Chapter 22.3.1, Grayscale Conversion* of the book *GPU Gems, Randima (Randy) Fernando, Addison Wesley*.

This book is publicly available on NVDIA's developer zone at `http://http.developer.nvidia.com/GPUGems/gpugems_ch22.html`.

Then, we use the `mix()` function, which applies a linear interpolation between the original color vector and the grayscale vector using the `u_amount` variable. The `gl_FragColor` variable is another predefined output variable of GLSL that determines the final pixel color of the fragment that is currently being processed.

Using the monochrome filter shader program in Canyon Bunny

Now that we have created our monochrome filter shader program, it is time to put it to use in Canyon Bunny. We want to use the shader's effect in the game screen, and apply it to the game world. This means that the GUI will remain colored like before. In addition to this, the shader program can be switched on and off with a new checkbox added to the debug section of the menu screen's **Options** dialog.

First, add these new constants to the `Constants` class that point to the files of our new shader program:

```
// Shader
public static final String shaderMonochromeVertex =
"shaders/monochrome.vs";
public static final String shaderMonochromeFragment =
"shaders/monochrome.fs";
```

After this, add the following line to the `GamePreferences` class:

```
public boolean useMonochromeShader;
```

Next, make the following changes to the same class:

```
public void load () {
showFpsCounter = prefs.getBoolean("showFpsCounter", false);
useMonochromeShader = prefs.getBoolean("useMonochromeShader",
    false);
}

public void save () {
prefs.putBoolean("showFpsCounter", showFpsCounter);
prefs.putBoolean("useMonochromeShader", useMonochromeShader);
prefs.flush();
}
```

Then, add the following line to the `MenuScreen` class:

```
private CheckBox chkUseMonoChromeShader;
```

After this, make the following changes to the same class:

```
private Table buildOptWinDebug () {
  Table tbl = new Table();
  // + Title: "Debug"

  // + Checkbox, "Show FPS Counter" label
  // + Checkbox, "Use Monochrome Shader" label
chkUseMonochromeShader = new CheckBox("", skinLibgdx);
tbl.add(new Label("Use Monochrome Shader", skinLibgdx));
tbl.add(chkUseMonochromeShader);
tbl.row();
return tbl;
}

private void loadSettings () {
```

Advanced Programming Techniques

```
        chkShowFpsCounter.setChecked(prefs.showFpsCounter);
        chkUseMonochromeShader.setChecked(prefs.useMonochromeShader);
    }

    private void saveSettings () {
    prefs.showFpsCounter = chkShowFpsCounter.isChecked();
    prefs.useMonochromeShader = chkUseMonochromeShader.isChecked();
    prefs.save();
    }
```

The last modifications to `GamePreferences` and `MenuScreen` just extended the settings handling by a new Boolean flag, which can now be toggled via the new checkbox added to the debug section of the **Options** dialog in the menu screen.

Next, add the following import lines to the `WorldRenderer` class:

```
        import com.badlogic.gdx.graphics.glutils.ShaderProgram;
        import com.badlogic.gdx.utils.GdxRuntimeException;
```

After this, add the following line to the same class:

```
        private ShaderProgram shaderMonochrome;
```

Also make the following changes to the same class:

```
        private void init () {
        batch = new SpriteBatch();
        camera = new OrthographicCamera(Constants.VIEWPORT_WIDTH,
        Constants.VIEWPORT_HEIGHT);
        camera.position.set(0, 0, 0);
        camera.update();
        cameraGUI = new OrthographicCamera(Constants.VIEWPORT_GUI_WIDTH,
        Constants.VIEWPORT_GUI_HEIGHT);
        cameraGUI.position.set(0, 0, 0);
        cameraGUI.setToOrtho(true); // flip y-axis
        cameraGUI.update();
          b2debugRenderer = new Box2DDebugRenderer();
        shaderMonochrome = new ShaderProgram(
        Gdx.files.internal(Constants.shaderMonochromeVertex),
        Gdx.files.internal(Constants.shaderMonochromeFragment));
        if (!shaderMonochrome.isCompiled()) {
            String msg = "Could not compile shader program: "
              + shaderMonochrome.getLog();
        throw new GdxRuntimeException(msg);
            }
          }
```

```
    private void renderWorld (SpriteBatch batch) {
    worldController.cameraHelper.applyTo(camera);
    batch.setProjectionMatrix(camera.combined);
    batch.begin();
    if (GamePreferences.instance.useMonochromeShader) {
    batch.setShader(shaderMonochrome);
    shaderMonochrome.setUniformf("u_amount", 1.0f);
        }
    worldController.level.render(batch);
    batch.setShader(null);
    batch.end();
    if (DEBUG_DRAW_BOX2D_WORLD) {
    b2debugRenderer.render(worldController.b2world,
    camera.combined);
        }
      }

    @Override
    public void dispose () {
    batch.dispose();
    shaderMonochrome.dispose();
    }
```

To load and initialize our shader program in the `init()` method, we pass both the shader files to the constructor of a new instance of `ShaderProgram`, which are then stored in the `shaderMonochrome` variable for later reference. It is good practice to ask whether a new shader program instance could be successfully compiled by calling its `isCompiled()` method. If this is not the case, the corresponding log message of the compile error can be retrieved by calling the `getLog()` method.

In the `renderWorld()` method, we wrapped the call that renders the actual game world with two `setShader()` calls. The first call activates our monochrome filter shader program while the next call passes null for the shader, which makes `SpriteBatch` switch back to LibGDX's default shader. Calling the `setUniformf()` method of an instance of a shader program allows us to set a float value for a uniform variable by a name. There are many more of these setter methods for different combinations of storage qualifiers and data types. We set the value of the uniform float variable named `u_amount` to the value `1.0f`. According to our code in the fragment shader, the linear interpolation will apply the grayscale effect in full to its target pixels.

Finally, we take care that the shader program's `dispose()` method is called to free any allocated memory when it is no longer needed.

Advanced Programming Techniques

Now, run the game, go to the **Options** dialog, and tick the checkbox to activate the monochrome filter shader program. The game screen should show up in a beautiful grayscale tone as soon as the game is started. A screenshot of the game with the enabled monochrome filter shader program is as follows:

$$\left[\begin{array}{c}\text{The blue background color, which is actually created using OpenGL's}\\\text{clear color, is not affected by our shader program. The reason behind}\\\text{this is that the shader's effect is only applied during the rendering}\\\text{of the game world where it is temporarily set in the sprite batch.}\\\text{Moreover, the game world is rendered on top of the (blue) clear color,}\\\text{which back then appeared to be a good idea just because it was an easy}\\\text{and cheap way of making the clear color a part of the scene and get a}\\\text{sky for free.}\end{array}\right]$$

Adding alternative input controls

The last and rather short topic in this chapter will show you how to use the peripheral devices using the example of accelerometers, which are very common types of sensors in today's smartphones and tablets. Accelerometers are subsystems that reliably and accurately detect and measure acceleration, tilt, shock, and vibration. Basically, we just need to read the sensor data that is being measured by the accelerometer hardware and later translate the data into values and/or ranges suitable for our game.

Accelerometers in Android and iOS devices are exposed by LibGDX using the three axes *x*, *y*, and *z*, which can be queried via the `Gdx.input` module. For instance, the current acceleration value for the *x* axis can be easily retrieved as follows:

```
float ax = Gdx.input.getAccelerometerX();
```

This is great, but what does the value that we just stored in `ax` actually mean? Moreover, what will influence it? So, to better understand how sensors work, we need to know what exactly is measured.

Let's start with the range of values. In the documentations of Android and LibGDX, the values for accelerometers are said to range between `-10.0f` and `10.0f`. This roughly resembles a value of what we know as the constant for gravity on earth, approximately 9.81 meters per square second. However, what we still do not know about is the internal orientation of the sensor hardware inside a device. This poses a problem to us because we cannot tell which axis is which. Luckily, LibGDX comes to the aid and is able to make an educated guess that is also reliable. There is a blog post by Mario Zechner that describes the issue about the different so-called native orientations in more detail at `http://www.badlogicgames.com/wordpress/?p=2041`.

All we have to remember is that LibGDX will make sure that the *y* axis always coincides with the bigger side while the *x* axis coincides with the smaller one. The *z* axis comes out of the screen.

An image taken from Android's SDK developer website that nicely illustrates the sensor coordinate system is as follows:

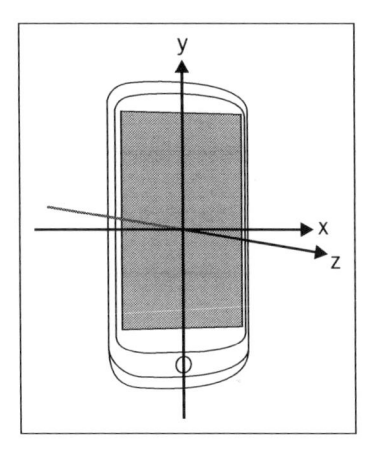

Advanced Programming Techniques

We will now move on to Canyon Bunny and implement alternative input controls using the accelerometer. The screen needs to be rotated by 90 degrees to the left in order to be able to play Canyon Bunny on a smartphone, since it is using the so-called landscape mode for display. It is important to understand that the orientation of the sensors will always remain the same no matter how the smartphone is moved and rotated around.

The new controls will allow you to tilt the screen to the left and right sides to move into the very same direction. The tilt angle for the *y* axis will determine the maximum velocity of the player character.

Add the following new constants to the `Constants` class:

```
// Angle of rotation for dead zone (no movement)
public static final float ACCEL_ANGLE_DEAD_ZONE = 5.0f;

// Max angle of rotation needed to gain max movement velocity
public static final float ACCEL_MAX_ANGLE_MAX_MOVEMENT = 20.0f;
```

Then, add the line of code to the `WorldController` class:

```
import com.badlogic.gdx.Input.Peripheral;
```

Next, add the following line to the `WorldController` class:

```
private boolean accelerometerAvailable;
```

After this, make the following changes to the same class:

```
private void init () {
    accelerometerAvailable = Gdx.input.isPeripheralAvailable(
    Peripheral.Accelerometer);
    cameraHelper = new CameraHelper();
    lives = Constants.LIVES_START;
    livesVisual = lives;
    timeLeftGameOverDelay = 0;
    initLevel();
}

private void handleInputGame (float deltaTime) {
    if (cameraHelper.hasTarget(level.bunnyHead)) {
        // Player Movement
        if (Gdx.input.isKeyPressed(Keys.LEFT)) {
            ...
        } else {
            // Use accelerometer for movement if available
```

```
if (accelerometerAvailable) {
        // normalize accelerometer values from [-10, 10] to [-1, 1]
        // which translate to rotations of [-90, 90] degrees
float amount = Gdx.input.getAccelerometerY() / 10.0f;
amount *= 90.0f;
        // is angle of rotation inside dead zone?
if (Math.abs(amount) <Constants.ACCEL_ANGLE_DEAD_ZONE) {
amount = 0;
        } else {
            // use the defined max angle of rotation instead of
            // the full 90 degrees for maximum velocity
amount /= Constants.ACCEL_MAX_ANGLE_MAX_MOVEMENT;
        }
level.bunnyHead.velocity.x =
level.bunnyHead.terminalVelocity.x * amount;
        }
    // Execute auto-forward movement on non-desktop platform
else if (Gdx.app.getType() != ApplicationType.Desktop) {
level.bunnyHead.velocity.x =
level.bunnyHead.terminalVelocity.x;
        }
      }
    }
  }
```

The new variable `accelerometerAvailable` is set once in the `init()` method, which in turn is used to select the input mode in `handleInputGame()`. If an accelerometer hardware is detected, the alternative input controls for player movement will be used. In this case, however, we first normalize the accelerometer values to make them stay in a range between `-1.0f` and `1.0f`, which can now also be interpreted by us as the percentage of desired movement in relation to the amount of tilt. The sign of the percentage also nicely describes the direction of the horizontal movement. A negative sign means movement to the left, whereas a positive sign means movement to the opposite direction. The percentage currently maps a movement of 100 percent in one direction to 90 degrees of tilting the screen in the same direction. It is very inconvenient to have to turn the device over the full range of 180 degrees, which also prevents fast player reactions.

This is why we introduced a new constant named `ACCEL_MAX_ANGLE_MAX_MOVEMENT` that allows you to define the maximum tilt angle that is needed to reach maximum velocity. The other new constant `ACCEL_ANGLE_DEAD_ZONE` is used to define a dead zone (here 5.0 degrees) in the positive and negative directions where no movement will occur. So, the dead zone makes it easier for the player to find a neutral position to let the bunny head stand still. Finally, we end up with a percentage of the desired movement stored in an amount that is simply multiplied with the terminal velocity to calculate the correct velocity value.

Summary

In this chapter, we covered the basics of the Box2D rigid body physics engine, and thereafter applied the newly gained knowledge, including all the individual parts (rigid body, body type, shape, fixture, and world) by creating a believable physics simulation of raining carrots. Also, two new game objects were added, which represented the carrot for physics simulations and a huge golden carrot statue symbolizing a level's goal or exit.

Then, we went down the graphics pipeline, more precisely the Programmable Pipeline of OpenGL (ES) 2.0 to explore the use of shaders. We created our own shader program to apply a monochrome filter effect of arbitrary intensity through a uniform variable that can be passed to the shader program at runtime in the application code. You learned about GLSL and created a simple pair of vertex and fragment shaders that are used in Canyon Bunny.

Finally, you learned how to use and work with peripheral devices using the example of an accelerometer. You also learned how to transform the data provided by a sensor into more suitable values. These values were then used as input to create an alternative way to control the player's movement just by tilting the screen to the left or to the right.

In the subsequent chapters, we will add animations to the game.

12
Animations

In this chapter, you will learn how to create and manage different kinds of animations using LibGDX's `Actions` and `Animation` classes. We will exemplify their usage by animating certain parts of the menu and game screen.

With regards to the menu screen, we will create time-based and event-based animations, including moving, scaling, and fading `Actor` objects via the so-called actions of the `Actions` class. Additionally, interpolation algorithms provided by LibGDX's `Interpolation` class will be used for added effects and for the smoothing of these animations.

The game screen, in a sense, is already animated according to the game logic, which takes care of coordinating the movement of every game object. However, each game object is rendered using a still image. In terms of animations, this is equivalent to a one-frame animation. With the help of the `Animation` class, we will define several sequences of individual frames to form animations for our game objects.

Manipulating actors through actions

The `Actions` class offers a large collection of common actions to easily manipulate the `Actor` objects. Besides action-specific parameters such as the position for a move action, some actions also allow you to specify the duration as well as the interpolation algorithm to be used. An action will always complete in an instant if the duration is either omitted or set to `0`. Interpolation algorithms are provided by LibGDX's `Interpolation` class.

> For a quick overview of the available interpolation algorithms in LibGDX, check out *Chapter 9, Screen Transitions*.

Animations

The following example illustrates the typical method signatures of two actions:

```
moveTo (x, y);
moveTo (x, y, duration);
moveTo (x, y, duration, interpolation);

rotateTo (rotation);
rotateTo (rotation, duration);
rotateTo (rotation, duration, interpolation);
```

Both the `moveTo()` and `rotateTo()` actions have their action-specific parameters x, y, and rotation, respectively, which is the absolute minimum requirement. In this case, both actions can also take an optional `duration` and `interpolation` parameter if needed.

> The methods of the `Actions` class are intended for static import. There are mainly two reasons for this: convenience and increased readability when chaining together multiple actions. The preceding example code and each following code using the `Actions` class will assume the use of static imports.
>
> In Java, a static import can be used to make static methods of one class available in the namespace of another class, thus removing the need to use the class qualification in order to call such methods.
>
> For more information about static imports, check out http://docs.oracle.com/javase/1.5.0/docs/guide/language/static-import.html.

Now, to add one or more actions to an actor, we simply need to call its `addAction()` method as follows:

```
Actor actor = new Actor();
float x = 100.0f, y = 100.0f, rotation = 0.0f, duration = 1.0f;
actor.addAction(sequence(
moveTo(x, y),
rotateTo(rotation),
delay(duration),
parallel(
moveBy(50.0f, 0.0f, 5.0f),
rotateBy(90.0f, 5.0f, Interpolation.swingOut))));
```

This example code shows a fictional actor that is completely initialized and manipulated via a chain of nested actions only. In this case, the added chain of actions starts as a sequence of more actions. This being said, the sequence comprises an absolute move action using `moveTo()` to a given point (`100, 100`), followed by an absolute rotation using `rotateTo()` (`0` degrees), followed by a short delay of `1` second, and finally followed by a parallel action that contains a list of even more actions. These parallel actions are a relative move using `moveBy()` (`50, 0`) and a relative rotation using `rotateBy()` (`90` degrees). Additionally, both actions use a duration of `5` seconds. Moreover, the relative rotation uses the `swingOut` interpolation algorithm.

So, the combined use of the `Actor` and `Actions` classes provides a very powerful way for us to express quite complex actor behaviors with relatively little code.

The next sections contain two lists with descriptions of the actions that are currently available.

Actions for manipulating actors

The following list describes actions that are useful to manipulate actors:

- `add()`: This adds an action to an actor
- `alpha()`: This sets the alpha value of an actor's color
- `color()`: This sets the color of an actor
- `fadeIn()` and `fadeOut()`: These are convenience actions to set the alpha value of an actor's color to `1` or `0`, respectively
- `hide()`: This sets the visibility of an actor to `false`
- `layout()`: This sets the actor's layout to `enabled` or `disabled`
- `moveBy()` and `moveTo()`: These move an actor by a relative amount or to a specific location
- `removeActor()`: This removes the actor to which this action is attached; alternatively, another actor that is to be removed can be specified
- `rotateBy()` and `rotateTo()`: These rotate an actor by a relative amount or to a specific angle of rotation
- `run()`: This runs a **Runnable** (the code will be executed in a separate thread)
- `scaleBy()` and `scaleTo()`: These scale an actor by a relative amount or to a specific scale

- `show()`: This sets the visibility of an actor to `true`
- `sizeBy()` and `sizeTo()`: These resize an actor by a relative amount or to a specific size
- `touchable()`: This sets the touchability of an actor (refer to the touchable enumerator)
- `visible()`: This sets the visibility of an actor

Controlling the order and time of execution

The following list describes actions that are useful for controlling the order and time of execution of other actions:

- `after()`: This waits for other actions of an actor to finish before its action is executed (note that this action will only wait for other actions that were already added to an actor prior to this)
- `delay()`: This delays the execution of an action
- `forever()`: This repeats an action forever
- `parallel()`: This executes a list of actions at the same time
- `repeat()`: This repeats an action for a given number of times
- `sequence()`: This executes a list of actions one after another

Animating the menu screen

Let's now discuss what we are actually going to animate in the menu screen. Basically, the first two bits of our animated menu involve the gold coins and the large bunny head.

Take a look at the following screenshot:

In this screenshot, you can see a rough sketch of the final animation divided into four essential steps. The following actions need to be taken for the shown steps:

1. The gold coins and bunny head are invisible at the beginning.
2. The gold coins fade in and scale up from 0 percent to 100 percent from the center screen as if they were jumping out of the water.
3. After a short pause, the bunny head appears in the top-right corner, which moves slightly until it reaches the edge of the rock that is visible in the background.
4. The bunny head moves as if it was jumping over to the other rock in front of it.

Animating the gold coins and bunny head actors

Add the following (static) import lines to the `MenuScreen` class:

```
import static com.badlogic.gdx.scenes.scene2d.actions.Actions.*;

import com.badlogic.gdx.math.Interpolation;
```

After this, make the following changes to the same class:

```
private Table buildObjectsLayer () {
  Table layer = new Table();
  // + Coins
  imgCoins = new Image(skinCanyonBunny, "coins");
  layer.addActor(imgCoins);
  imgCoins.setOrigin(imgCoins.getWidth() / 2,
    imgCoins.getHeight() / 2);
  imgCoins.addAction(sequence(
    moveTo(135, -20),
    scaleTo(0, 0),
    fadeOut(0),
    delay(2.5f),
    parallel(moveBy(0, 100, 0.5f, Interpolation.swingOut),
scaleTo(1.0f, 1.0f, 0.25f, Interpolation.linear),
alpha(1.0f, 0.5f))));
  // + Bunny
  imgBunny = new Image(skinCanyonBunny, "bunny");
  layer.addActor(imgBunny);
  imgBunny.addAction(sequence(
moveTo(655, 510),
delay(4.0f),
moveBy(-70, -100, 0.5f, Interpolation.fade),
moveBy(-100, -50, 0.5f, Interpolation.fade),
moveBy(-150, -300, 1.0f, Interpolation.elasticIn)));
  return layer;
}
```

All of the four steps are now expressed as actions in the code of the buildObjectLayer() method. This code replaces the setPosition() for the corresponding images. The origin of the gold coins' image that is stored in imgCoins needs to be adjusted so that it now points to its center. In this way, the image does not only grow or shrink when scaled but it will never move away from its original position. The first action of imgCoins is sequence() that merely groups all other actions. Then, the animation is initialized through the first three actions: moveTo(), scaleTo(), and fadeOut(). Next, a delay() action follows that creates a short delay of 2.5 seconds before the parallel action is executed.

The parallel action contains three more actions, moveBy(), scaleTo(), and alpha(), which are all executed at the same time. These three actions, when played together, create the impression that the gold coins appear to jump out of the water by moving them a bit downwards as well as fading them in and scaling them up from 0 percent to 100 percent. Interpolations are also used to support this effect. Choosing the right interpolation algorithm is usually a little trial-and-error at first, but after a while you will have a better understanding and feel for which one could work best for certain kinds of effects.

The animation for the bunny head is not that much different to the gold coins. It starts with a grouping sequence() that comprises an initializing moveTo() action followed by a delay() of 4 seconds. Then, three subsequent moveBy() actions are executed that describe the complete movement we discussed earlier.

Animating the menu buttons and options window

Now, for a final touch to the menu screen, let's animate the menu buttons in the bottom-right corner of the scene as well as the **Options** window that appears when the **Options** button is clicked. We want to let both buttons move out of the scene when the **Options** button is clicked on and let them move back into the scene after the **Options** window is closed again.

Add the following import lines to the MenuScreen class:

```
import com.badlogic.gdx.scenes.scene2d.actions.SequenceAction;
import com.badlogic.gdx.scenes.scene2d.Touchable;
```

Next, add the following lines of code to the same class:

```
private void showMenuButtons (boolean visible) {
  float moveDuration = 1.0f;
  Interpolation moveEasing = Interpolation.swing;
  float delayOptionsButton = 0.25f;

  float moveX = 300 * (visible ? -1 : 1);
  float moveY = 0 * (visible ? -1 : 1);
  final Touchable touchEnabled = visible ? Touchable.enabled
     : Touchable.disabled;
  btnMenuPlay.addAction(
moveBy(moveX, moveY, moveDuration, moveEasing));

  btnMenuOptions.addAction(sequence(
delay(delayOptionsButton),
moveBy(moveX, moveY, moveDuration, moveEasing)));

  SequenceAction seq = sequence();
  if (visible)
  seq.addAction(delay(delayOptionsButton + moveDuration));
  seq.addAction(run(new Runnable() {
    public void run () {
      btnMenuPlay.setTouchable(touchEnabled);
      btnMenuOptions.setTouchable(touchEnabled);
    }
  }));
  stage.addAction(seq);
}

private void showOptionsWindow (boolean visible,
boolean animated) {
  float alphaTo = visible ? 0.8f : 0.0f;
  float duration = animated ? 1.0f : 0.0f;
  Touchable touchEnabled = visible ? Touchable.enabled
   : Touchable.disabled;
  winOptions.addAction(sequence(
touchable(touchEnabled),
alpha(alphaTo, duration)));
}
```

The two new methods, `showMenuButtons()` and `showOptionsWindow()`, will allow us to easily show or hide the menu buttons and the **Options** window in an animated fashion. Any logic involved in the showing and hiding animation is encapsulated in these methods, which make it much more convenient to use.

The `showMenuButtons()` method has one parameter (`visible`) to control whether to show or hide the menu buttons. At the beginning of this method, we not only set many variables that are used to control the overall behavior of the animation, such as duration and easing, but also set some other variables whose values obviously depend on the visible flag. After the position, duration, and easing have been computed, we head over and add a couple of actions to both the menu buttons. The **Play** button is going to be directly moved to a relative position while the **Options** button does exactly the same but with an added delay prior to its move action. We will now discuss a pretty exciting example of how flexible actions are. We create a new and empty sequence and store it in `seq`. What follows is a conditional `delay()` action, so to say, which is only going to be added to the new sequence if the visible flag is set to `true`.

This means you can create and script actor behaviors in code while also being able to dynamically adjust and put them together as needed at a later time as we just did! Albeit, as a result of the prior condition, we always add a `run()` action to the sequence. The `run()` action takes a Runnable that is used in Java to put the code that is going to be executed in a separate thread. We use this and the conditional `delay()` action to call `setTouchable()` on the **Play** and **Options** buttons, which control whether the buttons receive and respond to touches and mouse clicks. Finally, the `sequence()` action stored in `seq` is added as a new action to the stage.

> In this case, we can safely do this to enqueue the `sequence()` action for execution because the sequence does not modify the stage with the `delay()` and `run()` actions.

The `showOptionsWindow()` method animates the options menu in the same way as described for the menu buttons in `showMenuButtons()`. The only difference here is that it takes a second flag that can be used to skip the animation.

Now, make the following changes to the `MenuScreen` class:

```
private Table buildOptionsWindowLayer () {
  ...
  // Make options window slightly transparent
  winOptions.setColor(1, 1, 1, 0.8f);
  // Hide options window by default
  showOptionsWindow(false, false);
  if (debugEnabled) winOptions.debug();
  // Let TableLayout recalculate widget sizes and positions
  winOptions.pack();
  // Move options window to bottom right corner
```

```
    winOptions.setPosition(Constants.VIEWPORT_GUI_WIDTH
- winOptions.getWidth() - 50, 50);
    return winOptions;
}

private void onOptionsClicked () {
  loadSettings();
  showMenuButtons(false);
  showOptionsWindow(true, true);
}

private void onCancelClicked () {
  showMenuButtons(true);
  showOptionsWindow(false, true);
  AudioManager.instance.onSettingsUpdated();
}
```

These changes simply put our animation methods in place where needed. The `buildOptionsWindowLayer()` method calls `showOptionsWindow()` with both parameters for visible and animated set to `false`. The reason for this is that we want the **Options** window to be hidden at the start like before and we also want this to happen in an instant. The `onOptionsClicked()` and `onCancelClicked()` methods call both show methods to either show or hide the menu buttons or the **Options** window, respectively.

Using sequences of images for animations

Up until now, all the animations we have created are based on changing attributes, such as the position, color value, and size, of still images. Therefore, our next enhancement is targeted toward the game objects that inhabit the game world of Canyon Bunny. We want to breathe life into the gold coin and bunny head game objects by creating several animations that are built from sequences of individual images. The resulting effect is very similar in comparison to an ordinary flip book where multiple images are perceived as a continuous animation when shown in rapid succession.

LibGDX provides a class called `Animation` that helps us define image sequences and also helps us to pick the right (key) frame from a sequence at a specific time which, for example, depends on the desired frame rate for playback. There is some clever mathematics and state-keeping involved for finding the right frame in an efficient way. Luckily, the `Animation` class saves us from having to go down that mathematical road and lets us just do animations the easy way with a variety of extra playback options.

Packing animations using TexturePacker

Before we look any further into the `Animation` class, let's first cover a great feature of LibGDX's TexturePacker that should be used when working with animations. Whenever TexturePacker builds a new texture atlas, it always scans the end of each image filename for an underscore followed by a number like `waterfall_03.png`. In this case, the number `03` is considered as the frame index of this animation, while the animation itself will be named and referred to as waterfall in the texture atlas.

Let's imagine that we have a five-frame animation called `waterfall`. So, according to the mentioned pattern for allowing animation frames to be recognized by TexturePacker, we would name our image files as follows:

- `waterfall_01.png`
- `waterfall_02.png`
- `waterfall_03.png`
- `waterfall_04.png`
- `waterfall_05.png`

The following short code example further illustrates the line of action to build animations:

```
TextureAtlas atlas = assetManager.get("atlas.pack");
AtlasRegion firstFrame = atlas.findRegion("waterfall");
AtlasRegion thirdFrame = atlas.findRegion("waterfall", 3);
Array<AtlasRegion> allFrames = atlas.findRegions("waterfall");
```

Animations

Let's assume that the `waterfall` animation is now available in the texture atlas (`atlas.pack`). To retrieve any given image from a texture atlas, we already know that we can simply call the `findRegion()` method and pass in the original filename without its extension to reference it. The preceding code example shows that you can also do this with an animation to get the first frame, or you can pass a second argument to specify a concrete frame index like index number 3 to get the third frame. The next line uses the `findRegions()` method instead of `findRegion()`. Notice the plural `s` in the method's name. This method returns a whole array of frames associated with the supplied name which is stored in the `allFrames` variable for now.

The following lines of code show how new animations are built using the `Animation` class:

```
float fps = 1.0f / 15.0f; // Time between frames in seconds
Animation aniFirst, aniFirstThird, aniAll, aniAllPingpong;
aniFirst        = new Animation(fps, firstFrame);
aniFirstThird   = new Animation(fps, firstFrame, thirdFrame);
aniAll          = new Animation(fps, allFrames);
aniAllPingPong = new Animation(fps, allFrames,
Animation.PlayMode.LOOP_PINGPONG);
```

The constructor of the class takes the time given in seconds that describes the time stepping or delay between the current and the next frame that is to be displayed. In this example, we use a frame rate of 15 frames per second. As the example code shows us further, we can pass in either an arbitrary number of `AtlasRegion` objects (our individual frames) or an array of those objects to define what frames should be used and in what particular order. Another feature of the `Animation` class is its play mode.

Choosing between animation play modes

There are six distinct play modes we can choose from. They are as follows:

- `NORMAL`: This plays the animation once (first frame to last)
- `REVERSED`: This plays the animation once (last frame to first)
- `LOOP`: This plays the animation in a loop (first frame to last)
- `LOOP_REVERSED`: This plays the animation in a loop (last frame to first)
- `LOOP_PINGPONG`: This plays the animation in a loop (first frame, to last, to first)
- `LOOP_RANDOM`: This plays the animation in a loop (random frames)

The `NORMAL` play mode is used as default if it is not explicitly set in the code.

Finally, the animations are now ready to be used and queried for their frames that should be currently displayed according to calculations. These calculations require one input value, which is the so-called state time, as shown in the following code. The state time is the elapsed time of an animation given in seconds. Usually, game objects keep track of their animation time, as we will see shortly:

```
TextureRegion region = aniAll.getKeyFrame(stateTime);
```

Assuming that the `stateTime` in the preceding code line yields a value of 0 seconds, the region variable will contain the first frame defined in the `aniAll` animation.

Animating the game screen

We are now going to animate the gold coin and bunny head game objects. However, before we can start building new animations, some preparations need to take place first, such as adding the actual image files to the project and rebuilding the texture atlas afterwards.

Copy the following files to `CanyonBunny-desktop/assets-raw/images/`:

- `anim_bunny_normal_XX.png` (where XX is 01, 02, and 03)
- `anim_bunny_copter_XX.png` (where XX is 01, 02, 03, 04, and 05)
- `anim_gold_coin_XX.png` (where XX is 01, 02, 03, 04, 05, and 06)

Now, set the `rebuildAtlas` variable to `true` and run the Canyon Bunny desktop application once to let the texture atlas be rebuilt with the newly added images for our animations.

Defining and preparing new animations

The following screenshot depicts all the frames, including their indices of the gold coin animation:

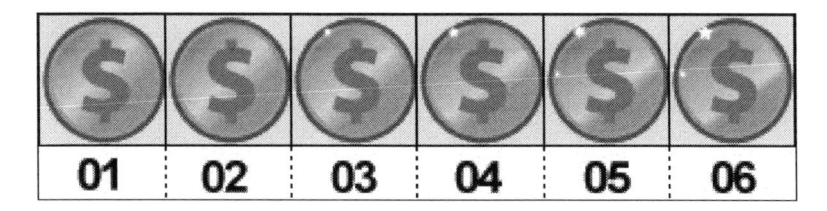

Animations

The shown frames are meant to be played back in a ping-pong loop (play mode: `LOOP_PINGPONG`) for the final animation. We will later refer to it as `animGoldCoin` in the code. The frame progression is as follows: 01, 02, 03, 04, 05, 06, 06, 05, 04, 03, 02, 01 [restart at the first frame].

The following screenshot depicts all the frames, including their indices of the bunny normal animation:

The shown frames are meant to be played back in a ping-pong loop (play mode: `LOOP_PINGPONG`) for the final animation and replace the current still image of the bunny head game object. We will later refer to this animation as `animNormal` in the code. The frame progression is as follows: 01, 02, 03, 03, 02, 01 [restart at the first frame].

The following screenshot depicts all the frames, including their indices of the bunny copter animation:

The shown frames are meant to be played back as three different animations:

- The first animation, `animCopterTransform`, plays all frames once (play mode: `NORMAL` and frame progression: 01, 02, 03, 04, 05)
- The second animation, `animCopterRotate`, plays the last two frames in a ping-pong loop (play mode: `LOOP_PINGPONG` and frame progression: 04, 05, 05, 04 [restart at the first frame])
- Lastly, the third animation, `animCopterTransformBack`, is simply the reverse of the first animation (play mode: `REVERSED` and frame progression: 05, 04, 03, 02, 01)

Now, let's put all these animations in our `Assets` class for later use. Add the following import lines to the `Assets` class:

```
import com.badlogic.gdx.graphics.g2d.Animation;
import com.badlogic.gdx.utils.Array;
```

Then, make the following changes to the same class:

```
public class AssetGoldCoin {
  public final AtlasRegion goldCoin;
  public final Animation animGoldCoin;

  public AssetGoldCoin (TextureAtlas atlas) {
    goldCoin = atlas.findRegion("item_gold_coin");

    // Animation: Gold Coin
    Array<AtlasRegion> regions =
    atlas.findRegions("anim_gold_coin");
    AtlasRegion region = regions.first();
    for (int i = 0; i < 10; i++)
    regions.insert(0, region);
    animGoldCoin = new Animation(1.0f / 20.0f, regions,
Animation.PlayMode.LOOP_PINGPONG);
  }
}

public class AssetBunny {
  public final AtlasRegion head;
  public final Animation animNormal;
  public final Animation animCopterTransform;
  public final Animation animCopterTransformBack;
  public final Animation animCopterRotate;

  public AssetBunny (TextureAtlas atlas) {
    head = atlas.findRegion("bunny_head");

    Array<AtlasRegion> regions = null;
    AtlasRegion region = null;

    // Animation: Bunny Normal
    regions = atlas.findRegions("anim_bunny_normal");
    animNormal = new Animation(1.0f / 10.0f, regions,
Animation.PlayMode.LOOP_PINGPONG);

    // Animation: Bunny Copter - knot ears
```

Animations

```
        regions = atlas.findRegions("anim_bunny_copter");
        animCopterTransform = new Animation(1.0f / 10.0f, regions);

        // Animation: Bunny Copter - unknot ears
        regions = atlas.findRegions("anim_bunny_copter");
        animCopterTransformBack = new Animation(1.0f / 10.0f, regions,
    Animation.PlayMode.REVERSED);

        // Animation: Bunny Copter - rotate ears
        regions = new Array<AtlasRegion>();
        regions.add(atlas.findRegion("anim_bunny_copter", 4));
        regions.add(atlas.findRegion("anim_bunny_copter", 5));
        animCopterRotate = new Animation(1.0f / 15.0f, regions);
    }
}
```

With regards to the code for the gold coin animation, you may have stumbled upon why we are inserting 10 additional copies of the animation's first frame at the beginning. Well, actually we are cheating here a little bit to achieve an artificial pause of the continuously looped animation that will now display the first frame for a much longer period of time in comparison to the other ones. Unfortunately, there is currently no way to define a per-frame duration and so we need to use a trick to create a short pause after a full animation cycle that basically avoids too flashy gold coins in our special case.

Animating the gold coin game object

Now, add the following import line to the `AbstractGameObject` class:

```
import com.badlogic.gdx.graphics.g2d.Animation;
```

Then, add the following lines of code to the same class:

```
public float stateTime;
public Animation animation;

public void setAnimation (Animation animation) {
  this.animation = animation;
  stateTime = 0;
}
```

After this, make the following changes to the same class:

```
public void update (float deltaTime) {
  stateTime += deltaTime;
  if (body == null) {
    updateMotionX(deltaTime);
    updateMotionY(deltaTime);

    // Move to new position
    position.x += velocity.x * deltaTime;
    position.y += velocity.y * deltaTime;
  } else {
    position.set(body.getPosition());
    rotation = body.getAngle() * MathUtils.radiansToDegrees;
  }
}
```

With these additions, we introduce two new common attributes that are shared with every game object in Canyon Bunny, the state time (stateTime) and the currently set animation (animation), which are going to be used for rendering the game object. We also added a convenience method called setAnimation() that allows you to change the current animation as well as reset the state time to 0. This is desirable because in almost every case, we do not want to start somewhere in the middle of a new animation but instead we want to start right from the beginning at the first frame. The change in the update() method simply makes sure that the state time is increased, which allows the animation to run.

Now, add the following import line to the GoldCoin class:

```
import com.badlogic.gdx.math.MathUtils;
```

After this, make the following changes to the same class:

```
private void init () {
  dimension.set(0.5f, 0.5f);

  setAnimation(Assets.instance.goldCoin.animGoldCoin);
  stateTime = MathUtils.random(0.0f, 1.0f);

  // Set bounding box for collision detection
  bounds.set(0, 0, dimension.x, dimension.y);

  collected = false;
```

```
}

public void render (SpriteBatch batch) {
  if (collected) return;

  TextureRegion reg = null;
  reg = animation.getKeyFrame(stateTime, true);
  batch.draw(reg.getTexture(),
position.x, position.y,
origin.x, origin.y,
dimension.x, dimension.y,
scale.x, scale.y,
rotation,
reg.getRegionX(), reg.getRegionY(),
reg.getRegionWidth(), reg.getRegionHeight(),
false, false);
}
```

In the `init()` method, we use the inherited `setAnimation()` method of `AbstractGameObject` to set the `animGoldCoin` animation. Also, the state time is initialized with a random value in the range from `0.0f` to `1.0f`. This is really a special use case here where we want each gold coin to use a different starting frame so that they look much more natural instead of being perfectly synchronized.

The following screenshot is of some gold coins that were initialized using the random state time:

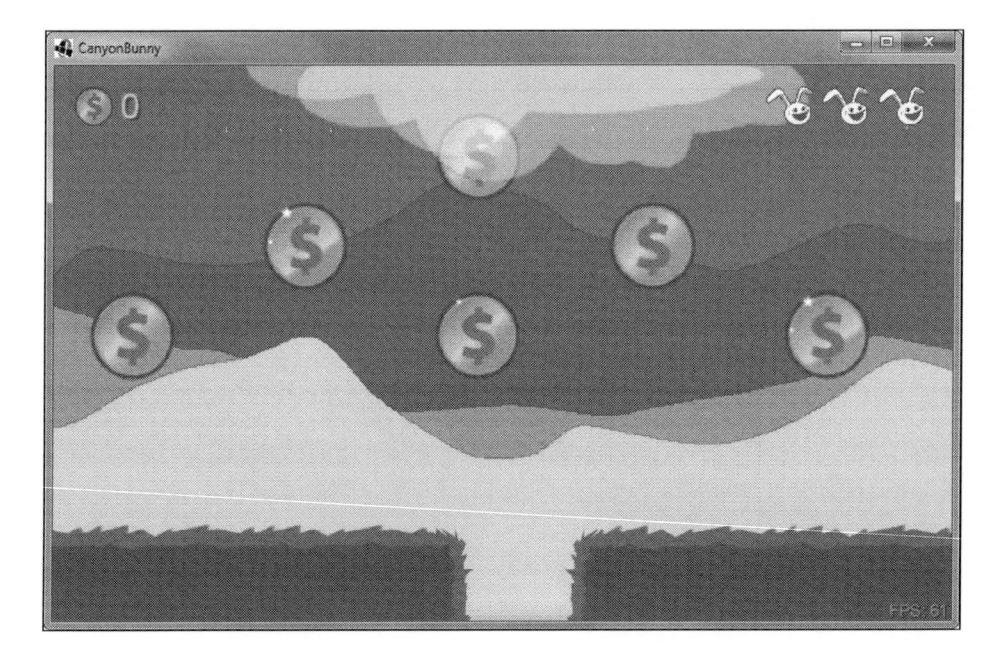

You can recognize the different state times by looking closely at the top-left corner of each gold coin where the little highlight either appears or disappears during the animation.

Animating the bunny head game object

Animating the bunny head is going to take a little more effort as we want to trigger all three of the available animations at certain events. The basic idea of having three animations is to have one standard animation (`animNormal`) that appears when nothing special is going on. Currently, when a feather power-up is picked up, the bunny head is tinted in an orange color to signalize that it is in the state of being able to fly at that very moment. Now, this is where the other three animations come into play. The first animation (`animCopterTransform`) shows a transformation from a normal bunny to a helicopter bunny by knotting its ears into something rotor-like. The second animation (`animCopterRotate`) will replace the original color-tinting effect by constantly rotating the knotted rotor ears of the bunny. Finally, there will be a reversed transformation animation (`animCopterTransformBack`) that unknots the bunny's ears again.

Animations

Take a look at the following diagram:

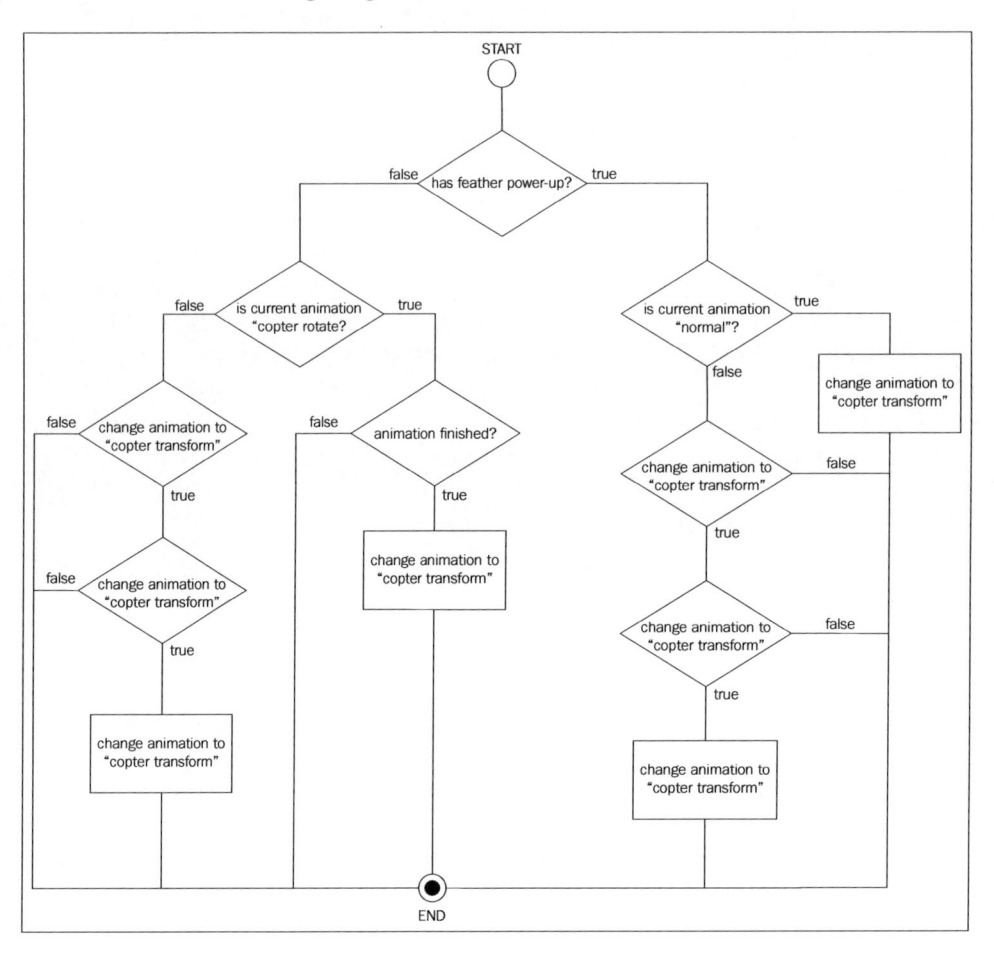

This diagram shows a state machine that we will need to implement to correctly change the states and animations of the bunny head game object. It begins with an overall check whether the feather power-up has been picked up (and is still active). Then, subsequent checks will try to find out what the current animation state is to take the correct actions accordingly.

> To find out more about (finite) state machines like the one we used in the preceding diagram, check out the wiki article at http://en.wikipedia.org/wiki/Finite_state_machine.

Now, add the following import line to the `BunnyHead` class:

```
import com.badlogic.gdx.graphics.g2d.Animation;
```

Then, add the following lines of code to the same class:

```
private Animation animNormal;
private Animation animCopterTransform;
private Animation animCopterTransformBack;
private Animation animCopterRotate;
```

After this, make the following changes to the same class:

```
public void init () {
  dimension.set(1, 1);

  animNormal = Assets.instance.bunny.animNormal;
  animCopterTransform = Assets.instance.bunny.animCopterTransform;
  animCopterTransformBack =
Assets.instance.bunny.animCopterTransformBack;
  animCopterRotate = Assets.instance.bunny.animCopterRotate;
  setAnimation(animNormal);

  // Center image on game object
  origin.set(dimension.x / 2, dimension.y / 2);

  ...
}
```

In the `init()` method, we store the references of every animation we are going to use in the corresponding local variables for much shorter names. Moreover, the starting animation is set to `animNormal`.

Now, make the following changes to the same class:

```
@Override
public void update (float deltaTime) {
  super.update(deltaTime);
  if (velocity.x != 0) {
    viewDirection = velocity.x < 0 ? VIEW_DIRECTION.LEFT
 : VIEW_DIRECTION.RIGHT;
  }
  if (timeLeftFeatherPowerup > 0) {
    if (animation == animCopterTransformBack) {
      // Restart "Transform" animation if another feather power-up
```

Animations

```
            // was picked up during "TransformBack" animation. Otherwise,
            // the "TransformBack" animation would be stuck while the
            // power-up is still active.
            setAnimation(animCopterTransform);
        }
        timeLeftFeatherPowerup -= deltaTime;
        if (timeLeftFeatherPowerup < 0) {
            // disable power-up
            timeLeftFeatherPowerup = 0;
            setFeatherPowerup(false);
            setAnimation(animCopterTransformBack);
        }
    }
    dustParticles.update(deltaTime);

    // Change animation state according to feather power-up
    if (hasFeatherPowerup) {
      if (animation == animNormal) {
        setAnimation(animCopterTransform);
      } else if (animation == animCopterTransform) {
        if (animation.isAnimationFinished(stateTime))
          setAnimation(animCopterRotate);
      }
    } else {
      if (animation == animCopterRotate) {
        if (animation.isAnimationFinished(stateTime))
          setAnimation(animCopterTransformBack);
      } else if (animation == animCopterTransformBack) {
        if (animation.isAnimationFinished(stateTime))
          setAnimation(animNormal);
      }
    }
}
```

The `update()` method now contains the logic that is shown in the preceding diagram. One detail that has not been covered yet is how we can find out if an animation is finished. The `Animation` class provides the `isAnimationFinished()` method for this purpose. However, this method is only possible if the animation is played without looping, given the state time.

Now, make the following final changes to the same class:

```
@Override
public void render (SpriteBatch batch) {
  TextureRegion reg = null;

  // Draw Particles
  dustParticles.draw(batch);

  // Apply Skin Color
  batch.setColor(
    CharacterSkin.values()[GamePreferences.instance.charSkin]
    .getColor());

  float dimCorrectionX = 0;
  float dimCorrectionY = 0;
  if (animation != animNormal) {
    dimCorrectionX = 0.05f;
    dimCorrectionY = 0.2f;
  }

  // Draw image
  reg = animation.getKeyFrame(stateTime, true);

  batch.draw(reg.getTexture(),
position.x, position.y,
origin.x, origin.y,
dimension.x + dimCorrectionX,
dimension.y + dimCorrectionY,
scale.x, scale.y,
rotation,
reg.getRegionX(), reg.getRegionY(),
reg.getRegionWidth(), reg.getRegionHeight(),
viewDirection == VIEW_DIRECTION.LEFT, false);

  // Reset color to white
  batch.setColor(1, 1, 1, 1);
}
```

In the `render()` method, we have removed the color-tinting effect in favor of our new animations. If an animation other than the standard one (`animNormal`) is detected, we will apply correcting values to the width and height for rendering. Since the standard animation is of a different dimension than the other animations, the other ones will look off-centered without the correcting values.

You can now run the game to check out all the animations we added throughout this chapter.

Summary

In this chapter, you learned how to manipulate the `Actor` objects using the `Actions` class. We discussed and used several complex chains of actions in Canyon Bunny's menu screen, which greatly demonstrate the power and flexibility of actions. Furthermore, we now know that the `Interpolation` class can also be used with these actions for added effects.

Apart from this, we have covered the `Animation` class and used the support of TexturePacker for packing animation frames which makes it easier to handle in the code. In addition to this, we have learned about the different play modes provided by the `Animation` class. Finally, we have implemented a state machine that is able to handle all events to trigger the right bunny head animations at the right time.

In the next chapter, you will learn about the latest LibGDX 3D API, where you will create basic models as well as import models exported from 3D animation software.

13
Basic 3D Programming

3D programming is an extremely complex topic, which cannot be explained completely in a single chapter. However, here I will provide very basic knowledge about the LibGDX 3D API. In this chapter, you will learn how to generate basic models (such as sphere, box, and cylinder) as well as loading models exported from 3D modeling software (such as Blender). Furthermore, we will see how to improve performance using frustum culling.

Selecting items in a 3D world is quite different, yet simpler, than in a 2D game. We will see how a user can interact with objects inside a 3D world using ray picking.

In this chapter, you will learn about the following topics:

- Create a basic model using the LibGDX 3D API
- Load a 3D model exported from Blender
- 3D frustum culling
- Ray picking

Light sources

Light clusters from the sun fall on an object, which reflect and reach our eye. This is how we see things. OpenGL ES allows us to create four types of light sources:

- **Ambient light**: This is not exactly a light source, but light reflected from other objects, thereby limiting the light intensity when compared with directional lights.
- **Directional light**: This comes from a faraway source. Light from sun is a perfect example of directional light.

- **Point light**: This is the light from a point source such as a bulb.
- **Spotlight**: This is similar to point light; however, it has a direction in which it shines. A flashlight/torch is a perfect example of a spotlight.

Environment and materials

OpenGL uses materials to refer to the properties of an object that determine how it interacts with light. In practice, when rendering you specify what (shape) to render and how to render. The shape is specified using the **Mesh** (or more commonly `MeshPart`), which defines the vertex attributes for the shader. The material is most commonly used to specify the uniform values for the shader.

Uniforms can be grouped into modelspecific (for example, the texture applied or whether or not to use blending) and environmental uniforms (for example, the lights being applied or an environment `cubemap`). Likewise, the 3D API allows you to specify a material and environment.

> To find out more about materials, environments, and attributes visit https://github.com/libgdx/libgdx/wiki/Material-and-environment.

Basic 3D using LibGDX

Here, we will explore the basis of the LibGDX 3D API and will create a basic scene with a sphere model at the center.

> You can also check the LibGDX wiki on the 3D API at https://github.com/libgdx/libgdx/wiki/Quick-start.

The project setup

First of all, let's create a new LibGDX project using `gdx-setup-ui.jar` as learned in *Chapter 1, Introduction to LibGDX and Project Setup*. Enter the values as shown here:

- **Name**: `ModelTest`
- **Package**: `com.packtpub.libgdx.modeltest`
- **Game Class**: `MyModelTest`
- **Destination**: `C:\libgdx`

You can see the following page after all the details are filled:

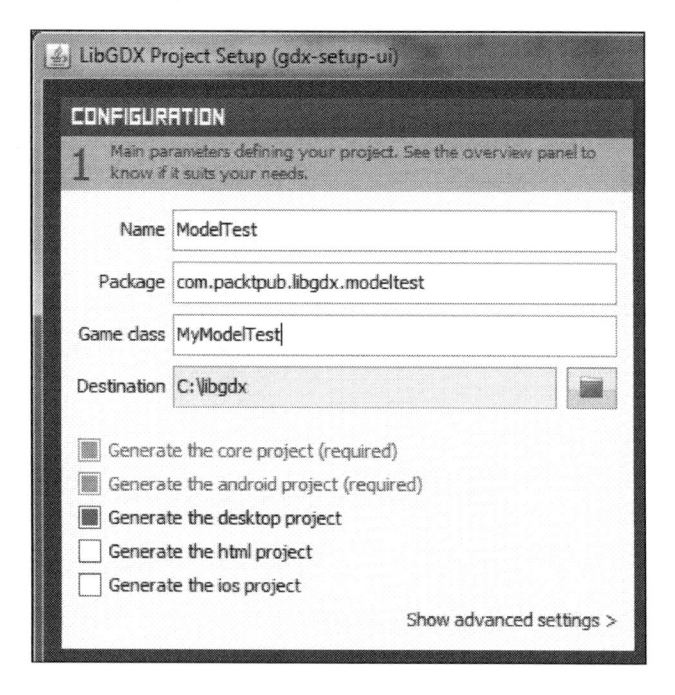

Here, you won't need the HTML or iOS project for testing models; however, if you want to simply check those devices, you can go ahead and enable those projects. Also, set the width and height to `800 x 480` in the project.

Open the `MyModelTest.java` file and remove all the auto-generated code and add the following code:

```
package com.packtpub.libgdx.modeltest;

import com.badlogic.gdx.ApplicationAdapter;
import com.badlogic.gdx.Gdx;
import com.badlogic.gdx.graphics.Color;
import com.badlogic.gdx.graphics.GL20;
import com.badlogic.gdx.graphics.PerspectiveCamera;
import com.badlogic.gdx.graphics.VertexAttributes.Usage;
import com.badlogic.gdx.graphics.g3d.Environment;
import com.badlogic.gdx.graphics.g3d.Material;
import com.badlogic.gdx.graphics.g3d.Model;
import com.badlogic.gdx.graphics.g3d.ModelBatch;
import com.badlogic.gdx.graphics.g3d.ModelInstance;
import com.badlogic.gdx.graphics.g3d.attributes.ColorAttribute;
```

Basic 3D Programming

```java
import com.badlogic.gdx.graphics.g3d.environment.DirectionalLight;
import com.badlogic.gdx.graphics.g3d.utils.CameraInputController;
import com.badlogic.gdx.graphics.g3d.utils.ModelBuilder;

public class MyModelTest extends ApplicationAdapter  {
    public Environment environment;
    public PerspectiveCamera cam;
    public CameraInputController camController;
    public ModelBatch modelBatch;
    public Model model;
    public ModelInstance instance;

    @Override
    public void create() {
        environment = new Environment();
        environment.set(new
ColorAttribute(ColorAttribute.AmbientLight, 0.4f, 0.4f,
0.4f, 1f));
        environment.add(new DirectionalLight().set(0.8f, 0.8f,
0.8f, -1f, -0.8f, -0.2f));

        modelBatch = new ModelBatch();

        cam = new PerspectiveCamera(67, Gdx.graphics.getWidth(),
Gdx.graphics.getHeight());
        cam.position.set(2, 2, 2);
        cam.lookAt(0, 0, 0);
        cam.near = 1f;
        cam.far = 300f;
        cam.update();

        ModelBuilder modelBuilder = new ModelBuilder();
        model = modelBuilder.createSphere(2, 2, 2, 20, 20, new
Material(ColorAttribute.createDiffuse(Color.YELLOW)),
Usage.Position | Usage.Normal);
        instance = new ModelInstance(model);

        camController = new CameraInputController(cam);
        Gdx.input.setInputProcessor(camController);
    }

    @Override
    public void render() {
```

```
            camController.update();

            Gdx.gl.glViewport(0, 0, Gdx.graphics.getWidth(),
    Gdx.graphics.getHeight());
            Gdx.gl.glClear(GL20.GL_COLOR_BUFFER_BIT |
    GL20.GL_DEPTH_BUFFER_BIT);

            modelBatch.begin(cam);
            modelBatch.render(instance, environment);
            modelBatch.end();
        }

        @Override
        public void dispose() {
            modelBatch.dispose();
            model.dispose();
        }

    }
```

Here, we made a basic scene and created a sphere model, as shown in the following screenshot:

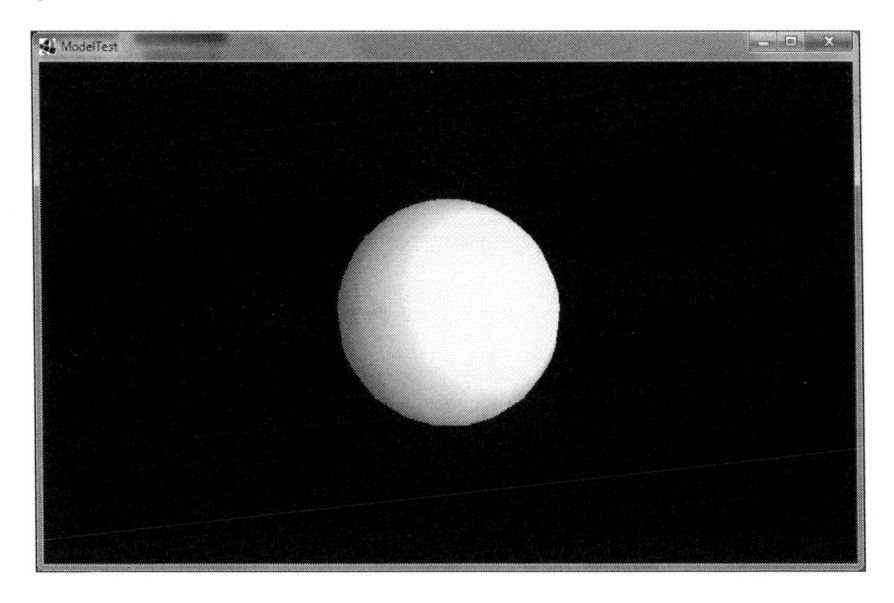

The camera

There are two types of cameras, namely orthographic and perspective. Here, we use the perspective camera to view the scene from a certain perspective, as shown here:

```
public PerspectiveCamera cam;

cam = new PerspectiveCamera(67, Gdx.graphics.getWidth(),
Gdx.graphics.getHeight());
cam.position.set(2, 2, 2);
cam.lookAt(0, 0, 0);
cam.near = 1f;
cam.far = 300f;
cam.update();
```

Using the preceding code, we create a perspective camera of field view 67 degrees keeping the current aspect ratio. The position of the camera is set at (x, y, z) coordinates (2, 2, 2) and is set by calling `cam.position.set(2, 2, 2)`. The coordinate system in LibGDX has the z axis aligned towards the viewer as visualized in the following figure:

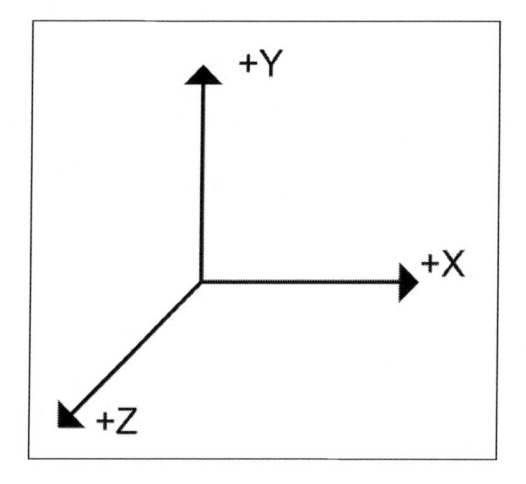

The camera is made to look at the origin (0, 0, 0) using the call `cam.lookAt(0, 0, 0)`. We set the near and far values to make sure we can always see our object. Finally, we update the camera so all the changes we made are reflected by the camera.

Model and ModelInstances

A model represents a 3D asset. It stores a hierarchy of nodes. A node has a transform and optionally a graphical part in the form of a `MeshPart` and `Material`. A model can be rendered by creating `ModelInstance` from it. This instance has an additional transform to position the model in the world, and allows the modification of materials and nodes without destroying the original model. The original model is the owner of any meshes and textures; all instances created from the model share these resources. Disposing of the model will automatically make all instances invalid.

We create a sphere model using LibGDX's `ModelBuilder`. It can create basic shapes such as box, sphere, cone, capsule, cylinder, and so on, as follows:

```
public Model model;
public ModelInstance instance;

ModelBuilder modelBuilder = new ModelBuilder();
model = modelBuilder.createSphere(2, 2, 2, 20, 20,
new Material(ColorAttribute.createDiffuse(Color.YELLOW)),
Usage.Position | Usage.Normal);

instance = new ModelInstance(model);
```

In the preceding code, a sphere is created with the width, height, and depth set to 2 units and the horizontal and vertical divisions are set to 20. You have to provide materials and attributes to create any model. Finally, `ModelInstance` is created from that model. After using the model, we dispose of it by calling `model.dispose()`.

The ModelBatch class

The `ModelBatch` class is used to render the model instance as follows:

```
modelBatch.begin(cam);
modelBatch.render(instance, environment);
modelBatch.end();
```

In the render method, we clear the screen, call `modelBatch.begin()`, render our `ModelInstance`, and then call `modelBatch.end()` to finish rendering. While rendering the model using `modelBatch.render()`, we provide the environment along with the rendering `ModelInstance`. The model batch is disposed of by calling `modelBatch.dispose()`.

The environment

The environment contains the uniform values specific for a location. For example, the lights are part of the environment. Simple applications might use only one environment, while more complex applications might use multiple environments depending on the location of `ModelInstance`. A `ModelInstance` class can only contain one environment though, as shown here:

```
public Environment environment;
...
environment = new Environment();
environment.set(new ColorAttribute(ColorAttribute.AmbientLight,
0.4f, 0.4f, 0.4f, 1f));
environment.add(new DirectionalLight().set(0.8f, 0.8f, 0.8f, -1f,
-0.8f, -0.2f));
...
modelBatch.render(instance, environment);
```

In the preceding code, a new environment is set and a directional light source is added. This environment is then rendered by calling `modelBatch.render()`.

Loading a model

In a game, we need an actual model exported from Blender or any other 3D animation software.

> The assets for our example are provided with the code bundle of this chapter.

Copy these three files to the `assets` folder of the `android` project:

- `car.g3dj`: This is the model file to be used in our example
- `tiretext.jpg` and `yellowtaxi.jpg`: These are the materials for the model

Replacing the `ModelBuilder` class in our `ModelTest.java` file, we add the following code:

```
assets = new AssetManager();
assets.load("car.g3dj", Model.class);
assets.finishLoading();
model = assets.get("car.g3dj", Model.class);
instance = new ModelInstance(model);
```

Additionally, a camera input controller is also added to inspect the model from various angles as follows:

```
camController = new CameraInputController(cam);
Gdx.input.setInputProcessor(camController);

camController.update();
```

This camera input controller will be updated on each `render()` by calling `camController.update()`.

The completed `MyModelTest.java` is as follows:

```
public class MyModelTest extends ApplicationAdapter {
    public Environment environment;
    public PerspectiveCamera cam;
    public CameraInputController camController;
    public ModelBatch modelBatch;
    public Model model;
    public ModelInstance instance;
    public AssetManager assets ;

    @Override
    public void create() {
    environment = new Environment();
    environment.set(new
ColorAttribute(ColorAttribute.AmbientLight, 0.4f, 0.4f, 0.4f,
1f));
        environment.add(new DirectionalLight().set(0.8f, 0.8f,
0.8f, -1f, -0.8f, -0.2f));

        modelBatch = new ModelBatch();

        cam = new PerspectiveCamera(67, Gdx.graphics.getWidth(),
Gdx.graphics.getHeight());
        cam.position.set(1,1,1);
        cam.lookAt(0, 0, 0);
        cam.near = 1f;
        cam.far = 300f;
        cam.update();

        assets = new AssetManager();
        assets.load("car.g3dj", Model.class);
        assets.finishLoading();
        model = assets.get("car.g3dj", Model.class);
```

Basic 3D Programming

```
            instance = new ModelInstance(model);

            camController = new CameraInputController(cam);
            Gdx.input.setInputProcessor(camController);

    }

    @Override
    public void render() {
            camController.update();
            Gdx.gl.glViewport(0, 0, Gdx.graphics.getWidth(),
    Gdx.graphics.getHeight());
            Gdx.gl.glClear(GL20.GL_COLOR_BUFFER_BIT |
    GL20.GL_DEPTH_BUFFER_BIT);

            modelBatch.begin(cam);
            modelBatch.render(instance, environment);
            modelBatch.end();
    }

    @Override
    public void dispose() {
            modelBatch.dispose();
    assets.dispose() ;
    }

}
```

The new additions are highlighted. The following is a screenshot of the render scene. Use the *W, S, A, D* keys and mouse to navigate through the scene.

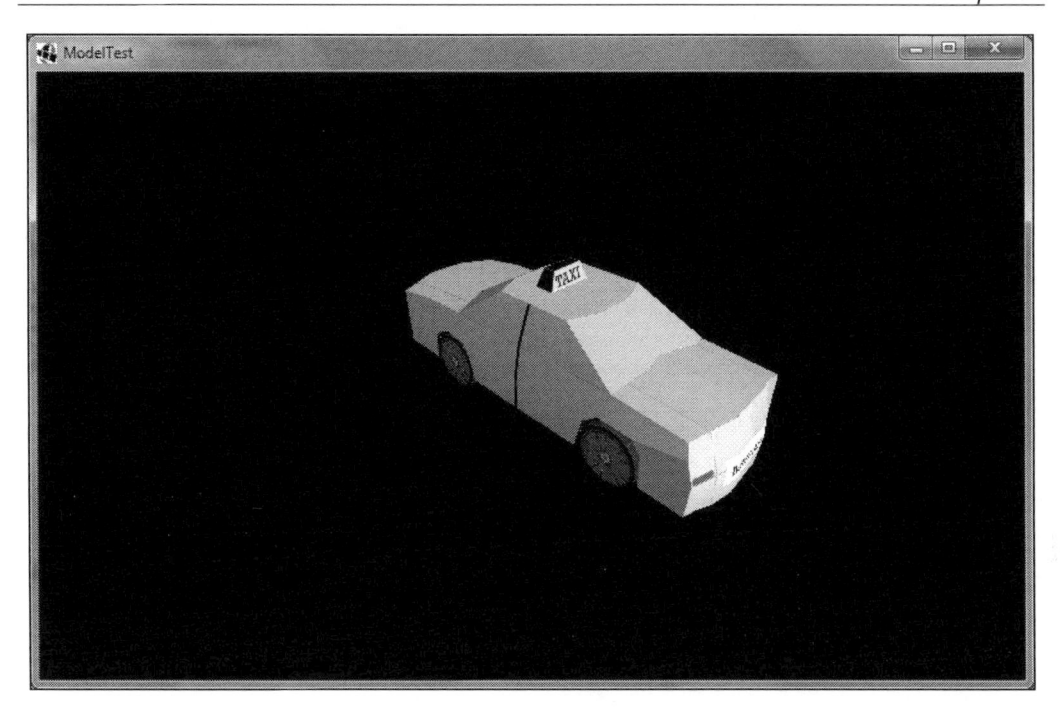

Model formats and the FBX converter

LibGDX supports three model formats, namely Wavefront OBJ, G3DJ, and G3DB. Wavefront OBJ models are intended for testing purposes only because this format does not include enough information for complex models. You can export your 3D model as .obj from any 3D animation or modeling software, however LibGDX does not fully support .obj, hence, if you use your own .obj model, then it might not render correctly. The G3DJ is a JSON textual format supported by LibGDX and can be used for debugging, whereas the G3DB is a binary format and is faster to load.

One of the most popular model formats supported by any modeling software is FBX. LibGDX provides a tool called FBX converter to convert formats such as .obj and .fbx into the LibGDX supported formats .g3dj and .g3db.

To convert `car.fbx` to a `.g3db` format, open the command line and call `fbx-conv-win32`, as shown in the following screenshot:

```
D:\>fbx-conv-win32.exe -o g3db -f car.fbx
```

Make sure that the `fbx-conv-win32.exe` file is in the same folder as `car.fbx`. Otherwise, you will have to use the full path of the source file to convert.

> To find out more about FBX converter visit https://github.com/libgdx/fbx-conv and https://github.com/libgdx/libgdx/wiki/3D-animations-and-skinning. Also, you can download FBX converter from http://libgdx.badlogicgames.com/fbx-conv.

3D frustum culling

In a 3D world, we have a lot of objects everywhere. However, only a small number of objects will be visible in the scene. Rendering all objects, including those that are not visible, can be a waste of our processing time and resources and will affect the speed of the game. Hence, we should only render those objects that are actually visible to the camera and ignore all other objects that are outside the field of view of the camera. This is known as frustum culling and there are several ways to accomplish this.

First, let's add an array of cars. The updated scene will look like this:

The `MyModelTest.java` file is as follows:

```
public class MyModelTest extends ApplicationAdapter  {
...
    public Array<ModelInstance> instances = new
Array<ModelInstance>();

    @Override
    public void create() {
        environment = new Environment();
        environment.set(new
ColorAttribute(ColorAttribute.AmbientLight, 0.4f, 0.4f,
0.4f, 1f));
        environment.add(new DirectionalLight().set(0.8f, 0.8f,
0.8f, -1f, -0.8f, -0.2f));

        modelBatch = new ModelBatch();
```

Basic 3D Programming

```
            cam = new PerspectiveCamera(67, Gdx.graphics.getWidth(),
Gdx.graphics.getHeight());
            cam.position.set(5, 20, 20);
            cam.lookAt(0, 0, 0);
            cam.near = 1f;
            cam.far = 100f;
            cam.update();

            assets = new AssetManager();
            assets.load("car.g3dj", Model.class);
            assets.finishLoading();
            model = assets.get("car.g3dj", Model.class);

            for (float x = -30; x <= 10f; x += 20) {
            for (float z = -30f; z <= 0f; z += 10f) {
                ModelInstance instance = new ModelInstance(model);
                instance.transform.setToTranslation(x, 0, z);
                instances.add(instance);
              }
            }

            camController = new CameraInputController(cam);
            Gdx.input.setInputProcessor(camController);

      }

      @Override
      public void render() {
            camController.update();

            Gdx.gl.glViewport(0, 0, Gdx.graphics.getWidth(),
Gdx.graphics.getHeight());
            Gdx.gl.glClear(GL20.GL_COLOR_BUFFER_BIT |
GL20.GL_DEPTH_BUFFER_BIT);

            modelBatch.begin(cam);
            for (ModelInstance instance : instances) {
                    modelBatch.render(instance, environment);
            }
            modelBatch.end();


      }
```

```
        @Override
        public void dispose() {
                modelBatch.dispose();
                assets.dispose();
        }
...
}
```

The difference from our previous `MyModelTest.java` file is that we added an array of model instances instead of one. Note that there is only one model and 12 model instances. The position of the camera is also changed to (5, 20, 20). The updated code is highlighted. You can use the mouse or *W, S, A, D* keys to navigate. However, with the current code, every model instance is drawn, whether they are in the scene or not.

In order to check this, let's update the code and add some strings to the scene as follows:

```
    ...
    public OrthographicCamera orthoCam;
    public SpriteBatch spriteBatch;
    public BitmapFont font;
    public StringBuilder stringBuilder = new StringBuilder();

    @Override
    public void create() {
    ...
    orthoCam = new OrthographicCamera(Gdx.graphics.getWidth(),
Gdx.graphics.getHeight());
    orthoCam.position.set(Gdx.graphics.getWidth() / 2f,
Gdx.graphics.getHeight() / 2f, 0);
            spriteBatch = new SpriteBatch();
            font = new BitmapFont();

    }

    @Override
    public void render() {
    ...
    modelBatch.begin(cam);
    int count = 0;
    for (ModelInstance instance : instances) {
            modelBatch.render(instance, environment);
            count++;
    }
    modelBatch.end();
```

Basic 3D Programming

```
        orthoCam.update();
        spriteBatch.setProjectionMatrix(orthoCam.combined);
        spriteBatch.begin();
        stringBuilder.setLength(0);
        stringBuilder.append("FPS: " +
    Gdx.graphics.getFramesPerSecond()).append("\n") ;
        stringBuilder.append("Cars: " + count).append("\n");
        stringBuilder.append("Total: " + instances.size).append("\n");
        font.drawMultiLine(spriteBatch, stringBuilder, 0,
    Gdx.graphics.getHeight());
        spriteBatch.end();

    }
```

Here, we add an orthographic camera to view 2D items in a 3D scene. Then, we print the FPS and total number of instances on the top-left corner of the game scene, as shown in the following screenshot:

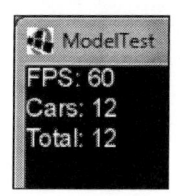

> **Want some 2D in 3D?**
>
> In your 3D game, you might want to add some 2D images such as a score icon or play/pause or mute button or maybe a permanent background image in the scene. We can use the orthographic camera and sprite batch to render 2D objects in the scene, just like we rendered the text here.

Now, we can see that there are a number of cars rendering and the total cars available are 12, even after navigating the scene using the mouse or keys. Hence, regardless of where the camera is at the moment, the number of instances rendered in the scene stays 12. Now, it is time to implement frustum culling.

> A frustum can be seen as a shape like a pyramid in 3D space with the converging end at the camera and the body containing everything the camera can see.
>
> Check this Wikipedia article on viewing frustum at http://en.wikipedia.org/wiki/Viewing_frustum.
>
> Also, read this wonderful article to get a good understanding about frustum and camera at http://www.badlogicgames.com/wordpress/?p=1550.

LibGDX provides some very easy methods to check if an object is inside the frustum. Add the following code to `MyModelTest.java`:

```
private Vector3 position = new Vector3();
private boolean isVisible(final Camera cam, final ModelInstance instance) {
    instance.transform.getTranslation(position);
    return cam.frustum.pointInFrustum(position);
}
```

Here, we added `Vector3` to hold the position. In the `isVisible()` method, we fetch the position of `ModelInstance` and next we check if that position is inside the frustum using the function `pointInFrustum()`.

Add `isVisible()` to the `render()` function:

```
@Override
public void render() {
...
modelBatch.begin(cam);
int count = 0;
for (ModelInstance instance : instances) {
    if (isVisible(cam, instance)) {
        modelBatch.render(instance, environment);
        count++;
    }
}
modelBatch.end();
...
}
```

Now, you can run the scene and navigate. You will find that the number of cars will change according to the position of the camera.

In the preceding `isVisible()` function, we check whether the position of the car is inside. What if only a part of the car is within the frustum? In order to check this, LibGDX provides a function, `boundsInFrustum`, to check whether the bounding box is completely within the frustum. A bounding box is a box that contains the entire model/instance. The following screenshot will give you a clear picture of this:

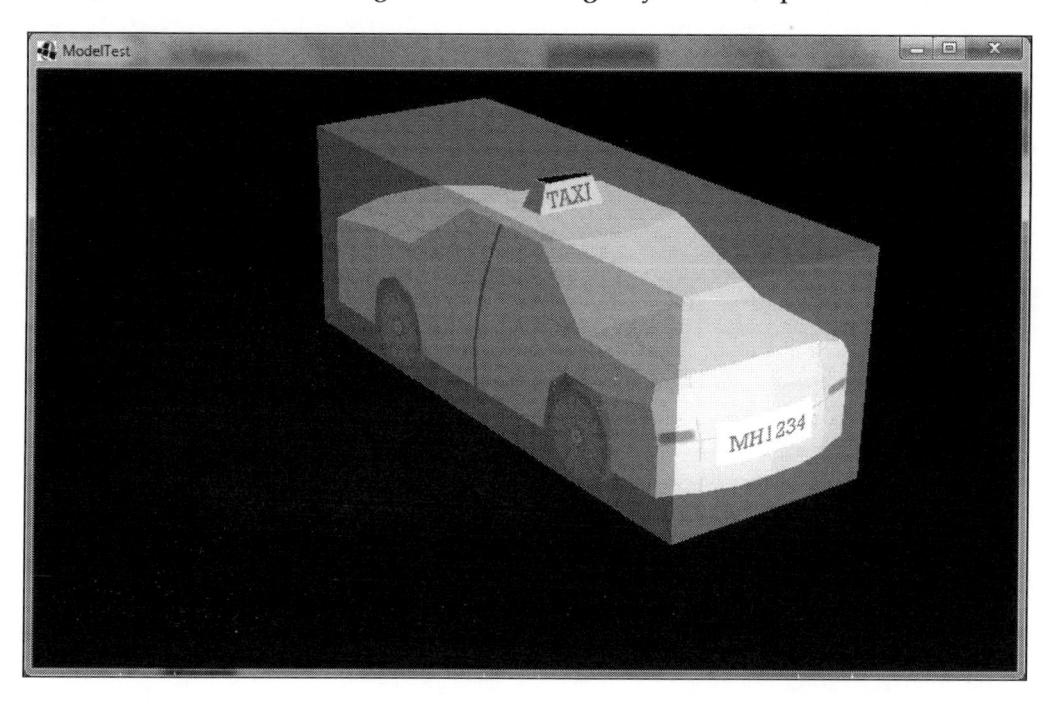

So, we can update our `isVisible()` function to check the bounding box in the following way:

```
private boolean isVisible(PerspectiveCamera cam, ModelInstance instance) {
instance.transform.getTranslation(position);
BoundingBox box = instance.calculateBoundingBox(new BoundingBox());
return cam.frustum.boundsInFrustum(position, box.getDimensions());
}
```

The `calculateBoundingBox` method will return the bounding box of that particular instance. Note, this function is a slow operation; hence, it would be better if you cache the result.

Similarly, we can calculate the bounding sphere. Checking against a radius is a bit faster, but it might cause more false positives, as shown here:

```
float radius = box.getDimensions().len()/2f ;
cam.frustum.sphereInFrustum(position, radius);
```

Here, `radius` is the radius of the bounding sphere.

Ray picking

It would be great if we could interact with the game objects. In a 2D scene, it is easy as we can map the 2D coordinates of the game object with the input coordinates. However, in a 3D game, it is different as the game object is positioned in 3D world coordinates and the input is available as 2D screen coordinates. A familiar scenario is a first person shooter game, wherein on shooting the bullet it is traced through the scene until a collision is detected. Ray picking is the process of shooting a line or ray from the camera through the 2D view port into the 3D game world until it hits an object, as shown here:

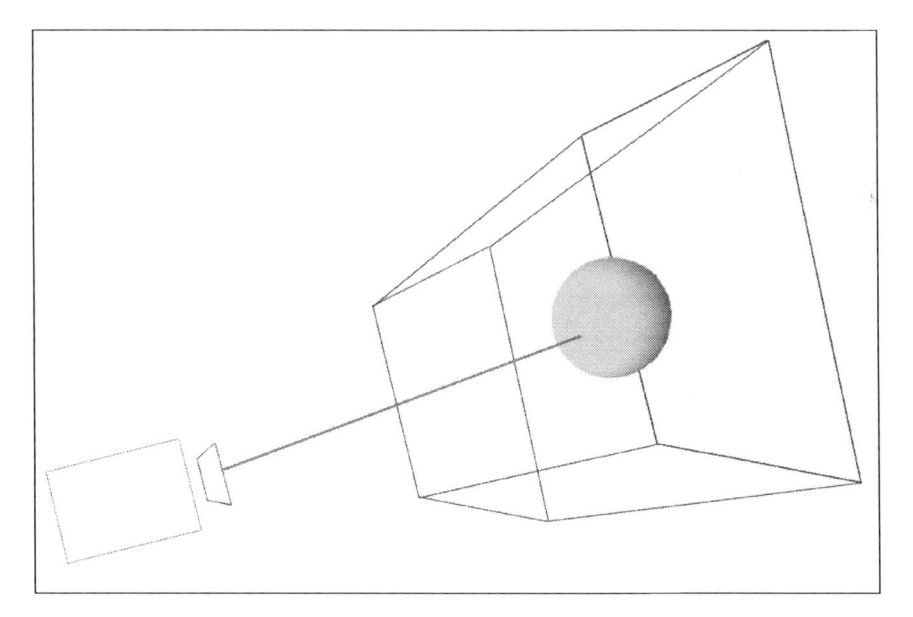

Basic 3D Programming

The following code will explain the process of ray picking in LibGDX. We will extend and update `CameraInputController` in the `create()` function as follows:

```
@Override
public void create() {
...
final BoundingBox box= model.calculateBoundingBox(new BoundingBox());
camController = new CameraInputController(cam) {
private final Vector3 position = new Vector3();

@Override
public boolean touchUp(int screenX, int screenY, int pointer, int button) {
Ray ray = cam.getPickRay(screenX, screenY);
for (int i = 0; i < instances.size; i++) {

ModelInstance instance = instances.get(i);
instance.transform.getTranslation(position);

if (Intersector.intersectRayBoundsFast(ray, position, box.getDimensions())) {
        instances.removeIndex(i);
        i--;
    }
}
return super.touchUp(screenX, screenY, pointer, button);
}
};
Gdx.input.setInputProcessor(camController);
}
```

Here, in `touchUp()`, the `getPickRay()` function creates a ray from the input coordinates. Now, we iterate through all the instances to check whether that ray hits an object. LibGDX provides a class `Intersector` that offers various static methods for intersection checking between different geometric objects. In order to check whether the ray collides with any game objects, we use the function `intersectRayBoundsFast()`. On collision, we remove that model instance from the instances array so when you touch any car in the game scene, it simply vanishes.

> Here, for simplicity, we extended the `CameraInputController` class. However, in your game, you need to implement your own event handler, `InputListerner` or `InputAdapter` class as learned in *Chapter 3, Configuring the Game*. To understand more about event handling, visit https://github.com/libgdx/libgdx/wiki/Event-handling.

Summary

In this chapter, you learned how to create a basic model and load 3D model of a car, frustum culling, rendering 2D text in a 3D scene, and ray picking.

You also learned about a standalone tool, FBX converter, to generate LibGDX supported 3D formats from `.obj` or `.fbx` models.

In the next chapter, you will learn how to include 3D physics in a game using Bullet Physics. This includes creating rigid bodies and applying physics properties just like you learned in Box2D.

14
Bullet Physics

In *Chapter 11*, *Advanced Programming Techniques*, you learned about 2D physics using Box2D. Now, we will enter the next dimension: 3D physics using the Bullet Physics engine. Bullet Physics itself is a huge topic, so, this chapter will focus on providing you with a basic idea about the 3D physics engine. Later, we will create a physics simulation using basic shapes.

In this chapter, we will cover the following topics:

- Create a project using `gdx-setup.jar`
- Focus on the basic concepts of bullet
- Create a simple application to simulate physics using Bullet

About Bullet Physics

Bullet is a 3D collision detection and rigid body dynamics library. It has been used in many Hollywood movies such as *Megamind*, *Shrek 4*, and *How To Train Your Dragon*, and popular games such as the *Grand Theft Auto* series. The Bullet Physics library was originally created by Erwin Coumans. Since 2005, the Bullet project has been open source with many other contributors as well. The Bullet library is published under the `zlib` license. It is written in C++ and has been ported to several frameworks and programming languages.

LibGDX integrates Bullet through a thin wrapper API. The wrapper tends to follow the original Bullet class names, which means that most classes are prefixed with bt as in the original library. This approach makes it easier to understand and transfer existing knowledge about Bullet by following tutorials and manuals that are not based on LibGDX. You can also use the official Bullet user manual and API documentation.

For more documentation related to the Bullet Physics engine, visit:

- `www.bulletphysics.org`
- `http://bulletphysics.org/mediawiki-1.5.8/index.php/Bullet_User_Manual_and_API_documentation`

For Bullet Physics tutorials, visit:

- `http://bulletphysics.org/mediawiki-1.5.8/index.php/Tutorial_Articles`
- `https://github.com/libgdx/libgdx/wiki/Bullet-physics`
- `http://blog.xoppa.com/using-the-libgdx-3d-physics-bullet-wrapper-part1`
- `http://blog.xoppa.com/using-the-libgdx-3d-physics-bullet-wrapper-part2`

A few basic concepts

Now, we will explore some basic ideas behind the vast Bullet library in the next sections.

Understanding rigid bodies

Rigid bodies are the basic building block of all physics simulations. Like in the real world, a rigid body has some properties such as mass, position, velocity, inertia as well as motion states, and so on. The rigid body is assumed to be solid and thus incapable of being deformed by the exerting forces.

Static, dynamic, and kinematic rigid bodies

There are three different types of objects in Bullet. They are as follows:

- Dynamic (moving) rigid bodies:
    - Positive mass
    - On every simulation frame, the dynamic world will update its world transform
- Static rigid bodies:
    - Zero mass
    - Cannot move or collide
- Kinematic rigid bodies:
    - Zero mass
    - They can be animated by the user, but there will be only one-way interaction and dynamic objects will be pushed away, however there is no influence from dynamics objects

Collision shapes

Like graphical meshes, collision shapes allow collision of a rich variety of different objects that one might encounter in the real world. Collision shapes don't have a world position; they are attached to collision objects or rigid bodies. The collision shape is for collisions only, and thus has no concept of mass, inertia, restitution, and so on. If you have many bodies that use the same collision shape, it is good practice to have only one Bullet collision shape, and share it among all those bodies. This helps save memory. Unlike graphical meshes, collision shapes are not always composed of triangles, but they can be represented as a primitive shape such as a box and a cylinder.

For more about collision shapes, visit the official manual at `http://bulletphysics.org/mediawiki-1.5.8/index.php/Collision_Shapes`.

MotionStates

MotionStates are a way for Bullet to do all the hard work for you by getting the objects being simulated into the rendering part of your program.

In most situations, your game loop would iterate through all the objects you're simulating before each frame render. For each object, you would update the position of the render object from the physics body. Bullet uses something called MotionStates to save you this effort.

MotionStates for objects communicate movement caused by forces in the physics simulation to your program. Static objects don't move, so there is no need to communicate movement. They don't need a motion state.

Kinematic objects are controlled by your program and the motion state works in reverse. It communicates movement of your object to Bullet so it can detect collisions with it.

> You can visit the official documentation at http://bulletphysics.org/mediawiki-1.5.8/index.php/MotionStates.

Simulating physics

In this physics engine, you can add and remove rigid bodies, set and apply properties to the bodies as well as the Bullet world itself, thereby creating a wonderful world similar to our living world inside our computer.

Being a feature-rich engine, there are more features to be explored, but that's not in the scope of this book. However, for in-depth information, you can download the manual at https://github.com/erwincoumans/bullet2/blob/master/Bullet_User_Manual.pdf?raw=true.

Learning Bullet with LibGDX

In the next sections, you will learn how to use Bullet libraries in LibGDX.

Setting up a project

If you are using the old LibGDX project generation (gdx-setup-ui.jar) method, then you'll need to add gdx-bullet.jar to your main project. Alternatively, you can add the gdx-bullet project to the projects of the build path of your main project. For your desktop project, you'll need to add the gdx-bullet-natives.jar file to the libraries. For your android project, you'll need to copy the armeabi/libgdx-bullet.so file and armeabi-v7a/libgdx-bullet.so file to the libs folder in your android project.

Bullet isn't supported for GWT at the moment. Alternatively, we can use the LibGDX Gradle Project Setup (gdx-setup.jar) tool where Bullet will be linked altogether and you don't have to worry about it.

Open the gdx-setup.jar file and enter the following details:

- **Name**: CollisionTest
- **Package**: com.packtpub.libgdx.collisiontest
- **Game class**: MyCollisionTest
- **Destination**: C:\libgdx
- **Android SDK**: <Path to your android-sdk>

Select the latest LibGDX version and check Android, Desktop, iOS as **Sub Projects**. We will avoid **Html** as Bullet does not support GWT at the moment. Now, select **Bullet** under the **Extensions** menu and click on **Generate**, as shown in the following screenshot. Now, you can follow the steps in *Chapter 1*, *Introduction to LibGDX and Project Setup*, under the *Creating a new application* section, to generate and import the LibGDX project.

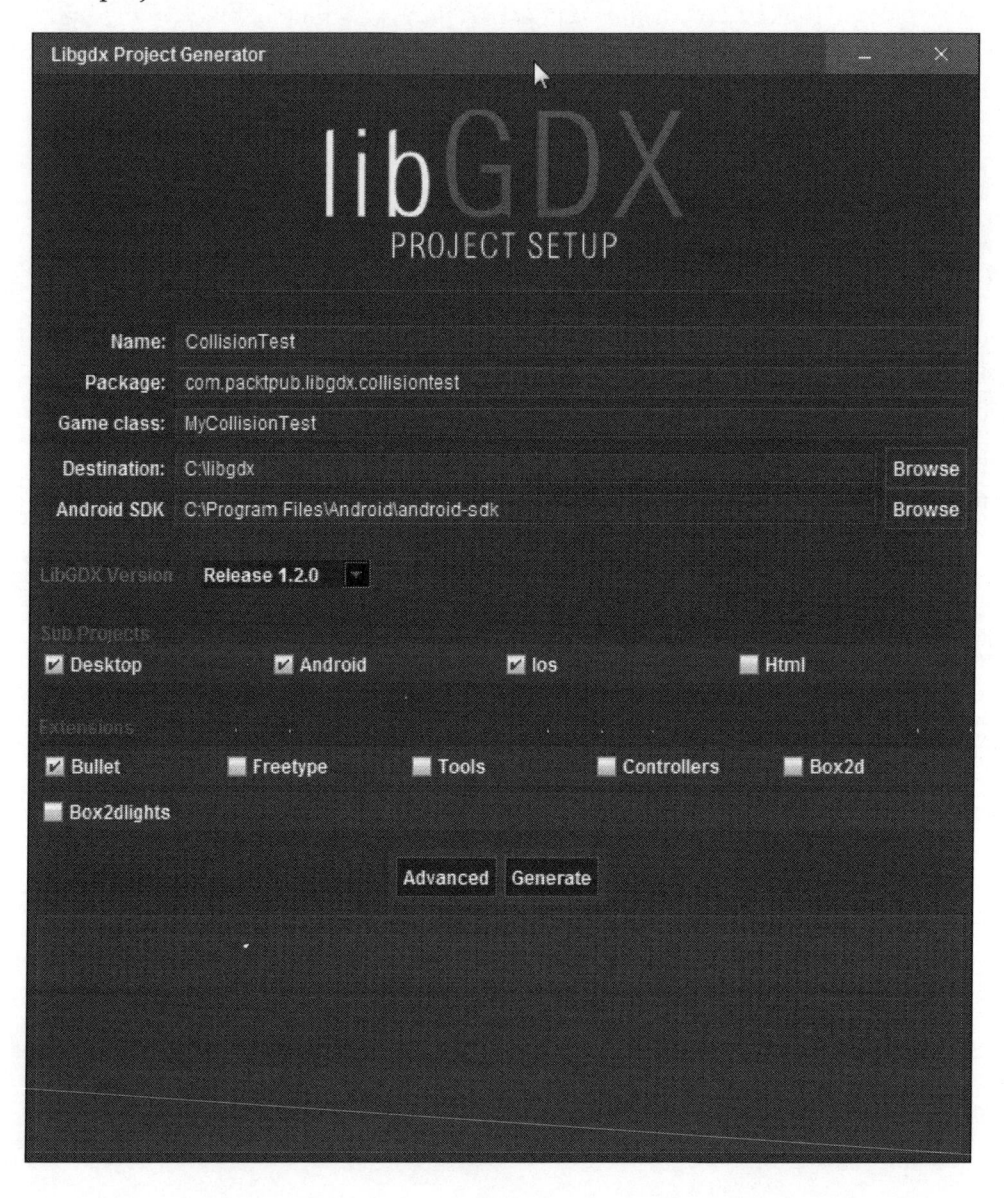

Creating a basic 3D scene

In *Chapter 13, Basic 3D Programming*, you learned how to create a basic model. Let's do it again. Create a simple scene with a ball and ground, as shown in the following screenshot:

Add the following code to `MyCollisionTest.java`:

```
package com.packtpub.libgdx.collisiontest;

import com.badlogic.gdx.ApplicationAdapter;
import com.badlogic.gdx.Gdx;
...
import com.badlogic.gdx.utils.Array;

public class MyCollisionTest extends ApplicationAdapter {
PerspectiveCamera cam;
ModelBatch modelBatch;
```

Bullet Physics

```java
Array<Model> models;
ModelInstance groundInstance;
ModelInstance sphereInstance;
Environment environment;
ModelBuilder modelbuilder;

@Override
public void create() {
    modelBatch = new ModelBatch();

    environment = new Environment();
    environment.set(new ColorAttribute(ColorAttribute.AmbientLight,
0.4f, 0.4f, 0.4f, 1f));
    environment.add(new DirectionalLight().set(0.8f, 0.8f, 0.8f, -
1f, -0.8f, -0.2f));

    cam = new PerspectiveCamera(67, Gdx.graphics.getWidth(),
Gdx.graphics.getHeight());
    cam.position.set(0, 10, -20);
    cam.lookAt(0, 0, 0);
    cam.update();

    models = new Array<Model>();

    modelbuilder = new ModelBuilder();
    // creating a ground model using box shape
    float groundWidth = 40;
    modelbuilder.begin();
    MeshPartBuilder mpb = modelbuilder.part("parts", GL20.GL_TRIANGLES,
Usage.Position | Usage.Normal | Usage.Color,
new Material(ColorAttribute.createDiffuse(Color.WHITE)));
    mpb.setColor(1f, 1f, 1f, 1f);
    mpb.box(0, 0, 0, groundWidth, 1, groundWidth);
    Model model = modelbuilder.end();
    models.add(model);
    groundInstance = new ModelInstance(model);

    // creating a sphere model
    float radius = 2f;
    final Model sphereModel = modelbuilder.createSphere(radius,
radius, radius, 20, 20, new Material(ColorAttribute.
createDiffuse(Color.RED),
ColorAttribute.createSpecular(Color.GRAY),
FloatAttribute.createShininess(64f)), Usage.Position
| Usage.Normal);
```

```
        models.add(sphereModel);
        sphereInstance = new ModelInstance(sphereModel);
        sphereinstance.transform.trn(0, 10, 0);
    }

    public void render() {
        Gdx.gl.glViewport(0, 0, Gdx.graphics.getWidth(), Gdx.graphics.
getHeight());
        Gdx.gl.glClearColor(0, 0, 0, 1);
        Gdx.gl.glClear(GL20.GL_COLOR_BUFFER_BIT |
GL20.GL_DEPTH_BUFFER_BIT);

        modelBatch.begin(cam);
        modelBatch.render(groundInstance, environment);
        modelBatch.render(sphereInstance, environment);
        modelBatch.end();
    }

    @Override
    public void dispose() {
        modelBatch.dispose();
        for (Model model : models)
            model.dispose();

    }
}
```

The ground is actually a thin box created using `ModelBuilder` just like the sphere. Now that we have created a simple 3D scene, let's add some physics using the following code:

```
public class MyCollisionTest extends ApplicationAdapter {
...

private btDefaultCollisionConfiguration collisionConfiguration;
private btCollisionDispatcher dispatcher;
private btDbvtBroadphase broadphase;
private btSequentialImpulseConstraintSolver solver;
private btDiscreteDynamicsWorld world;

private Array<btCollisionShape> shapes = new
Array<btCollisionShape>();
private Array<btRigidBodyConstructionInfo> bodyInfos = new
Array<btRigidBody.btRigidBodyConstructionInfo>();
```

Bullet Physics

```java
    private Array<btRigidBody> bodies = new Array<btRigidBody>();
    private btDefaultMotionState sphereMotionState;

    @Override
    public void create() {
    ...
        // Initiating Bullet Physics
        Bullet.init();


        //setting up the world
        collisionConfiguration = new btDefaultCollisionConfiguration();
        dispatcher = new btCollisionDispatcher(collisionConfiguration);
        broadphase = new btDbvtBroadphase();
        solver = new btSequentialImpulseConstraintSolver();
        world = new btDiscreteDynamicsWorld(dispatcher, broadphase,
solver, collisionConfiguration);
        world.setGravity(new Vector3(0, -9.81f, 1f));


        // creating ground body
        btCollisionShape groundshape = new btBoxShape(new Vector3(20, 1 /
2f, 20));
            shapes.add(groundshape);
        btRigidBodyConstructionInfo bodyInfo = new
btRigidBodyConstructionInfo(0, null, groundshape, Vector3.Zero);
        this.bodyInfos.add(bodyInfo);
        btRigidBody body = new btRigidBody(bodyInfo);
        bodies.add(body);

        world.addRigidBody(body);

        // creating sphere body
       sphereMotionState = new
btDefaultMotionState(sphereInstance.transform);
        sphereMotionState.setWorldTransform(sphereInstance.transform);
        final btCollisionShape sphereShape = new btSphereShape(1f);
        shapes.add(sphereShape);

        bodyInfo = new btRigidBodyConstructionInfo(1, sphereMotionState,
sphereShape, new Vector3(1, 1, 1));
        this.bodyInfos.add(bodyInfo);

        body = new btRigidBody(bodyInfo);
        bodies.add(body);
```

```
      world.addRigidBody(body);
   }

   public void render() {
      Gdx.gl.glViewport(0, 0, Gdx.graphics.getWidth(),
   Gdx.graphics.getHeight());
      Gdx.gl.glClearColor(0, 0, 0, 1);
      Gdx.gl.glClear(GL20.GL_COLOR_BUFFER_BIT | GL20.GL_DEPTH_BUFFER_
   BIT);

      world.stepSimulation(Gdx.graphics.getDeltaTime(), 5);
      sphereMotionState.getWorldTransform(sphereInstance.transform);

      modelBatch.begin(cam);
      modelBatch.render(groundInstance, environment);
      modelBatch.render(sphereInstance, environment);
      modelBatch.end();
   }

   @Override
   public void dispose() {
      modelBatch.dispose();
      for (Model model : models)
            model.dispose();
      for (btRigidBody body : bodies) {
            body.dispose();
      }
      sphereMotionState.dispose();
      for (btCollisionShape shape : shapes)
            shape.dispose();
      for (btRigidBodyConstructionInfo info : bodyInfos)
            info.dispose();
      world.dispose();
      collisionConfiguration.dispose();
      dispatcher.dispose();
      broadphase.dispose();
      solver.dispose();
      Gdx.app.log(this.getClass().getName(), "Disposed");
   }
}
```

The highlighted parts are the addition to our previous code. After execution, we see the ball falling and colliding with the ground.

Initializing Bullet

We know that LibGDX uses a wrapper to call the C++ Bullet library. So, before calling any of the Bullet functions, we have to load the Bullet library to memory. To do this, we call `Bullet.init()` in the `create()` method. Calling any of the Bullet functions, for example, `btDefaultCollisionConfiguration()` before `Bullet.init()` will result in an error.

Creating a dynamics world

After initializing Bullet, we create the virtual physics world where everything happens. To do this, we add the following code:

```
collisionConfiguration = new btDefaultCollisionConfiguration();
dispatcher = new btCollisionDispatcher(collisionConfiguration);
broadphase = new btDbvtBroadphase();
solver = new btSequentialImpulseConstraintSolver();
world = new btDiscreteDynamicsWorld(dispatcher, broadphase,
solver, collisionConfiguration);
world.setGravity(new Vector3(0, -9.81f, 1f));
```

Collision detection in a 3D world is complex. We can use specialized collision detection algorithms, however, they are very expensive if we use them to check all bodies at a time. Ideally, we'd first check whether the two objects are near each other, for example, using a bounding box or bounding sphere, and only if they are near each other, we'd use the more accurate and specialized collision algorithm. This two phase method has benefits. The first phase, where we find collision objects that are near each other, is called the broad phase. Then, the second phase, where a more accurate specialized collision algorithm is used, is called the near phase. In practice, the collision dispatcher is the class we've used for the near phase.

To construct the dynamics world, we'll need a constraint solver and a collision configuration. The constraint solver is used to attach objects to each other. Also, `btCollisionConfiguration` allows the Bullet collision detection stack allocator and pool memory allocators to be configured. This collision configuration is also fed to the collision dispatcher through its constructor and then we create our dynamic world by calling `btDiscreteDynamicsWorld`. The `btDiscreteDynamicsWorld` class is a subclass of `btDynamicsWorld`, which is a subclass of `btCollisionWorld`. When the world is created, we define its gravity using the `setGravity()` function.

A custom MotionState class

In a 3D world with many physics objects, all might not be at motion at the same time. For each frame render, if we iterate and update positions of all render objects we're simulating, it would require a lot of time especially if the game has a lot of physics bodies. Luckily, the Bullet wrapper offers callback methods that will be called when a certain event occurs. We create a custom interface extending the btMotionState class where we include what to do when something happens. For example, create a new MyMotionState.java file in the com.packtpub.libgdx.collisiontest package and add the following code:

```
public class MyMotionState extends btMotionState {
final ModelInstance instance;
public MyMotionState (ModelInstance instance) {
   this.instance = instance;
}
@Override
public void getWorldTransform(Matrix4 worldTrans) {
   worldTrans.set(instance.transform);
}
@Override
public void setWorldTransform(Matrix4 worldTrans) {
   instance.transform.set(worldTrans);
}

}
```

The setWorldTransform() function will set the transformation of the render object, whereas the getWorldTransform() function returns the transformation of the current render object. This custom class will update the render instance when Bullet updates the position of respective physics object.

A simple ContactListener class

LibGDX Bullet wrapper offers callback methods to notify us when a collision occurs. Here, we can define what should happen when a collision occurs. This is similar to contact listener in Box2D. However, this callback class, ContactListener, is not a Bullet class but a class specifically created for the Bullet wrapper. For this reason, we do not have to inform Bullet to use ContactListener.

Bullet Physics

Create a new `MyContactListener.java` file in the `com.packtpub.libgdx.collisiontest` package and add the following class:

```
public class MyContactListener extends ContactListener {
@Override
public void onContactStarted(btCollisionObject colObj0,
btCollisionObject colObj1) {
    Gdx.app.log(this.getClass().getName(), "onContactStarted");

}
}
```

In the `create()` method of our game class, we simply call the following method:

```
MyContactListener contactListener = new MyContactListener();
```

> Bullet contact listener provides a lot of methods for various collision states. For more information, visit https://github.com/libgdx/libgdx/wiki/Bullet-physics#contact-listeners.

Adding some rigid bodies

Now, we will create individual bodies and set their properties and put them into our dynamics world, as follows:

```
    modelbuilder.begin();
MeshPartBuilder mpb = modelbuilder.part("parts",
GL20.GL_TRIANGLES, Usage.Position | Usage.Normal | Usage.Color,
new Material(ColorAttribute.createDiffuse(Color.WHITE)));
    mpb.setColor(1f, 1f, 1f, 1f);
    mpb.box(0, 0, 0, 40, 1, 40);
    Model model = modelbuilder.end();
groundInstance = new ModelInstance(model);


    btCollisionShape groundshape = new btBoxShape(new Vector3(20, 1 / 2f, 20));
    btRigidBodyConstructionInfo bodyInfo = new
btRigidBodyConstructionInfo(0, null, groundshape, Vector3.Zero);
    btRigidBody body = new btRigidBody(bodyInfo);
    world.addRigidBody(body);
```

[428]

The preceding steps are to create the ground. In our program, the ground is simply a box with very low height. Using the mesh builder, we create a box with width, height, and depth as 40, 1, and 40 units respectively. Remember, this is simply a visual model that we created. For actual collision, we need to create a physics body with btCollisionShape. However, btCollisionShape is a base class intended for low-level usage. Hence, we use btBoxShape, which inherits btCollisionShape that creates a box primitive around the origin, its side axis aligned with length specified by half extents, in local shape coordinates. Similar to the box shape, we can also create a sphere, a cone, a cylinder, a capsule, an arrow, and so on.

To create btRigidBodyConstructionInfo, we need to specify the mass, motion state, collision shape, and the local inertia. Here, we we defined the mass as zero zero and local inertia as zero vector. This is because our ground body is static. Zero mass isn't physically possible. It is used to indicate that the ground should not respond to any forces applied to it. It should always stay at the same location (and rotation), regardless of any forces or collisions that may be applied to it. This is called a static object. The other objects (with a mass greater than zero) are called dynamic objects. Since our ground is static, we don't have to provide any motion state either.

> Static objects do not need a motion state because they do not move.

Finally, we create the rigid body feeding bodyInfo to the btRigidBody constructor. This rigid body is then added to our dynamics physics world by calling world.addRigidBody(body).

Stepping the world

In Bullet, we need to call a function to update the dynamic physics world so that the game world continues to progress. This is achieved by the stepSimulation() call. We provide three parameters, the delta time, maximum substeps, and a fixed time step. The following code will explain everything:

```
world.stepSimulation(Gdx.graphics.getDeltaTime(), 5 , 1/60f);
```

Bullet will perform as many (but not more than the specified maximum) calculations using the specified 1/60f delta time, until it reaches the specified actual elapsed delta time. Obviously, it's very unlikely that the delta value is always exactly a multiple of 1/60f. In fact, it is possible in some cases that the value of delta is less than specified 1/60f, causing Bullet not to perform any calculations at all. Using this along with custom btMotionState will provide a smooth transition in our game.

> To find much more about the step simulation in the standard wiki, visit `http://bulletphysics.org/mediawiki-1.5.8/index.php/Stepping_the_World`.

Ray casting in Bullet

Ray casting is like shooting a virtual laser between two points and seeing whether it hit anything and what it hit. There are a number of useful things you can do with ray casting, such as firing weapons. This is similar to what we learned in *Chapter 13, Basic 3D Programming*, under the *Ray picking* section.

To do a ray cast, you need to:

1. Create a `RayResultCallback` object.
2. Do the ray test.
3. Process the results of the ray cast.

The ray test is done by calling the `world.rayTest(rayFrom, rayTo, rayTestCB);` function where `rayFrom` and `rayTo` are objects of the `Vector3` class and `rayTestCB` is an object of the `ClosestRayResultCallback` class. The `world` object is the dynamics world where physics is simulated. The result of this method is stored in `rayTestCB`.

A simple test game

We will create a simple physics game just like the previous one. Here, we will include basic shapes such as a box, sphere, cylinder, and cone and do a simple ray testing. The program will have a ground shape upon which objects (such as a box and sphere) will be thrown on touch. There will be buttons on screen, which after selected will allow the related item to be thrown. The last button demonstrates ray picking. Your screen will look like this:

![MyCollisionTest screenshot]

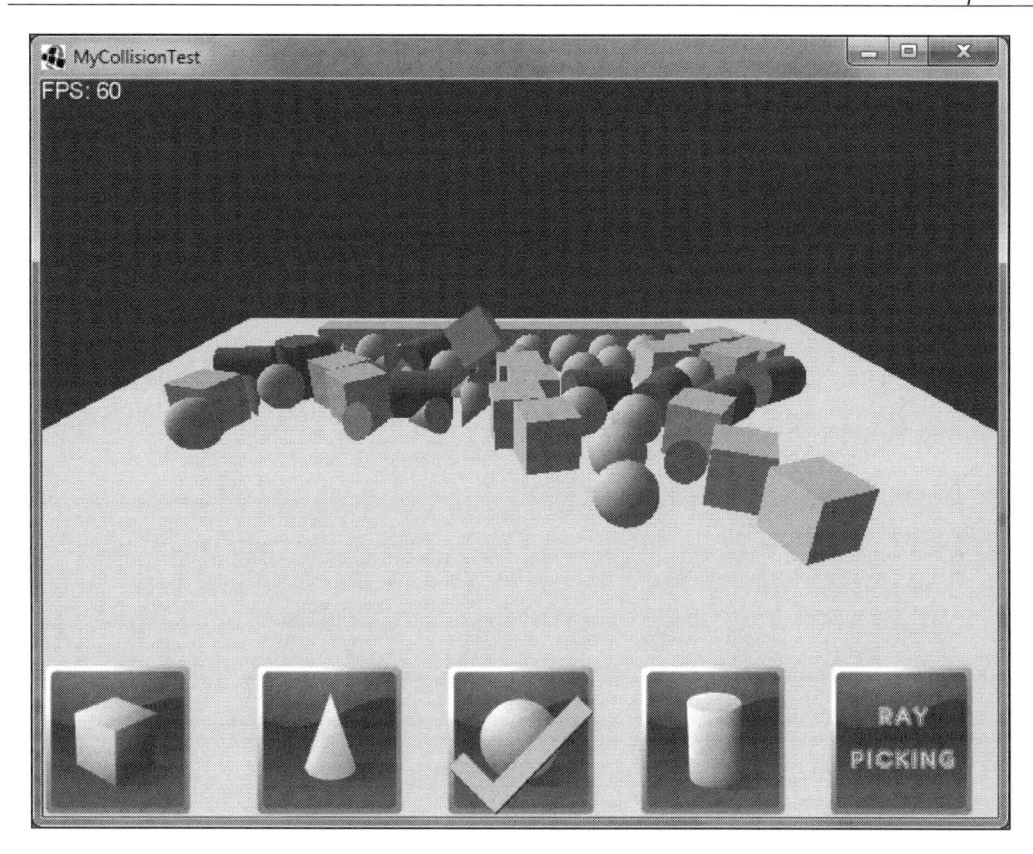

The whole code and art can be found in code bundle section of this chapter.

We have already created the MyContactListener.java and MyMotionState.java files in our com.packtpub.libgdx.collisiontest package. The following is a list of Java files we will be creating:

- MyBulletInterface.java: This is a custom Bullet interface.
- BulletWorld.java: This is the class that contains the dynamics world. This class implements MyBulletInterface.
- BulletObjects.java: This class inherits BulletWorld. It will have functions to create a box, a cone, the ground body, and so on.
- MyCollisionWorld.java: This simple class inherits BulletObjects.
- Items.java: This is an enum object that has the basic shapes.
- UserData.java: As the name indicates, this stores the specific data related to each rigid body.

Bullet Physics

Now, we will create the previously listed Java files as follows:

1. Add the following code to `MyBulletInterface.java`:

    ```
    public interface MyBulletInterface extends Disposable {

    public void init();

    public void update(float delta);

    public void remove(btRigidBody body);

    public btDiscreteDynamicsWorld getWorld();

    }
    ```

2. Add the following code to `BulletWorld.java`:

    ```
    public class BulletWorld implements MyBulletInterface {
        protected btDefaultCollisionConfiguration collisionConfiguration;
        protected btCollisionDispatcher dispatcher;
        protected btDbvtBroadphase broadphase;
        protected btSequentialImpulseConstraintSolver solver;
        protected btDiscreteDynamicsWorld world;

        protected BulletWorld() {

        }

        @Override
        public void init() {
            Bullet.init();
            collisionConfiguration = new btDefaultCollisionConfiguration();
            dispatcher = new btCollisionDispatcher(collisionConfiguration);
            broadphase = new btDbvtBroadphase();
            solver = new btSequentialImpulseConstraintSolver();
            world = new btDiscreteDynamicsWorld(dispatcher, broadphase, solver, collisionConfiguration);
            world.setGravity(new Vector3(0, -9.81f, .1f));

        }
    ```

```
        @Override
        public void update(float delta) {
              world.stepSimulation(delta, 5 , 1/60f);
        }
        @Override
        public void dispose() {
              world.dispose();
              collisionConfiguration.dispose();
              dispatcher.dispose();
              broadphase.dispose();
              solver.dispose();
        }
        @Override
        public btDiscreteDynamicsWorld getWorld() {
              return world ;
        }
        @Override
        public void remove(btRigidBody body) {
              world.removeRigidBody(body);
              ((UserData) body.userData).dispose();
        }
}
```

As you can see, `BulletWorld` implements `MyBulletInterface`. Here, Bullet is initiated and the dynamics world is created by providing the properties of the dynamics world. The `update()` function will step the dynamics world and `remove()` will remove and dispose of the given rigid body from the dynamics world.

Also, observe that while disposing, the `btDiscreteDynamicsWorld` parameter is disposed before all other world parameters such as `dispatcher` and `broadphase`. Otherwise, you will get a runtime exception while disposing of the following files:

3. Add the following to `BulletObjects.java`:

   ```
   public class BulletObjects extends BulletWorld {
   private static final Vector3 temp = new Vector3();
   private static final Vector3 localIneria = new Vector3(1,
   1, 1);

   private btCollisionShape boxShape, coneShape, sphereShape,
   cylinderShape, groundShape;
   private Model boxModel, coneModel, sphereModel,
   cylinderModel, groundModel;
   ```

Bullet Physics

```java
    protected BulletObjects() {
       super();
    }

    @Override
    public void init() {
       super.init();
       final ModelBuilder builder = new ModelBuilder();
       float width, height, radius;

       width = 20;
       builder.begin();
       MeshPartBuilder mpb = builder.part("parts",
    GL20.GL_TRIANGLES, Usage.Position | Usage.Normal |
    Usage.Color, new Material(ColorAttribute.createDiffuse(Color.
    WHITE)));
       mpb.setColor(1f, 1f, 1f, 1f);
       mpb.box(0, 0, 0, 2 * width, 1, 2 * width);
       groundModel = builder.end();
       groundShape = new btBoxShape(new Vector3(width, 1 / 2f,
    width));

       width = 2f;
       boxModel = builder.createBox(width, width, width, new
    Material(ColorAttribute.createDiffuse(Color.GREEN)), Usage.
    Position | Usage.Normal);
       boxShape = new btBoxShape(new Vector3(width, width,
    width).scl(.5f));

       width = 1.5f;
       height = 2f;
       coneModel = builder.createCone(width, height, width, 20,
    new Material(ColorAttribute.createDiffuse(Color.LIGHT_GRAY)),
    Usage.Position | Usage.Normal);
       coneShape = new btConeShape(width / 2f, height);

       radius = 2f;
       sphereModel = builder.createSphere(radius, radius,
    radius, 20, 20, new Material(ColorAttribute.createDiffuse(Color.
    ORANGE)),
    Usage.Position | Usage.Normal);
       sphereShape = new btSphereShape(radius / 2f);

       width = 2f;
```

```
    height = 2.5f;
    cylinderModel = builder.createCylinder(width, height,
width, 20, new Material(ColorAttribute.createDiffuse(Color.RED)),
Usage.Position | Usage.Normal);
    cylinderShape = new btCylinderShape(new Vector3(width,
height, width).scl(.5f));

}

private btRigidBody createRigidBody(Model model,
btCollisionShape CollisionShape, Vector3 position, boolean
isStatic) {
   if (isStatic)
           return createStaticRigidBody(model,
CollisionShape, position);

    final ModelInstance instance = new ModelInstance(model);
    final btMotionState motionState = new
MyMotionState(instance);
    motionState.setWorldTransform(instance.transform.trn
(position).rotate(Vector3.Z, MathUtils.random(360)));
    final btRigidBodyConstructionInfo bodyInfo = new
btRigidBodyConstructionInfo(1, motionState, CollisionShape,
localIneria);
    final btRigidBody body = new btRigidBody(bodyInfo);
    body.userData = new UserData(instance, motionState,
bodyInfo, body);
    world.addRigidBody(body);
    return body;
}

private btRigidBody createStaticRigidBody(Model model,
btCollisionShape CollisionShape, Vector3 position) {
    final ModelInstance instance = new ModelInstance(model);
    instance.transform.trn(position);
    final btRigidBodyConstructionInfo bodyInfo = new
btRigidBodyConstructionInfo(0, null, CollisionShape,
Vector3.Zero);
    final btRigidBody body = new btRigidBody(bodyInfo);
    body.translate(instance.transform.getTranslation(temp));
    body.userData = new UserData(instance, null, bodyInfo,
body);
    world.addRigidBody(body);
    return body;
}
```

```java
public btRigidBody create_box(Vector3 position, boolean isStatic) {
    return createRigidBody(boxModel, boxShape, position, isStatic);
}

public btRigidBody create_cone(Vector3 position, boolean isStatic) {
    return createRigidBody(coneModel, coneShape, position, isStatic);
}

public btRigidBody create_sphere(Vector3 position, boolean isStatic) {
    return createRigidBody(sphereModel, sphereShape, position, isStatic);
}

public btRigidBody create_cylinder(Vector3 position, boolean isStatic) {
    return createRigidBody(cylinderModel, cylinderShape, position, isStatic);
}

public btRigidBody create_ground() {
    return createRigidBody(groundModel, groundShape, Vector3.Zero, true);
}

@Override
public void dispose() {

    super.dispose();
    boxModel.dispose();
    coneModel.dispose();
    sphereModel.dispose();
    cylinderModel.dispose();
    groundModel.dispose();

    boxShape.dispose();
    coneShape.dispose();
    sphereShape.dispose();
    cylinderShape.dispose();
    groundShape.dispose();
}

}
```

This class will generate the rigid bodies with specific sizes. Observe that we have only created a single instance of btCollisionShape and Model for each basic shape in the init() function. However, they are called in other functions repeatedly. This is because we only need a single instance of btCollisionShape and Model to create a rigid body and a model instance. This helps save memory.

4. Add the following to MyCollisionWorld.java:

```
public class MyCollisionWorld extends BulletObjects {
    public static final MyCollisionWorld instance = new MyCollisionWorld();

    private MyCollisionWorld() {
        super();
    }

    @Override
    public void init() {
        super.init();
    }

}
```

Observe that the constructor is private. Hence, this class cannot be called from other classes. Similarly, the constructors of the base classes are all protected so that only MyCollisionWorld can call it. However, we have a static final instance of MyCollisionWorld, which is public. This is to ensure that only one instance of the dynamics world is available in the game.

5. Add the following to Items.java:

```
public enum Items {
        GROUND, CONE, BOX, CYLINDER, SPHERE, RAY_PICKING;
}
```

6. Add the following to UserData.java:

```
public class UserData implements Disposable {

    public static final Array<UserData> data = new Array<UserData>();
    private static final Vector3 temp = new Vector3();
    final ModelInstance instance;
    final btMotionState motionState;
    final btRigidBody body;
```

```java
        final btRigidBodyConstructionInfo bodyInfo;

    public UserData(ModelInstance instance, btMotionState 
motionState, btRigidBodyConstructionInfo bodyInfo, 
btRigidBody body) {
            this.instance = instance;
            this.motionState = motionState;
            this.bodyInfo = bodyInfo;
            this.body = body;
            data.add(this);
    }

    public btRigidBody getBody() {
            return body;
    }

    public ModelInstance getInstance() {
            return this.instance;
    }

    public boolean isVisible(Camera cam) {
            return 
cam.frustum.pointInFrustum(instance.transform.
getTranslation(temp));
    }

    @Override
    public void dispose() {
            if (motionState != null) {
                    motionState.dispose();
            }
            bodyInfo.dispose();
            body.dispose();

            data.removeValue(this, true);
            Gdx.app.log(this.getClass().getName(), " Rigid 
body removed and disposed.");
    }

}
```

All the user data created is stored in the static array data declared at the beginning of this class.

Now, we will update the `ModelTest.java` file as follows:

- Code for ray picking
- Orthographic camera for displaying FPS and the buttons
- `InputAdapter` to handle the input from user

First, add the code to `MyCollisionTest.java` as follows:

```
public class MyCollisionTest extends ApplicationAdapter {
PerspectiveCamera cam;
ModelBatch modelBatch;
Environment environment;

MyCollisionWorld worldInstance;
btRigidBody groundBody;
MyContactListener collisionListener;
Sprite box, cone, cylinder, sphere, raypick, tick;
ClosestRayResultCallback rayTestCB;
Vector3 rayFrom = new Vector3();
Vector3 rayTo = new Vector3();

BitmapFont font;
OrthographicCamera guiCam;
SpriteBatch batch;

...
}
```

Here, we added the custom classes that implement the physics as well as the images, font, camera, and `SpriteBatch` to control the 2D plane. We also added the `Vector3` objects for ray testing.

Next, we update the `create()` method to initialize our classes as follows:

```
@Override
public void create() {

...

worldInstance = MyCollisionWorld.instance;
worldInstance.init();
groundBody = worldInstance.create_ground();

int w = -10;
for (int i = 0; i < 10; i++) {
```

Bullet Physics

```java
            worldInstance.create_box(new Vector3(w += 2, 1.5f, 10), true);
        }
        rayTestCB = new ClosestRayResultCallback(Vector3.Zero, Vector3.Z);

        font = new BitmapFont();
        guiCam = new OrthographicCamera(Gdx.graphics.getWidth(), Gdx.graphics.
        getHeight());
        guiCam.position.set(guiCam.viewportWidth / 2f, guiCam.viewportHeight /
        2f, 0);
        guiCam.update();
        batch = new SpriteBatch();

        float wt = Gdx.graphics.getWidth() / 5f;
        float dt = .1f * wt;
        box = new Sprite(new Texture("cube.png"));
        box.setPosition(0, 0);

        cone = new Sprite(new Texture("cone.png"));
        cone.setPosition(wt + dt, 0);

        sphere = new Sprite(new Texture("sphere.png"));
        sphere.setPosition(2 * wt + dt, 0);

        cylinder = new Sprite(new Texture("cylinder.png"));
        cylinder.setPosition(3 * wt + dt, 0);

        raypick = new Sprite(new Texture("ray.png"));
        raypick.setPosition(4 * wt + dt, 0);

        tick = new Sprite(new Texture("mark.png"));
        enableButton(sphere);

        collisionListener = new MyContactListener();
        Gdx.input.setInputProcessor(adapter);

    }


    public void enableButton(Sprite sp) {
        tick.setPosition(sp.getX(), sp.getY());
    }
```

Next, we update the `render()` method as follows:

```
@Override
public void render() {
Gdx.gl.glViewport(0, 0, Gdx.graphics.getWidth(), Gdx.graphics.
getHeight());
Gdx.gl.glClearColor(.2f, 0.2f, 0.2f, 1);
Gdx.gl.glClear(GL20.GL_COLOR_BUFFER_BIT | GL20.GL_DEPTH_BUFFER_BIT);

float delta = Gdx.graphics.getDeltaTime();
worldInstance.update(delta);

for (UserData data : UserData.data) {
if (!data.isVisible(cam)) {
worldInstance.remove(data.getBody());

}
}

modelBatch.begin(cam);
for (UserData data : UserData.data) {
modelBatch.render(data.getInstance(), environment);
}
modelBatch.end();

batch.setProjectionMatrix(guiCam.combined);
batch.begin();
font.draw(batch, "FPS: " + Gdx.graphics.getFramesPerSecond(), 0, Gdx.
graphics.getHeight());
box.draw(batch);
cone.draw(batch);
cylinder.draw(batch);
sphere.draw(batch);
raypick.draw(batch);
tick.draw(batch);
batch.end();
}
```

We have already created a singleton instance of the dynamics world in `MyCollisionWorld`. This instance is accessed here and initiated as follows:

```
worldInstance = MyCollisionWorld.instance;
worldInstance.init();
```

Bullet Physics

This dynamics world is stepped by calling `worldInstance.update()` in the `render()` method.

Game objects that are not visible in our camera are destroyed immediately. The following code will check whether the rigid body is within the view. If not, then the object will be removed and disposed:

```
for (UserData data : UserData.data) {
    if (!data.isVisible(cam)) {
        worldInstance.remove(data.getBody());
    }
}
```

Add `InputAdapter` and ray testing as follows:

```
private final InputAdapter adapter = new InputAdapter() {
    private Items item = Items.SPHERE;
    private final Vector3 temp = new Vector3();

    public boolean touchUp(int screenX, int screenY, int pointer, int button) {
        guiCam.unproject(temp.set(screenX, screenY, 0));
        if (box.getBoundingRectangle().contains(temp.x, temp.y)) {
            enableButton(box);
            item = Items.BOX;
            return true;
        } else if (cone.getBoundingRectangle().contains(temp.x, temp.y)) {
            enableButton(cone);
            item = Items.CONE;
            return true;
        } else if (sphere.getBoundingRectangle().contains(temp.x, temp.y)) {
            enableButton(sphere);
            item = Items.SPHERE;
            return true;
        } else if (cylinder.getBoundingRectangle().contains(temp.x, temp.y)) {
            enableButton(cylinder);
            item = Items.CYLINDER;
            return true;
        } else if (raypick.getBoundingRectangle().contains(temp.x, temp.y)) {
            enableButton(raypick);
            item = Items.RAY_PICKING;
            return true;
```

```
        }

        Ray ray = cam.getPickRay(screenX, screenY);
        Vector3 position = ray.origin.cpy();
        btRigidBody body;
        switch (item) {
        default:
        case BOX:
        body = worldInstance.create_box(position, false);
        break;
        case CONE:
        body = worldInstance.create_cone(position, false);
        break;
        case CYLINDER:
        body = worldInstance.create_cylinder(position, false);
        break;
        case SPHERE:
        body = worldInstance.create_sphere(position, false);
        break;
        case RAY_PICKING:

        rayFrom.set(ray.origin);
        rayTo.set(ray.direction).scl(50f).add(rayFrom); // 50 meters max
        rayTestCB.setCollisionObject(null);
        rayTestCB.setClosestHitFraction(1f);
        worldInstance.getWorld().rayTest(rayFrom, rayTo, rayTestCB);

        if (rayTestCB.hasHit()) {
        final btCollisionObject obj = rayTestCB.getCollisionObject();
        body = (btRigidBody) (obj);
        if (body != groundBody)
                worldInstance.remove(body);
        }

        return true;
        }
        body.applyCentralImpulse(ray.direction.scl(20));

        return true;
        };
    };

    }
```

Bullet Physics

The buttons are simply sprites that on selection will be ticked with a green tick mark. The `InputAdapter` interface processes the touch input from the user. The `touchup()` function in `InputAdapter` will check whether the current touch is inside any button. If the user selects any button, then the button is set, or the program will continue with the throw/raypicking functions.

To throw the physics object, the `applyCentralImpulse()` function is called. The object is thrown at the direction cast by the ray.

The following is the code for ray picking:

```
Ray ray = cam.getPickRay(screenX, screenY);
Vector3 position = ray.origin.cpy();
rayFrom.set(ray.origin);
rayTo.set(ray.direction).scl(50f).add(rayFrom); // 50 meters max
rayTestCB.setCollisionObject(null);
rayTestCB.setClosestHitFraction(1f);

worldInstance.getWorld().rayTest(rayFrom, rayTo, rayTestCB);
if (rayTestCB.hasHit()) {
      final btCollisionObject obj = rayTestCB.getCollisionObject();

/**
Do something
*/
}
```

Here, a ray is created from the input coordinates by the `getPickRay()` function. The `rayFrom` value, a `Vector3` value, is set to the origin of the ray, whereas `rayTo` is set at a distance of 50 units from the origin point in the ray direction. The callback object, `rayTestCB`, is cleared by setting `null` to the `setCollisionObject()` function. Finally, by calling `rayTest()`, we check whether the ray has hit any object within the `rayFrom` and `rayTo` points.

Finally, dispose everything as shown here:

```
@Override
public void dispose() {
for (UserData data : UserData.data) {
data.dispose();
}
worldInstance.dispose();
```

```
modelBatch.dispose();

box.getTexture().dispose();
cone.getTexture().dispose();
cylinder.getTexture().dispose();
raypick.getTexture().dispose();
sphere.getTexture().dispose();
Gdx.app.log(this.getClass().getName(), "Disposed.");
}
```

Having fun with shadows

It appears that something is missing since we have light and reflection but no shadows. Shadow in LibGDX is still evolving. The way of using shadows might change in the next version. However, we will simply put a shadow here just to make the scene look more complete:

```
DirectionalShadowLight shadowLight;
ModelBatch shadowBatch;
@Override
public void create() {
. . .
environment = new Environment();
environment.set(new ColorAttribute(ColorAttribute.AmbientLight,
.4f, .4f, .4f, 1f));
environment.add(new DirectionalLight().set(0.8f, 0.8f, 0.8f, -1f,
-0.8f, -0.2f));

    shadowLight = new DirectionalShadowLight(1024, 1024, 60, 60,
1f, 300);
    shadowLight.set(0.8f, 0.8f, 0.8f, -1f, -.8f, -.2f);
    environment.add(shadowLight);
    environment.shadowMap = shadowLight;
    shadowBatch = new ModelBatch(new DepthShaderProvider());
    . . .

}
@Override
public void render() {
   //update the world
   . . .

    shadowLight.begin(Vector3.Zero, cam.direction);
    shadowBatch.begin(shadowLight.getCamera());
```

```
        for (UserData data : UserData.data) {
              shadowBatch.render(data.getInstance());
        }
        shadowBatch.end();
        shadowLight.end();
    . . .

    // draw the modelBatch
}

@Override
public void dispose() {
    . . .
    shadowBatch.dispose();
    shadowLight.dispose();

}
```

The `shadowLight` object is an object of `DirectionalShadowLight` and `shadowBatch` is `ModelBatch` with a depth shader. The model instances are rendered using `shadowBatch` to simulate the shadows near the actual model instances.

Here is the screenshot of the scene with shadows enabled:

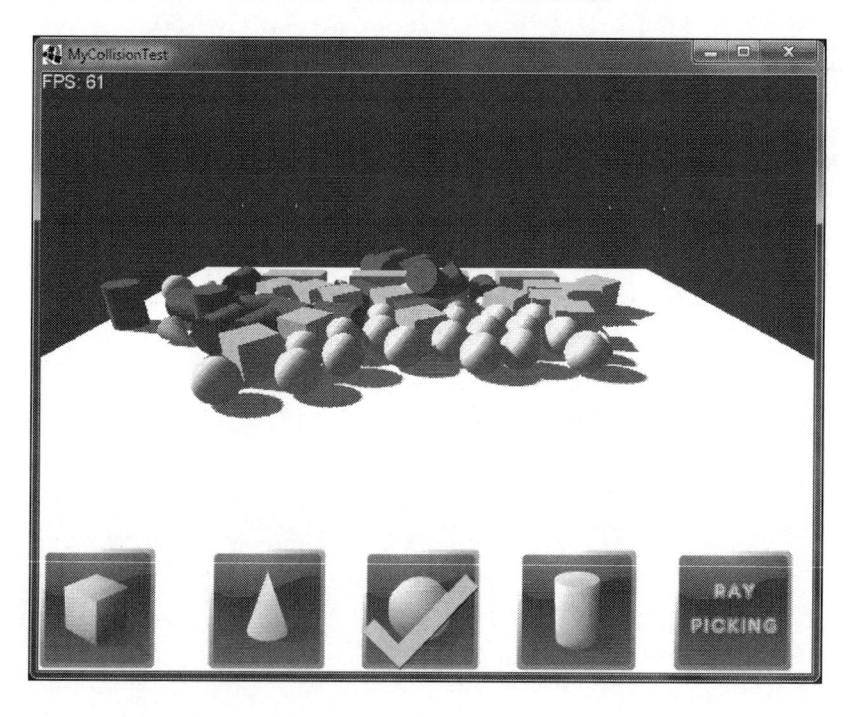

> To know about shadow mapping, visit the Wikipedia page at http://en.wikipedia.org/wiki/Shadow_mapping.

Summary

In this chapter, you learned the basics of Bullet Physics. You learned to create a rigid body and apply physics and ray testing in Bullet. You also experimented with basic physics shapes such as a box, a sphere, a cylinder, and so on. You understood callbacks such as contact listeners and motion states. Finally, you applied shadows to make the scene look more complete.

A special note from the author to you:

Congratulations! You have just finished reading this book and I really hope you enjoyed it just as much as I did while writing it. You should now feel confident enough about using the LibGDX framework to start developing your very own games.

You can take a look at the wonderful games that have already been made with LibGDX at http://libgdx.badlogicgames.com/gallery.html. All that's left to say is that I wish you good luck in your future projects that will hopefully make great use of LibGDX.

Index

Symbols

3D frustum culling 404-410
3D programming 393
3D scene
  camera, using 398
  creating 421-425
  creating, LibGDX used 394
  environment 400
  model 399
  ModelBatch class, using 399
  ModelInstances, creating 399
  project setup 394-397

A

accelerometers
  used, for adding alternative input controls 364-368
actions
  actors, manipulating through 369-371
  add() method 371
  alpha() method 371
  color() method 371
  execution order, controlling 372
  execution time, controlling 372
  fadeIn() method 371
  fadeOut() method 371
  hide() method 371
  layout() method 371
  moveBy() method 371
  moveTo() method 371
  removeActor() method 371
  rotateBy() method 371
  rotateTo() method 371
  run() method 371
  scaleBy() method 371
  scaleTo() method 371
  show() method 372
  sizeBy() method 372
  sizeTo() method 372
  touchable() method 372
  visible() method 372
actions, execution time
  after() method 372
  delay() method 372
  forever() method 372
  parallel() method 372
  repeat() method 372
  sequence() method 372
actor game objects
  implementing 195-198
ADT Plugin
  URL 15
alternative input controls
  adding, accelerometers used 364-368
ambient light 393
Android
  demo application, running on 79-83
  URL, for API guide 66
Android API levels
  URL 29
Android Developer
  URL 140
Android SDK
  installing 21-29
  URL, for downloading 21
animations
  packing, TexturePacker used 379, 380
  play modes, selecting 380, 381
  sequences of images, using 378

Apple Developer
  URL 141
application
  creating 37
  creating, Gradle-based setup used 46-51
  creating, old setup tool used 37-46
application life cycle, LibGDX 74-76
application module
  about 68
  Android API level, querying 69
  data persistence 69
  graceful shutdown 68
  logging facility 68
  memory usage, querying 70
  multithreading 70
  platform type, querying 70
Application Programming Interface (API) 10, 67
as3sfxr
  about 314
  URL 315
assets
  loading 148
  organizing 149-157
  testing 157-160
  tracking 148
audio device
  accessing, directly 312
  AudioDevice interface 313
  AudioRecorder interface 314
audio files
  .mp3 (MPEG-2 Audio Layer III) 310
  .ogg (Ogg Vorbis) 310
  .wav (RIFF WAVE) 309
audio module
  about 71
  music, streaming for playback 72
  sounds, loading for playback 71

B

backends, LibGDX
  about 65
  Android 66
  LWJGL 66
  RoboVM 67
  URL, for list of unresolved issues 67
  WebGL 66
background layer
  adding 246
bfxr generator
  about 314, 317
  URL 317
Blender
  used, for loading model 400-402
Box2D
  about 329, 330
  adding 333
  adding, for non-Gradle users 337
  body types, selecting 331, 332
  dependency, adding in Gradle 334-336
  exploring 331
  fixtures, using 332
  Physics Body Editor 333
  physics, simulating 330, 332
  reference link 330
  rigid bodies 331
  shapes, using 332
  URL 332
Box2D, features
  constraints 332
  contact listener 332
  joints 332
  sensors 332
Bullet
  about 331, 415
  collision shapes 417
  initializing 426
  MotionStates 418
  physics, simulating 418
  ray casting 430
  rigid bodies 417
  simple test game, creating 430-444
  step simulation 429
  URL, for downloading manual 418
Bullet Physics
  about 415
  reference link 416
  URL, for documentation 416
Bullet, with LibGDX
  3D scene, creating 421-425
  Bullet, initializing 426
  ContactListener class, defining 427, 428
  custom MotionState class, creating 427

dynamics world, creating 426
project, setting up 419, 420
bunny head object
  creating 201-210

C

camera
  about 398
  fixing 220-222
  orthographic camera 398
  perspective camera 398
CameraHelper class
  implementing 130-132
  used, for adding camera debug
      controls 132-135
Canyon Bunny
  about 58, 59, 107
  camera debug controls, adding Camera-
      Helper class used 132-135
  CameraHelper class, adding 130-132
  class diagram, using 110-112
  creating 57
  debug controls, adding 126-130
  game loop, building 117-121
  implementing 117
  music and sound effects, adding 318-327
  project, setting with gdx-setup-ui
      tool 108, 109
  raining carrots, adding 338
  resources, gathering 137
  scene, creating 165
  screen transitions, implementing 287-296
  test sprites, adding 121-126
CanyonBunnyMain class
  implementing 114
cfxr generator
  about 314-316
  URL 316
clouds
  moving 274
clouds object
  creating 174-176
code hot swapping 100-105
collision detection
  adding 213-220

collision shapes
  about 417
  URL 417
community, LibGDX project
  reference link 14
complex effects
  creating, with particle systems 264-270
Constants class
  implementing 113
ContactListener class
  defining 427, 428
controls layer
  adding 247, 248
core modules, LibGDX
  about 67
  application 68
  audio 71
  files 73
  graphics 71
  input 72
  network 73
create() method 95, 97
custom Android application icon
  setting up 138-140
custom iOS application icon
  setting 140
custom MotionState class
  creating 427

D

**Dashboards section, Android developer
      website**
  URL 79
debugger
  using 100-105
demo-android project 62
demo application
  about 62-64
  actual code 94
  create() method 95-97
  dispose() method 98
  example code, inspecting of 94, 95
  render() method 97
  running, in iOS device 88-93
  running, in WebGL-capable
      web browser 83-88

running, on Android 79-83
running, on desktop 77, 78
demo-desktop project 62
demo project 62
device capabilities
  URL, for official documentation 93
directional light 393
dispose() method 98
dust particle effect
  adding, to player character 270-272
dynamic rigid bodies 332, 417

E

Eclipse
  about 9
  installing 19
  running 30-36
  URL, for downloading 19
Eclipse 4.3.2 (Kepler)
  URL 31
Eclipse Integration Gradle
  URL 15
environment
  about 394, 400
  reference link 394
event handling
  reference link 413
extra lives, game GUI
  implementing 191, 192

F

fade transition effect
  creating 298-300
FBX 403
FBX converter
  about 403
  URL, for downloading 404
feather icon
  adding, to GUI 222-225
feather object
  creating 200, 201
files module
  about 73
  external file handle, obtaining 73
  internal file handle, obtaining 73

finite state machine
  reference link 388
fixtures
  using 332
FPS counter, game GUI
  implementing 192, 193
fragment shaders 357
Framebuffer Objects (FBO) 288
Freenode
  URL 14
frustum
  about 409
  reference link, for viewing 409
frustum culling 404

G

G3DB 403
G3DJ 403
game
  basic concepts 55, 56
game assets 55
game GUI
  enhancing 280
  extra lives, implementing 191, 192
  feather icon, adding 222-225
  FPS counter, implementing 192, 193
  game score, displaying 283, 284
  implementing 186-190
  player lives, displaying 280-282
  rendering 193
  score, implementing 190, 191
game logic
  about 55
  adding 213
  camera, fixing 220-222
  collision detection, adding 213-220
  feather icon, adding to GUI 222-225
  game over 220-222
  game over text, adding 222-225
  lives, losing 220-222
game objects
  actor game objects, implementing 195-198
  bunny head object, creating 201-210
  clouds object, creating 174-176
  creating 166, 167
  feather object, creating 200, 201

gold coin object, creating 198-200
mountains object, creating 171-173
rock object, creating 167-210
water overlay object, creating 173, 174
game screen
animating 381
bunny copter animation, defining 381-384
bunny head game object, animating 387-391
gold coin animation, defining 381-384
gold coin game object, animating 384-387
game settings
using 260-262
game world
assembling 182-185
Garbage Collector (GC) 115
gdx-setup.jar file
URL, for downloading 46
gdx-setup-ui tool
used, for setting up Canyon Bunny project 108, 109
versus gdx-setup 52-54
Glyph Designer
about 186
URL 186
GNU Image Manipulation Program (GIMP)
about 161
URL 161
gold coin object
creating 198-200
Google Web Toolkit (GWT)
about 63
URL 66
Gradle
Box2D dependency, adding 334-336
Gradle-based setup
used, for creating application 46-51
graphical particle editor
using 265
Graphical User Interface (GUI) 166
graphics module
about 71
delta time, querying 71
display size, querying 71
frames per second (FPS) counter, querying 71
Graphics Processing Unit (GPU) 329

H

Head-Up Display (HUD) 166
Hiero
about 186
URL 186

I

icons, iOS version
reference link 64
images
used, for animations 378
Independent Game Developers (Indies) 9
Info.plist keys
CFBundleIconFiles 92
CFBundleIdentifier 92
CFBundleName 92
UIRequiredDeviceCapabilities 92
UISupportedInterfaceOrientations 92
URL, for official documentation 93
Inkscape
about 59
URL 59
input module
about 72
accelerometer, reading 72
Android's soft keys, catching 73
keyboard/touch/mouse input, reading 72
vibrator, canceling 72
vibrator, starting 72
installation, Android SDK 21-29
installation, Eclipse 19
installation, Java Development Kit (JDK) 15-18
installation, plugins 30-36
Integrated Development Environment (IDE) 9, 19
interface, LibGDX 74-76
interpolation algorithms
using 296-298
iOS device
demo application, running on 88-93

[453]

J

Java Development Kit (JDK)
  installing 15-18
  URL, for downloading 15
Java Perspective 30
Java Runtime Environment (JRE) 16
Java Virtual Machine (JVM) 10
Joint Photographic Experts Group (JPEG)
  about 59
  reference link 59
jumpState, bunny head object
  FALLING 207
  GROUNDED 207
  JUMP_FALLING 207
  JUMP_RISING 207
JVM Code Hot Swapping feature 61

K

kinematic rigid bodies 331, 417

L

Lerp
  about 263, 275
  used, for creating rocks movement 276, 277
  using 275
level data
  handling 161, 162
level loader
  completing 210-212
  implementing 177-182
LibGDX
  about 10
  application life cycle 74-76
  core modules 67
  downloading 20
  interface 74-76
  URL, for downloading 20
  used, for creating 3D scene 394
LibGDX 1.2.0, features
  audio 12
  file I/O 12
  graphics 11, 12
  input handling 12
  math and physics 13
  storage 12
  tools 13
  URL 11
  utilities 13
LibGDX 3D API
  reference link 394
LibGDX backends
  about 65
  Android 66
  LWJGL 66
  RoboVM 67
  WebGL 66
LibGDX installation
  prerequisites 14
LibGDX reflection
  URL 239
light sources
  about 393, 394
  ambient light 393
  directional light 393
  point light 394
  spotlight 394
Lightweight Java Game Library. *See* **LWJGL**
linear interpolation. *See* **Lerp**
lives
  losing 220-222
log levels
  LOG_DEBUG 68
  LOG_ERROR 68
  LOG_INFO 68
  LOG_NONE 68
logos layer
  adding 247
LWJGL
  about 66
  URL 66

M

Main loop thread 70
manifest file, Android
  icon 82
  label 82
  minSdkVersion 82
  name 82
  screenOrientation 82
  targetSdkVersion 82
  URL, for official documentation 81

materials
  about 394
  reference link 394
menu screen
  animating 372, 373
  background layer, adding 246
  bunny head actors, animating 374, 375
  controls layer, adding 247, 248
  gold coins, animating 374, 375
  logos layer, adding 247
  menu buttons, animating 375-377
  objects layer, adding 246
  Options window, animating 375-377
  Options window layer, adding 249-253
  scene, building 240-245
menu UI
  creating, scene graph used 236-240
Mesh 394
model
  about 399
  loading, Blender used 400-402
ModelBatch class
  using 399
model formats
  about 403
  FBX 403
  G3DB 403
  G3DJ 403
  Wavefront OBJ 403
ModelInstances
  creating 399
monochrome filter shader program
  creating 358-360
  using 360-364
MotionStates
  about 418
  URL, for documentation 418
mountains object
  creating 171-173
multiple screens
  managing 227-234
music and sound effects
  adding 318-327
  Music interface 312
  playing back 309, 310
  Sound interface 310, 311

N

native orientations
  reference link 365
network module
  about 73
  client/server sockets, creating 74
  HTTP requests, making 73
  URI, opening in web browser 74
Non-Power-Of-Two (NPOT)
    textures 80, 141

O

objects layer
  adding 246
old setup tool
  URL, for downloading 37
  used, for creating application 37-46
OpenGL (ES) 2.0
  reference link 358
OpenGL ES 2.0 Reference Card
  URL 358
OpenGL Shading Language (GLSL) 358
Options, particle editor
  Additive 269
  Aligned 269
  Attached 269
  Behind 269
  Continuous 269
Options window layer
  adding 249-253
  building 253-260
  game settings, using 260-262
orthographic camera 398

P

Paint.NET
  URL 161
parallax scrolling
  about 278
  adding 278-280
Particle Editor, properties
  Angle 268
  Count 267
  Delay 267
  Duration 268

Emission 268
Gravity 268
Image 267
Life 268
Life Offset 268
Options 269
Rotation 268
Size 268
Spawn 268
Tint 268
Transparency 268
Velocity 268
Wind 268
X Offset 268
Y Offset 268
ParticleEffect class, methods
 allowCompletion() 264
 dispose() 265
 draw() 264
 load() 265
 reset() 264
 save() 265
 setDuration() 265
 setFlip() 265
 setPosition() 265
 start() 264
 update() 264
particle.png file
 about 271
 reference link 271
particle systems
 complex effects, creating with 264-270
permissions, Android
 URL, for official documentation 82
perspective camera 398
physics
 simulating, with Box2D 330-332
 simulating, with Bullet 418
Physics Body Editor
 about 333
 reference link 333
pixel bleeding. *See* **texture bleeding**
pixel shaders. *See* **fragment shaders**
planning, game projects 56
player character
 dust particle effect, adding to 270-272

play modes
 LOOP 380
 LOOP_PINGPONG 380
 LOOP_RANDOM 380
 LOOP_REVERSED 380
 NORMAL 380
 REVERSED 380
 selecting 380, 381
plugins
 installing 30-36
point light 394
Portable Network Graphics (PNG)
 about 59
 reference link 59
prerequisites, LibGDX installation
 Android SDK, installing 21-29
 Eclipse 19
 Eclipse, running 30-36
 Java Development Kit (JDK) 15-18
 plugins, installing 30-36
Programmable Pipeline 357
Pulse Code Modulation (PCM) 309

R

raining carrots
 adding 338
 assets, adding 338
 carrot game object, adding 339
 goal game object, adding 340, 341
 implementing 345-356
 level, extending 342-344
raster graphics
 reference link 59
ray casting 430
ray picking 411, 412
red, green, blue, and alpha (RGBA) 118
render() method 97
Render to Texture (RTT) 287
rigid bodies
 about 331, 417
 adding 428, 429
 features 331
 selecting 331, 332
rigid bodies, types
 dynamic 332, 417
 kinematic 331, 417

[456]

static 331, 417
RoboVM
  about 67
  URL 67
rock object
  creating 167-170, 210
  rendering 170

S

Scene2D
  about 227
  URL, for documentation 235
Scene2D UI
  about 235
  URL, for documentation 236
scene, Canyon Bunny
  building, for menu screen 240-245
  creating 165
scene graph
  about 235
  used, for creating menu UI 236-240
score, game GUI
  implementing 190, 191
screen transitions, Canyon Bunny
  implementing 287-296
  transition effects, implementing 296
sfxr generator
  about 315
  URL 315
shaders
  about 329, 357
  advantages 357
  fragment shaders 357
  monochrome filter shader program, creating 358, 359
  monochrome filter shader program, using 360-364
  reference link 358
  vertex shaders 357
shadow mapping
  reference link 447
shadows 445, 446
shapes
  using 332
simple test game
  creating 430-444

singleton 151
skins
  about 235
  URL, for documentation 236
slice transition effect
  creating 304-306
slide transition effect
  creating 301-303
sound generators
  about 314
  bfxr generator 314, 317
  cfxr generator 314, 316
  sfxr generator 315
  using 314
Sound interface 310, 311
SoundManager2 (SM2)
  about 66
  URL 67
spotlight 394
sprite sheet. *See* texture atlases
starter classes
  about 76
  demo application, running in WebGL-capable web browser 83-88
  demo application, running on Android 79-83
  demo application, running on desktop 76-78
  demo application, running on iOS device 88-93
static imports
  reference link 370
static rigid bodies 331, 417
step simulation
  about 429
  reference link 430

T

TableLayout
  about 235
  URL, for documentation 236
texture atlases
  about 80, 141
  creating 141-147
texture bleeding 144

TexturePacker
  about 148
  URL 148
  used, for packing animations 379, 380
TexturePacker-GUI
  about 147
  URL 147
time stepping strategies
  reference link 293
transition effects, Canyon Bunny
  fade transition effect, creating 298-300
  implementing 296
  interpolation algorithms, using 296-298
  slice transition effect, creating 304-306
  slide transition effect, creating 301-303

U

Unified Modeling Language (UML) class diagram 107
Uniform Resource Identifier (URI) 74

V

vector graphics
  reference link 59
vertex shaders 357
vertical synchronization (vsync) 115

W

water overlay object
  creating 173, 174
Wavefront OBJ 403
WebGL
  URL 67
WebGL-capable web browser
  demo application, running in 83-88
widgets 235
WorldController class
  implementing 115
WorldRenderer class
  implementing 116

[PACKT] open source
PUBLISHING
community experience distilled

Thank you for buying
Learning LibGDX Game Development
Second Edition

About Packt Publishing

Packt, pronounced 'packed', published its first book, *Mastering phpMyAdmin for Effective MySQL Management*, in April 2004, and subsequently continued to specialize in publishing highly focused books on specific technologies and solutions.

Our books and publications share the experiences of your fellow IT professionals in adapting and customizing today's systems, applications, and frameworks. Our solution-based books give you the knowledge and power to customize the software and technologies you're using to get the job done. Packt books are more specific and less general than the IT books you have seen in the past. Our unique business model allows us to bring you more focused information, giving you more of what you need to know, and less of what you don't.

Packt is a modern yet unique publishing company that focuses on producing quality, cutting-edge books for communities of developers, administrators, and newbies alike. For more information, please visit our website at www.packtpub.com.

About Packt Open Source

In 2010, Packt launched two new brands, Packt Open Source and Packt Enterprise, in order to continue its focus on specialization. This book is part of the Packt Open Source brand, home to books published on software built around open source licenses, and offering information to anybody from advanced developers to budding web designers. The Open Source brand also runs Packt's Open Source Royalty Scheme, by which Packt gives a royalty to each open source project about whose software a book is sold.

Writing for Packt

We welcome all inquiries from people who are interested in authoring. Book proposals should be sent to author@packtpub.com. If your book idea is still at an early stage and you would like to discuss it first before writing a formal book proposal, then please contact us; one of our commissioning editors will get in touch with you.

We're not just looking for published authors; if you have strong technical skills but no writing experience, our experienced editors can help you develop a writing career, or simply get some additional reward for your expertise.

[PACKT] open source
PUBLISHING — community experience distilled

Libgdx Cross-platform Game Development Cookbook

ISBN: 978-1-78328-729-1   Paperback: 516 pages

Over 75 practical recipes to help you master cross-platform 2D game development using the powerful Libgdx framework

1. Gain an in-depth understanding of every Libgdx subsystem, including 2D graphics, input, audio, file extensions, and third-party libraries.

2. Write once and deploy to Windows, Linux, Mac, Android, iOS, and browsers.

3. Full of uniquely structured recipes that help you get the most out of Libgdx.

Unity Game Development Blueprints

ISBN: 978-1-78355-365-5   Paperback: 318 pages

Explore the various enticing features of Unity and learn how to develop awesome games

1. Create a wide variety of projects with Unity in multiple genres and formats.

2. Complete art assets with clear step-by-step examples and instructions to complete all tasks using Unity, C#, and MonoDevelop.

3. Develop advanced internal and external environments for games in 2D and 3D.

Please check **www.PacktPub.com** for information on our titles

[PACKT] open source
community experience distilled
PUBLISHING

Learning Cocos2d-x Game Development

ISBN: 978-1-78398-826-6   Paperback: 266 pages

Learn cross-platform game development with Cocos2d-x

1. Create a Windows Store account and upload your game for distribution.
2. Develop a game using Cocos2d-x by going through each stage of game development process step by step.

HTML5 Game Development [Video]

ISBN: 978-1-84969-588-6   Duration: 1:58 hrs

Build two HTML5 games in two hours with these fast-paced beginner-friendly videos

1. Create two simple yet elegant games in HTML5.
2. Build games that run on both desktops and mobile browsers.
3. Presented in a modular approach with elegant code and illustrated concepts to help you learn quickly.

Please check **www.PacktPub.com** for information on our titles

Printed in Great Britain
by Amazon